Mastering Novell
Directory Services

Mastering™ Novell® Directory Services®

Dave Kearns

San Francisco • Paris • Düsseldorf • Soest • London

SYBEX®

Associate Publisher: Guy Hart-Davis
Contracts and Licensing Manager: Kristine O'Callaghan
Acquisitions & Developmental Editor: Maureen Adams
Associate Acquisitions & Developmental Editor: Diane Lowery
Editor: Elizabeth Hurley
Project Editor: Donna Crossman
Technical Editor: Art Brieva
Book Designer: Bill Gibson
Graphic Illustrators: Andrew Benzie, Tony Jonick
Electronic Publishing Specialist: Rhonda Ries
Project Team Leader: Shannon Murphy
Proofreaders: Phil Hamer, Jennifer Putman
Indexer: Ted Laux
CD Coordinator: Kara Schwartz
CD Technician: Keith McNeil
Cover Designer: Archer Design
Cover Illustrator/Photographer: FPG International

Library of Congress Card Number: 99-67591
ISBN: 0-7821-2632-4

Manufactured in the United States of America

10 9 8 7 6 5 4 3 2 1

For Maura, David, Liam, and Katie.

Keep those networks up!

Dave Kearns

Foreword

We have entered an exciting new phase of growth in business networking and the Internet. The earlier phases were all about connecting to networks, both within organizations and globally on the Internet. The new wave is all about managing the relationships among the myriad people, applications, services, and devices that now populate the Net. Perhaps no software technology will play as large a role in meeting this challenge as directory-based networking platforms and applications.

Simply put, now is the time for Novell Directory Services (NDS), and now is the time for this book. Dave Kearns, a true networking expert, has created an excellent resource for understanding, using, and programming with Novell's full-service directory. Network administrators and managers, CIOs, and software developers will all benefit from the strong grounding in directory-enabled computing that *Mastering Novell Directory Services* provides. Each of these groups looks at the problems of managing relationships on the network in slightly different ways. Together, they reinforce the message that directory services are becoming central to the way information is accessed and managed in an interconnected world.

For IT professionals, directory services have become bread and butter technology for everyday network administration and management. This is Novell's heritage: providing technology that hardcore networking professionals need to do more with less. Administrators use NDS to manage and control all resources and relationships on the network from a single location and login, reducing the time and budget required to keep the network running and keep users happy. Typical business users may not know it, but they have the directory to thank for a more secure and reliable network, access to new applications and services, and the freedom to access their applications and resources anywhere, any time.

New directory-based tools and utilities, arriving in the marketplace virtually every day, continue to advance the art of network management and control. Novell's ZenWorks, for example, uses the directory to automate such ordinarily time-consuming chores as creating new user passwords and IDs, distributing software upgrades to desktops, protecting workstations against viruses, and auditing for Y2K compliance. In addition, IT staff can use policy information stored in the directory to control network equipment such as routers and switches. For example, businesses can establish policies to allocate bandwidth to critical applications and business processes, a key to reliable performance and mission-critical operations.

While becoming a favorite technology of professionals at the front lines of networking, NDS is also capturing the respect of CIOs and other business leaders. From the executive point of view, the issue is of one of bridging the gap between the enterprise and the Internet and intelligently managing the necessary change. Directory-based networks help accomplish these missions by providing a unified management and security infrastructure that spans the enterprise and the Web. Businesses are using this software infrastructure to preserve their existing investments, deploying NDS eDirectory across NetWare, NT, and UNIX platforms (and soon Linux, Windows 2000, and Tru64 UNIX) to create a heterogeneous network that looks, feels, and works as a single entity.

This same directory-based network integrates seamlessly with the Internet, with the directory merging the private and the public into a secure global network that stays open and flexible for upgrades and expansion. The highly scalable NDS eDirectory extends Novell's traditional directory strengths in network management and security to the broader world of Internet Service Providers and e-commerce. Businesses can thus deploy new Internet applications and e-commerce services, but in a planned and phased way that makes sense for the present and future.

For software developers, NDS spells opportunity in the form of new applications and services that tap the digital profiles stored in the directory. Ultimately, it's not directory services themselves that will make the biggest impact on our customers and industry, but the applications and activities that directory services make possible. That's where much of the magic created by people reading this book will be realized. This is an opportunity, I believe, comparable to what the SQL marketplace represented ten years ago. New directory-enabled applications will encompass leading programs in database, messaging, network management, resource planning, and every aspect of e-commerce and business on the Web.

On the Internet, directories are becoming central to locating resources and tailoring services and applications to the needs of individual users. Directory-based Internet services enable profile marketing that respects relationships and provides custom content to the user. In addition, organizations can securely extend their supply-chain management to the Internet by using directory applications to authenticate users, safeguard transactions, and provide selective access to enterprise data. Teachers, meanwhile, are using directory-based applications to structure the Internet for our children and protect them from inappropriate content.

Directory-based applications are reaching into every area of business, and soon, I believe, will cross into a new frontier of consumer solutions. In a networked world, individuals too will need a directory to manage and control the digital identity information that defines where they can go, what they can do, and who they are on the Net. Today, the situation is not so clear for the millions of consumers who shop and do business transactions on the Web. Every time users register with a Web site, they are creating a relationship with an outside organization. The trail of data individuals leave behind when they use the Internet—what some call digital fingerprints—is a rich source of information about their habits, their preferences, and the company they keep. But in doing so, users provide information about their lives, some of it quite personal. When you visit a Web site, the site is actually visiting you.

New directory-based technology, however, may offer the right solution to turn the situation around. For example, Novell's new DigitalMe product gives users personal control of digital identity information such as passwords and IDs, e-mail addresses, the "cookies" that indicate their past Web behavior, and records of past transactions such as retail purchases. The range of potential applications for this technology is vast, ranging from financial services and other online retailers to human resources databases, student directories, and new kinds of messaging and collaboration programs that leverage personal identity. Trusted third parties will serve as back end "identity vaults," leveraging NDS to provide their e-commerce customers with unprecedented levels of personalized service, privacy, and control over life on the Web. Currently, Novell is working with major financial institutions and other partners to evaluate and deploy DigitalMe in new Internet services.

CIOs, network managers, developers, and users are all now using directory services to capture the full benefits of the Internet's new wave. If you represent any of these groups, this fine book on NDS will help you harness that momentum by putting the world's leading directory service to work. It's time to take control of your networks and the Internet, along with all those digital relationships on which the future of your business depends.

Dr. Eric Schmidt
Chairman and CEO
Novell, Inc.

Acknowledgments

While my name is on the cover, and I deserve the blame for any errors or mistakes, innumerable people have contributed to whatever success this book might have, both directly (by working on it with me) and indirectly (by encouraging me or evangelizing NDS).

First, my deepest thanks to David Fugate of Waterside Productions, as well as Guy Hart-Davis, Neil Edde, and Maureen Adams of Sybex. I consider them all friends as well as co-workers on this project.

Donna Crossman, the Project Editor, has been a ray of sunshine and always believed any excuse for missing a deadline, or at least managed to find a way to restructure the schedule. Our Editor, Elizabeth Hurley, fought mightily to get my prose under control and, for the most part, she succeeded. Any glaring errors are mine alone. Jim Henderson, who contributed Chapter 19 on programming for NDS, is an old friend and a successful author in his own right. Technical Editor Art Brieva waded through a huge amount of detail and sorted the fact from the fiction in a way that immensely improved the book. I'd be remiss if I forgot Shannon Murphy, our Production Team Leader, who effortlessly streamlined the production efforts with Publication Services. The Publication Services team of Jan Fisher, Rhonda Ries, and Rob Siedenburg did a wonderful job. A superhuman effort by all, right down to the wire, got this book out the door on time.

I couldn't have written this book without Novell (which, after all, created NDS). I am grateful for the help and support of many people at Novell Technical Services, especially the people I work closely with on the Novell Support Connection: Kim Groneman and the NSC volunteers, especially Jim Henderson, Dave Parkes, Marcus Williamson, Peter Kuo, Marcel Cox, Sandra Harrell, Suzanne Miles, and everyone else who's graduated from the NETW4X forum on CompuServe to the NDS forums on support.novell.com. I owe you a round (one round, Dave!) the next time we get together.

Finally, thanks go to Eric Schmidt and his executive team at Novell, as well as all those on the NDS product teams—including Michael Simpson, Samm DiStasio, Michael Bryant, and Brian Faustyn—Novell's PR team, and their cohorts at Cunningham Communications. They've all spent countless hours helping me to understand the directory and all of its implications.

Contents at a Glance

Table of Contents

Introduction

Over 50 million people worldwide—connected to more than 25 percent of the enterprise networks that exist—are using Novell Directory Services. Since its introduction, more networks have been installed using NDS than any other directory system.

Part of the reason for this is Novell's excellent reputation as a networking vendor; but mostly it's because NDS works, and works better than any other network directory system currently in use or scheduled for release in the next few years.

Yet, with all that success, up until now there have been no books that presented the full story of NDS. Yes, there are a few books out there about repairing and troubleshooting the directory. NDS has also been mentioned in the numerous books about NetWare versions 4.0, 4.01, 4.02, 4.1, 4.11, 4.2, 5.0, and 5.1. This is the only book to tell the complete story of NDS: how (and why) it was created, how it evolved, what it's used for, how it works, and where it's going.

Who Should Read This Book

The author believes everyone should read this book, but the publisher has asked me to be a bit more specific about our intended audience. This book is for you if

- You administer a NetWare network

- You administer a Windows NT or UNIX network

- You write software for networks

- You make purchasing decisions for networks

- You are a "power user" of networks

- You simply want to know more about networking

How This Book Is Organized

Mastering Novell Directory Services is divided into three parts. Part I contains an introduction to directories, an overview of existing directory systems, and a guide to existing standards for directories. Part II delves deeply into NDS: its structure, use, and development. Part III goes beyond NetWare to other products—from Novell and other vendors—that make use of NDS, help you manage NDS, or depend on NDS. I finish up in Chapter 18 with a look at what the future may hold for NDS, and I present a brief introduction to programming with NDS in Chapter 19.

At the back of the book you'll find two handy sources of NDS-related information. Appendix A is a glossary of NDS terms, and Appendix B points you to a site that provides an up-to-date listing of providers of directory utilities and applications.

If you're interested only in NDS, you might start with Chapter 4. There's no real need to read the book from page one through to the end. Jump around as your fancy takes you. Start with the parts you're most interested in, then follow the references to other chapters as you find you need to.

Conventions Used in This Book

Unless otherwise indicated, comments regarding NetWare refer to versions 4.10, 4.11, 4.2, and 5. Things specific to versions 4.1 and 4.2 are usually referenced as 4.*x*, while things specific to versions 5 and 5.1 are usually referenced as 5.*x*. Likewise, NetWare 3.11 and 3.12 are grouped as 3.1*x*.

I've organized the information in this book using some conventions that I hope you'll find useful. I've placed key facts and useful kernels of information in Notes, Tips, and Warnings that can be found throughout the text. (You'll want to pay special attention to the Warnings, which can save you from making common mistakes that are time-consuming to fix.) In some of the chapters, you'll also come across sidebars that contain material related to the topic being discussed, but which isn't necessarily central to it.

What's on the CD

The CD-ROM accompanying this book contains a large selection of programs—full versions, evaluation versions, and demo versions—that can help you to manage and troubleshoot NDS and other aspects of your network. Each directory on the CD-ROM has a readme file explaining what the program does and how to install it. The CD-ROM alone is well worth the price of the book, but you really should read the book anyway.

Keeping in Touch

I'd love to hear your comments about *Mastering Novell Directory Services*. Send e-mail to ndsbook@vquill.com; I promise to answer every one I receive. But please don't send technical questions there. Should you have a technical question, post it to the NDS forum available as part of Novell's Support Connection (NSC) (http://support.novell.com/). As a NSC volunteer, the author reads the messages there every day. (And answers them, too!)

PART

I

Anatomy of a
Directory Service

CHAPTER

1

An Introduction
to Network Directories

Directories are something we use everyday without considering the abstract concept behind them. To understand Novell Directory Services, you'll need to have a firm grasp of this concept both in the limited sense of a network directory, as well as with the more general concept of a directory that is commonly associated with telephone directories and other organized listings. The material presented in this chapter will seem abstract at times, even rather dry; the goal is to provide a solid conceptual base from which you'll be able to understand network directories, particularly Novell Directory Services. Some of the terminology that is useful when discussing the structure of Novell Directory Services is introduced in this chapter.

Throughout the book, the term network directory will be used to refer to the various forms of network, system, and application directories that can exist in a networking environment. Novell Directory Services is but one example of this type of directory.

We'll begin with a brief discussion of the purpose of a network directory and then go on to survey the various aspects of the general directory concept. Next, we'll examine the telephone directory as an example to illustrate how these aspects can interact. Finally, we'll close with a discussion of the unique characteristics of a network directory and how they relate to the general directory concept.

Why a Network Directory?

Network directories can be used to store and organize information about network resources such as computers, users, printers, hubs, routers, web sites—indeed, pretty much everything connected to the network. Network directories can also be used to provide a variety of services, such as supplying users with information about system or application resources, as well as controlling access to those resources.

NOTE Network directories should not be confused with directories associated with file systems. File system directories (now generally known as folders on Windows 95/98/NT/2000 desktops) provide an organizational structure for files stored on a system. While network directories are used to organize information about network resources, both of these directory types are applications of the more general directory concept that will be covered later in this chapter.

Most network directories are an integral part of network operating systems (NOS) or an application. Other directories, though, transcend the boundaries of any single system or application to encompass a group of systems or applications. Organizations with networks often have multiple directories in place and each is associated with the various systems or applications that exist in the network environment. In most cases, such directories operate independently of each other and require separate administrative procedures for maintenance. Users employ those directories that provide information for, or control access to, resources that they use. An emerging concept, called a *metadirectory*, envisions using a single product to administer and view the many disparate directories an enterprise may be using. Novell's DirXML initiative (see Chapter 15, "NDS and Novell Products," for more on metadirectory services) is one approach to unifying our view of the data in multiple directories.

Some network directories are dedicated solely to providing information about system or application resources, while others are used to provide security services to control access to system or application resources. When a network directory is responsible for providing security services, it not only contains information about the resources being secured but it also contains information about users or systems allowed to access those resources. In such cases, the information about users or systems contained in a network directory is used for authentication by a security service so when these users or systems are allowed access to secured resources they cannot be impersonated.

Mapping a Directory's Conceptual Framework

As a concept, network directories do not differ greatly from other examples of the more general concept of a directory, such as telephone directories or other organized lists that provide information. All directories share certain aspects, and these shared aspects explain the manner in which the information in directories is maintained and presented. In the following sections, we'll explore some aspects of the general directory model as discrete elements of a conceptual framework for directories.

Directory Scope

A directory is merely a specialized type of database. It can be distinguished from other databases by its purpose: It is designed, built, and populated with data to allow users to locate objects using information associated with the objects. The directory can be further distinguished by its *scope,* which can be defined as the types of objects it contains combined with its range—that portion of all objects in the real world included within that particular directory. Like any database, a directory is a logically coherent collection of data with some inherent meaning; that is the data are related in some way and have a useful purpose. In order for the directory to maintain its usefulness over time, changes that occur in the portion of the real world encompassed by it need to be reflected in it. That part of the real world represented by a directory can usually be defined as a collection of discrete objects that can take many forms, from physical objects to abstract ideas.

As an example, an employee directory for a company will include all (or a logical subset of all) employees of that company (and no one who is not an employee) and certain types of information associated with those employees.

Since the purpose of an employee directory is to allow users to locate employees or certain information about the employees represented in the directory, all useful information must be systematically associated with the entry for each employee in the directory. As changes occur within the organization (new hires, terminations, promotions, job changes, etc.), the directory needs to be updated to reflect the changes.

In this example, we've made no assumptions about how the data maintained in the directory would be structured or how it would be presented to users. The specification for the directory was primarily concerned with its scope, or the combined description of the types of objects represented in the directory (employees and associated data) and the range (all employees of the company) of the directory.

The scope serves as the specification of the type of information that must be contained within the directory to achieve the directory's purposes. For instance, it would probably be necessary to include information about departments and positions for each employee represented in the directory, since users would likely need to find an employee who holds a particular position within a department. Other useful information that could be contained in an employee directory would be telephone numbers and mail stops so that users can easily contact employees represented in the directory.

Directory Structure

Once the scope of a directory has been defined, a *structure* needs to be established for the directory so that information within the directory can be maintained on an ongoing basis. This structure serves two purposes: ensuring that all objects within a directory can be uniquely identified so that they will map to an object unambiguously within the portion of the real world encompassed by the directory; and providing a framework that can be used to segment maintenance of logical subsets of the objects contained in the directory.

It is not a requirement that the structure established for a directory look the same as the way information within the directory will be presented to users. In other words (in database terms), the fields and field order of the directory do not have to mirror the forms or reports used to add, modify, or view the data. Instead, the structure should be considered the authoritative directory, or superset, from which the various other ways the directory might be presented—the subsets—are derived. These two aspects of structure are called *object identification* (the method used to ensure the uniqueness of each object's name) and *object organization* (the method through which objects are stored and retrieved).

Object Identification

Object identification is the means by which data elements within the directory can be uniquely identified and mapped to objects that exist in the portion of the real world defined in the directory's scope. This can be compared to the use of a master key (or index) in other database systems, where some unique characteristic of the objects represented by data elements in the database is used for the unique identification of each data element. As an example, each employee in an organization could be identified by full name; but since it is possible for employees to have identical names, it is often necessary to use some other characteristic, such as an employee number or social security number, to uniquely identify each employee.

The range of identifiers available for assignment to data elements for unique identification within a directory is often referred to as the *namespace*. Assignment of identifiers from the namespace usually needs to be managed in some way to ensure that no two discrete objects represented in a directory are given the same identifier.

Namespaces in a directory can be specified in one of two ways: each object type can have its own namespace (so that the same identifier can be used for different types of objects); or multiple object types can share a namespace (so that no two types of objects can share the same identifier). When each object type has its own namespace, the various object namespaces can still be mapped to a single namespace for the entire directory (meaning separate namespaces for each object type with another namespace encompassing all object types). Thus a unique identification for each object is achieved by combining identifiers for the objects within the namespace for the object class with an identifier for the object type.

As an example, an employee directory could be structured so that managers and staff are maintained separately. If the two types of objects—managers and staff—represented in the directory had separate namespaces, then data elements representing both a manager and a staff member could use the same identifier. If the two types of objects shared the same namespace, then it would not be possible for the same identifier to be used for both a manager and a staff member.

Let's say you have a convention of creating identifiers by using a person's first initial and last name. Further, let's suppose that the company employs a manager named Jean Smith and a staff member named Joe Smith. With only a single namespace for the organization, both would end up as Jsmith, which wouldn't work since the identifier must be unique. But if managers and staff had separate namespaces, then the identifiers might be Jsmith.MGR and Jsmith.STAFF, which are unique.

Object Organization

The other aspect of the directory structure, the organization of objects within the directory, can be useful in achieving the goals of object identification while also serving other purposes. If objects are grouped in some structured way within the directory, it might be possible to define separate namespaces for each group of objects that are subordinate to the main namespace for the directory. In such a case, the various group namespaces can be considered subsets of a single namespace (encompassing the entire directory) by combining identifiers for the objects within the subordinate namespace with a namespace identifier. This can provide a structured way to deal with name clashes that can occur within a directory.

As we noted earlier, it is entirely possible that two employees in an employee directory could share the same first and last names. Although there might be methods available to deal with such name clashes (such as using middle names or initials to differentiate between the employees), defining groups such as departments or divisions with separate namespaces would decrease the total number of objects sharing a particular namespace and could decrease the chances that name clashes would occur within each group.

Even though a large organization might have more than one employee named Paul Jones, it is less likely that a smaller unit within the organization (such as a department, division, or region) would have more than one employee named Paul Jones. If one Paul Jones was in the Eastern region and another Paul Jones was in the Midwest region, each employee would be known locally as just Paul Jones. Within the entire organization each employee could be uniquely identified in the directory as Paul Jones in the Eastern region and Paul Jones in the Midwest region.

The organization of objects represented in a directory can also serve to make access to information about the objects in the directory easier and to allow for portability of parts of the directory. These are related somewhat to directory presentation, which is covered in the next section. Good organization can also assist in the management of information in the directory through the grouping of objects in some structured manner, so that the groups of objects can be managed separately.

In the case of the employee directory example, a directory encompassing all employees in a large organization could grow too large to be managed effectively or used conveniently. An example of a structure that might address this problem might be to organize the employee directory along divisions or regions within the organization so that each portion of the directory can be maintained independently.

Directory Presentation

Once the structure of a directory has been established in such a way that the information contained in the directory can be maintained effectively, the directory is ready for presentation to users. This means that the raw contents of the directory, otherwise known as the authoritative directory, are made available to users. This can be as simple as printing the contents of the directory and distributing copies to all users. Presentation of the directory in this manner is often not ideal; the results might be too voluminous or difficult to use since it is probably structured in a way that makes it easy to maintain.

There are four objectives that influence the ways in which a directory can be presented to users:

- Completeness

- Accessibility

- Accuracy

- Efficiency

These objectives act not only as goals but also as constraints, because each objective can influence the presentation of a directory in ways that seem to contradict other objectives. Deciding whether a particular presentation of a directory is effective requires that the interests of completeness, accessibility, accuracy, and efficiency be evaluated and then compared with the advantages of using other methods for presenting the directory. It is not uncommon for a directory to be presented using more than one method, each of which is chosen because it satisfies a particular objective more completely than the others.

Completeness: Is All of the Information Available?

Completeness is a necessity for a directory presentation because if a directory cannot be counted on to contain information about all of the objects that inhabit the portion of the real world encompassed by the directory, it cannot be relied on. This is an obvious point when considering a directory presentation that includes all elements represented in a directory. When only a subset of a directory will be presented, completeness dictates that the subset contain all elements that can be expected to be included in the subset.

Accessibility: Can Any Object Be Retrieved?

Much of the usefulness of a directory presentation is determined by accessibility. This objective requires that a directory be available to users in situations where they need to get information from the directory. Accessibility can also be thought of as requiring that information presented from the directory be organized in a way that makes it easy for the user to locate what they are looking for. In the case of the employee directory, this could be accomplished by printing it on a sheet of paper or in a booklet and distributing copies to all employees—the resulting directory presentation could then be kept in desk drawers or posted in cubicles for easy reference by users. Other techniques for improving the accessibility of such an employee directory presentation could involve posting it on Intranet Web sites that can be searched or using an online database system such as Lotus Notes.

Accuracy: Is the Information Correct?

Accuracy is another objective that regulates much of the usefulness of a directory presentation. If the directory information being presented to users cannot be relied upon for accuracy, then all information (including accurate information) contained in the directory presentation will be considered suspect and will decrease the total value of the directory presentation for users. Accuracy requires not only that information from the directory presented to the user be correct (accurately recorded in the directory) but also current (reasonably up-to-date or timely). Constant changes to objects and information in a directory will constrain the ways in which the directory can be presented to users, since some methods will be more difficult to keep up-to-date than others.

Efficiency: Is the Retrieval Process Cost-Effective?

Efficiency is what balances the often-conflicting objectives of completeness, accessibility, and accuracy. The quest for efficiency comes from the need to minimize the costs associated with presenting directories without sacrificing achievement of the other objectives.

In the employee directory example, printing the contents of the employee directory and distributing copies to users as a method of directory presentation might be considered inefficient if accuracy were a critical objective. This is because such a directory presentation would be inaccurate as soon as a change occurred in the organization, unless new editions were constantly being printed and distributed. Since this would be very costly, a method for directory presentation that would allow for online access to current information would more readily satisfy the efficiency objective, although such a method could decrease accessibility for users when they don't have access to online resources.

Meeting the Objectives

The process of balancing the objectives of completeness, accessibility, accuracy, and efficiency is what determines the optimal methods for presenting information from a directory. Using the employee directory as an example once again, it is reasonable to expect that it could be presented in some static form (via a printed list or booklet) that is distributed to users.

The objective of completeness would be achieved by a printed directory as long as the intention were that all employees in the organization be included in the directory presentation. The objective of accessibility would be achieved as long as the information contained in the directory presentation made it easy to locate desired information (printed directories are often convenient for users).

As it has already been pointed out, the objective of accuracy would not likely be optimally achieved by such a method, since it is likely that the printed list would be out-of-date in a strict sense as soon as it was printed and distributed to users. But having a printed directory at one's fingertips is so convenient and the information in it is often "good enough" in aggregate terms to sacrifice some measure of accuracy. The objective of efficiency would limit the frequency of updates to the directory presentation because time and effort are required to print and distribute the employee directory to users. Efficiency would be measured in terms of balancing the need for accuracy of the directory presentation with the costs of printing and distribution.

Putting It Together: The Complete Directory Model

The three aspects of the conceptual framework of a directory that have been examined in this section—scope, structure, and presentation—can now be consolidated in a fashion that allows for the evaluation of directory implementations, including network directories, at a conceptual level. One way to represent such a framework is with a layered model that represents the aspects as building blocks of a complete directory (Figure 1.1).

FIGURE 1.1

A layered directory model

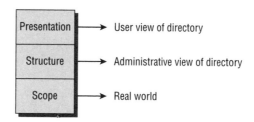

The base layer of the directory model is the scope component that represents the physical or conceptual elements of a directory. The process of defining the scope involves selecting the portion of the real world that we will represent by information in the directory and determining the ways in which the information will be used. The form and content of data elements specified for the directory will depend on the ability of the organization responsible for the directory to collect information for inclusion in it.

The next layer of the directory model is the structural component, representing the administrative elements of a directory. The process of defining the structure involves determining how data elements contained in the directory can be identified so that they can be associated unambiguously with objects that exist in that portion of the real world represented by the directory (as defined in the scope). This is also the realm where an administrative structure for the directory is defined so that information contained in the directory can be maintained effectively.

The administrative structure is not required to be defined in a way that is related to how the information contained in the directory is presented. However, one important thing to keep in mind is that the way the structure is defined could make it difficult to present directory information effectively for users.

The top layer of the directory model is the presentation component that represents the user interface elements of a directory. The objectives of completeness, accessibility, accuracy, and efficiency influence the process of defining the ways in which the information in the directory is presented to users. The presentation component will generally include multiple methods for presenting directory information since certain methods will better satisfy some objectives at the expense of other objectives.

It might be helpful to apply this newly created directory model to another example of a directory implementation to provide some perspective on the concepts covered here. The next section uses this directory model to isolate the conceptual elements of a telephone directory to provide a better understanding of the reasons behind the various ways such a directory is presented.

Illustrating the Directory Model

You're already familiar with the various forms of telephone directories, which provide a great opportunity to illustrate how the model can be applied to an actual implementation of a directory. This section describes a telephone directory using the directory model that was developed in the previous section. Examining a telephone directory with the directory model helps to illustrate the reasons behind the way a telephone directory is structured and presented to users.

Scope: What's in a Phone Book?

In its simplest form, a telephone directory is simply a database of telephone numbers that includes information about the individuals or entities to which the telephone numbers are assigned. In the largest sense possible, the portion of the real world encompassed by the telephone directory would be the collection of all telephone numbers that have been assigned to individuals or entities around the world. We quickly realize, though, that this would be inefficient due to the sheer number of entries needed, so instead we segment the directory to include only those phone numbers assigned within a particular geographical area. To put it another way, the scope of the typical white pages telephone directory is the collection of unique telephone numbers in a given area, along with the name of the person each number is assigned to (presented as an alphabetical listing of the names).

The reason for developing a telephone directory is to allow users to locate information about people or organizations that have been assigned telephone numbers. The information in the telephone directory that will be of most interest to users is the actual telephone number that will allow the user to contact the person or organization that has been assigned the telephone number by the telephone service provider.

Since telephone service providers are responsible for assigning telephone numbers to individuals and entities, it makes sense that the telephone service providers would be responsible for creating the telephone directory. For purposes of day-to-day operations (including service and billing activities), telephone service providers have a wealth of information about the people to whom they have assigned telephone numbers. Some of this information, such as street addresses, could also be of interest to users of a telephone directory, so including this information in the presentation provides an alternate purpose for a telephone directory.

Telephone Directory Structure

Worldwide telephone service is facilitated by an interconnected network of telephone switches that allow connections to be established between most points on the globe. All of these points are connected to local switches and can be uniquely identified by telephone numbers that are assigned by local telephone service providers. Each local telephone company is responsible for assigning telephone numbers to lines connected to switches under its control using a preallocated domain of numbers that could be thought of as the namespace for the group of switches.

A country will often have a number of these local administrative regions. This allows more than one group to carry out the tasks of assigning telephone numbers to lines and maintaining information associated with the lines. In the United States, this partitioning occurs at a regional level using area codes that are administered by RBOCs (Regional Bell Operating Companies). For international communication, countries have been incorporated into a larger namespace through the creation of country codes that are based on agreed-upon conventions.

In this case, the structure of the telephone directory is segmented along administrative lines in such a way that multiple local groups working independently can manage the global namespace. At the same time, the system ensures that all objects represented in the directory can be uniquely located using a combination of the country code, the area or local code, and the local phone number. This telephone number is then used as an address when establishing the telephone connection. The various parts of the telephone number are used as instructions that tell all intervening switches how to route the call.

Telephone Directory Presentation

The most common method for presenting a telephone directory is to print telephone books and distribute them to users of services in the areas they cover. Because of the sheer volume of information that comprises what could be described as the "global telephone directory," only a portion of this directory is presented to users in the form of telephone books. These portions of the global telephone directory that are presented to users contain information about people and organizations that have been assigned telephone numbers in the user's local area. This is acceptable in most cases because the majority of telephone communications occur between people and organizations in the same area. (Well, at least that was true when the system was being first set up.)

Telephone service providers usually distribute two different types of telephone books to users—white pages and yellow pages. Both types of directory presentations are designed to make the information contained in the directory more accessible. The information is organized in ways that make it easy to find telephone numbers using different types of information associated with the person or organization you're looking for.

White pages typically provide an alphabetized list of names that can be used for locating telephone numbers or addresses. Sometimes white pages will provide separate listings for government, business, and residential lines. Yellow pages present listings of businesses organized by categories that can also be used for locating telephone numbers or addresses. Such telephone books, although often rather bulky, are convenient and satisfy the accessibility objective of directory presentation by making telephone directory information available near most phones.

These telephone books also satisfy the completeness objective, as long as they include telephone numbers and other information about all people or organizations that have been assigned telephone numbers in the area that is covered by the telephone book. The objective that suffers with telephone books is accuracy because telephone books are only published periodically (typically once per year). Since changes will occur over time, some of the information in the telephone book will become outdated. Inaccuracy that grows over time is often considered acceptable for telephone books since they are so convenient and the vast majority of the information remains accurate.

The objective of efficiency is the factor that partly explains why telephone books are not published more often, since the publishing schedule for a telephone directory is determined by balancing publishing costs with the amount of information that changes over time.

Telephone service providers also maintain online telephone directory presentations that compensate for the shortcomings of the printed telephone book. Users can often call an operator or information line and obtain a telephone number by providing a name and, if necessary, some information about where the individual or entity might be located. Such a service is convenient for users, because it only requires picking up the phone and asking someone for the desired information. The service is also more accurate than a telephone book because the information provided by the operator will be more current than the information found in a telephone book.

The problem with such an online service is that it is very expensive to provide, and since many of the requests could just as easily be satisfied by referencing the published telephone book it is necessary to discourage such "abuse" by charging for the service in some way. This allows the service to remain available for those who truly need the up-to-date information it provides.

Recent technological trends are also being exploited to improve the accuracy and efficiency of directory presentations. Some telephone service providers have deployed Web-based telephone directories that allow users to search for telephone numbers using a variety of criteria. Web-based directories are advantageous because they provide the same level of accuracy available with a phone-based information service in a more efficient manner because they do not cost nearly as much to maintain. In cases where users have easy Internet access, such a service can also be more accessible than a telephone book.

The Network Directory's Special Features

In the previous examination of the telephone directory as an application of the directory model, we indulged in a fair amount of sleight-of-hand to avoid discussing some of the more technical aspects behind the structural, or administrative, aspects of the directory. Subjecting the phone directory to a more careful examination would have betrayed the true identity of the telephone directory. The telephone directory is, after all, a network directory.

What aspects of the telephone directory allow it to make its way into the territory of network directories? The first clue can be found in the definition of the scope, where the telephone system is characterized as an interconnected network of telephone switches. In addition, the key objects represented in the directory are telephone numbers, which act as addresses for establishing connections between points attached to switches over the telephone network. The primary purpose for presenting the directory is to allow users to locate telephone numbers using names or categories that are easier to remember than numbers.

Additional investigation of some of the details of telephone switch management and network routing would have revealed the integral role of the directory in the operation of the telephone network. This integration of the directory into the operation of the network is the critical factor that distinguishes network directories from the more general forms of directories (such as an employee directory). The network directory acts as more than a simple listing of the resources available. By interacting with the user, the network directory can control access to the objects on the network and the directory itself. Aside from the presentation of network-related information to users, one of the more common purposes of a network directory is to provide a means by which system or application resources can be managed.

Using Access Control

Network directories do have one unique characteristic when compared to other directories: the role they play in controlling access to system or application resources on the network. A network directory's security role is defined as part of the directory's scope. When that is done it is also necessary to specify, within the scope, the methods available for controlling access to resources.

Access to a network resource within the scope of a directory can be controlled simply by requiring a password before the resource can be accessed.

This type of authentication is usually considered to be *weak*. When the password is associated with a resource, it is usually shared by multiple users in such a way that one of the principles of system security, individual accountability, cannot be achieved without great difficulty. For example, if every member of a group uses the same password to access the resource there is no way to be sure which member is accessing it at any given time. Some measure of individual accountability for users could be achieved by assigning unique passwords to each user for each resource being protected, but that would require $N \times R$ passwords, where N is the number of users and R is the number of resources. This could quickly become an administrative nightmare!

There are methods for controlling access to resources that more adequately provide for individual accountability. They usually involve specifying methods for reliably determining the identity of users accessing secured resources. In order to identify users allowed to access system or application resources, the definition of the scope of the directory must incorporate user identification object types, such as system identifiers or user accounts. When system identifiers are used, a reasonable level of assurance is required that an unauthorized system cannot easily impersonate an authorized system by co-opting its identifier. When user accounts are used, a reasonably strong form of authentication needs to be performed so that an unauthorized user cannot easily impersonate an authorized user. General security principles are covered in greater detail in the discussion of NDS security in Chapter 12.

Working with Multiple Network Directories

As systems and applications proliferate in a networking environment, the number of directories within that environment is also likely to increase. Since the directories often operate independently, this proliferation of directories places burdens on users, as well as on the staff responsible for maintaining the directories associated with the systems and applications. These burdens are especially acute when multiple independent directories participate in securing access to network resources.

From an administrative perspective, the use of multiple independent directories requires redundant procedures to maintain the system identifiers or user accounts needed to identify authorized users. From a user's perspective, users are required to identify themselves in some way to the various directories they interact with. This means that users are often responsible for maintaining several different user accounts and passwords.

The burdens introduced by the use of multiple independent network directories often motivate organizations to analyze their network directory environment to identify opportunities for the integration of directory information across disparate systems and applications. By integrating directory information across multiple systems and applications, organizations can eliminate some of the redundant and costly administration procedures that are required to manage network directories and also reduce the number of separate user accounts and passwords that users are required to maintain. In some cases, the ideal goal of such an exercise is the selection of a universal network directory that can eliminate redundant directory administration while also allowing for a single point of user authentication (single sign-on). We firmly believe that NDS is that universal directory system.

Of course, while the ideal is to have only one directory system, the reality is that multiple directories will be present on our networks for the foreseeable future. The pioneering work Novell has done with NDS, including dirXML and Single Sign-On, goes a long way towards allowing a single point of administration as well as a single point of access for all of the directories an administrator and a user need to interact with.

Summary

In this chapter, you've been introduced to the directory concept as a general purpose listing through the example of an employee directory. By looking at the generally understood concept of a telephone directory, which was expanded to a generic definition of a network directory, you've gotten an idea of some of the principles behind a directory. A directory is defined by its scope—the collection of objects it contains, their unique identifier, and the directory's access methods.

This chapter has examined the individual components common to most types of directories and has developed a conceptual directory model to aid in the development of an understanding of how directories can be implemented. Four factors—completeness, accessibility, accuracy, and efficiency—are important to a directory's implementation. All of these concepts are examined in greater detail throughout the first section of this book.

The next chapter examines network directories in more concrete terms by presenting examples of some of the more common ones that inhabit networking environments.

CHAPTER

2

The Evolution of
Network Directories

As you learned in Chapter 1, network directories share most of the characteristics of the general directory concept, differing primarily in their specialized network—or system-related—purposes. Network directories are often characterized as services (directory services or naming services) because they are usually implemented in a manner similar to other network services, such as file and print, but with the express purpose of associating names with network resources in order to hide some of the underlying complexities of network systems.

The most typical role for a directory or naming service in a network is a complementary one in which the directory assists users with locating and accessing resources provided by other network services, while also used in support of security services that implement user-level security controls.

The services aspect of network directories relates to both the structural and presentation facets of the conceptual directory framework presented in Chapter 1. Information in network directories is usually managed (structural) and made available (presentation) through the operating system or as part of applications in the form of add-on programs, libraries, or application program interfaces (APIs). Programs to maintain information in a network directory are often distinct from those used to present the directory information, although in some cases the functions will use the same facilities.

Directory management is usually considered a privileged activity that is delegated to select individuals or groups who are authorized to perform such management. Access to directory information is also considered a privileged activity in some cases. When either is the case, security controls are usually implemented by the directory or by the systems or applications providing directory services to protect the directory information from unauthorized access and tampering by systems or personnel.

This chapter provides brief overviews of several common directories in use within the computer-networking world as well as those directory services used by Novell in NetWare before NDS. The network directories included in this chapter were chosen more for their representative value than out of a desire for completeness, so the exclusion of a directory implementation from this discussion should not be taken as a value judgment of any kind. Two network directories are deliberately missing from this chapter: X.500 and its related Lightweight Directory Access Protocol (LDAP), which will be discussed in the next chapter; and Novell Directory Services, which is the focus of the rest of this book.

Even though the common roles for directories can be defined with a certain amount of clarity, it is not often clear how to identify a directory. In other words, when looking at a system, where do we look for a directory?

The first hint is to look for some of the common network functions where directories usually play the roles that were identified earlier and assume that a directory is there performing its duties. For example, directories are often integral to the identification and authentication process that is so important to system security. So, if we look at how security is implemented within a system, we will probably find a directory performing its duties. In addition, directories often assist in allowing for easy location of network resources, therefore if we look at how network resources are located, we will probably find a directory performing its duties. This is the approach taken in this chapter in the case of systems within which directories were not self-evident.

Network Name Resolution

We'll begin our discussion of network directory implementations with one of the simpler forms—services dedicated to performing the essential function of providing network name resolution to simplify access to network resources. Network name resolution is a process that allows names to be associated with network resources so that the resources can be accessed through names instead of network addresses, since names are more easily remembered than addresses. Three naming services are covered in this section: Domain Naming System (DNS) for TCP/IP; Windows Internet Naming Systems (WINS) for NetBIOS over TCP/IP; and Service Advertising Protocol (SAP) for IPX/SPX.

Domain Naming System (DNS)

The Domain Naming System is without a doubt the most widely deployed network directory in use today. The Domain Naming System (DNS) is a centralized naming service for the TCP/IP protocol suite that provides host-name-to-IP address resolution services to systems on private networks or on the Internet. Name resolution is used for the TCP/IP protocol suite to allow network hosts to be identified using names rather than numeric addresses, since names are usually easier for humans to remember.

The default way to provide host name resolution services for the TCP/IP protocol suite is to use local *hosts* databases that map IP addresses to host names. On most systems, the hosts database usually is a whitespace-delimited file called `/etc/hosts` that simply consists of records (lines) containing IP addresses using dotted decimal notation (e.g., `10.55.243.1`) and one or more names associated with each address. (In a whitespace-delimited file, fields within a record are separated by blank spaces or simple punctuation—commas or semicolons.) When a process attempts to contact a TCP/IP resource using a name instead of an address, the *hosts* database on the local workstation is automatically consulted to find the first IP address associated with the name. Once an address-to-name association is located, the associated IP address is used to contact the destination host. If an association can not be found, then the connection attempt fails just as if an incorrect address had been provided.

There are several problems that usually present themselves when using local hosts databases for name resolution as network environments grow. First, when a node is added to a network or changes its location, the hosts databases for all systems that wish to converse with this node need to be updated in some way. Since it is usually difficult to predict the systems with which a given system will need to communicate, it is usually easier to distribute changes to all systems on a network. Such a scheme is manageable as long as there are not many systems that need to be updated, and as long as there is little or no communications occurring with systems on other networks.

In fact, in the early days of the Internet a centralized distribution scheme was used where a central authority distributed an authoritative hosts database to sites connected to the Internet. As the number of connected sites grew, maintenance and distribution of this authoritative database became difficult. Keeping the database current would have required making many changes each day and distributing current copies of the authoritative hosts database to an increasing number of sites at an accelerated pace. In addition, the size of this authoritative hosts database was growing too large to be distributed easily. It was obvious that another method was needed to provide name resolution for the Internet.

What was needed was a way to provide access to current host name resolution information for systems connected to the Internet while allowing local administrative control over name resolution information related to local resources. The resulting design of the Domain Naming System (DNS), described in RFCs (Requests For Comments) 1034 and 1035 and implemented in products such as the Berkeley Internet Name Domain (BIND), satisfied these requirements. DNS adopted a client-server model where servers contain host-name-to-IP-address mapping information about a portion of the network and make this information available to clients.

Nameservers

DNS servers, called *nameservers,* manage portions of a hierarchical namespace—a term used to denote a group of related objects contained within a small subset of the realm of the network. The entire namespace is hierarchical to allow for the unique identification by name of every system attached to the connected networks and registered in databases maintained by nameservers. The DNS hierarchy is divided into domains, or zones, that form an inverted tree that starts at the root and branches downward through independently managed domains. Authority to manage host-name-to-IP-address mappings within a domain is delegated by an administrator of a domain holding a position in the hierarchy directly above the domain.

Any given nameserver knows only about the domains that it is directly responsible for managing, as well as the nameservers for any domains directly above and below its managed domains in the DNS hierarchy. Systems that are represented by entries in a domain database on a nameserver can be uniquely identified within the DNS hierarchy using a combination of host name and domain name. For example, if a system has a host name of "snoopy" within the domain database for `foo.bar.com`, it can be contacted by a client system outside the domain using the name `snoopy.foo.bar.com` as long as the client system resolves names with a nameserver within the same hierarchy. This combination of host name and domain name is sometimes referred to as an FQDN (Fully Qualified Domain Name).

Resolvers

Client systems, called *resolvers,* resolve names by interacting with nameservers using simple queries and responses. It is necessary for a client system to specify one or more nameservers that it will use to originate all host name resolution operations. When multiple nameservers are specified, the resolver will use the first nameserver in the list as long as it is available—other nameservers often are used only when the first nameserver is unavailable. On Unix systems, the nameservers used by a resolver usually are specified in the `/etc/resolv.conf` file that contains a default domain name and the IP addresses of one or more nameservers.

Name resolution operations usually begin with the resolver sending a query to a nameserver containing a host name that needs to be resolved to an address. The response that the nameserver sends to the resolver depends on a number of factors. If the name being requested is for a domain directly managed by the nameserver, and the requested host has an entry in the local database, the nameserver will immediately send a response containing the requested host's IP address, and the operation will be complete once the resolver receives the response. If the name being requested is for a domain that is not directly managed by the nameserver, the nameserver will do one of three things depending on the configuration:

- The nameserver will usually first consult its cache that is used to hold the results of recent or frequent name resolution requests. The cache is used to cut down on name resolution traffic and to increase the speed with which responses can be provided to resolvers. If the requested information is not in cache, one of the traditional name resolution methods is used instead and the result is stored in cache.

- The nameserver will provide *iterative* name resolution by responding to the resolver with one or more referrals to other nameservers (either above or below the nameserver in the DNS hierarchy) that would better allow the host's DNS entry to be located. At this point, the resolver is responsible for contacting a referred nameserver in the same manner that it contacted the previous nameserver. The resolver will continue chasing down referrals as necessary until the host name can be resolved to an IP address, it runs out of referrals, or it receives a response that the host cannot be found.

- The nameserver will provide *recursive* name resolution by contacting another nameserver on behalf of the resolver and taking control of the name resolution process until it can provide a response to the resolver. In this case, the nameserver is responsible for chasing down referrals as necessary, and the only response the resolver receives will be an IP address or a response that the host cannot be found.

When navigating the DNS hierarchy to resolve host names, a resolver could encounter nameservers that provide either iterative or recursive name resolution, although recursive name resolution is more commonly provided by nameservers.

Database Replication and Management

The information residing on a particular nameserver may be replicated to other servers that will provide identical name resolution services to resolvers for fault tolerance and load balancing purposes. Administration of host-name-to-IP-address mappings within a particular domain occurs at the primary nameserver for the domain, and copies of the DNS database are downloaded periodically by replica nameservers in a process called *zone transfer*. As long as replication occurs frequently and consistently, resolvers can use any primary or replica nameserver for name resolution without worrying about whether the information is current or accurate.

Due to the cross-platform nature of DNS (numerous types of servers and clients can participate in DNS name resolution), there is no single method that is used to manage the DNS database. Depending on the operating system platform acting as a nameserver as well as the software used to provide name resolution services, the DNS database could be maintained directly through manipulation of the database tables or indirectly through utilities. Client name resolution operations are always performed using the protocols defined in the DNS specification.

DNS and the Internet

The Domain Naming System is important as a network directory due to its current status as an official Internet standard and its wide acceptance by users and organizations as the authoritative naming service for hosts and networks connected to the Internet. Even if a network is not connected to the Internet, DNS is still used by organizations with TCP/IP networks since it provides a reasonably elegant method for management of name-to-address mappings for TCP/IP hosts on an Intranet. DNS is also used as the basis for some electronic mail addressing systems to allow for the unique identification of users in the same way that systems are uniquely identified. The only differences between the DNS hierarchy of the Internet and one that is used by organizations not connected to the Internet come down to administration of the top-level domains.

The official DNS domain hierarchy for the Internet has long been supervised by the Internet Assigned Number Authority (IANA), the Internet Network Information Center (InterNIC), and Network Solutions Inc. (NSI). These organizations have authorized a limited number of top-level domains covering generic organizational and geographic groupings. Table 2.1 lists the seven top-level organizational domains and some of the top-level geographical domains. Currently, if an organization wants to participate on the Internet, it must register its first-level name with the InterNIC or NSI as a subdomain of one of the top-level domains. This is changing, and the newly organized Internet Corporation for Assigned Names and Numbers (ICANN) was formed to take over responsibility for the IP address space allocation, protocol parameter assignment, domain name system management, and root server system management functions.

The governance by the various Internet authorities of the top-level and first-level domains in the Internet DNS hierarchy has been an increasingly controversial topic in recent years as the networking community has been forced to deal with two types of scarcity due to the explosion of the Internet. The first type of scarcity, that of IP addresses, is technological and results from the limited 32-bit address space of the present specifications for the IP protocol. This will be addressed with the implementation of version 6 of the IP protocol (IPv6; the present version is IPv4) with its larger address space.

The second type of scarcity, that of names within the top-level domain name spaces, is largely arbitrary and has led to many well-publicized conflicts between organizations and individuals trying to stake claims to Net identities. The two types of scarcity are not necessarily related, but the challenges caused by the scarcity of IP addresses have overshadowed the ease with which the scarcity of domain names could be addressed.

The process of registering Internet domain names, and even the fees charged for the administration of the registration process, has been the source of dissatisfaction for many in recent years and has led to litigation in some cases. This can be attributed to the unclear nature of rules governing the assignment of Internet domain names. For instance, it is still not clear whether or how trademarks (like those from countries outside the United States) can be protected for or applied to Internet domain names under the .com top-level domain.

TABLE 2.1	**Domain Name**	**Covers**
Internet Top-Level Domains	com	Commercial organization
	edu	Educational institution
	gov	Government agency or organization
	int	International organization
	mil	U.S. military
	net	Networking organization
	org	Nonprofit organization
	us	United States
	de	Germany
	nl	Netherlands
	jp	Japan
	fr	France
	uk	United Kingdom

The technical and political issues surrounding the Domain Naming System that have emerged over time highlight some of the challenges that exist when developing and maintaining any universal network directory. DNS was able to achieve its present ubiquity due to its simplicity and the essential name resolution function it performed. Although the political issues could increasingly cripple the growth of the official Internet DNS hierarchy, the simplicity of DNS could ultimately contribute most to its demise as other alternatives that have more features or flexibility are evaluated and adopted.

DNS primarily provides a single function: the resolution of host names to IP addresses. The problem with this is that users and organizations often would like to be able to access more information about systems, services, and other network resources, but doing so would require another directory to store this additional information. Since this other directory could also easily contain information about host names and IP addresses for name resolution, a separate DNS database would be tautological. The emergence of LDAP (Lightweight Directory Access Protocol) as an official Internet standard for accessing a variety of directories could make this scenario a reality.

DHCP

Another problem with DNS as it was originally specified is that the host-name-to-IP-address database maintained on nameservers is static, meaning that administrative intervention is required to change the contents to reflect changes to the networking environment. This requirement is inconsistent with techniques that have been developed to address the scarcity of IP addresses. One such technique, Dynamic Host Configuration Protocol (DHCP), allows a system to lease an IP address on a network for a certain period of time when necessary from a pool of addresses. With DHCP it is possible and perhaps probable (depending on how leases are arranged) that any given system will have different IP addresses over a period of time.

Because administrators do not directly control which system gets a particular IP address, it is not feasible for the DNS database to be updated each time a system obtains a new IP address. The way this is somewhat addressed is for administrators to reserve a range of IP addresses for static resources such as servers so that name resolution information for resources that are accessed by users can remain current in the DNS database. As information becomes increasingly mobile or distributed on multiple systems, though, this practice could defeat the purpose of DHCP because an increasing number of systems will require static addresses. Several vendors, including Novell, are attempting to address this issue by providing a means for DHCP to communicate with DNS to allow name resolution for dynamic resources. In fact, the newest versions of NDS include both DNS and DHCP within the directory service.

Windows Internet Naming System (WINS)

Windows Internet Naming Service (WINS) is a name resolution service designed by Microsoft for network resources using the NetBIOS protocol. NetBIOS (originally developed by IBM), and its successor NetBEUI, has been the protocol of choice (rather than Unix's TCP/IP or Novell's IPX/SPX) for Windows networking.

The use of NetBIOS/NetBEUI is dropping as Microsoft has encouraged the use of TCP/IP and NWLink (its implementation of IPX/SPX) for Windows networking beginning with Windows 95 and Windows NT 4. Nevertheless, WINS is still used in Windows peer-to-peer networks as well as for DHCP in Windows NT.

WINS is similar in function to the Domain Naming System, although it adds functionality through interaction with DHCP by ensuring that NetBIOS names are unique and by allowing the name resolution database to be maintained dynamically. The name resolution services provided by WINS are meant to replace the manual method of maintaining name resolution information for NetBIOS resources on TCP/IP networks that was first introduced with Microsoft's LAN Manager. This original method involved the use of lmhosts databases (actually, a flat, whitespace delimited file similar to DNS's /etc/hosts database) stored on client workstations or servers. Just as with the base IP protocol suite, it is possible to use DNS to provide name resolution for NetBIOS resources, but WINS is generally preferred due to its added functionality.

Updating WINS Databases: Push Partners and Pull Partners

WINS cooperates with the DHCP service running on a Windows NT/Windows 2000 Server. This server is used for centralized administration and configuration of additional WINS servers, static name tables, and replication information. Additional WINS servers that contain replicas of the main WINS database are used to distribute NetBIOS name resolution services and traffic for fault tolerance and load balancing. Any given WINS server will be a *push partner* or *pull partner* with at least one other WINS server. Pull partners receive WINS database updates from other WINS servers, while push partners send information to other WINS servers. It is possible for a WINS server to be both push and pull partners with various other WINS servers.

All NetBIOS-name-to-IP-address-mapping records in the WINS database are assigned version numbers so that push and pull partners can determine which records need to be updated during replication. Both push and pull partners can initiate replication sessions based on a predefined replication threshold based on the time since the last replication. Push partners can also initiate replication once a threshold based on the number of updates has been exceeded.

When a pull partner initiates a replication session, it requests all records with a higher version number than the records it currently possesses from its partner. When a push partner initiates a replication session, it notifies its partners and they proceed as if they were initiating the replication session by requesting all records with a higher version number than those records they currently possess.

WINS and the Internet

The implementation of WINS by organizations connected to the Internet has been limited to providing name resolution for NetBIOS resources only within the organizations. This is partly due to the fact that WINS servers provide a flat namespace which must realistically be maintained centrally by an organization, so unlike the case of DNS, there is not a network of independently managed WINS databases that interact with each other to provide universal name resolution services.

Another factor that limits the possibility that the enhanced functionality of WINS could allow it to replace DNS, despite the fact that it provides the same basic functions to a certain extent, is that WINS is dedicated to providing name resolution for NetBIOS resources. This factor keeps WINS from being used to provide name resolution for other TCP/IP services.

Service Advertising Protocol (SAP)

Service Advertising Protocol (SAP) is a naming service for the IPX/SPX protocol designed by Novell for its NetWare operating system. SAP allows systems (such as file servers, print servers, and gateway servers) to advertise their services and addresses so they can be located on the network using names instead of addresses.

SAP is typically implemented as a dynamic naming service where systems advertise their presence periodically during operation so that routers can build tables of available services. Routers dynamically remove services from the tables they maintain either when they are informed by an advertising service that it will stop functioning or when they do not hear from an advertising service for a specified period of time. The form of service information tables differs by systems; for example, NetWare servers (where routing is integral) store SAP entries in the bindery as dynamic objects.

Information about services is propagated to routers that maintain service information tables by service-providing systems and by other routers. Service-providing systems provide first-hand information about their services by periodically broadcasting IPX packets containing information about all services available on the system on their local network segments. Routers provide second-hand information about network services by periodically broadcasting all SAP information maintained in their tables on their local interfaces. Routers will not, however, broadcast SAP information on an interface from which they learned of the service.

Each SAP packet contains one or more SAP entries, and each SAP entry consists of a type identifier, a service name, and an IPX network address. Type identifiers provide a standard numeric representation of the type of service being advertised, and each type identifier encompasses an independent flat namespace. For example, it is perfectly reasonable for the same name to be advertised with multiple SAP types as long as the same name is not advertised with the same SAP type. There is no way for SAP to prevent a service from advertising a name for a service using a name associated with a service that is already in use on a network, but it will be difficult to establish reliable communications when such a name clash occurs.

Network clients use SAP to locate services by issuing queries for services either by sending a broadcast on the local network or by contacting a specific router. When a SAP query is sent to a specific router, the router will respond with all services from its service information tables that satisfy the query. When a SAP query is issued as a broadcast, all routers connected to the local network will respond with services that satisfy the query.

An example of a common broadcast request on a NetWare network is Get Nearest Server, which allows a client system to obtain the network address of the nearest server for its initial attachment to the network.

SAP is a highly effective name resolution service and its simplicity has allowed it to remain in wide use in NetWare networks despite some serious problems with the way it operates on large networks. The most serious problem is that SAP can require a tremendous amount of broadcast traffic to propagate current service availability information that allows routers to keep their service information tables current. This characteristic has lead to the router broadcasts that occur on network segments being characterized as freight trains since hundreds of packets can be broadcast every minute on network segments throughout a network. In response to this, most organizations with large NetWare networks implement SAP filtering to control the propagation throughout the network of information about certain types of services, but this can lead to the unavailability of some services that might be needed occasionally even though they would normally be reachable.

Several services have been developed by Novell to reduce the need for such broadcast traffic to maintain current service information that makes SAP much more manageable, such as NetWare Link Services Protocol (NLSP), NetWare/IP and its Domain SAP Services (DSS), and Novell Directory Services (NDS). However, SAP continues to play a role in IPX networks because many networks have older devices that require it and because it is still an effective way for client systems to learn about nearby services.

Unix Services

The Unix operating system differs from the others we are examining in this chapter in that it is not a single operating system developed by a vendor for one or more specific system architectures. Instead, Unix can be thought of as a family of operating systems developed by many different vendors for a wide array of system architectures. The different "flavors" of Unix that have been developed over the years share some common characteristics, such as a preemptive multitasking kernel, modularity of key components, and integral support for the TCP/IP protocol suite. These common characteristics allow Unix to be considered as if it were a single operating system despite numerous differences in the details of the various vendor implementations.

The many paths leading from the origins of Unix to its proliferation offer an explanation for the unique state of the Unix operating system. Unix was originally designed and written for PDP-7 systems by engineers at AT&T's Bell Labs, after a group writing the Multics operating system was spun off. (This had left Bell Labs without an operating system of its own.)

The original Unix code was eventually rewritten using the newly invented C language in 1973, and the portability of the C language allowed Unix to be ported away from the original PDP systems to newer systems. Also, at this time Unix was becoming popular in academic institutions due to the ease with which the source code could be obtained and the lessons about operating system design and implementation that could be learned by studying the source code. The portability of the operating system code also made it popular with designers of new systems. This was because all that was necessary to provide the Unix operating system for their new systems was to write a C compiler for the particular system and make some minor hardware-specific modifications to the source code.

Design and porting efforts by system designers and educational institutions in the early days of Unix generally included the addition of custom "improvements" to address perceived shortcomings of the original Unix operating system. Since most development efforts were undertaken independently, many of the improvements were redundant or were not compatible with each other, so consequently interoperability between Unix implementations suffered.

Various drives to improve the interoperability between Unix implementations have resulted in the establishment of some standards and the broad acceptance of other *de facto* standards. The standardization process developed to the point where two major versions of Unix emerged: System V from AT&T's Unix System Laboratories (USL)—subsequently controlled by Novell and then the Santa Cruz Operation (SCO)—and BSD (Berkeley Software Distribution). Today, most Unix implementations incorporate most aspects of both major versions to enhance interoperability between different vendors' implementations.

One certainly does not need to look hard to identify directories within the various Unix implementations. The previously discussed *hosts* and DNS databases are examples of directories that were originally implemented on Unix systems to provide essential functionality for the TCP/IP protocol suite, which has been implemented along with the directories on so many other platforms. Other directories can be found that help users locate services on other systems. Despite the fact that security was not a consideration in the original plans for Unix, most Unix implementations now share a standard user-focused security model that can use several types of user and group directories to store the information needed to implement security.

The basic user directory used by the Unix security mechanism consists of lists of users and groups stored in the `/etc/passwd` and `/etc/group` files. Records containing information about users, such as user name, user ID (uid), default group ID (gid), password, and GECOS (the user's full name or other information about the user) are typically stored in the `/etc/passwd` file in colon-delimited fields. Security considerations often dictate that the password information be stored in a "shadow" password file so that the encrypted password cannot be directly accessible to all users on the system as is usually the case when the passwords are stored in the /etc/passwd file.

GECOS originally stood for General Electric Comprehensive Operating System, an OS developed by GE around 1970. When GE's computer division was sold to Honeywell, it was changed to GCOS. Bell Labs had a few GCOS machines, running print spooling and other services, and incorporated a field into early Unix /etc/passwd files to store information about these machines, calling it the "GECOS field". Today, long after GCOS has passed from the scene, the field is still used for the user's full name and other human-ID information on many Unix systems.

Even though the passwords are encrypted using a one-way hash algorithm, the encrypted passwords are still subject to offline brute force or dictionary attacks if they are directly readable by users. The group directory is stored in the /etc/group file and each record consists of a colon-delimited field containing a group name, group ID (gid), and a comma-delimited member list. A user is a member of a group if the user appears in the group's member list or if the user's gid maps to the group. The numeric uid and gid are used internally by Unix to track privileges—assigning privileges at the group level allows for the privileges to affect all members of the group.

The Unix user and group directories encompass independent flat namespaces, so it is possible for a user and a group to have the same name without being related in any way. In addition, user and group directories on one system do not necessarily have any relation to user and group directories on other systems.

Some facilities that allow interaction between multiple systems make assumptions about the equivalence of uid and gid information on the communicating systems, and some facilities allow for the possession of a uid on one system to serve as a credential for gaining access to another system. Despite the obvious negative security implications of such connectivity schemes, they are popular in some cases due to their simplicity, and attempts are made to maintain common uid and gid schemes across systems.

To ease user maintenance for multiple systems, the Network Information Service (NIS) can be used as a distributed name service to map a centralized directory on top of the basic user and group directories for multiple systems. Some installations also use NFS (Network File System) to allow systems to use a common set of directory files in a shared /etc directory. When security is of greater concern in a multisystem environment, Kerberos can be used to provide a centralized directory while replacing some of the standard Unix security mechanisms that are considered weak by most people in the security community. Both facilities are discussed in the following sections.

Network Information Service (NIS)

The Network Information Service (NIS) is a distributed name service developed by Sun Microsystems that extends or replaces many of the basic /etc directories used by Unix systems to allow directory information to be stored on a single system and shared by many hosts.

NIS was originally called Yellow Pages (YP), but since Yellow Pages is a trademark in the United Kingdom the name was changed to Network Information Service. Many of the commands associated with NIS retain the "yp" prefix.

NIS Systems Organization

Systems using NIS are organized into domains within which one or more NIS servers provide information for other machines within the domain. NIS domains are similar in concept to DNS domains except they lack its hierarchy. NIS servers maintain shared directory information in files called *maps* that are usually derived from files that make up the Unix /etc directories (such as /etc/passwd, /etc/group, /etc/hosts, etc.).

Within an NIS domain, one NIS server is designated as the master and other servers that provide NIS services act as slaves to allow for fault tolerance and load balancing. There can be only one master server for each NIS domain, although it is possible for a single server to act as a master for multiple domains. All maintenance activities are performed on the master server, and the slave servers obtain their information from the master whenever changes are made.

All NIS maps have version numbers associated with them, and slave servers use this version information to detect changes that occur on the master server so they can initiate a transfer to keep the copies of their maps current. Master servers are also capable of initiating the transfer of maps by pushing updated information to slave servers.

NIS Client Systems

NIS client systems are configured to request directory information from one or more servers within the system's domain via a process called *binding*. It doesn't matter whether the information comes from a master or slave server since all information within a domain should be identical. Binding is a three-step process that consists of a program running on the client system obtaining the address of an active NIS server and then sending the request to the NIS server, which returns the requested information directly to the program making the request. This type of client-server directory model allows a large number of systems to use the same directory data without requiring that the data be maintained on each system.

In order for a client configured for NIS to obtain user information from an NIS server, its /etc/passwd file must contain a special NIS redirection record (typically taking the form +: or +::0:0:::) that instructs the NIS client software to query NIS for all further information when it is encountered. Since programs access the /etc/passwd file sequentially, any records that appear before this special record are treated as normal user records while all other records following the NIS redirection record are ignored. This means that user accounts that appear in the /etc/passwd file before the NIS redirection record can be thought of as local resources, whereas user accounts that are accessed via an NIS server are domain resources.

Client system access to group information is handled in a similar manner with a special NIS redirection record (typically taking the form +:) occurring after local groups in the /etc/group file. The mail aliases file (/etc/aliases or /usr/lib/aliases) is another directory file where local information can be accessed before an NIS lookup takes place. Local information in other directory files (such as /etc/hosts, /etc/hosts.equiv, /etc/netgroups, /etc/protocols, and /etc/services) is ignored when NIS is used to distribute directory information within a domain.

NIS Security Issues

Several security issues have been identified with the original specifications of the Network Information Service, almost all of which center around the lack of authentication requirements for NIS servers to disseminate directory information. For example, this might allow an anonymous host on a network to request user information from an NIS server and receive the equivalent of an /etc/passwd record containing the encrypted password as a response.

With this information, an intruder can use an offline brute force or dictionary attack to obtain a password from this information and gain unauthorized access to systems, all without obtaining any authorized access at all to any system within the NIS domain. It is also conceivable that an anonymous host could convince a slave NIS server to accept unauthorized updates that might allow an intruder to gain unauthorized access to a system within the server's NIS domain.

As a result of these vulnerabilities and other scalability problems, the original specification of NIS is not considered robust. It does not address other security and deployment issues that exist in Unix networking environments. Various techniques for enhancing the security of NIS have been proposed, such as keeping an NIS domain name secret, but this *security by obscurity* approach does not inspire a great deal of confidence in network administrators. Sun has developed an enhanced directory service called Network Information Service Plus (NIS+), which addresses many of the security and scalability limitations of the original NIS, but its implementation has been hampered by its lack of full interoperability with other NIS servers and its limited third-party support.

Kerberos

Kerberos is a network security system originally developed for Project Athena at MIT (Massachusetts Institute of Technology) that provides trusted third-party authentication and key management for secure communications between network nodes. With Kerberos, centralized key distribution hosts mediate the establishment of network sessions between systems in such a way that both ends of a session can authenticate to each other while agreeing on keys used for encryption or integrity validation of secure communications. Versions 4 and 5 of Kerberos (commonly referred to as Kerberos V4 and Kerberos V5) are the two most recent implementations of the Kerberos system and are the most common versions in use. Kerberos is receiving increasing attention today, since it is the default authentication method used in Windows 2000 networks implementing Microsoft's Active Directory Service (ADS).

Kerberos V4 and V5 Implementation

The implementation details of Kerberos V4 and V5 differ significantly, but the concepts behind the two versions are similar enough to allow them to be covered together. The key idea behind Kerberos is that a central host acts as Key Distribution Center (KDC) that mediates communications between principals that trust it. As Kerberos views things, a *principal* is anything using the authentication system, be it a user or a network service running on a server. There may be more than one service being provided by a given server that uses Kerberos, just as there may be more than one user requesting a given service with the involvement of Kerberos.

The primary component of the Kerberos system is a master database residing on a server that maintains a list of each of its principals (users or services) and their private keys. Only the Kerberos servers and their principals know the private keys, and a Kerberos server uses these keys to create messages that are used to convince one principal that another is authentic. In Kerberos V4, each principal is assigned a three-part identifier that consists of a name, instance, and realm. Instances are somewhat redundant for normal users, but they are often used to identify services on a server that is identified by a name. Kerberos V5 dropped the instance component for principal identification so each client is assigned only a two-part identifier that consists of a name and realm.

Realms are the administrative units of Kerberos: Each realm contains at least one KDC that holds the master copy of the Kerberos database to which all updates are made. Additional read-only copies of the Kerberos database can be replicated to additional KDCs within a realm so that authentication can continue in the event that the KDC holding the master copy of the Kerberos database is unavailable. When replicated KDCs for a realm are available on a network, the only operations that cannot be performed when the master copy of the Kerberos database is unavailable are adding or deleting users and password changes.

In Kerberos V4, principals can request sessions with other principals in different realms as long as the realm of the requested principal is directly registered as a principal in the requesting client's realm. Chaining of realms not directly related is not allowed in Kerberos V4, so in an environment with multiple realms, each realm must be registered as a principal in all other realms to support communications between all realms. In Kerberos V5, chaining of realms is allowed but the ways that principals can use to discover a chain of realms is not specified. Implementations of Kerberos V5 usually create a hierarchy of realms (denoted by multipart realm names similar to DNS domain names) so that the hierarchy can be traversed to discover the required chain. In this case, it is not necessary for all realms to be registered as principals in all other realms since each realm only needs to be registered as a principal with realms directly above and below it.

The Authentication Process

Kerberos authentication uses two types of credentials, called *tickets* and *authenticators*. Tickets are used to pass authoritative principal information between a KDC and a principal. Authenticators contain additional information that can be used to verify the information contained in a ticket and establish a session. Tickets and authenticators are issued during the authentication process when principals establish sessions with other principals. When a principal such as a user initially logs in, the user is assigned a ticket-granting ticket that is used to obtain additional tickets when it is necessary to establish sessions with other principals.

The Kerberos authentication process begins when a principal requests that a KDC provide it with the information necessary to establish a session with another principal. The KDC responds with a message encrypted with a request for the principal's key that contains another message encrypted with the requested principal's key. These messages are the tickets and authenticators. The requesting principal is then responsible for decrypting the message provided by the KDC with its key and sending the resulting message to the desired principal. This message contains information about the requesting principal, and because it is encrypted with the requested principal's key the recipient can be assured that it originated from a trusted KDC once it is successfully decrypted and the requesting principal's information is validated. Once the authentication process is completed, both principals share a session key that can be used to ensure the confidentiality and integrity of communications between the clients.

Both Kerberos V4 and V5 represent major improvements over the ways that security is normally handled in a Unix environment, while also providing for centralized management of user, service, and resource naming. Although originally developed for Unix, the Kerberos specifications, especially Kerberos V5, are generic enough to allow their use in environments outside of Unix.

Because Kerberos is a radical departure from the ways security is usually provided on Unix systems, deployment of Kerberos is often difficult since it requires "kerberized" utilities and services instead of the standard Unix versions. They replace most of the utilities and services provided with standard Unix implementations so that Kerberos services can be used.

IBM Mainframes (MVS)

Mainframes have historically been the hub of all computer activity within organizations, and in many respects they remain there today due to their support of high volume transaction processing and high availability to support mission-critical applications. In most cases, mainframes are necessarily centralized resources due to their size, complexity, environmental factors, and the activities necessary to maintain them and the information that is processed on them. Due to IBM's long-standing dominance of the mainframe market, the term *mainframe* is often used as a generic term for mainframes provided by IBM that run the VSE/ESA, VM (Virtual Machine), or MVS (Multiple Virtual Storage) operating systems. Other vendors such as Unisys, Amdahl, and Fujitsu provide mainframes as well, but the conceptual differences between these machines and IBM's mainframes are not that great.

VSE/ESA is the operating system used primarily with IBM's small to midrange ES/9000 uniprocessor systems. Its primary use is in batch and transaction-processing environments, although it is also used to provide file services in multiplatform distributed environments. The support requirements for VSE are not as good as they are for the other more complex operating systems such as VM and MVS, so VSE is often implemented into smaller organizations or distributed mainframe-processing environments.

VM (Virtual Machine) is both an operating system and an operating environment that has, as its primary advantage, the capability to allow multiple operating systems (such as MVS and VSE) to share the same processor complex. This is accomplished through facilities that present a virtual machine interface to each hosted operating system that allows each operating system to behave as if it had absolute control over the host system.

VM also supports CMS (Conversational Monitor System), IBM's primary interactive environment. The support requirements for VM are greater than for VSE, so VM is often implemented in larger organizations that require CMS or its virtual machine capabilities (such as organizations migrating from VSE to MVS).

MVS is IBM's most complex mainframe operating system and runs on IBM's largest ES/9000 uniprocessor and multiprocessing systems. MVS is primarily used in mission-critical batch and transaction processing environments, although interactive processing capabilities are available through TSO (Time Sharing Option), CICS (Customer Information Control System), or IMS (Information Management System). One of the main advantages of MVS is its ability to support multiprocessing so that large time-critical applications can run processes in parallel on multiple processors to increase the speed of processing and transaction response times. Due to its complexity, the support requirements for MVS can be tremendous so most often it is implemented by large organizations with heavy processing requirements for mission-critical applications that require high availability.

Based on the wide usage by organizations of IBM mainframes and the conceptual similarity (primarily the concepts of centralization and control) of other mainframes and their operating systems, this section will focus on directory implementations for IBM mainframes running MVS. The most common way that a directory is implemented in an MVS environment is through the installation of a security package. MVS by itself does not provide for the security of the system's resources, and since security is often an important consideration for the information processed by a mainframe, organizations usually install packages that allow for the system's resources to be secured.

The three main packages that are implemented by organizations for security are IBM's RACF (Resource Access Control Facility), Computer Associates' Top Secret, and Computer Associates' ACF2 (Access Control Facility). The implementation of one of these packages can usually be thought of as constituting the implementation of a directory for MVS, and these packages are briefly covered in the following sections.

RACF

RACF (Resource Access Control Facility) is an IBM software product providing data security protection for IBM's MVS and VM operating systems.

RACF provides data protection by restricting initial entry to the system via services (TSO, CICS, and IMS) or batch processes, and by protecting resources through rules that define access authorizations. Security protection is usually extended only to resources that have profiles with security information established in the RACF database, which is normally referred to as resources that are defined to RACF. This default implementation of the "allow everything except that which is explicitly prohibited" security policy means that resources with no profiles are afforded no specific protection by the RACF security facilities. RACF does have the option to protect everything by default, so that resources cannot be accessed unless they are defined to RACF with appropriate access rules.

All information necessary for RACF to perform its security functions is maintained in one or more RACF databases installed on the mainframe's permanent DASD (Direct Access Storage Device—a hard drive on midrange and mainframe IBM computers). Security administrators responsible for maintaining information in RACF databases interact indirectly with RACF through utilities, and the only operations that require direct access to the RACF databases are structural changes and backups. Resource information and access rules for RACF are stored in database records called *profiles,* and five types of profiles can be defined to RACF:

User Profiles   Contain information about users that can access various system services, including information about groups to which the users belong.

Group Profiles   Contain information about groups and the users that are members. Group Profiles are used to assign access rules to users with similar roles without needing to assign the rights individually.

Connect Profiles   Establish connections between users and groups. There is a separate Connect Profile for each group membership.

Data Set Profiles   Store access authorizations and other information for data sets (similar to files and directories although there are additional structures possible).

General Resource Profiles   Store access authorizations and other information for system resources such as DASD, tape volumes, terminals, programs, and transactions.

Each type of profile within a RACF database has its own flat namespace, and the databases encompassed by a RACF directory normally do not extend beyond a single mainframe system. Despite this, RACF is still viewed as a universal directory for organizations, since systems running RACF are centralized and the scope of services controlled by RACF access control is comprehensive.

Top Secret

Top Secret is an access control security package marketed by Computer Associates (CA). It is primarily designed to protect the MVS and VM system environments against unauthorized access and to permit authorized users to perform only authorized functions. Top Secret limits access to system resources by limiting system entry through passwords and other restrictions (such as time of day or terminal addresses) and by allowing only authorized actions to be performed with resources.

Top Secret implements a user-oriented security architecture where users are associated with a set of specific resource access authorizations. Consequently, users are the focus of Top Secret security and all access control processing is performed when users are authenticated rather than each time resources are accessed.

Accessor Identification

With Top Secret, a user is assigned an Accessor Identification (ACID—pronounced like the chemical term) that uniquely identifies them on the system. The ACID acts as a key to access the Security File that stores information about resources the user is allowed to access and the operations the user is allowed to perform on the resources. Each ACID for a user is specific to an access facility (such as TSO, CICS, or IMS) that is part of a flat namespace that is shared by all access facilities, so a user could possess several unique ACIDs. Authentication of a user with an ACID is accomplished with a password, and a user's password is typically not required to be unique for each of the user's ACIDs.

ACIDs are related to resources through ownership or authorization. Ownership of a resource allows unlimited access to that resource and allows the owner ACID the discretionary ability to grant access authority to other users. If a user's ACID is not defined as the owner of a resource, an appropriate authorization is required to perform operations on the resources.

All administrative operations for Top Secret are performed using the TSS command and one of its many functions. Various TSS functions access or manipulate information in the Top Secret database that is shared by all of the system's processors. Information in the database is stored in encrypted form on shared DASD. The database contains security records for users, profiles, departments, divisions, zones, defined resources, and access rules. When a user session is initiated (via batch or an interactive login), Top Secret retrieves the user's security record from the database and places it in the user's address space. From that point forward throughout the session, all required access validations are performed with the information stored in the address space.

Operation Modes

There are four modes of operation for Top Secret that control its behavior during access validation:

Dormant Mode   When in this mode, Top Secret does not provide default protection of resources but instead only protects critical resources that are identified with the special ACTION(FAIL) flag by exception.

Warn Mode   This mode provides the same resource protection by exception as Dormant mode, but warnings are generated when access rules for resources without the ACTION(FAIL) flag are violated, so that the security can be fine-tuned without interrupting processing.

Implement Mode   Users with ACIDs defined to Top Secret will not be able to access resources when access rules are violated, but users that are not defined to Top Secret can access resources that are not defined to Top Secret.

Fail Mode   All resources are protected by default and all users must be defined to Top Secret with ACIDs.

Different modes can be implemented concurrently for specific groups of users, so that all users within a particular division or with a certain profile could operate under Warn mode while others would operate under Dormant mode.

Like RACF, Top Secret can be viewed as a universal directory because it can be used to define and protect all resources on one or more systems.

ACF2

The Access Control Facility (ACF2) is a data security system marketed by Computer Associates (CA) for the MVS operating system. It is aimed at protecting data sets from unauthorized access. By default, ACF2 provides complete data set protection (similar to the alternative behavior of RACF) by denying access to any data set unless a specific rule has been established for that data set to allow some form of access. Within the ACF2 rule set, there are four types of access that can be specified:

READ   Permits a data set to be opened for input.

WRITE   Permits a data set to be opened for output.

ALLOC   Permits a data set to be allocated, scratched, or have its catalog entry changed.

EXEC   Permits a data set to be accessed to load a program into memory to be executed.

Two terms occurring frequently in discussions regarding ACF2 rules are *LID* and *UID,* which are related, yet serve different functions. The LID (login identification) identifies an account performing an operation, and the UID (user identification) identifies users to whom rules can be applied. The LID is a subset of the UID, and any given LID could be associated with more than one UID. A UID is associated with other UIDs through a group field, and each individual UID maps to a specific LID. UIDs are used in ACF2 rule definitions, and LIDs and UIDs share the same namespace within an ACF2 database.

Because of the comprehensive nature of ACF2 interfaces to MVS facilities, ACF2 can also be considered a universal directory for MVS like RACF and Top Secret, due to the central position of MVS systems within many organizations.

IBM OS/400

OS/400 is the operating system for IBM's AS/400 series of midrange processors that provide batch processing and online transaction processing capabilities similar to those provided by larger mainframes and their operating systems. When compared with IBM's current large mainframe systems, AS/400 systems are smaller in terms of overall processing power and storage support. Accordingly, the AS/400 typically serves in environments that need mainframe-like capabilities on a smaller scale than is typically handled by a mainframe.

The AS/400 platform also serves as a migration path for legacy applications running on IBM's previous lines of midrange systems, the System/36 and System/38.

OS/400 was developed concurrently with the AS/400, and the two are integrally packaged with each other. As a result of this integration, the terms *AS/400* and *OS/400* are often used interchangeably to refer to the OS/400 operating system. The design of the operating system reflects its recent development (the AS/400 and OS/400 were introduced in the late 1980s), as it implements an object-oriented architecture where all types of information maintained on the system are integrated into a single object model. Among the many advantages of this approach is the capability to include security information with every type of object. Because all individual objects share the same basic security qualities, objects such as user profiles, print queues, files, and database columns can be secured in the same way.

The AS/400's object model extends to the storage and representation of data on the system. The hardware and operating system handle all aspects of data storage, such as whether the data is stored on disk or in memory at any given moment or how data is physically represented within the system's storage. Data integrity checks performed by the operating system allow for only operations defined as valid for an object to be performed with or to the object. For example, it is not possible to add a text item to a numeric object.

The operating system also handles all type conversions so that operations with mixed data types are performed automatically with predictable results. Security information is also associated with each object, and security authorization is checked for every interaction between objects. When an object is copied, all information, including the security information, is copied to the new object along with the data so the new object will behave in the same manner as the original object.

Users are defined within the OS/400 object model as user profile objects with properties unique to users or services. Group profiles can be used to provide default settings that member user profiles can inherit in order to ease administration of profiles for similar types of users.

There are two important properties of user profiles within OS/400: The user object is the focus of identification and authentication within the system; and each object defined on the system is owned by a user profile. The identification and authentication aspects of user profiles in OS/400 do not differ from what is associated with representations of users in most other directories that participate in security functions. Users access the system using a user profile, and all processes execute under the control of a specific user profile. An object is initially owned by the user profile that created it, but the original owner can transfer ownership to other user profiles.

 Ownership allows a user profile to control the security and all other user-definable properties of the object regardless of the type of object that is owned.

This single object model serves as OS/400's object-oriented implementation of a network directory where information about all types of objects within the system is accessible using techniques that are shared across all object types. All objects contain a header that includes information about the object, including the security information noted previously.

The aggregation of information associated with the system's objects and the ways that it can be presented to users can be thought of as the AS/400's implementation of a directory. In most cases, this particular directory implementation is limited in scope to a single system, but the object-oriented architecture allows for a great deal of management granularity and pervasiveness within the system so that it is not usually necessary to implement other directories within an AS/400 system.

DEC OpenVMS

OpenVMS is the most recent generation of the VMS operating system for Digital Equipment Corporation (DEC, now part of Compaq) minicomputers based on the VAX and Alpha AXP processor architectures. OpenVMS has evolved from the original VAX-based VMS operating system and its PDP-based predecessors to earn the designation of "open" based on its support for the more recent RISC-based Alpha AXP processor architecture and the increasingly pervasive implementation of open systems technologies commonly associated with Unix systems and the Internet.

VAX- and AXP-based systems running OpenVMS are capable of supporting numerous tasks within organizations, including interactive transaction processing, batch processing, and file sharing for network-connected systems. Systems running VMS and OpenVMS have supported clustering, or sharing storage subsystems between multiple independent systems, as a standard capability for some time to provide fault tolerance while also improving performance for some types of concurrent operations.

OpenVMS is organized into four execution layers and all of them have corresponding levels of privilege: Kernel (highest privilege level), Executive, Supervisor, and User (lowest privilege level). All operations, including interactive user sessions using DCL (Digital Command Language), occur in an environment called a *process,* which exists within one of the layers. Processes are the basic scheduling entities of OpenVMS that consist of several elements including a timeslice, allocated storage, code, and data. Depending on whether sufficient privileges are granted to a given process when it is created, a process can spawn additional processes or allocate additional storage for itself within certain limits. All processes, whether they are used for interactive user sessions or batch operations, are associated with user identification codes (UICs) for security and data integrity purposes.

Processes for batch operations or system programs are created when the code is executed, while processes for interactive sessions are created when a user opens a terminal connection and authenticates to the system. The identification and authentication procedure is usually controlled by the LOGINOUT.EXE program, which validates usernames and passwords against the SYS$SYSTEM:SYSUAF.DAT file. This file contains information that is used during authentication and process initialization, such as the username, UIC, priority, and maximum detached threads.

Beyond providing information for authentication and process initialization, the SYSUAF.DAT file is used for resolving names to UICs, which are used internally by OpenVMS to uniquely identify each user. The UIC consists of a pair of numbers [*n*,*m*], the first of which is the user number and the other is the number of the default group. User account information in the SYSUAF.DAT file is maintained by the administrator using the AUTHORIZE utility.

Protection of files, devices, and queues in OpenVMS is based on UICs and ACLs (Access Control Lists), and a wide variety of additional security information associated with users is stored in the SYS$SYSTEM:RIGHTSLIST.DAT file. This additional information takes the form of rights identifiers, which are flags used to provide protection to system resources such as files, devices, and queues in a more modular way than the basic UIC-based protection. The additional security information is maintained by a variety of Access Control List (ACL) commands.

OpenVMS implements a flat namespace for its user directory, consisting primarily of the contents of the SYSUAF.DAT and RIGHTSLIST.DAT database files, and the directory has no relation to directories that might exist on other systems. It is possible, though, for multiple systems to share the same user directory if the database files are located on clustered storage shared by the systems.

Windows Networking: Workgroups and Domains

Microsoft's networking software (such as LAN Manager, Windows for Workgroups, Windows 95, and Windows NT) typically is capable of implementing either of two models for organizing networked systems into groups for administrative purposes. The simplest model is the *workgroup* where all systems that are members of a workgroup are loosely related for the purpose of allowing shared resources such as directories and printers to be easily located. *Domains,* on the other hand, go beyond the resource-sharing aspects of workgroups by implementing a shared security service that can be used (by all systems in the domain that support security) to control access to local resources. This section focuses on directories implemented on Windows NT systems that support security services provided by individual systems and domains.

All Windows NT systems, regardless of whether they exist in a workgroup or a domain, provide security services to control access to resources and services located on the system. These security services allow for access to be controlled at the user and group levels and are enforced upon initial entry to the system.

Users can typically access Windows NT systems either locally or from across the network—in both cases access to resources is controlled by the same security services. These security services use directories that contain information about users and groups that are identified by name and associated with internal object IDs that are assigned by the system. The names for users and groups share a common namespace, so it is not possible to have a user and group with the same name on a system.

Rights assignments for resources within the system are based on object IDs rather than names, and object IDs are not reused once an object is deleted. This means that if an object is renamed, its rights assignments will remain intact as long as the object ID has not changed, whereas if an object is deleted and recreated with the same name, the object ID for the new object will be different and all previous rights assignments will be lost.

Domains implement a separate directory that contains information about machines, users, and groups that are part of the domain. Unlike workgroups, which systems can join at will and where they can advertise their services, systems must be added to a domain explicitly in order to participate in the domain's security services.

The privilege of adding machines to a domain is typically reserved for administrators, but it can be delegated to other users or groups as desired. It is not necessary, however, for a system to be a member of a domain to access most resources on systems within that domain.

The properties for users and groups defined in a domain's directory are similar to those for stand-alone systems, except that the domain's directory is shared by all systems that are members of the domain rather than being restricted to a single system.

The domain directory database is maintained on a server designated as a Primary Domain Controller (PDC), and additional copies of the domain directory database can be replicated to one or more Backup Domain Controllers (BDCs). Users can authenticate to any domain controller in the domain, so if the PDC is unavailable, user authentication can continue uninterrupted. All administrative activities for a domain must occur at the PDC since the PDC contains the only read-write copy of the domain's directory database, and each domain can have only one PDC at any given time.

In the event that a domain's PDC is unavailable, activities such as adding and deleting users and groups, or changing passwords, cannot be performed, but a BDC can be promoted to a PDC if the PDC cannot be returned to service in a reasonable amount of time.

All systems that are members of a domain, and that are not designated as domain controllers, retain their local directories. This requires that a distinction be made between local and domain resources when assigning rights on each system in a domain. Domain users and group objects are identified by a two-part name that includes the domain name and the object name. While system names are identified either by the object name itself (within the context of the system) or by a two-part name that includes the system name and the object name. This requires that domain names and system names be unique within the same namespace, and this is enforced by the name resolution that is used for the network (which depends on the communication protocols being used).

Because the namespaces for users and groups within domain and local system directories are independent, it is allowable for different objects to have the same names within both the domain and local system directories. The local objects can be distinguished from domain objects through the two-part names, and it is possible for a domain user or group object to be a member of a local group residing on a system.

Any given system can be a member of only one domain. This means allowing users defined in one domain to access resources located in another domain would be difficult without the concept of trust that exists in the domain security model. Without trust, separate accounts would need to be created in the directories for other systems or domains for users wishing to access those resources, and the users would be required to authenticate each time they needed to access those resources even though they had already authenticated to their primary domain. This is not necessary since domains can be configured to trust other domains, so that users in one domain can access resources in other domains using their existing domain credentials as long as the resource domains trust the user's domain. Domain trust relationships are directional, which means that trust relationships between domains need not be mutual.

Although the trust model allows for flexible access to resources across domain boundaries, managing trust relations can become quite difficult as networks grow and the number of domains increase. Part of the reason it's so difficult is that the currently implemented trust model does not allow chaining of trust relationships. So, it is not possible for a user to access resources in a domain that trusts a domain that in turn trusts the user's domain unless the resource domain explicitly trusts the user's domain. If every domain in a network required a two-way trust with every other domain on the network, each domain would require an explicit trust relationship with every other domain on the network. The total number of required trust relationships would grow exponentially with each domain added to the network.

These problems are usually addressed by creating a distinction between authentication domains and resource domains. Authentication domains are dedicated to maintaining user and group accounts and they do not trust any other domains (except perhaps each other). Resource domains are dedicated to providing resources and services for the network and are satisfied to leave the authentication tasks to the authentication domains that they trust. This configuration makes trusts much more manageable since authentication domains do not normally need to maintain trust relationships, and each resource domain needs only to maintain one-way trust relationships with the authentication domains.

Banyan StreetTalk

StreetTalk is a network naming service originally developed for Banyan's VINES (Virtual Networking System), a network operating system loosely based on Unix for servers running on Intel processors. Even though VINES itself has not experienced a great deal of success in the network industry, StreetTalk has achieved distinction as an innovative directory service due to the unique way it provides for globally identifying network resources (including services, users, and lists) in a loosely structured yet coherent manner. Due to the strength of StreetTalk, Banyan has extended its reach through its ENS (Enterprise Network Services) products to allow StreetTalk to coordinate access to services for network operating systems other than VINES such as Unix, NetWare, and Windows NT.

Every network resource associated with systems encompassed by a StreetTalk directory has a name and a set of attributes that allows it to be uniquely identified within the directory. The names of resources are independent of the particular network in which the server they reside on is located, making it possible for users to connect to services or resources attached to different servers without knowing where they reside. The names assigned to resources map to network addresses that are tracked by the StreetTalk directory, and all management activities use the StreetTalk names for resources rather than other identifiers. Attributes assigned to resources can also be used to assist with locating or categorizing them.

StreetTalk names consist of three components separated by the @ sign, and each component maps (moving left to right) to an item, group, and organization. Conceptually, items can be thought of as users or resources that belong to a group, which in turn belongs to an organization. As an example, the StreetTalk (ST) naming service for a server called "Quest" would be identified as ST@Quest@Servers, where "Quest" is a group created to contain all services associated with the server and "Servers" is the default organization created to contain all servers. This three-part naming scheme is often viewed as mapping naturally to a hierarchical scheme, but such hierarchy is not rigidly defined for StreetTalk although it is often the case in practice.

Certain types of resources such as users, lists, and services can be assigned one or more nicknames that allow for the resources to be identified more easily than might be the case if full names were always required. Nicknames are pointers that can be used interchangeably with the full names of the resources. Nicknames inhabit the same namespace that is used for full StreetTalk names. Usage of nicknames is sensitive to context with respect to default groups and organizations, but nicknames can refer to resource names that exist outside the group and organization containing the nickname.

Every StreetTalk service maintains a directory database on the server where the service is running, and this database is distributed among multiple servers when they are present. There are no centralized servers providing naming services for StreetTalk, as there are for other network directories, so there is no single point of failure for the naming service in a multiserver environment.

The directory databases maintained on servers contain detailed information about the items associated with groups on those servers, and each server maintains tables that map all known groups to servers. Organizations, in contrast, do not exist primarily in any single place but instead exist only as logical entities allowing groups to be associated with each other. Directory information is distributed among servers periodically at a fixed interval or when servers or groups are added or deleted.

Administrators are responsible for maintaining StreetTalk names and for managing the distribution of names throughout the network. Administrators gain their privileges through membership in special list items called "Admin-List" that are associated with groups. Lists behave in the same manner as groups in most other directories with the added property of being able to contain names for multiple types of objects (including other lists).

Resource names can be located in a StreetTalk directory using flexible search capabilities that allow searches based on parts of names or attributes associated with resources. Resource types (such as users, services, or groups) share a common set of attributes that have a name, type, and value. One of the interesting features of StreetTalk is that administrators can add custom attribute specifications for resource types to provide additional information about resources or to allow for additional associations between resources.

StreetTalk is integrated with the security services of operating systems hosting StreetTalk naming services so that the StreetTalk directory can provide the information necessary to control initial entry to the system and access to system resources. Initial entry is controlled through the identification and authentication process, which typically involves a user presenting a StreetTalk name or nickname and a password to the Login program that interacts with the security service. The security service uses the StreetTalk name to determine which server can provide the information necessary to validate the authentication request, and then opens a connection with the StreetTalk service on that server to continue the authentication process.

Electronic Mail Directories

This section discusses electronic mail as a generic application—rather than looking at specific products—for the purpose of illustrating a common type of directory that is shared by many electronic mail systems. Electronic mail systems are typically implemented as a service distributed across many servers that act as post offices to participate in the delivery of messages.

Post offices are usually servers containing mailboxes for local users, and the directories implemented on post office servers contain information about other post offices as well as information about the users mapped to their mailbox addresses. An electronic mail address often consists of all the information necessary for a message to be delivered and usually contains two parts that unambiguously identify a mailbox at a post office: a mailbox (or user) name and a post office name.

Most electronic mail systems allow a user sending a message to directly enter a recipient's address without requiring access to the directory on the recipient's post office server. But in cases where a user wants to send a message but doesn't know the exact address of a recipient, finding the address could be difficult—especially when the sender doesn't know the name of the recipient's post office. When faced with such a situation, a user could search likely post offices for the recipient's mail box, but this could be time consuming and perhaps ultimately unsuccessful if the directories maintained on post office servers are not directly accessible.

This problem can usually be addressed by consolidating the information from the multiple independent directories into a single database, called a *directory catalog,* which can be consulted by users sending messages to obtain the addresses of recipients. Such directory catalogs can be maintained automatically or manually. Automatic catalog maintenance usually occurs within organizational electronic mail systems, where the directory catalog database could be updated when mailboxes are added or deleted from post offices.

It is also possible for an agent running on a server containing a directory catalog database to dredge up user and mailbox information from all known post offices. Users often maintain their own directory catalogs, as well, when centrally maintained catalogs are not feasible (due to size or disparate mail systems) or available, especially when they need to compose messages when they are not connected to the networks that might contain such centrally maintained catalogs.

NetWare

Novell's directory systems have evolved from a relatively simple one in the first versions of NetWare through NDS—the most sophisticated directory service available for PC networks. We'll look at three distinct versions of NetWare's server-based directory systems (called the bindery): pre-NetWare 2.*x*, NetWare 2.*x*, and NetWare 3.*x*. We'll also briefly look at NetWare Name Service, a stop-gap attempt to expand NetWare Bindery Services to multiple servers. Finally, we'll look at the issues facing the engineers who had the job of designing the NDS system.

Early NetWare

"Early NetWare" encompasses the years from 1985 through 1988 when NetWare 2 was released. Version numbers become confusing, because the first NetWare released on the Intel platform was called version 4. This was succeeded by Advanced NetWare 1.0, which in turn gave way to NetWare 286/2.0.

Although the bindery in these systems was similar to that of 2.0, it was of little concern to administrators and programmers because the details were hidden from public view.

We do know that there were two files—NET$BIND.SYS and NET$BVAL.SYS—that contained the data. System administrators used a program called PASSWORD to create and maintain user accounts, trustee assignments, and login scripts. With this same program users could make changes to their own scripts.

Passwords were not encrypted. Supervisor equivalent users could read and change the passwords of all users.

This early bindery access program did know the concept of "home directory," which was lost in the NetWare 2 version only to reemerge later.

Judging by today's standards, the early bindery doesn't seem like much from either an administrative or security perspective. Nevertheless, it was head and shoulders above the competition, Microsoft's MSNet, which used password-protected directories (and had no concept of "users") for its security mechanism. Each time you changed directories, you entered another password!

NetWare 2.*x* Bindery

The biggest change with NetWare 2.0 was that the bindery objects and properties were finally opened up to public view and manipulation. Novell released an API (Application Programming Interface) so that third-party programmers could read from and write to the bindery.

NetWare 2.*x* Bindery Objects

Bindery objects were found to have six components:

Object ID   This component is a 4-byte hexadecimal number assigned by the operating system when the object is created. This means that there's an absolute limit of 65,536 bindery objects. Because of the algorithm used to create the ID, the same object will undoubtedly have a different object ID on different servers. In fact, if you create, then delete, then re-create an object, it's almost certain to be given a different object ID on the second creation.

Object Type   A classification of the object. Novell created a large number of object types (called *well-known object types*) including user, group, printer, print server, etc. This is also a 4-byte hex number. Object types 0000–8000 are reserved by Novell, as is FFFF (a "wildcard" value programmers can use when browsing or searching the bindery without wishing to limit the object types found). Third parties could register an object type with Novell, or use a number greater than 8000h (and hope no one else used the same one).

Object Name   48-bytes to hold the name of the object, be it a user, group, printer, server, or whatever.

Object Flag   The Object Flag has one of two possible values: dynamic or static. Dynamic objects are removed from the bindery when the server is downed, while static objects remain until deleted from the bindery. Users and groups are static objects, while file servers are dynamic—their identity is "discovered" by the server after it's booted.

Object Security   The Object Security component is another flag indicating other objects' access to this object. (See Table 2.2 for the possibilities.) There are two numbers associated with each object, one for READ access and one for WRITE access.

Properties Flag   This component is used to identify if the object has associated properties. While most objects will have properties, a third-party application could use an entry here to simply identify that it had been installed. Properties themselves fall into two categories: Items or Sets. Items (such as the properties PASSWORD, ACCOUNT_BALANCE, FULL_NAME, etc.) have a 128-byte associated value, while Sets (such as GROUPS_I'M_IN) can have up to 32 Object IDs stored within the 128-byte value. Only Object IDs can be part of the value of a Set property.

T A B L E 2.2	Value	Access Level	Description
Possible Values and Meanings of the Object Security Flag	0	Anyone	Access allowed by anyone, logged in or not
	1	Logged	Access allowed by all logged-in users
	2	Object	Access allowed only by the object itself or someone logged in as the object
	3	Supervisor	Access allowed only by the Supervisor object or an object that is supervisor-equivalent
	4	NetWare	Access allowed only by the operating system

NetWare 2.*x* Bindery Properties

Each bindery object can have one or more properties associated with it. The property, in turn, has the following attributes:

Property Name   Up to 15 characters. Common properties are PASSWORD, FULL_NAME, ACCOUNT_BALANCE, and GROUPS_I'M_IN.

Property Flags   Two flags, one indicating if the property is static or dynamic, the other indicating if it is an item or a set. Dynamic properties are lost when a server is rebooted.

Property Security   Uses the same coding as Object security (see Table 2.2) to determine who has access to read or write the property.

Since third-party programmers could access and manipulate bindery objects and properties, bindery size grew, as did access time. This was addressed in NetWare 3.

NetWare 3.*x* Bindery

One of the major headaches involved in upgrading from NetWare 2.*x* to NetWare 3.*x* is migration of the bindery. This is, in part, because the bindery in NetWare 3 had grown from two to three files (one for objects, one for properties, and one for values), while some of the fields had also changed. The Object ID, for example, was now 6 bytes (rather than four) allowing over 16 million (instead of NetWare 2's 65,000) bindery objects to be defined.

The changes introduced were a response to the growing size of NetWare—more users per server, more servers per LAN. Not much was changed about the functionality of the bindery, though, and most of the information detailed earlier about NetWare 2's bindery still applied. But networks continued to grow.

One change was the introduction of a new object type, the User Access Manager, with new security provisions. This was an object type that would have separately assignable bindery access rights. In NetWare 2, this was all or nothing—either an object was Supervisor-equivalent with access to all other objects, or a "normal" object with bindery access only to itself.

Because the bindery database wasn't indexed, finding a particular record meant searching from the first one until the one you wanted was found. This is called a "flat file" database. As networks grew, this took longer and longer to occur. It was at about this point that definite work on what would become NDS began.

As networks grew, users (and other bindery objects) needed to access more than one server—in some cases, much more than one. Administrators began beseeching Novell for some way to enter an object's information once and have it propagated to other servers.

Microsoft's LAN Manager operating system and its spin-offs—IBM's LAN Server, Digital's PathWorks, et al.—had introduced the domain concept. At the time, this looked like a much easier way to administer a large network (the concept of "large" being much smaller back then). User information was added once with rights to all objects within the domain (servers, printers, etc.) being accessible from the user entry screen.

NetWare administrators needed to go to each server's bindery and enter the user's information for every server the user needed to access. Because the users were clamoring for a change, because the real possibility of losing market share was apparent, and because NetWare 4 with NDS wasn't quite ready to ship, Novell introduced a product that never got beyond release 1.0. That product became something of an embarrassment to Novell; it was called *NetWare Name Service*.

NetWare Name Service

In late 1990, with the release of NetWare 4 still thought to be a year away (in actuality, it was another two and a half years before the release), Novell needed to stem the tide of criticism about the server-centric bindery system.

Because Novell's programmers were hard at work on NetWare 4, there was no one to spare for this problem. So an outside contractor was found who, over the course of a long weekend, created NNS.

NNS could, under ideal conditions, synchronize the binderies on a group of NetWare servers called a "domain." The synchronization had to be performed manually, as often as necessary. While there was no concept of a "master" server, all administration of the domain needed to be done from one preselected administrative workstation.

In theory, there was no limit to the number of servers in the domain. In fact, because of the brute force nature of the synchronization, domains of more than eight servers either took far too long to synchronize or were prone to errors when connections dropped during the synchronization.

The synchronization was done one server at a time as the application performing the sync first attached to, then logged out of, each server in turn.

No further versions of NNS were shipped, and all support for NNS was dropped in the fall of 1994. Because of the poor implementation of NNS, the vastly superior NDS was slow in being accepted.

The Beginnings of NDS

NDS's designers began with the notion that the network and the server were not the same. The server was simply one more object in the network. So the bindery's server-centric view had to be expanded to a network-centric view.

The designers learned that, even though NetWare 3's bindery allowed for over 16 million objects, there would always be networks that needed to have 17 million or more.

A fully relational database was needed to overcome the search-time penalty of the bindery. Further, in a brilliant insight, the idea of a distributed database was included. This meant that parts of the database could be in different places, even multiple places, so that the loss of a single data repository (such as a server) would not totally crash the directory system. NNS had shown that brute force copying of the database from server to server was a resource hogging, time-intensive, disaster-prone method.

For security reasons, as well as to further move the bindery/directory from server-centric to network-centric, the file system supervisor and the directory system supervisor were not necessarily the same person. Additionally, although some object needed all rights to a particular object and its properties, this ability might need to be held by different user objects for different parts of the network.

What NDS Designers Learned from Other Efforts

While the experience of NetWare's bindery, and in particular the disaster-prone experience of NetWare Name Service, formed a solid core of knowledge for the NDS designers, they also studied other directory systems to learn what was desirable for NDS as well as what should be avoided.

LAN Manager's Domain system, although suffering from many of the same drawbacks as NNS, showed that a network-centric, rather than server-centric, view was desirable, as was the ability to have more than one instance of the directory's database. But the domain system still required the entire database to be present on a domain controller (the "head" server), so it wasn't completely divorced from server-centricism. By making the server simply one more directory object, NDS immediately became more scalable to even larger networks.

Banyan Systems VINES network operating system had been known for years because of its naming service, in which each object within the network had a unique name as well as an alias, or "friendly name," which users could use to access the object. Both concepts were incorporated into NDS.

Finally, in the mid-1980s the CCITT (Consultative Committee for International Telegraphy and Telephony) had begun defining a message handling and transport specification called X.400. As a consequence, a method of constructing a worldwide directory of message users was needed and codified as the X.500 specification. The hierarchical structure of X.500, its tree-like design, and much of its nomenclature were used to create NDS. This foresight was well repaid in 1996 when LDAP (Light Directory Access Protocol), a protocol for quickly accessing an X.500 directory, became prominent as the best way to query directory databases across the Internet. Novell was able to quickly adapt an LDAP interface to NDS (released in early 1997), further distancing Novell from other network operating system vendors.

X.500 is so essential to understanding NDS that we've devoted all of Chapter 3 to it. You should read and understand it in order to assimilate the basic concepts designed into NDS.

Summary

This chapter has attempted to illustrate some of what can constitute a directory by exploring the many ways that directories are implemented in various systems. The purpose of this exercise has been to illustrate that network directories are neither a new nor a unique concept, but are instead integral to the operation of most network systems. This should serve as groundwork allowing us to point out the important ways that Novell Directory Services and the related X.500 standards differ from most of these examples of what might be considered legacy directories.

The most difficult part of this chapter has been deciding which directories within the various systems under consideration should be included or excluded from this discussion. Some directories are easy to identify since they operate independently—such as the Domain Naming System that is so important conceptually for the following chapters—but others are more difficult to identify since they are embedded in other systems. When directories were embedded in systems, the decision to isolate certain directory components was based on how they satisfied the roles for directories identified in the previous chapter. These roles included assisting users with locating network resources and supporting system security services.

Obviously, some directories that fit these criteria were not covered even though they can be found in systems under consideration. For example, file system directories found on NetWare and Windows NT servers can often be considered network directories, especially when facilities such as the Universal Naming Convention (UNC) allow direct access to files or directories on network systems regardless of context. We are painfully aware that many of the decisions to not include directories that met our criteria were indeed capricious, but we hope that the discussion has still been valuable.

CHAPTER

3

The Directory: X.500

Our general discussion continues in this chapter with the review of an actual international standard for network directories. Although the previous chapter dealt to some degree with standards for directory services (such as DNS and WINS), it primarily covered actual implementations of directories that do not necessarily conform to widely acknowledged industry standards.

The directory specifications described in this chapter (called simply the *Directory* in the standards documentation), represent an effort on the part of international standards groups to define a framework for directory services that would be useful for a variety of systems and applications. This framework is commonly referred to as X.500 and is described in a series of documents developed in collaboration by the CCITT (Consultative Committee for International Telegraphy and Telephony), the ISO (International Standards Organization), and the IEC (International Electrotechnical Commission).

The most recent edition of the Directory Specifications consists of two nearly identical sets of nine separate documents that were published in 1993 by the ITU-T (International Telecommunications Union, formerly the CCITT) and the ISO/IEC JTC 1 (a joint technical committee of the ISO and IEC). The ITU-T version of the documents is referred to as the X.500 Recommendations, whereas the ISO/IEC version is known as International Standard 9594. The only differences between the ITU-T and ISO/IEC documents are minor variations in wording. The working documents are kept aligned by having common draft documents that combine both sets of wording. The ISO/IEC 9594 documents served as the primary sources for much of this chapter (although it would have made little or no difference if the ITU-T X.500 documents had been used instead).

Standards are considered important in networking since they are usually the means by which independently developed systems or applications can interoperate—as long as they conform to the rules established for those standards. This generally is not the case with ITU-T and ISO documents, such as the specification for the X.500 Directory, since they are usually not complete specifications. While they are spoken of as standards, two different vendors' implementations, conforming to the specification in every way, might still not interoperate because of the extensions each would necessarily have to add to make X.500 functional.

Throughout this chapter the term *Directory* (uppercase *D*) refers to the directory specified in the X.500 documents. The term *directory* (lowercase *d*) refers to a generic implementation of the standard or to nonspecific directories in general (such as, a telephone directory).

No matter how inadequate the X.500 specifications might appear compared to the goals of most standards, they are extremely valuable as a conceptual framework for network directory services for a number of reasons. First, X.500 presents comprehensive specifications that have accumulated a high level of support within academia and the networking industry. They are now almost universally acknowledged as the prototypical framework for network directory services. In addition, the standards have benefited from a wealth of practical experience in the field that has contributed to their ongoing development.

Although there are many examples of directories implementing various aspects of the X.500 Directory specifications, it would not be useful to use such implementations to illustrate the standards. This chapter focuses instead on the concepts and terminology described in the X.500 Directory standards documentation. We'll begin with a brief discussion of X.500's background and history, then move on to a review of the actual elements specified in the standards. The conceptual directory model developed in the first chapter is used to organize the concepts and terminology introduced with the X.500 Directory specifications.

Tracing the Directory's Origins

The X.500 Directory specifications were developed originally to play a significant role in the OSI (Open Systems Interconnection) basic reference model for network communications. They were aimed specifically at addressing the requirement for an Electronic Directory Service (EDS) defined by the ISO for the OSI Application Layer. The goal of OSI is to allow, with a minimum of technical collaboration outside of the standards themselves, the interconnection of information processing systems from different manufacturers, under different management, of different levels of complexity, and of different ages. The documents that currently make up the ITU-T X.500 Recommendations and ISO/IEC International Standard 9594 combine to provide a comprehensive and detailed specification for a general-purpose directory service capable of allowing access to a variety of information. This directory information could be distributed widely and yet appear within a single logical framework.

The process of creating a standard is long, complex, and usually very politically charged, since at least two entities must collaborate. In the case of what eventually became known as the first edition of the X.500 Directory standards, the entire process required about six years beginning in 1983, when both the CCITT and the ISO began work on proposals for a standard directory specification. Both organizations presented proposals and counter-proposals based on this work, and they completed a draft proposal for a "convergent document" to unify the standard in late 1986. Finally in 1988, the Directory became a standard when the ISO ratified International Standard 9594, and the CCITT accepted the proposals as the X.500 Recommendations.

In the years following the 1988 publication, X.500 steadily gained the support of other standards bodies, academic institutions, and network software developers. The Internet community was perhaps the area of the networking world where X.500 initially generated the most enthusiasm. Many recognized the potential for a directory to support global communications by defining a framework for a global service making information about network resources universally available (similar to the way the white pages of a telephone book work). The Internet community contributed a great deal of development and publicity to the evolution of X.500. Several RFCs (Requests for Comments, the semiofficial documentation for

Internet standards and protocols) were written about various aspects of X.500 implementation. These RFCs provided implementation details as well as guidance for future development of the standards.

Despite all the interest in X.500 within the Internet community, the Directory has been unable to make the transition from technical journals, textbooks, and pilot projects to actual deployment of a global directory serving Internet users in the same way that white pages directories serve telephone customers. Even though directories based on X.500 do not yet play a central role in global communications, the concepts and terminology associated with X.500 became the framework for the development of network directories. Vendors implementing directories for systems or applications routinely use the models codified within the X.500 Directory standards as integral parts of the design of their directories.

The initial 1988 standards presented the components of a distributed directory service that served as the basis of several pilot projects and reference implementations. Probably the most influential of these initial implementations was Quipu, named for the intricate record-keeping devices consisting of color-coded strings used by ancient Inca tribes in South America. Quipu was included in the ISODE (ISO Development Environment) and addressed many of the underspecified or missing issues with the original X.500 specifications, such as access control and replication. It was influential in the development of the second edition of the standards, published in 1992 and 1993.

Another pilot implementation, Paradise (Piloting An inteRnationAl DIrectory SErvice), focused on stimulating and extending the use of the X.500 Directory as a white-pages-type service. Paradise paid particular attention to technical and organizational aspects of global directory implementation based on the X.500 Directory standards.

One of the important characteristics of the Paradise effort has been its use of an IP (Internet Protocol) infrastructure rather than the OSI infrastructure specified in the Directory standards.

Many of the lessons learned during pilot and reference implementations using the 1988 edition of the Directory specifications contributed to the development of the current 1993 edition. The evolution of the Directory specifications over the years has resulted in many document revisions being passed around among the various organizations involved in the standardization process. These different versions of the standards have contributed to the confusion of those attempting to implement directories conforming to X.500 Directory standards. The second edition revised (but did not replace) the first edition, so both editions are labeled as version 1 of the Directory. Due to this overlap, any directory implementations claiming conformance to version 1 of the Directory specifications are required to specify the edition to which they conform.

Understanding Standards Documents

The technically aligned Directory standards published in 1993 consist of nine documents known as the ITU-T X.500 Recommendations and the ISO/IEC 9594 International Standards. The individual documents are:

- ITU-T Recommendation X.500 (1993) | ISO/IEC 9594-1:1993, *Information Technology—Open Systems Interconnection—The Directory: Overview of Concepts, Models, and Services*. Introduces the concepts of the Directory and the DIB (Directory Information Base) and provides an overview of the services and capabilities they provide.

- ITU-T Recommendation X.501 (1993) | ISO/IEC 9594-2:1993, *Information Technology—Open Systems Interconnection—The Directory: Models*. Provides a number of different models for the Directory as a framework for the other Recommendations in the X.500 Series. These are the models: the overall (functional) model; the administrative authority model; the generic Directory Information models (providing Directory User and Administrative User views of Directory information); the generic Directory Systems Agent (DSA) and DSA information models and Operational Framework; and a security model.

- ITU-T Recommendation X.511 (1993) | ISO/IEC 9594-3:1993, *Information Technology—Open Systems Interconnection—The Directory: Abstract Service Definition*. Defines in an abstract way the externally visible service provided by the Directory, including bind and unbind operations, read operations, search operations, modify operations, and errors.

- ITU-T Recommendation X.518 (1993) | ISO/IEC 9594-4:1993, *Information Technology—Open Systems Interconnection—The Directory: Procedures for Distributed Operations*. Specifies the procedures by which the distributed components of the Directory interoperate in order to provide a consistent service to its users.

- ITU-T Recommendation X.519 (1993) | ISO/IEC 9594-5:1993, *Information Technology—Open Systems Interconnection—The Directory: Protocol Specifications*. Specifies the Directory Access Protocol, the Directory System Protocol, the Directory Information Shadowing Protocol, and the Directory Operational Binding Management Protocol (fulfilling the abstract services specified in Recommendations X.501, X.511, X.518, and X.525).

- ITU-T Recommendation X.520 (1993) | ISO/IEC 9594-6:1993, *Information Technology—Open Systems Interconnection—The Directory: Selected Attribute Types*. Defines a number of attribute types and matching rules that may be useful across a range of applications of the Directory. One particular use for many of the attributes defined is in the formation of names, particularly for the classes of object defined in Recommendation X.521.

- ITU-T Recommendation X.521 (1993) | ISO/IEC 9594-7:1993, *Information Technology—Open Systems Interconnection—The Directory: Selected Object Classes*. Defines a number of selected object classes and name forms that may be useful across a range of applications of the Directory. An object class definition specifies the attribute types that are relevant to the objects of that class. A name form definition specifies the attributes to be used in forming names for the objects of a given class.

- ITU-T Recommendation X.509 (1993) | ISO/IEC 9594-8:1993, *Information Technology—Open Systems Interconnection—The Directory: Authentication Framework*. Defines a framework for the provision by the Directory of authentication services to its users. It describes two levels of authentication: simple authentication, using a password as a verification of claimed identity; and strong authentication, involving credentials formed using cryptographic techniques. While simple authentication offers some limited protection against unauthorized access, only strong authentication should be used as the basis for providing secure services.

- ITU-T Recommendation X.525 (1993) | ISO/IEC 9594-9:1993, *Information Technology—Open Systems Interconnection—The Directory: Replication*. Specifies a shadow service that DSAs may use to replicate

Directory information. The service allows Directory information to be replicated among DSAs to improve service to Directory users, and provides for the automatic updating of this information.

- ITU-T Recommendation X.581 (1993), *Protocol Implementation Conformance Statement (PICS)—Directory Access Protocol Proforma*. There is no equivalent ISO/IEC document for this recommendation.

- ITU-T Recommendation X.582 (1993), *Protocol Implementation Conformance Statement (PICS)—Directory System Protocol Proforma*. There is no equivalent ISO/IEC document for this recommendation.

Many of the terms and acronyms used in the descriptions of the various documents are defined in the following sections. This part of the chapter presents the specifications for the Directory. The discussion of Directory specifications is organized according to the specified conceptual directory model and consists of sections defining the scope, structure, and presentation aspects of the Directory.

The Basics of Directory Scope

The scope of a directory defines the boundary surrounding the portion of the real world represented by the elements within the directory, as well as the types of information, associated with those elements, that need to be maintained in the directory. The environment within which the directory exists and its intended uses determine the portion of the real world represented in the directory.

The Directory specifications were designed to provide a framework for directory services, rather than a fully specified directory to support a predetermined set of applications. Since the Directory was designed with many possible uses in mind, those people responsible for implementing directories or designing applications to make use of directory services make their own decisions about how to support the Directory.

This arrangement required the introduction of a conceptual information model to allow those responsible for implementing directories to define a scope suitable for the environments and applications supported by their particular directories. The designers envisioned some generic applications for the Directory to provide examples of how the conceptual information model could be applied to define their scope. This section looks first at the generic applications described in the standards and then at the conceptual information model used to define the scope of a directory implementation.

Planning for Applications and the Directory

During the design process, several assumptions were made about the environment within which the Directory would provide services. First, it was assumed that the telecommunications networks that the Directory would provide services for could be arbitrarily large and subject to constant changes. Resources on the network could enter or leave at any time without warning; paths between resources could be added or removed; and various characteristics of these resources (such as addresses, availability, and physical locations) could change at any time. Second, although the overall rate of change of information associated with network resources might be rapid, the useful lifetime of such information would not be short. This meant that generally the information associated with a given resource would be accessed by users more often than the information would change. Finally, there was the assumption that resources involved in telecommunications services are typically identified by addresses or other identifiers selected for their ease of allocation or efficiency of processing, rather than for their ease of use by humans.

The designers envisioned the Directory as a tool with the primary role of allowing users to access information about network resources while providing for the maintenance, distribution, and security of that information. Users could include people and computer programs. Network resources could include servers providing network services, printers, and users.

The network information maintained in the Directory was intended to satisfy two needs of users: to be isolated from changes that occur to information associated with resources; and to have access to a user-friendly view of the network and its resources. The introduction of a "level of indirection" between the users and the resources isolates users from changes to information associated with resources. This can be accomplished by associating names with resources. Allowing users to locate resources using a variety of characteristics (which rarely change) associated with resources other than fully qualified names or addresses (which could change arbitrarily) provides a user-friendly view of the network and its resources.

Three generic applications for which the Directory would play an integral role were envisioned: interpersonal communications, intersystem communications, and authentication. In interpersonal communications applications (such as electronic mail), the Directory would play the role of providing humans or their agents with the information necessary to communicate with other humans or their agents. Intersystem communications applications would use the Directory to provide the information necessary for services to communicate with services running on other systems. Applications requiring authentication would use the Directory to verify identities by requiring users or resources taking part in communications to provide some proof of their identities.

Setting Up Object Classes and Attributes

Since only generic applications were defined in the standards for the Directory, there was no way to determine the portion of the real world encompassed by a directory service conforming to the standards. Therefore, the Directory specifications introduced a conceptual information model to allow for a consistent definition of scope for directory implementations. The support by the Directory for multiple applications drawn from a wide range of possibilities is the main characteristic of the Directory design that contributes to this information model. As you learned earlier, applications drive the definition of scope for a directory implementation. So it was expected that the nature of the applications supported would govern the information contained in the Directory and the ways in which it would be accessed.

The generic applications defined for the Directory assume that certain types of information would be available within the directory. These might include:

- Information about people (such as electronic mail addresses, phone numbers, and public key identity certificates) that would be of interest to users attempting to establish communications with them.

- Information about servers and services that could be used to learn their location and availability.

- Operational information such as access controls and internal consistency data used to maintain the integrity of information in the directory.

The information model was meant to generalize the constructs used to specify the way such information (and other types of information not envisioned by the Directory designers) would be represented in directory implementations.

The information model specifies a directory database consisting of a collection of entries (or object instances), each of which is associated with one or more attributes. Each attribute is defined with a data type, and can contain one or more values. Using standard database terms to describe this information model, the Directory database is analogous to a table, while objects and attributes are analogous to records and fields, or rows and columns. The Directory, however, was not intended to be a general-purpose database, although it was conceivable that a directory implementation could be built on database systems. Instead, it was assumed that there would be a much higher frequency of read operations rather than updates, which could limit the scope of information suitable for inclusion in a directory implementation.

Each instance of an object created in the Directory must contain object class attributes that define a name for the instance and the type of real world object the instance represents. Names are used to uniquely identify each object instance in the Directory, and object classes are used to define the attributes that are available to hold information associated with each object instance. Typical object classes include people, computers, and network services, and each object class definition includes a predetermined set of attributes associated with it. The rules determining the attributes associated with object classes are defined in the directory schema that is established by whoever implements a directory and, optionally, by whoever has the responsibility for maintaining information in the directory implementation.

Individuals responsible for maintaining information in a directory implementation have the ability to modify the schema to define new object classes and attributes. This allows directory implementations to be useful for applications that were not anticipated by the directory implementation designers.

Attributes are defined independently of object classes, so it is possible that a given attribute could be used by more than one object class. Within the Directory specifications, data types for the values associated with attributes are defined using ASN.1 (Abstract Syntax Notation One), which is a standard language for defining data types. Directory implementations can, and often do, use alternate methods for defining attribute data types such as BER (Basic Encoding Rules), Unicode, simple string syntax, or data type rules associated with a specific programming language. Object classes are defined through inheritance (a new object class is built upon the attributes of a base class) or superclassing (a new object class is defined by combining the attribute associations of one or more existing base classes and, optionally, with associations with additional attributes). The attributes associated with an object class are divided into mandatory and optional associations. An instance of an object class must have legal values for all mandatory attributes.

Defining the scope for a directory implementation consists of defining object classes and attributes to provide a framework for creating directory entries (object instances). For example, a directory implementation might define an object class of User that would be associated with the following attributes: Object Class, Common Name, Given Name, Middle Name, Surname, Description, E-Mail Address, Telephone Number, and Fax Number. The Common Name field could be designated the distinguished attribute that is required for uniquely identifying each object instance. The mandatory attributes would then likely be the Object Class and Distinguished Name attributes, with the rest of the attributes defined as optional.

The Directory provides opportunities to exploit commonness among applications through the recognition that specific information associated with an object class may be relevant to more than one application. Based on the generic applications envisioned for the Directory to support, a number of object classes and attribute types were defined in the Directory specifications that could be useful across a range of applications. The rules established for the default object classes, and their respective attribute definitions and assignments, make up the default schema for the Directory. The schema also defines permitted relationships between objects, a topic that is covered in the next section because it is a structural concept.

What's behind the Directory Structure

As we saw in Chapter 1, the structure of a directory specifies the way that information is stored and managed within the directory. The structure is the administrative aspect of a directory, and it serves two primary functions: object identification and object organization. Object identification ensures that each object within a directory can be uniquely identified so that it will map to an object unambiguously within the portion of the real world encompassed by the directory. Object organization provides a framework that can be used to segment maintenance of logical subsets of the objects contained in the directory.

The Directory specifications provide a detailed framework for defining the structure of directory implementations that goes beyond fulfilling the two primary functions of the directory structure. Object identification and organization are addressed in the definition of the constructs and rules of the Directory Information Base (DIB) covered in the next section. Additional structural elements, such as provisions for distributed operation, replication, and access control are also addressed in the Directory specifications through models and protocols, and are examined in the following sections.

The Directory Information Base (DIB)

The previous section, *The Basics of Directory Scope,* describes an information model consisting of object classes and attributes that serve as the basis for defining the scope of a directory implementation. The information held in the directory database for entries and attributes, or object instances, is collectively known as the Directory Information Base (DIB). The entries correspond to objects in the network, and the associated attributes describe the properties of each object.

The entries in the DIB are organized hierarchically as part of an inverted tree structure, known as the Directory Information Tree (DIT), that represents the logical organization of the directory's contents. Entries higher in the tree (nearer the root) often represent entities with an organizational purpose such as countries, localities, organizations, or organizational units (such as divisions or departments). Such intermediate entries act as containers for additional subordinate entries that combine with those entries above them to form a subtree. Entries lower in the tree typically represent people, computers, or services, and act as leaf entries instead of containers. They do not form subtrees since leaf entries are not allowed to have subordinate entries.

A mandatory attribute associated with every object class, referred to as the *distinguished attribute,* is specified in the Directory information model to provide for object instance naming. The distinguished attribute is known as the Relative Distinguished Name (RDN) for the entry in the Directory Information Base, which uniquely identifies each object instance within the context of its location in the Directory Information Tree. Unique identification of every object instance in the DIT, independent of context, is accomplished by combining the RDNs of every container between the root and the object instance to form the Distinguished Name (DN).

Object instances can have more than one DN through the use of alias entries that point to specific object instances. Alias entries are instances of object classes, derived from the Alias class, that usually serve the sole purpose of pointing to other object instances. They normally allow specific object instances to be accessed using alternative names or to be made available in an alias entry's context without requiring the use of the DN of the object instance.

Accessing an object instance through an alias entry can be accomplished by de-referencing the alias entry (at the option of the user) and using the pointer to the object instance.

The Directory schema is maintained as part of the DIB to ensure that entries in the DIB remain well formed as modifications occur over time. The Directory schema serves two purposes: It defines the object classes, attributes, and allowable associations (mandatory and optional) between object classes and attributes (covered in the discussion of the information model) available in the Directory. It also defines the allowable superior and subordinate relationships, known as *name bindings,* between object instances within the DIT.

The Directory schema rules governing object classes and attributes to ensure that an object instance cannot be defined with the wrong attributes for its object class, with a missing mandatory attribute, or with the wrong type of data within an attribute value. The Directory schema rules governing name bindings between object classes ensure that the hierarchical structure of the DIT cannot be compromised by arbitrary superior or subordinate relationships between object instances, such as not allowing leaf entries to be used as intermediate entries. Figure 3.1 shows a hypothetical DIT.

The collection of RDNs that make up the Distinguished Name of an object instance provide information about the entry's relative location in the DIT. For example, the object instance for Mary Smith in Figure 3.1 would

FIGURE 3.1

A hypothetical
Directory Information
Tree

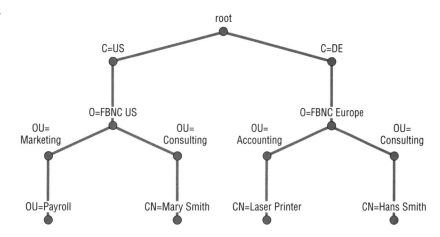

have a DN of {C=US, O=FBNC US, OU=Consultants, CN=Mary Smith},
which corresponds to a logical location in the DIT:

- C, which represents *Country,* is the highest grouping entry in the DIT.
  The Directory schema restricts such entries to appearing only below
  the root.

- O, which represents *Organization,* is the next highest grouping entry
  after Country. The Directory schema restricts such entries to
  appearing only below the root or directly below a Country entry.

- L, which represents *Locality,* is a grouping entry that can occur at any
  point in the tree except directly under the root.

- OU, which represents *Organizational Unit,* is another grouping entry.
  The Directory schema restricts such entries to appearing only below
  an Organization entry.

- CN, which represents *Common Name,* is the distinguished attribute
  (or RDN) for an object instance, in this case probably an instance of
  the object class User. CN is commonly used in full DNs to refer to the
  RDN of a leaf entry. The Directory schema usually restricts leaf entries
  to appearing only below certain container object instances such as
  Organization or Organizational Unit.

You'll notice that the order used here for the Distinguished Name is the reverse of that used in NDS (where the Common Name comes first). The order presented here is that used for X.400 electronic mail addresses.

The hierarchical structure of the logical directory embodied in the tree-like shape of the DIT is meant to provide for a multitiered structure so that maintenance of directory information can be divided and subdivided among multiple authorities. Local administrative authorities can be given authority for maintenance of directory information within a subtree. Administrative authorities responsible for a given subtree can subdivide authority within the subtree by delegating authority. Administrative authority over a subtree brings with it the responsibility to ensure, for example, that all of the entries in the subtree have unambiguous DNs. Responsibility is passed down the tree from superior to subordinate authorities, with control being enforced by means of the schema.

Distribution and Replication

The Directory specification takes into account that in order to ensure efficient access to directory information, the contents of the DIB might need to be distributed or replicated to multiple locations in a network or internetwork. Distributing information in the DIB typically facilitates local management of local resources within a network-wide framework. When information in the directory is distributed, the DIT is still seen by users as an integrated whole.

Replication of information in the directory, called *shadowing* in the Directory standards, consists of maintaining multiple copies of the same information in different locations. This often helps to improve the quality of service by increasing the performance and availability of the directory. Replication improves performance by allowing distributed network information held in the directory to be located near users so they don't have to traverse wide area network links (which are often slow or congested) to access the information. Replication improves availability by eliminating the impact of a single point of failure, because users can access information in a replica in the event that the original is unavailable. In the event of a system failure, replicated information can be used to reconstruct any directory information that was lost as well.

The Directory System Agent (DSA) is defined in the functional model of the Directory, illustrated in Figure 3.2, as an application process that is given the role of providing access to the DIB from external entities such as users or other DSAs. DSAs maintain a portion (or the whole) of the DIB; and when multiple DSAs are responsible for maintaining separate portions of the DIB, they must communicate with each other to facilitate distributed operation. The Directory System Protocol (DSP) was specified to allow DSAs to communicate with each other. When DSP is being used, a DSA stores information about other DSAs, called knowledge information, in order to locate the other DSAs on the network.

FIGURE 3.2

The functional model
of the Directory

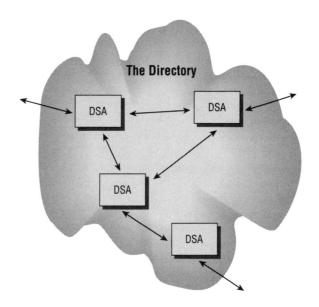

The DSA may use information in its local database, interact with other DSAs, or direct a requester to other DSAs to provide access to information in the directory. The role of the DSA in providing access to the DIB for users (for both centralized and distributed operation) is covered in the section called "The Power of Directory Presentation," while this section describes the role of the DSA in facilitating replication of directory information.

DSAs may maintain two types of replicated entry information: cache copies and shadowed information. Cache copies, consisting of entry and knowledge information from other parts of the Directory obtained by the DSA to satisfy requests of users or other DSAs, are maintained to improve the response time to future requests for the same information. Caching procedures are not covered in the Directory specifications since they were considered to be implementation-specific and beyond the scope of the standards.

Shadowed copies contain information replicated from other DSAs for the purpose of maintaining copies of directory information in multiple locations. The DSAs responsible for maintaining shadowed directory information communicate with each other to ensure that the contents of the copies remain current. It was not a requirement of the Directory that changes to shadowed directory information occur immediately within all copies—transient conditions where both old and new versions of the same information are available were considered acceptable.

Before shadowing can occur between two DSAs, they require an agreement, called a *shadow operational binding,* that covers the conditions under which replication will occur. The Directory Operations Protocol (DOP) is defined in the Directory specifications to establish, modify, and terminate shadow operational bindings between pairs of cooperating DSAs. Once a pair of DSAs has established a shadow operational binding, they can communicate with each other using the Directory Information Shadowing Protocol (DISP) to transfer directory information between them for replication.

The functional model for directory shadowing allows a DSA to assume one of two roles with respect to its shadow partner when a shadow operational binding has been established: It can be either a shadow supplier or a shadow consumer. A DSA can assume both roles for the same or different directory information as long as each role is defined for a different DSA. Typically, the shadow supplier holds the master copy of directory information for its portion of the DIB, and it establishes primary shadow operational bindings with other DSAs that act as shadow consumers.

It is also possible for a DSA acting as a shadow consumer for a certain portion of the DIB to provide indirect shadows (shadows of a shadow) of the same information to other DSAs. This is facilitated by establishing secondary shadow operational bindings where the DSA acts as the shadow supplier to other DSAs for the replicated portion of the DIB it contains.

In all cases, there can be only one master copy of a given portion of the DIB and all updates are directed to that copy and replicated to shadow copies according to the shadow operational bindings that exist.

Directory Access Control

The directory specifications assume that the directory exists in an environment where various administrative authorities need to control access to certain elements of the directory information. Some of the directory elements the designers identified as needing various levels of protection included information related to the DIT structure, directory user information, and directory operational information (including access control information). To help prevent unauthorized access to directory elements, it was determined that the identity of users and DSAs should be verified so that access to directory information can be controlled adequately. An authentication framework was defined in the directory specification consisting of two levels of authentication:

- Simple authentication, which requires just a password for verification of a user's identity

- Strong authentication, which is based on credentials that are formed using public key cryptographic techniques

While simple authentication is capable of providing some limited protection against unauthorized access, it was suggested that strong authentication was necessary for the directory to provide secure services. The Directory specifications also include guidelines for the use of digital signatures, public key certificates, and Certificate Revocation Lists (CRLs), including specification of how the information necessary for the operation of such systems may be stored and accessed in the directory.

An access control scheme, referred to as *basic access control,* is defined in the Directory specifications to provide the means by which local security policies are enforced through mechanisms within the directory that control access to directory information. Such control over access to directory information can be exercised to prevent unauthorized detection, disclosure, or modification of the information. When determining whether an authenticated user is allowed to access directory information, the access control mechanisms consider the following:

- The component within the directory being accessed

- The user requesting the operation

- The specific right required to complete the portions of the operation

- The defined security policy governing access to that information

The Power of Directory Presentation

In Chapter 1, we learned that a directory's presentation scheme specifies the methods available to users for accessing information contained in the directory. The methods that are typically available for presenting directory information can be evaluated qualitatively in terms of four primary factors: completeness, accessibility, accuracy, and efficiency (see Chapter 1 for a detailed discussion of these factors). Some methods for accessing directory information will emphasize certain objectives at the expense of others. A particular method is generally selected based on an evaluation of the relative strengths of available methods weighed against any necessary trade-offs.

The Directory specifications provide a well-defined set of access capabilities—known as the *abstract services* of the directory—for presenting directory information to users. Access to information in the directory is accomplished via a *Directory User Agent (DUA),* which is an application process that acts on behalf of users. The DUA interacts with DSAs to allow simple modification and retrieval capabilities. DUA access to the directory is illustrated in Figure 3.3. At the time the specifications were developed, the designers expected that the basic access capabilities would be extended in specific directory client implementations with local DUA functions to provide more advanced capabilities that might be required by end-users.

FIGURE 3.3

DUA access to the Directory

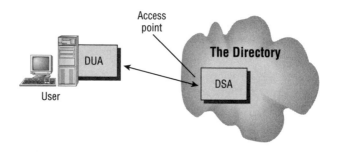

Directory Access Protocol (DAP)

At the time it was developed, several patterns of use of information or requests for information contained in the Directory were anticipated in support of the generic applications envisioned for it. They include:

- *Look-up,* the classic form of information retrieval, where users request specific information related to a known resource.

- *Name resolution,* where resources are located using names that can be easily predicted or remembered by users. This can be considered a special case of look-up.

- *Browsing,* allowing users to select resources from a list when the name of the desired resource might not be known without seeing it.

- *Searching* and *filtering,* where information associated with resources is used to locate individual resources or groups of resources.

- *Authentication* (presented earlier as a generic application), which verifies the identity of users and resources.

The Directory Access Protocol (DAP) was designed to provide a standardized way for DUAs to interact with DSAs to access information in the directory. The idea was to support the anticipated patterns of use as well as other complementary operations. Bind and Unbind functions are provided to manage connections between DUAs and DSAs, although it is not necessary for a DUA to bind with a DSA to submit requests. DAP specifies requests as functions, allowing interrogation of the directory as well as allowing modification of directory information. The requests result in outcomes specific to each type of request.

Five functions are included in DAP for interrogating the directory: Read, Compare, List, Search, and Abandon. They perform in the following manner:

- A *read* request is aimed at a particular entry and causes the values of some or all of the attributes of that entry to be returned. Where only some attributes are to be returned, the DUA supplies the list of attribute types of interest.

- A *compare* request is aimed at a particular attribute of a particular entry and causes the directory to check whether a supplied value matches a value of that attribute. For example, this can be used to carry out password checking, where the password held in the directory might be inaccessible for *read* but accessible for *compare*.

- A *list* request causes the directory to return the list of immediate subordinates of a particular intermediate entry in the DIT.

- A *search* request causes the directory to return information from all of the entries within a certain portion of the DIT that satisfy some filter condition. The information that is returned from each entry consists of some or all of the attributes of that entry, as with *read*.

- An *abandon* request, as applied to an outstanding interrogation request, informs the directory that the originator of the request is no longer interested in the request being carried out. The directory may, for example, cease processing the request and may discard any results achieved so far.

Four functions are included in DAP for modifying information in the directory: Add Entry, Remove Entry, Modify Entry, and Modify Distinguished Name. They work as follows:

- An *add entry* request causes a new entry to be added to the DIT.

- A *remove entry* request causes an entry to be removed from the DIT.

- A *modify entry* request causes the directory to execute a sequence of changes to a particular entry. Either all or none of the changes are made, and the DIB is always left in a state consistent with the schema. The changes allowed include the addition, removal, or replacement of attribute values.

- A *modify distinguished name* request is used to change the Relative Distinguished Name (RDN) of an entry or to move an entry to a new container in the DIT. If an entry has subordinates, then all subordinates are renamed or moved accordingly.

A number of controls can be applied to the various requests, primarily to allow the user to impose limits on the use of resources consumed by the directory when satisfying requests. Among the controls available are limits on the amount of time for an operation, limits on the size of the results set, scope limits for the search, and the priority of the request. Requests may be accompanied by security parameters that directory security mechanisms may need to control access to directory information. Filters may also be established to limit the entries that can be included in the result of a request that acts on multiple entries.

Distributed Operation

The interaction between DUAs and DSAs is straightforward when only a single DSA needs to be involved to satisfy a request from a DUA. When the DIB is distributed and multiple DSAs are required to satisfy requests, the interaction between the DUA and DSAs is much more complex. In such environments, requests initiated by a DUA can be satisfied by the DSA that accesses its own database or interacts with other DSAs. Alternatively, the DSA may redirect the request to another DSA to help provide the requested information.

A number of cases of request handling have been identified. They can be reduced to three major cases for the purposes of simplification: chaining, multicast, and referral. *Chaining* is what happens when all DSAs are connected and a DUA issues a query. The query travels the predefined chain and the reply follows the same path back to the DUA. *Multicast* has two variations: parallel and sequential. *Parallel* is when a DUA issues a query that goes out to all DSAs and all of them reply. *Sequential* uses the same model, except that a DUA issues queries sequentially until a DSA replies with the requested information. *Referral* has two variants: where DSAs are chained and where DSAs are not chained. When DSAs are chained, the first DSA makes the call to other DSAs (with the referral information). Otherwise, the DUA has to make the call.

Lightweight Directory Access Protocol (LDAP)

Directory client software that implements DAP is subject to significant resource requirements due to the heavy overhead required to support the upper layers of the OSI stack and the complexity required to handle referrals when operating in a distributed environment. The resource requirements have made it difficult to deploy directory implementations since many client machines, especially PC and Macintosh systems, lack the resources necessary to properly support directory client software using DAP. This difficulty fostered the development of the Lightweight Directory Access Protocol (LDAP), which specifies a simpler client interface to the directory than was specified for DAP.

LDAP is not defined in the directory specifications, but was developed to provide a client interface for directories conforming to the X.500 directory standards. The choice of attribute names and the hierarchical structure of LDAP are clearly derived from the X.500 directory specifications.

It is important to remember that LDAP does not specify an X.500 directory, but instead provides a protocol suitable for use by users interacting with any hierarchical, attribute-based directory.

Version 2 of the Lightweight directory Access Protocol (LDAPv2), documented in RFC 1777 *Lightweight Directory Access Protocol,* RFC 1778 *The String Representation of Standard Attribute Syntaxes,* and RFC 1779 *A String Representation of Distinguished Names,* serves as the basis of most current client implementations of the protocol. LDAP has recently been adopted as an official Internet standard for a directory access protocol and has garnered the support of most influential network software developers. Version 3 (LDAPv3), an update recently approved by the IETF, addresses some limitations found during deployment of LDAPv2. It also adds new features, improves compatibility with the second edition (1993) of the directory specifications and better specifies how LDAP can be used with non-X.500 and stand-alone directories.

LDAP uses the same information model as that defined in the X.500 directory specifications, as well as many of the functional client-server characteristics for interaction between users and the directory. When operating with directories conforming to the X.500 directory standards, an LDAP client interacts exclusively with LDAP providers (usually running as server processes) that are responsible for interacting with DSAs on behalf of the client. LDAP is used as the protocol governing communications between the LDAP client and the LDAP provider, and DAP is used as the protocol governing communications between the LDAP provider and the DSAs. This model is illustrated in Figure 3.4.

When using LDAP to access information contained in non-X.500 directories, only the LDAP provider is different since that is the only component required to communicate natively with the directory. It is even possible to implement "native" LDAP directories where the LDAP provider acts as the sole access point to information residing in the directory.

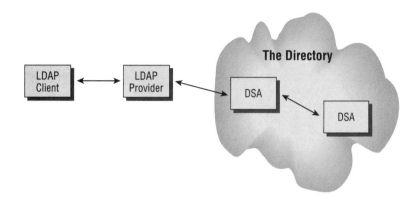

LDAP is simpler and less resource-intensive to implement on client systems than DAP (owing to the fact that implementation of DAP is reserved for server systems). In addition, since LDAP was designed with the objective of interacting with other (non-X.500) directories, it is finally feasible to build directory access capabilities into more applications. This is because adding LDAP support could allow interaction with a variety of directories.

The simplicity of LDAP is a result of a number of design considerations that were intended to reduce the protocol's resource requirements when compared with DAP. They include:

- The implementation of only a subset of the functions defined for DAP

- The offloading of complicated operations required in a distributed environment (such as referral handling) from the client to the LDAP provider

- Simplified encoding of attribute types and values using a lightweight form of BER (Basic Encoding Rules)

- Simplified encoding of protocol data elements (such as distinguished names) using ordinary strings

- Its use of the TCP transport (and possibly other simple transports) instead of the complex OSI protocols

LDAP includes a Bind operation that is simpler than the equivalent Bind function used to initiate sessions between the client and a server in DAP. The LDAP Unbind operation used to terminate sessions is virtually identical to the Unbind function included in DAP. Three operations are included in

LDAP for interrogating the directory, while DAP includes five functions for this purpose. The functions in LDAP are compare, search, and abandon. They can be defined as:

- The LDAP *compare* request is equivalent to its DAP counterpart, where the directory compares a client's assertion for an entry's attribute value with the value of the attribute for the entry in the directory.

- The LDAP *search* request is similar to its DAP counterpart, where the directory returns all of the entries consisting of all or some of the entry's attributes within a certain portion of the DIT that satisfy some filter condition. LDAP also uses the *search* request to emulate the DAP Read and List functions through definition of filter conditions aimed at obtaining equivalent results.

- The LDAP *abandon* request is equivalent to its DAP counterpart, where the client can inform the directory that it should abandon an outstanding interrogation request in the event that the client is no longer interested in the request being carried out.

LDAP includes four operations for modifying information in the directory. They are equivalent to the four functions included in DAP for this purpose. The LDAP functions are modify, add, delete, and modify RDN. They perform as follows:

- The LDAP *modify* request is similar to its DAP counterpart, where the client can request that the directory modify an entry. LDAP defines simplified semantics for the *modify* request by supporting three operations: add values, delete values, and replace values.

- The LDAP *add* request is equivalent to its DAP counterpart, where a new entry can be added to the DIT.

- The LDAP *delete* request is equivalent to its DAP counterpart, where an entry can be removed from the DIT.

- The LDAP *modify RDN* request is similar to its DAP counterpart, where its functionality is limited to allowing changes to the last component of an entry's distinguished name.

LDAP provides a subset of the controls that can be applied to various requests, including those used to impose limits on the use of resources consumed by the directory when satisfying requests. Handling of alias entries is simplified in LDAP by allowing de-referencing options to be selected as arguments for requests rather than requiring a separate operation, as is the case in DAP.

Lightweight Directory Update Protocol (LDUP)

LDAP provides a mechanism for searching and reading multiple directories with a single query. LDAP also provides a mechanism for modifying a directory. Missing, however, is a method for distributing modifications to multiple directories in order to keep their information synchronized. A new IETF working group, LDAP Duplication/Replication/Update Protocol (LDUP), has been organized to define how LDAP-enable can share data and keep each other up-to-date. Participants in the working group include people from all the major LDAP enabled directory vendors, and subteams are working now to prepare draft proposals for the whole group to consider. Currently, plans are to have a version 1 specification in place before the end of 1999.

Summary

Even though directories completely conforming to the X.500 directory standards are rare, directories implementing important conceptual or functional elements of the directory have been around for a long time. For example, the Domain Naming System (DNS) and Novell Directory Services (NDS) provide services similar to those defined in the X.500 directory standards. Such directory or naming services usually adopt the X.500 architecture (entries and attributes organized in a tree structure) and some amount of the X.500 functionality. Other elements of the directory specifications such as the specific protocols and the ASN.1 notation are less likely to be adopted in such implementations.

The wide acceptance of the concepts and models defined in the X.500 directory can be attributed to the following advantages that were outlined in RFC 1309 *Technical Overview of Directory Services Using the X.500 Protocol*, which introduced the X.500 directory standards to the Internet community:

- Decentralized Maintenance: Each site within a global X.500 directory is responsible only for its local part of the directory, so updates and maintenance can be done instantly.

- Powerful Searching Capability: X.500 provides powerful searching facilities that allow users to construct arbitrarily complex queries.

- Single Global Namespace: Much like the Domain Naming Systems (DNS), X.500 provides a single homogeneous namespace to users. The X.500 namespace is more flexible and expandable than which is available for DNS.

- Structured Information Framework: X.500 defines the information framework used in the directory, allowing local extensions.

- Standards-Based Directory: As X.500 can be used to build a standards-based directory, applications which require directory information (e-mail, automated resource locators, special-purpose directory tools) can access a planet's worth of information in a uniform manner, no matter where they are based or currently running.

Implementing directories based on the X.500 directory specifications has been slow due, in part, to the complexity and resource requirements of directory client software. The slow rate of implementation could also partly be attributed to developers waiting for the 1992 revisions for both X.500 and the X.400 Message Handling Services (MHS), which rely heavily on X.500 services. The problems caused by the complexity and resource requirements of directory client software have been addressed when Lightweight Directory Access Protocol (LDAP) emerged, and now that updates to both X.500 and X.400 have appeared, directory implementations are rapidly conforming to the X.500 directory specifications in more significant ways.

PART

II

Novell Directory
Services

CHAPTER

4

NDS Concepts
and Terminology

ike just about every other computer-based technology, Novell Directory Services has its own concepts as well as its own terms to describe these concepts. First-time users of NDS might be intimidated by terms that they are not familiar with, but the concepts behind the terms should be easy enough to grasp. The creators of NDS chose specific terminology to describe its workings simply to remove any associations the user might have with terms that are more familiar but also more generic.

Few, if any, of the terms and concepts used for NDS are unique to NDS. They're drawn from those used in the database world (after all, NDS is a distributed, replicated database) modified by or coupled with those used for user authentication and security.

As always, Novell defines the terms used by reference to NetWare concepts, so don't assume you understand the meaning of a word that seems familiar. Be sure you know the Novell definition of a term you may be familiar with in a different context. For example, the word *domain* means different things to an NT network administrator than it does to a Unix network administrator. Currently, *domain* is not used at all as an NDS term, although a domain might be an NDS object. Confused? Read on...

In this chapter, we'll define the terms and introduce the concepts of NDS. Later chapters will go into more depth explaining the uses of the concept. Not every term or phrase associated with NDS will be found here—see the glossary for a complete list of definitions. In this chapter we'll look at the basic principles of NDS and some of its basic units.

The NDS Schema

A *schema* is a definition of the structure of a database. In it are defined the *physical structure*—tables, rows, fields, field types, keys, etc.—as well as the *metaphysical structure*. By this we mean that the schema identifies the basic, or atomic, units and their properties, along with rules for adding to or combining the atomic units into constructs usable in everyday activities. In particular, the NDS schema contains the rules that define how the directory tree is constructed.

Figure 4.1 shows how hypothetical objects are constructed from the base schema. At the top of the image is the atomic unit *thing*. It has the properties of Name, Location, and Extensible. From this the three object classes— *device, person,* and *resource*—are created, each inheriting the properties of *thing* and adding additional properties. For example, the *resource* class may have the property of Server (i.e., the server where the resource is accessible) added to the base property Location. Each of these classes is then extended to create discrete objects. Notice that *printer* is an object of the class *device,* as is *computer.* To the properties of a *device,* the object *printer* adds such things as page definition, layout, and paper source. This not only makes the object more useful but differentiates it from the object *computer,* even though both are based on the same class. This is a simplified abstraction of NDS. For example, the atomic unit (the base object class, from which all others are derived) is called "Top" in NDS. Top also has a larger, and richer, group of attributes than those shown in the figure.

The NDS schema is stored within the directory in what is called the *schema partition.* This is one of the four partitions (Bindery, Schema, System, and External References) which are installed on every NetWare 4.*x*/ 5.*x* server regardless of whether the server holds a replica of the directory tree.

If you are a developer, you can think of the schema as a Class Library that contains basic object class definitions. In order to create a new object class, you take an existing object class and add new features to it. In this way, the class that was inherited remains intact and the new object type is placed in the Class Library, as well. An application that needs to know about an object type does not need to have this information hard coded but reads the schema definition of the object.

FIGURE 4.1

The objects in the bottom row are instances of the classes in the middle row, which are all based on the atomic unit *thing*.

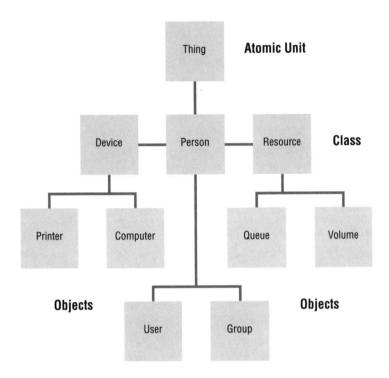

From a user's or administrator's perspective, you might think of the schema as the "social rules" that are passed between object classes and objects. Each generation inherits a set of rules, adds new features to them, and passes the new set on to the next generation.

If you are using Novell's ManageWise to monitor your network, note that it uses the term *schema* to refer to the Management Information Base (MIB) for an object. While its definition is similar to that of the NDS schema, they are not interchangeable.

The NDS schema defines:

- The types of objects that can exist in an NDS tree
- The possible locations of these object in the NDS tree
- The information (stored as attributes) that can be and must be maintained about the object

Schema Components

The NDS schema consists of three basic components:

- Object classes

- Attribute types

- Attribute syntaxes

The set of rules that controls the creation of a particular object is called an object class. Each object class is defined in terms of attributes. An attribute is a specific piece of information that can exist for an object. (NetWare utilities and documentation sometimes call attributes, *properties.*)

For example, NDS contains an object class for users, called *User object.* This User object class defines many attributes (over 80), including attributes for such items as the user's name, telephone number, address, and group memberships.

Attributes are defined in terms of a base set of data types called *attribute syntaxes,* and the attribute syntaxes define the primary data types for values stored in the NDS database.

For example, some attributes, such as Password Minimum Length or Minimum Account Balance, take integer values whereas other attributes, such as a user's Full Name or Given Name, take string values.

NDS has a set of built-in classes and attribute types that accommodate general categories of network objects, such as organizations, users, and devices. This set is called the *base schema.* The base schema is extensible: NDS developers can build on the base schema to create new classes and new attributes for objects. However, these new classes and attributes must be defined in terms of the existing syntaxes. Defining new syntaxes is not allowed.

Schema Structure

The schema defines the set of rules that govern the types of objects that can exist in an NDS tree. Each object belongs to an object class that specifies what attributes can be associated with the object. All attributes are based on a set of attribute types that are, in turn, based on a standard set of attribute syntaxes.

The NDS schema not only controls the structure of individual objects but also controls the relationship among objects in the NDS tree. The schema rules allow some objects to contain other subordinate objects. Thus the schema gives structure to the NDS tree.

The attribute syntaxes define the primary data types for values stored in the NDS tree. Attribute types are defined from the attribute syntaxes and define the possible attributes an object can have. Object classes are defined using a subset of the possible attributes and determine the types of objects that can be in the tree. The tree structure rules define how the object classes can be organized and nested in the tree and, therefore, determine the tree's structure.

NDS in NetWare 5: New Schema Features

The base schema in NetWare 5 has added a number of new attributes and one new object class while also making changes in containment rules and syntax matching. In addition, the inheritance of ACLs (Access Control Lists) has been modified. The following sections describe these new features.

Containment Changes

NetWare 4 allowed either an Organization object or a Country object to be the root of the NDS tree. NetWare 5 allows a user to select the tree root from the following object classes:

- Tree Root
- Country
- Organization

The Tree Root object can contain Country and Organization objects.

Syntax Matching Changes

NetWare 4.x versions of the NDS schema documented only two syntaxes that supported approximate matching: Object ACL and Octet List. The NetWare 5.x schema supports approximate matching for all syntaxes with lists of strings and with distinguished names of objects. The approximate match allows two strings to match without requiring all strings in the list to match. It also allows the distinguished names of objects, such as Servers, Volumes and Users, to match while ignoring the other fields in the syntax.

New Object Classes

The NDS base schema added only one new object class: Tree Root. This object allows the tree name to be part of the object's distinguished name. When a NetWare 4.11 tree is upgraded to NetWare 5, Tree Root becomes the base object of the NDS tree.

New Attribute Definitions

Attributes were added for transitive synchronization (which allows the NDS database to synchronize in mixed IPX and IP networks), and guaranteed globally unique IDs, bindery restrictions, and password management. The following attributes are new:

- Bindery Restriction Level
- GUID
- Obituary Notify
- Other GUID
- Password Management
- Purge Vector
- Synchronized Tolerance
- T (Tree Name)
- Timezone
- Transitive Vector
- Used By
- Uses

ACL Enhancements Affecting Attributes

NetWare 4.*x* allows the inheritance of ACLs granted to [All Attribute Rights] to flow down the NDS tree but blocks the inheritance of ACLs granted to specific attributes.

NetWare 5.*x* allows the network supervisor to select whether ACLs granted to specific attributes or (All Attribute Rights) are inherited. The control comes with the Inheritance Control right that has been added to the rights bit mask. This right controls whether the privilege set in the ACL flows to subordinate objects.

Allowing the inheritance of ACLs to specific attributes enables the network supervisor to set up managers who can manage specific attributes, such as phone numbers, addresses, and passwords, without granting Supervisor rights to the objects. If the ACL to a specific attribute is granted at the container level, the right can be inheritable to an entire branch of an NDS tree.

For example, you can create a telephone number manager by granting the manager an ACL to the Telephone Number attribute of an NDS container object. The privilege set should include the Read, Write, and Inheritance Control rights. The Password Management attribute was added specifically so that network supervisors could set up password managers for the entire NDS tree or portions of the tree.

ACL Enhancements Affecting Objects

In NetWare 4.x, when a user, or trustee, is given (Entry Rights) to a container object, the trustee is given the same rights to all of the subordinate objects of that container. These rights automatically flow down the tree unless an Inherited Rights Filter blocks them.

In NetWare 5.x, (Entry Rights) can behave just as they did in NetWare 4.x, but NetWare 5.x allows them to be configurable. An Inheritance Control right has been added to the bit mask for entry rights, and it controls whether the trustee of the ACL can inherit the rights.

This enhancement has only specialized uses because most of the time the network administrator granting entry rights will want the trustee to inherit the rights. However, this functionality allows the network administrator to create a partition manager who has the rights to create and manage replicas but does not have the rights to modify objects in the containers of the partitions.

Schema Extensions

The NDS schema is extensible. Developers can define new object classes and attributes in addition to those provided by the base schema. In fact, the NetWare operating system and NetWare utilities extend the schema.

When developers define new attribute types or new object class definitions, they must register them with Novell Developer Support to ensure uniqueness. On registering, the developer receives a unique prefix that is prepended to the names of the new attribute and object class definitions. The developer also receives an ASN.1 (Abstract Syntax Notation One) ID for object classes and one for attribute definitions. These IDs can be expanded to include as many unique IDs as needed for object classes and attributes.

In NetWare 4.11 and below, object classes and attributes may have, but are not required to have, an ASN.1 ID. In NetWare 5, ASN.1 IDs are required for applications to pass Novell certification. ASN.1 serves as a common syntax for transferring information between two end systems.

Object Class Definitions

Object classes define the types of objects that can exist in the NDS database. Database entries are created by selecting an object class and then supplying the required attribute information for the entry. For example, to create an entry for a user, you must select the User object class and then supply a name for the user.

In the base schema, all object classes are non-removable; that is, they cannot be deleted or in any other way removed from the schema. Object classes that extended the schema are removable.

An object class is defined by its characteristics, which consists of the following kinds of information:

- Structure rules for naming and containment
- Super classes
- Object class attributes
- ACL templates
- Object class flags

An object class does not have to specify definitions for all characteristics because it can inherit characteristics from super classes.

Structure Rules

All object classes possess two types of structure rules:

- Naming attributes, which determine how objects of the class are named.
- Containment classes, which determine where in the NDS tree hierarchy objects can be placed.

The structure rules for an object class define the possible structural relationships of objects in the NDS tree. The structure rules are either explicitly defined by the class or inherited from a super class. If the class defines them, the class definitions take precedence over inherited definitions.

Naming Attributes

Objects are identified by their own name and the name of their parent objects. An object's name is called its *partial name* or *relative distinguished name* (RDN). An object's RDN is determined by its naming attribute.

The object's full name (with all its parent names included) is called the complete name or distinguished name (DN). An object's DN is determined by all the objects it is subordinate to. Hence, containment rules, which control subordination in the tree, effectively control the formation of distinguished names.

Each class has one or more attributes designated as naming attributes. These attributes can be either mandatory or optional attributes, but at least one must be given a value when creating an object of that class. If the only naming attribute is declared as optional, it is, in effect, mandatory.

Naming attributes specify the rules for the partial name of the object. For example, Organization objects are named by the O (Organization Name) attribute. This attribute is the only attribute value that can appear in an organizational entry's partial name.

Multivalued Naming Attributes   Naming attributes can be multivalued; in other words, more than one name (value) can be added to the naming attribute. For example, an organization can have both "Testing" and "Engineering" as values for the O (Organization Name) attribute. However, only one value will be flagged as the naming value, and that value is used in search operations.

Some object class definitions specify multiple naming attributes. For example, the Locality object class is named by the L (Locality Name) and S (State or Province Name) attributes. Thus, an RDN for locality can include just an L (Locality Name) attribute, just an S (State or Province Name) attribute, or both attributes.

For example, the name for the Austin, Texas, locality could be:

L=Austin

S=Texas

L=Austin + S=Texas

The last example uses both attributes with a plus sign (+) to indicate where the second attribute's value begins. When the type specifiers (in this case L and S) are used as shown, the name is referred to as a typed name. A typeless name has the following format: "Austin+Texas."

Shareable Naming Attributes   A naming attribute does not necessarily reflect the class an object belongs to. Many classes, such as Computer, User, and Server, are named by their CN (Common Name) naming attribute. In fact, CN is the recommended naming attribute for leaf objects. In such cases, the naming attribute itself does not indicate which class the object belongs to, but the value of the naming attribute may suggest the nature of the object. However, some naming attributes are closely tied to specific classes. For example, the C (Country Name) naming attribute is used to name only Country objects in the base schema.

Inheritance of Naming Attributes   Naming attributes for effective classes must follow the inheritance rules. Effective classes can inherit naming attributes only if the naming attributes of the super classes are identical and do not conflict. If they are different and therefore ambiguous, the effective class must define its own naming attributes. Noneffective classes may have ambiguous naming attributes, but often define the naming attributes so subordinate objects can inherit them. For example, the Server class defines naming attributes that are inherited by the AFP Server, NCP Server, CommExec, Messaging Server, and Print Server classes.

Containment Classes

Objects that can contain other objects are called *container objects* or *parent objects*. Container objects are the branches of the NDS tree and provide a structure that is similar to a directory in a file system. Objects that cannot contain other objects are called *noncontainer* or *leaf objects*. Leaf objects represent the actual network resources that perform some function in the NDS tree, such as users, printers, modems, servers, or volumes.

Containment Class Rules   For each object class, a list of containment classes specifies where an object of that class may appear in the hierarchical structure of the NDS tree. An object can be immediately subordinate to only those objects whose classes appear in the containment list of the object's expanded class definition. An expanded class definition includes all the characteristics defined for the class as well as all the characteristics that the class can inherit from super classes.

Effective classes can inherit containment classes from super classes only if the inheritance does not make containment ambiguous. If the inherited containment is ambiguous, the class must define containment. Class-defined containment overrides containment defined for super classes.

Effective classes are those object classes that can be used to create entries in the NDS database. Noneffective classes cannot be used to create entries and are used by the schema so that multiple object classes can inherit a common set of schema characteristics. Noneffective classes can have ambiguous containment.

Containment classes limit the possible location of an object in the Directory tree, thus restricting the order and types of partial names that appear in the object's complete name. Containment helps to ensure that the NDS tree expands in a consistent and logical fashion. For example, an Organization object can be the topmost object of the NDS tree or subordinate to the Tree Root object. A User object can be subordinate to an Organization object but not to a Tree Root object. Before users can be added to an NDS tree, the tree must contain either an Organization object or an Organizational Unit object, which are the containment classes for the User object.

While helping to control the structure of the Directory, containment classes must also be flexible enough to accommodate a variety of organizational situations. An example is the relationship between the Organization and Locality classes. Each class specifies the other as a containment class. This allows an administrator to decide which hierarchical order best represents the company's organization.

Containment Classes in the Base Schema   The table below lists the classes in the base schema that can contain other objects and the object types that they can contain.

	Object Class	Contained Classes
T A B L E 4.1 Container Objects and Their Contained Classes	Tree Root	Country
		Organization
	Country	Locality
		Organization
	Locality	Locality
		Organization
		Organizational Unit
	Organization	Locality
		Organizational Unit
		Leaf Objects
	Organizational Unit	Locality
		Organizational Unit
		Leaf Objects

Tree Root, Organization, and Country can be the topmost object in the tree. Country and Organization can be, but are not required to be, subordinate to Tree Root.

The base schema defines all effective leaf objects as subordinate to either Organizational Unit or Organization. Applications, which extend the schema, can define leaf objects that are subordinate to any container in the tree. They can also define new container objects. Such applications cannot, however, define new container objects for the root of the tree.

Containment of Leaf Objects   The following table lists the leaf objects (effective and noneffective), the object classes that can be their parent container, and the object that defined the containment.

T A B L E 4.2 Leaf Objects and Their Containers	**Object Class**	**Contained By**	**Class Defined For**
	AFP Server	Organization Organizational Unit	
	Alias	Special case—inherits containment from the referenced object	Alias
	Bindery Object	Organization Organizational Unit	Bindery Object
	Bindery Queue	Organization Organizational Unit	Queue
	Comm Exec	Organization Organizational Unit	Server
	Computer	Organization Organizational Unit	Device
	Device	Organization Organizational Unit	Device
	Directory Map	Organization Organizational Unit	Resource
	External Entity	Organization Organizational Unit	External Entity
	Group	Organization Organizational Unit	Group

	Object Class	Contained By	Class Defined For
T A B L E 4.2 *(cont.)* Leaf Objects and Their Containers	List	Organization	List
		Organizational Unit	
	Message Routing Group	Organization	Group
		Organizational Unit	
	Messaging Server	Organization	Server
		Organizational Unit	
	NCP Server	Organization	Server
		Organizational Unit	
	Organizational Person	Organization	Organizational Person
		Organizational Unit	
	Organizational Role	Organization	Organizational Role
		Organizational Unit	
	Partition	Special case	Partition
	Person	None	Top
	Print Server	Organization	Server
		Organizational Unit	
	Printer	Organization	Device
		Organizational Unit	
	Profile	Organization	Profile
		Organizational Unit	

T A B L E 4.2 *(cont.)* Leaf Objects and Their Containers	**Object Class**	**Contained By**	**Class Defined For**
	Queue	Organization	Resource
		Organizational Unit	
	Resource	Organization	Resource
		Organizational Unit	
	Server	Organization	Server
		Organizational Unit	
	Unknown	Special case	Any
	User	Organization	Organizational Person
		Organizational Unit	

Noneffective classes cannot be used to create an object in the NDS tree, but they are often used to define containment classes for other object classes to inherit.

A couple of effective object classes are unique: Alias and Partition. Alias inherits its containment classes from the object that it references. Since all leaf objects have Organization and Organizational Unit as their containment classes, an Alias will usually inherit these containment classes. However, an Alias can reference a container, and when it does, the Alias inherits the container's containment classes.

Partition inherits its containment class from its root container object. Since a partition can be defined for any container object in the tree, a partition can have the containment rules of Tree Root, Country, Organization, Locality, and Organizational Unit in the base schema.

The Person class defines no containment classes and inherits no containment class from its super class, Top. Thus, Person is like Top in that they both do not affect containment classes of any objects in the NDS tree.

Containment Classes and Inheritance   Containment classes create the hierarchy of the NDS tree and determine where an instance of an object can be created in the NDS tree. A special flag, (Nothing), allows the three objects, Tree Root, Country, and Organization, to have no superior object.

Once an instance of an object (or an entry) is created in the NDS tree, the entry inherits rights from its container objects, and the container objects are part of the entry's distinguished name. However, the object classes in the schema do not inherit anything from their containment classes.

Object classes can inherit containment definitions, but such inheritances come from the schema's super class structure.

Super Classes

Super classes create the hierarchy of the schema and determine the characteristics that an object class can inherit from another object class. Inheritance simplifies the rules of the schema because it allows some characteristics to be defined once, while multiple object classes can use and enforce these common characteristics.

The sections below describe the following characteristics of super classes:

- Root schema object

- Super class rules

- Class hierarchy

- Object class inheritance rules

Root Schema Object   The Top object class is the root of the schema. Because all other object classes inherit characteristics from the Top class, the Top class specifies information that pertains to all other classes. For example, the Top class defines the following optional attributes:

- ACL

- Back Link

- Last Referenced Time

- Obituary

- Used By

NDS uses these attributes to maintain information. Since these attributes are defined for Top, all object classes inherit these attributes.

Entries in the NDS tree have them available whenever NDS needs to assign a value to one.

Super Class Rules   Each object class must define an object class as its super class. Super classes cannot be recursive; therefore an object class cannot list itself as a super class. The complete definition of each object class is derived from the characteristics of the object class itself as well as the characteristics of all classes in its super class lineage. Hierarchies of classes develop through class inheritance in this manner. The classes at the top of the hierarchy provide general characteristics, whereas those at the bottom become more and more specialized. The complete set of rules for an object class is called the *expanded class definition*.

The object class from which an entry is created is called the entry's base class. The expanded class definition for an object class includes the base class and the sum of the information specified by all its super classes. For the purpose of searching the NDS tree, an entry is considered a member of all of its super classes. For example, the base class for creating a user is the User class. The User class inherits from the following super classes: Organizational Person, Person, and Top.

Although the schema is stored with the rest of the NDS database, schema data is logically separated from the NDS tree and must be accessed through different functions. Also, the schema's class hierarchy does not necessarily form a simple tree graph because a class can list more than one class as a super class. Listing multiple classes as super classes is called *multiple inheritance*. (None of the objects in the NDS base schema uses multiple inheritance.)

Object Class Inheritance Rules   While a class automatically inherits some characteristics in the schema, a class can select to inherit or block the inheritance of other characteristics. The schema follows the following inheritance rules:

- A class must declare another class as its super class. The class then automatically inherits any super classes of its defined super class. (Top is the only class that has no super class.)

- A class may, but is not required to, define mandatory or optional attributes. The class, however, always inherits all the attributes, both mandatory and optional, of its super classes.

- A class may, but is not required to, define a default ACL template. The class always inherits all the default ACL templates of its super classes. Classes that extend the schema cannot define new default ACL templates.

- A class can inherit containment classes and naming attributes, but if the class defines them, any definitions made in super classes are not applied to the class.

Object Class Attributes   An attribute is a single piece of information that is stored in the database about an object. The attributes assigned to an object class can be mandatory or optional:

- If an attribute is mandatory, a value must be assigned to the attribute before an instance of the object can be created.

- If an attribute is optional, a value does not need to be assigned to create an instance of the object. The only exception is an optional naming attribute. If the optional naming attribute is the only attribute used for naming the object, this optional attribute becomes a mandatory attribute.

Both mandatory and optional attributes are always inherited from super classes. There is no way to block the inheritance. Also, mandatory definitions take precedence over optional designations. For example, a subordinate class can define an attribute as mandatory that is optional in a super class. For that class it is now mandatory. However, if a subordinate class tries to define an attribute as optional that a super class defines as mandatory, the attribute is still mandatory for the subordinate class.

A client cannot associate an attribute with an object unless the attribute is listed among the mandatory or optional attributes of the object's expanded class definition. If a client must associate an attribute with a particular object and the attribute is not specified by the object class, the client must extend the schema by:

- Adding the new attribute to the class or a super class as an attribute

- Defining a new class that inherits from the original class and adds the new attribute as an attribute

If the attribute is added to a nonremovable class, the attribute becomes nonremovable. Attributes are only removable when they are not assigned to any class.

Object Class Flags There are five object class flags that can be "set" (turned On) or "not set" (turned Off). Applications extending the schema can set two: Container and Effective. NDS sets three: Nonremovable, Ambiguous Naming, and Ambiguous Container.

Container Flag

The Container flag indicates whether the object can contain other objects. The flag is turned On for those object classes that are designated as container classes. The flag is turned Off for all leaf object classes.

Effective Flag

The Effective flag indicates whether an object class is effective or noneffective. The Effective flag is turned On for those classes that can be used both to provide definition and to create objects. The Effective flag is turned Off for those classes that provide definition but cannot be used to create objects.

Only effective classes are:

- Used to create entries in the NDS database

- Assigned as base classes to the entries they create in the NDS database

Most of the object classes in the base schema are effective classes. Since effective classes are the active building blocks from which an NDS tree is created, their structure rules must be complete. This means that the naming attributes and containment classes cannot be ambiguous.

For example, if naming attributes or containment classes are not specified for a new effective class, they are inherited from the new class's super classes. If the new effective class inherits from multiple super classes, the naming attribute and containment classes must be identical. If they aren't identical, the structure rules conflict and are ambiguous. In this case, an effective class must define its naming attributes and containment classes.

If the structure rules are incomplete or ambiguous, NDS automatically flags the class as noneffective. The effective or noneffective flag is assigned to a class when it is originally defined. The value cannot be modified after the class is created.

The noneffective classes are not active and thus cannot be used to create objects in an NDS tree. They are typically used as super classes to define class information that is shared by multiple effective classes. The effective classes can then inherit the class information from the noneffective super class rather than repetitively defining it.

The base schema defines the following noneffective classes:

- Device
- Organizational Person
- Partition
- Person
- Resource
- Server

Top is the one special case for the Effective flag. Although Top is flagged as an effective class, no object can be created from the Top class.

Nonremovable Flag

The Nonremovable flag indicates whether the object class can be removed from the schema. The flag is turned On for objects that cannot be removed. The flag is turned Off for object classes that can be removed. All base schema object classes are flagged nonremovable. Object classes added to extend the schema are the only classes that may have the nonremovable flag turned Off.

Ambiguous Naming Flag

The Ambiguous Naming flag indicates whether the object class has clearly defined naming attributes. As a general rule, noneffective classes can be created with ambiguous naming, but effective classes must have nonambiguous naming attributes. Only in special cases can effective classes be created with ambiguous naming. The Alias class object is one of these special cases since it needs to inherit the naming attributes of its reference object class.

For most object classes in the base schema, the Ambiguous Naming flag is turned Off. The only object classes where this flag is turned On are Top, Alias, Person, and Partition.

Ambiguous Container Flag

The Ambiguous Container flag indicates whether the object class has clearly defined containment classes. As a general rule, noneffective classes can be created with ambiguous containment, but effective classes must have non-ambiguous containment. Only in special cases can effective classes be created with ambiguous containment. The Alias class object is one of these special cases since it needs to inherit the containment classes of its reference object class.

For most object classes in the base schema, the Ambiguous Container flag is turned Off. It is turned On for object classes Top, Alias, Person, and Partition.

Default ACL Templates   Every object in the NDS tree has an Access Control List (ACL) attribute. This attribute holds information about which trustees have access to the object itself (entry rights) and which trustees have access to the attributes for the object. This information is stored in sets of information containing:

- The trustee name

- The affected attribute—(Entry Rights), (All Attributes Rights), or a specific attribute

- The privileges

Default ACL templates are defined for specific classes in the base schema and provide a minimum amount of access security for newly created objects. Only base schema objects can have default ACL templates. Developers extending the schema cannot create default ACL templates for new objects.

Because the Top object class defines a default ACL template, all object classes inherit a default ACL template. The ACL defined for Top allows the object that creates another object the right to supervise the created object. This ACL ensures that every object added to an NDS tree has a supervisor.

An object inherits the default ACL templates that are defined for any of the object's super classes. For example, the NCP Server object inherits default ACL templates from Top and Server, and then defines one for itself.

Developers extending the schema cannot create templates that overwrite or add to the templates in the base schema. However, when an object is created in an NDS tree, the creation process can set the object's ACLs to any value, including one that changes a value that comes from a default ACL template.

Construction Rules for Object Classes   The following rules regulate the construction of new object classes. Developers who need to define the new object classes should pay close attention to these rules:

- Object class definitions cannot be recursive. That is to say, an object cannot have itself as a super class.

- Only classes with complete structure rules can be flagged as effective and, thus, used to create objects. This means the super classes, containment, and naming attributes must be complete.

An effective class can be constructed in three ways:

- The class defines its own structure rules.

- The class inherits structure rules from its super classes.

- The class defines part of the structure rules (such as naming) and inherits the other part of the structure rules (such as containment) from a super class.

Structure rules that might be inherited from its super classes are ignored for a class that defines its own structure rules. If structure rules of an effective class are inherited, they must be nonambiguous.

Attribute Type Definitions   All attributes found in an NDS tree consist of an attribute type and an attribute value, which can be multivalued. The attribute type identifies the nature of information the attribute stores, and the value is the stored information.

The attribute type definition can do any of the following:

- Identify the attribute syntax used for the value.

- Specify the constraints that are imposed on the syntax.

These constraints are also known as attribute flags. Attributes are assigned to objects according to the object's class definition.

An example of an attribute type is CN (Common Name) which uses the "Case Ignore String" syntax. CN (Common Name) constrains this syntax to a range from 1 to 64 Unicode characters. This attribute is used by many object classes, including Server, Person, Group, and Bindery Object.

Attribute types can be added to the NDS schema. However, once an attribute type has been created, it can't be modified.

Attribute types can be removed from the NDS schema, but only if the attribute is not part of the base schema and only if the attribute type isn't assigned to a class. All attribute types in the base schema are always flagged nonremovable.

Attribute Syntaxes   The attribute syntax controls the type of information that can be stored in the value (for example, integer, string, or stream data). The syntax must be selected from the set of predefined attribute syntaxes. The syntax also controls the type of compare operations that can be performed on the value.

Attribute Constraints The attribute constraints restrict the information that can be stored in the data type and constrain the operations of NDS and NDS clients. The constraints specify whether the attribute:

- Allows only a single value or multiple values

- Has a range or size limit to the value

- Is synchronized immediately, at the next scheduled interval, or never

- Is hidden or viewable

- Is writable or read-only

The table below lists all of the attribute constraints.

T A B L E 4.3 Attribute Constraints	**Constraint**	**Description**
	DS_SINGLE_VALUED_ATTR	Indicates that the attribute has a single value with no order implied.
	DS_SIZED_ATTR	Indicates that the attribute has an upper and lower boundary. This can be the length for strings or the value for integers. The first number indicates the lower boundary and the second, the upper boundary.
	DS_NONREMOVABLE_ATTR	Prevents the attribute from being removed from an object class definition. The client cannot set or modify this constraint flag and thus cannot modify the attribute. All base-schema attribute-type definitions have the nonremovable flag set.
	DS_READ_ONLY_ATTR	Prevents clients from modifying the attribute. The NDS server creates and maintains the attribute.
	DS_HIDDEN_ATTR	Marks the attribute as usable only by the NDS server. The client cannot set or modify this flag and thus cannot see or modify the attribute.

T A B L E 4.3 *(cont.)* Attribute Constraints	**Constraint**	**Description**
	DS_STRING_ATTR	Labels the attribute as a string type. You can use attributes of this type as naming attributes.
	DS_OPERATIONAL	Indicates that NDS uses the attribute internally and requires the attribute to function correctly.
	DS_PUBLIC_READ	Indicates that anyone can read the attribute without read privileges being assigned. You cannot use inheritance masks to prevent an object from reading attributes with this constraint.
	DS_PER_REPLICA	Marks the attribute so that the information in the attribute is not synchronized with other replicas. The client cannot set or modify this constraint flag and thus cannot modify the attribute.
	DS_SCHEDULE_SYNC_NEVER	Allows the attribute's value to change without such a change triggering synchronization. The attribute can wait to propagate the change until the next regularly scheduled synchronization cycle or some other event triggers synchronization.
	DS_WRITE_MANAGED	Forces users to have managed rights on the object that contains this Attribute before they can change the attribute's value.

T A B L E 4.3 *(cont.)*	Constraint	Description
Attribute Constraints	DS_SERVER_READ	Indicates that Server class objects can read the attribute even though the privilege to read has not been inherited or explicitly granted. You cannot use inheritance masks to restrict servers from reading attributes with this constraint.
	DS_SYNC_IMMEDIATE	Forces immediate synchronization with other replicas when the value of the attribute changes. Attributes without this constraint are synchronized at the next synchronization interval. In NetWare 5 (NDS release 599 or later) all attributes have this constraint except Back Link, Bindery Property, Bindery Object Restriction, Bindery Restriction Level, Bindery Type, Last Login Time, Last Referenced Time, Login Time, Purge Vector, Reference, Synchronize Up To, Timezone, Transitive Vector, Unknown, and Unknown Base Class.

Attribute Syntax Definitions   An attribute syntax defines a standard data type that an attribute uses to store its values in the NDS tree. The syntax definitions are static definitions represented in basic C-code format. For example, the schema includes the following attribute syntaxes:

SYN_CI_STRING   The Case Ignore String syntax is used by attributes whose values are strings and the case (upper or lower) is not significant.

SYN_INTEGER   The Integer syntax is used by attributes whose values are signed integers.

An attribute syntax consists of a single data type for which syntax matching rules and qualifiers have been specified. Matching rules indicate the characteristics that are significant when comparing two values of the same syntax. There are three primary matching rules:

Equality To match for equality, two values must be identical, use the same attribute syntax, and conform to the data type of the attribute syntax. Most syntaxes specify a match for equality. NDS checks that the values being matched conform to the data type of the syntax. NDS will not attempt to match two values if the syntax does not specify a match for equality.

Ordering To match for ordering, a syntax must be open to comparisons of "less than," "equal to," and "greater than." For example, 50 is less than 100, and N is greater than B.

Substrings To match substrings, a syntax must be open to search and comparison patterns that include the asterisk (*) wildcard. For example in a syntax using substring matching, "n*v*l" would match "naval," "navel," and "novel."

An approximate comparison rule can be used in searches and comparisons on syntaxes with lists of strings and syntaxes with distinguished names:

Strings The approximate rule determines whether a string is present in a syntax with a string list.

Distinguished Names The approximate rule determines whether a distinguished name matches the distinguished name in a corresponding field while ignoring the other fields in the syntax. To increase performance, NDS replaces distinguished names with IDs in the comparison and search operations.

A syntax can specify one or more of these matching rules. For example, the Case Ignore String syntax specifies matching rules of equality and substrings.

A syntax can also specify qualifiers for comparison that ignore characters such as dashes, leading spaces, trailing spaces, and multiple consecutive internal spaces. All string syntaxes use comparison operations that ignore extra spaces. Other qualifiers allow only digits or only printable characters.

Attribute type definitions are built on attribute syntaxes. Developers extending the schema can create new attribute types using these syntaxes, but they cannot create any new syntax definitions.

Interaction with File Systems

Up through NetWare 5, files and file-system directories are not present as objects within the NDS directory, although servers and volumes are. At least one product, the Internet Caching Server (sold only by computer manufacturers as part of a hardware device) makes use of a new file system called the Unified File Object Directory (UFOD), originally developed for the Wolf Mountain clustering initiative, which was abandoned in 1998. UFOD may reappear in an upcoming version of NetWare.

Servers and Server Objects

Server is a generic term for a software application that responds to requests from clients—which could be other applications, users, or computers. In NetWare terminology, *server* is used as a synonym for file server and—more specifically—a NetWare Core Protocol (NCP) file server. Other types of servers—such as message servers, fax servers, print servers, Apple Filing Protocol (AFP) servers, etc.—are almost always referred to by qualifying the term *server*. That is the meaning used in this book; references to *servers* mean NCP File Servers.

Servers are important to NDS for a number of reasons. First, of course, is that the NDS database is stored on servers as ordinary database files. Second, one part of NDS stored on every server is the Bindery partition in which dynamic objects (server routing information, for example) needed for Bindery emulation is stored. Users and other objects using non-NDS enabled client tools need to have bindery emulation so that they can access the server as if it were a NetWare 2.*x* or 3.*x* environment yet still be part of your directory tree. Third, because your directory tree needs to reflect the location of each server for such things as bindery context, the server must exist within a container in the tree.

Note that the "server object" is a representation of the physical server. It's quite possible for the object to have a different name than the actual server—avoid this at all costs, it will only lead to confusion later on.

WARNING   You should exercise care in placing the server object within the tree. It should, ideally, reside in the same container as the users who will access the server.

When NDS is first installed, the server it is installed to is automatically placed within the tree as a server object, and the NDS administrator's password is automatically given to the user "Supervisor" for that server, who has all rights to its file system.

Although the user "Supervisor" is given the same password as the user "Admin," there is no equivalence or synchronization between the two user objects. The Supervisor password does not change when Admin's does, but must be manually changed if you wish to keep them synchronized.

Volumes and Volume Objects

Volume objects (called SERVER_VOLNAME), like server objects, are part of the tree for location information. That means the User object's Home Directory property references the Volume object as well as the path to the directory. As with the Server object, assigning rights to the Volume object does not grant any particular right to the file and directory structure of the volume—that must be done through the file system utilities.

Also as is possible with the Server object, it is possible to name the Volume object differently from the physical volume, something you would be wise to avoid doing.

Directories and Files

The server's files and directories do not exist as objects within the tree at this time (see the reference to UFOD at the beginning of this section, though). Rights and privileges within the file system are set and maintained on each server by the user known as Supervisor or another user security equivalent to Supervisor (among whom are the user Admin). In smaller networks, the tree administrator (ADMIN) and the file system administrator (SUPERVISOR) will frequently be the same person, but you will do well to remember that their roles within the network are quite different.

Directory Map Object

While files and directories don't exist as objects within the tree, there is an object that appears to reference a directory in the file system: the Directory Map Object.

This object is used by the NetWare Application Launcher (NAL—part of the ZENWORKS product) but can be used without it. It holds the path (*server_name/volume_name:directory\ subdirectory*) used to access an application.

Traditionally, you would map the application's path to a drive letter in a login script. If the path to the application changed, you'd need to change all of the login scripts. Now, you can map the drive letter to the Directory Map object for the application. Should the path change, you just change an attribute of the Directory Map object—no changes to login scripts are necessary!

File System Security

NDS plays a very limited role in providing for file system security, through granting of ownership and granting of access to Server and Volume objects. The actual security information for files and directories is stored within the Directory Entry Table (DET) on the server on which the file or directory is physically present. The advent of UFOD may—and most likely will—change this.

There is nothing in the nature of directories, files, or their security that makes it difficult or impossible to include them as objects within the directory. Rather, it was the need for backward compatibility with NetWare 3 and non-NDS-aware clients, with their server-centric view of the network, that led to the separation of the file system from the directory.

Summary

This chapter has introduced the basic concepts of NDS and the terminology used for those concepts. Objects and object classes (the abstraction of an object) are the basic building blocks. The NDS schema is used to describe the object classes. NDS comes with a base schema, defining those objects and classes found in all instances, but the schema can be extended to encompass other objects and classes. It is extremely important that all NDS replicas within a network understand the same schema extensions.

This chapter has also presented the terminology and definitions used to describe NDS security. Finally, we've looked at the place of the file system within NDS.

C H A P T E R

5

Replication and
Partitioning

Replication refers to the ability to make identical copies of data available on separate platforms. For example, when I wrote this chapter of the book, a copy was sent to my editor. The data in the chapter was replicated on both my computer and the editor's computer. Both copies were identical. Searching on a word or sentence within the chapter could be done on either copy. Changes could be made to either copy. If the editor made changes, they were sent to me; if I made changes, they were sent to the editor. In this way, each replica is kept synchronized with the other.

Partitioning refers to the ability to separate different parts of the data within the database into subsets of the entire database. The subsets are usually internally related in some way. In the above example, I might send the text of the chapter to a copy editor and the graphics from the chapter to an art editor. The text partition and the art partition together constitute the chapter.

Novell's NDS stands out among all competing directory services because of the rich environment it provides for replication and partitioning. In this chapter, we'll look at both concepts, explain why a directory system needs them, and delve into the Novell implementation of them. First, though, let's examine why having a single copy of the directory—one that holds all objects—can be a problem.

A Centralized Directory: Good or Bad?

NetWare 2.*x* and 3.*x* both worked on a centralized directory called the *bindery*. To access information on the network, it was necessary to log in to the server whose bindery held your user information. If that server were down—or otherwise unavailable—you couldn't log in to the network.

Network operating systems (NOS) based on Microsoft's LAN Manager (such as IBM's LAN Server and Warp Server, Digital's PathWorks, and Microsoft's own NT Server), allow the Domain database to be replicated, but do not allow you to administer the database unless you are logged into the Primary Domain Controller. If it's unavailable, you can still log in to the network, but you can't make changes to the database.

Most Unix systems are similar to NetWare 2.*x* and 3.*x*—the directory for a host is kept on that host, and nowhere else.

For all of these scenarios, if the server, host, or network you wish to access is on the other side of a slow WAN link, it can take many minutes for you to authenticate and gain access.

So, with a centralized directory system, all users (including administrators) have the following problems:

- A specific server, host, or domain controller must be up and accessible in order to log in.

- If the server, host, or domain controller is on the other side of a WAN link, authentication may be very slow.

Additionally, administrators have these problems:

- If the server, host, or primary domain controller is down or unavailable, no administrative changes can be made.

- For NetWare 2.*x* and 3.*x* and for Unix, if the server or host's file system is trashed, the entire directory may be unrecoverable.

Breaking Down Partitioning

It's important to remember that NDS is a *distributed* database. Partitioning is simply the process of breaking up your NDS tree into smaller portions that can then be distributed throughout your network. The main purpose of doing this is to provide scalability—as your network grows so does the size of your directory tree. Since there should always be more than one copy of your tree as the tree grows it takes longer and longer to synchronize the replicas.

Synchronization takes place at the partition level. The more partitions there are of a given tree, the faster the synchronization of each can occur.

Balance this, though, with the fact that the time it takes to synchronize is also dependent on the number of replicas. See Chapter 8, "Directory Design," for tips on balancing the number of partitions and the number of replicas.

Also, logging in to the network will generally be faster for users if the partition that holds their context is stored on a server that is physically (or logically) close to them.

Partitions are named for the topmost container within the partition. Thus, when NDS is first installed there is only one partition, called *Root*.

An object must be part of one—and only one—partition. So, partitions cannot overlap, but every tree is created with at least one partition: the Root partition.

An Example of Partitioning

Figure 5.1 shows the initial design of a directory tree for the Virtual Quill company. Both Organizational Units (OU)—USA and Europe—are contained in the same partition: the Root partition. Even though Virtual Quill is a very small company (3 users, 1 server) the network administrator—Andy S. Tree—has begun to think about scaling the directory as the company grows.

Note that even though the company occupies only one room, Andy has planned for future expansion by creating two containers named for geographic locations (USA and Europe). By using location (or some other logical division) as the determining factor for placement of OUs, he has laid the foundation for efficient partitioning of the tree. Later in the tree design process, partitioning around geographic boundaries will have a positive influence on the performance of day-to-day activities, such as user logins. This design also helps the tree's administrators by increasing the speed and efficiency of object changes and major partition operations.

Figure 5.2 shows the changes Andy made when Virtual Quill grew to two rooms and three servers. New OU containers have been created in line with the company's future expansion plans and Andy has partitioned off the branch beginning at OU=USA so that the tree now has two partitions: Root and USA. He could just as easily have made OU=Europe the partition point, but because Virtual Quill is located in London, Andy kept the container in which his user object was contained (OU=UK) in the Root partition for his own convenience.

F I G U R E 5.1

When first installed, NDS creates a single partition for all containers.

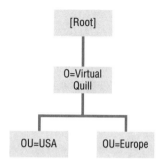

F I G U R E 5.2

Virtual Quill's tree is divided into two partitions.

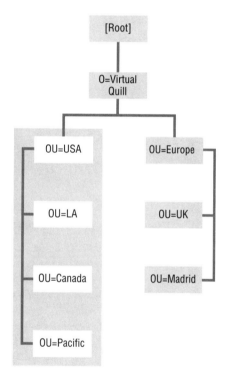

As Virtual Quill continues to grow, remote offices are established in Los Angeles and Sydney, Australia. Andy creates new OUs for these offices and their subdivisions and then further partitions his directory tree. Root and USA partitions remain, but he's partitioned OU=UK from Root and created the new Pacific partition. Figure 5.3 shows the results. Even though the users in the Pacific partition are physically located in the Los Angeles office, their activities are separate from those of the users in the USA partition, so there are few instances of users in one partition needing resources in the other. If they should need those resources, Andy could easily create a Group object in one partition that included users from the other or simply grant access to objects in one partition—a printer, for example—by users in the other.

FIGURE 5.3

Virtual Quill's tree is further partitioned to meet its geographic objectives.

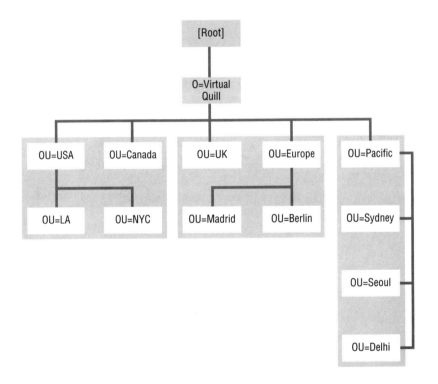

Virtual Quill keeps on growing, as shown in Figure 5.4. But company executives have decided that Canadian operations will no longer be handled from the L.A. office. Instead, the Canadian workers will report to the U.K. headquarters. Andy creates a new partition (Europe) out of the UK partition and then moves OU=Canada from the USA partition to the UK partition. Even though there are now offices (and servers) in London, Madrid, Los Angeles, New York, Sydney, and Seoul, Andy does the partitioning and moving from his desk in London using NetWare Administrator's NDS

Manager option (see below) It takes only a few minutes, and all of the changes are quickly synchronized on all of the servers within the Virtual Quill network.

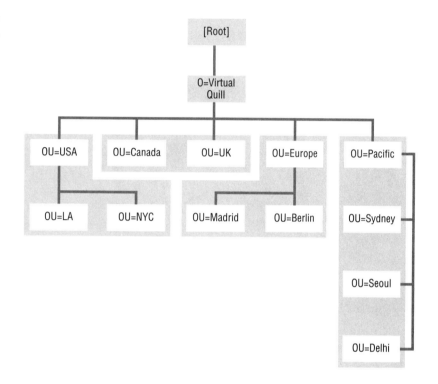

More company growth leads to a beefing up of the New York, Canada, Madrid, and Seoul offices. Andy repartitions his directory tree to reflect the actual needs of the company by creating the Canada, Madrid, NYC, and Seoul partitions. Even though Asian sales are handled by personnel in the Los Angeles office, Andy creates a separate partition for Seoul (and Delhi, which is contained in Seoul) in anticipation of future expansion. Andy can easily give access to objects within the USA partition to users within the Seoul partition, as they need it. Figure 5.5 shows the Virtual Quill directory tree after these operations have been performed.

More growth brings further partitioning as Andy S. Tree seeks to keep his network and directory optimized.

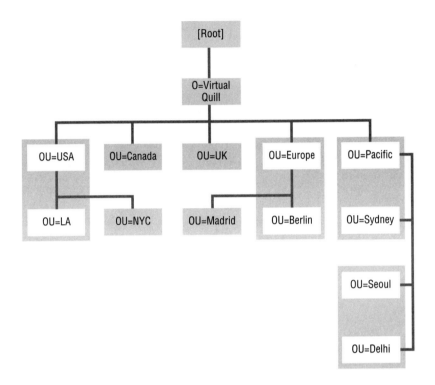

Child Partitions and Subordinate References

The directory in the example above has been partitioned and distributed among a group of servers so that users can be authenticated from a server physically or logically close to them. Despite this, we said that the administrator, Andy S. Tree, could handle all maintenance quickly and easily from his desktop.

Every partition except the Root partition is said to be a *child partition* and to have as its parent that partition directly above it going toward Root. In Figure 5.5, the partitions USA, Canada, UK, Europe, and Pacific are all child partitions of Root. NYC is a child of USA, Madrid is a child of Europe, and Seoul is a child of Pacific. You would also refer to USA as the *parent partition* of NYC, Europe as the parent of Madrid, and Pacific as the parent of Seoul. Carrying the analogy further, children of the same parent are referred to as *siblings*. Those are the only genealogical references, though—there are no grandparents, cousins, or other types of relatives.

While a partition can have only one *parent,* it can have many children. It's wise, though, to limit the number of children—especially those needing subordinate references—to speed up synchronization services. See Chapter 8 for more information on the proper design of your tree.

If a parent partition is stored on a server that does not have copies of its child partitions, then a special entity called a subordinate reference is created. This is simply a reference to the topmost container object of the child partition, including the locations of the child's replicas. In this way, the administrator—or any user with the proper rights—can start at the Root and "walk the tree" to any point, moving from server to server following each branch through the various partitions. This is all done transparently by whatever application is being used. To the user, it appears that the entire tree is stored locally. Contrast this to NetWare 3's bindery system, or Windows NT's domain system, where the user (or administrator) must keep logging in to different servers, or logging in to different domains, in order to see every object in the network.

What Makes Replication Tick

We mentioned above that LAN Manager-based networks allow you to keep more than one copy of your directory database available by establishing Primary Domain Controllers and Backup Domain Controllers. We refer to this as a *replicated database*. NDS is also replicated, in addition to being distributed (see *Breaking down Partitioning*, earlier), an attribute that LAN Manager's domains do not share.

The main goals of replication are fault tolerance and availability. Fault tolerance is maintained by distributing identical information to multiple servers so that if the information on one or more servers becomes unavailable, the network can continue operating since the information is available from other servers. This distribution of identical network information to multiple servers introduces the need to keep the information synchronized; NDS does this automatically by keeping all replicas loosely consistent.

Increased availability is achieved by allowing for the distribution of identical network information to different areas of the network.

Replication is implemented at the *partition* level. Some partitions may have fewer or more replicas than others, as your needs warrant.

Types of Replicas

There are three types of replicas: Master, Read/Write, and Read-Only. You will see Subordinate References referred to as Subordinate Reference Replicas, but because only the attributes of the base container of the child partition are stored there, this is not a true replica. The three types of replicas allow the following operations:

Master   Clients can create, modify, and delete entries, and they can perform operations that deal with partitions.

Read/Write   Clients can create, modify, and delete entries.

Read-Only   Clients cannot make changes. They can only read information.

An object must be part of one—and only one—partition. So, partitions cannot overlap, but every tree is created with at least one partition: the In practice, Read-Only replicas, intended as a security measure, are rarely used. Instead, assigning proper trustee rights and Inherited Rights Filters protects your tree, while allowing maintenance to be performed on any available replica.

Every partition is required to have one and only one Master replica. This is created automatically either at installation (for the Root partition) or at the time a partition is created. NDS does not require more than the Master Replica, nor does it limit the number of Read/Write or Read-Only replicas you can create. It is highly recommended, though, that there be at least three replicas (one Master, two Read/Write) of every partition to ensure fault tolerance. By the same token, it is recommended that there be no more than 15 replicas to minimize bandwidth usage during synchronization. Should it become necessary to change a Read/Write replica to a Master (in a case where the server holding the Master replica is being removed), this will automatically change the old Master replica's type to Read/Write.

An object must be part of one—and only one—partition. So, partitions cannot overlap, but every tree is created with at least one partition: the Any server that will offer bindery services must hold either the Master or a Read/Write replica of the partition in which the server is setting its bindery context.

The administrator specifies the servers on which each replica is stored. There is no limit to the number of replicas that a single server can hold, but it should be obvious that only one replica of a particular partition can be stored on a single server.

NDS maintains a list of all of the servers holding replicas of a particular partition, called the *replica ring* of that partition.

Updating through Synchronization

NDS is described as *loosely consistent*. This means that all the replicas are not instantaneously updated whenever a change is made. Instead, each change is marked with a date and time stamp. Periodically, the changed information is distributed to other replicas in the ring and applied to their copies of the database. The date and time stamp assures that changes are applied in the same order on all replicas of the partition.

It is not necessary for all replicas to be present during synchronization. Should one server be down, the synchronization information would continue to be sent to it until it comes back up.

This can create a large amount of network traffic, however. So, if you are planning to take a server down for any length of time (to replace hardware, because of an anticipated power outage, etc.) you should first remove any replicas stored on it and then replace them after the server is brought back up. If it contains any Master replicas, you should "promote" a Read/Write replica to be Master so that one is always present.

The Magic of Automatically Created Replicas

Whenever you install a new NetWare Operating System and at the same time create a container in which you place the server, a new partition is created starting with that container, and its Master replica is placed on that server.

When you install a new NetWare Operating System and place the server within an already existing container, a Read/Write replica of that container's partition is placed on the server. However, this applies only for the first three servers created within that container. Once three replicas of that partition exist, no more are automatically created.

The Art of Replica Placement

Deciding how many replicas to create and where to place them is an art rather than a science. This will be covered in more detail in Chapter 8, "Directory Design." The following guidelines should be taken into consideration:

- More replicas mean greater fault tolerance. At least three replicas of every partition should exist to ensure continuous accessibility of the database.

- More replicas mean greater use of bandwidth for synchronization. There shouldn't be any reason to create more than 15 replicas (and usually far fewer) of any partition.

- The more replicas a particular server holds, the greater its use of bandwidth during synchronization. Minimize the number of replicas to maximize a server's throughput.

- Partitions containing a user's context should be replicated to a server either physically or logically close to the user in order to minimize the amount of time needed for authentication.

- Subordinate references participate in the synchronization process. Minimize the number of subordinate references to maximize throughput. Remember that you only indirectly affect the placement of subordinate references through your placement of parent and child partitions.

- Bindery services require that each server have at least a Read/Write replica of the partition where the server is setting its bindery context. Minimize bindery services to minimize the number of replicas needed.

As an example of replica placement, Table 5.1 shows how Virtual Quill's administrator, Andy S. Tree, placed his replicas for the partitions shown earlier in Figure 5.5, given a network connectivity layout shown in Figure 5.6. For the sake of simplicity, consider that each OU contains one server named after the OU with serv appended (OU=USA contains server USA_serv, and so on).

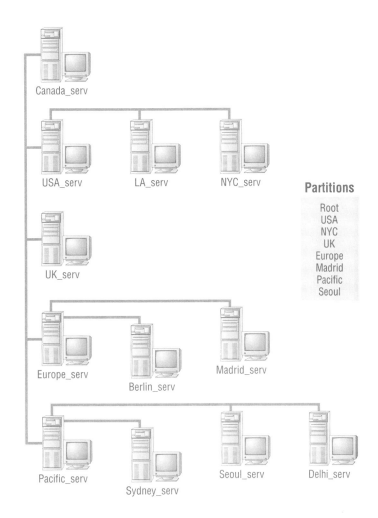

FIGURE 5.6

A network diagram
for the Virtual Quill
network

Note that Andy has created at least three replicas of each partition. A partition's replicas are placed on each server within the partition and at least one is placed outside the partition. Further note that partition synchronization should only be taking place among servers directly connected to each other. For example, Sydney_serv holds only one replica, a Read/Write for the Pacific partition; and it synchronizes only with Pacific_serv, the only other server it directly connects to. Remember that Subordinate References are created automatically whenever a server holds a replica of a parent partition but not its child partition.

T A B L E 5.1 Distribution of Replicas in the Virtual Quill Network	Server	Partition	Type
	UK_serv	Root	Master
		UK	Master
		Europe	Read/Write
		Canada	Read/Write
	Canada_serv	Canada	Master
		Root	Read/Write
		UK	Read/Write
		USA	Read/Write
	USA_serv	USA	Master
		NYC	Read/Write
		Canada	Read/Write
	LA_serv	USA	Read/Write
		NYC	Read/Write
	NYC_serv	NYC	Master
		USA	Read/Write
	Europe_serv	Europe	Master
		Root	Read/Write
		UK	Read/Write
		Madrid	Read/Write
		Pacific	Read/Write
	Berlin_serv	Europe	Read/Write
		Madrid	Read/Write
	Madrid_serv	Madrid	Master
		Europe	Read/Write
	Pacific_serv	Pacific	Master
		Europe	Read/Write
		Seoul	Read/Write
	Sydney_serv	Pacific	Read/Write
	Seoul_serv	Seoul	Master
		Pacific	Read/Write
	Delhi_serv	Seoul	Read/Write

Given the number of partitions and the number of servers participating, it would be difficult to reduce the number of Subordinate References, but Andy should keep trying. The diagrams and tables do not take into consideration the possibility that bindery Services might create a need for other replicas. Andy, after all, is a forward-looking administrator and has included nothing on his network that requires bindery emulation.

For more information on planning your partitions and replicas see Chapter 8, "Directory Design." Creating, migrating, and maintaining partitions and replicas is covered in detail in Chapters 10 and 11.

Table 5.2 lists the Subordinate References held by each server in the Virtual Quill network.

TABLE 5.2	Server	Subordinate Reference
Subordinate Reference Distribution in the Virtual Quill Network	UK_serv	USA Pacific Madrid
	Canada_serv	Europe Pacific
	Europe_serv	USA Canada Seoul
	Pacific_serv	Madrid
	Sydney_serv	Seoul

Manipulating Partitions and Replicas

NDS Manager is the tool used to create, maintain, and remove partitions and replicas in NetWare 4.11 and above (earlier versions used Partition Manager, a part of NWADMIN). Container objects that are the starting point of a partition are shown in blue, while servers storing replicas are shown in red. The following sections present a brief overview of partition and replica operations. More information about the uses of NDS Manager can be found in Chapter 11, "NDS Maintenance."

Adding a Partition

To add a partition, highlight the container object that will be the starting point for the new partition and then click the Create as New Partition button in the NDS Manager. Remember that all containers that cascade from the highlighted one will be part of the new partition.

Removing Partitions

Partitions cannot be deleted. They must be merged into the partition sitting directly above them in the tree. To remove a partition, highlight it and then click the Merge Partition button in the NDS Manager. The partition will become a part of its Parent partition. Note that this can be a time-consuming process to carry out.

Moving a Container Object

In order to move a container object to a different part of the directory tree, the object must satisfy two conditions: It must be the starting point of a partition, and it must not have any child partitions. If there is a child partition, first merge it with the parent. If the container you wish to move is not the starting point of a partition, use the Create a New Partition button in the NDS Manager to make it the starting point.

Once these conditions are satisfied, highlight the container, and then click the Move Partition button. You'll be asked to select a new place on the tree for the partition, and you'll be able to browse to select one. Select a container and confirm your choice. The partition will be moved and become a child partition of the new container's partition.

You should also check the box labeled Create Alias in Place of Moved Container. This will automatically redirect users whose context is set to the former location of the container to its new location until you can change their configuration files. This happens without the user being aware of it.

Adding a Replica

In NDS Manager, highlight the partition you wish to replicate, and then click the Replicas button. The list of existing replicas, their types, and the servers holding them is displayed. Click the Add Replica button, and select the Read/Write or Read-Only type, then browse the server list, select the one to hold this replica, and click OK.

Changing a Replica Type

Since we suggested not creating Read-Only replicas and since you cannot directly change the type of a Master replica, the only choice is to change a Read/Write replica to a Master. This will automatically change the former Master to a Read/Write replica. To do this, highlight the replica in the Partition Replicas dialog box, and click the Change Type button. Choose Master, and then click OK.

Removing a Replica

A Master replica cannot be removed. Should you wish to remove one, first change a Read/Write replica to be Master. (This changes the old Master to Read/Write automatically, and you'll be able to delete it.)

Highlight the replica you wish to remove, and then click the Delete Replica button.

Rebuilding Replicas

If directory information becomes corrupted or if you have made extensive changes to your tree and wish them to synchronize as quickly as possible, you can use NDS Manager to rebuild the replicas in the ring.

If it's a Read/Write replica that needs to be rebuilt, highlight it, and then click Receive Updates. This will cause the Master replica to send its information to the Read/Write replica.

If it's a Read/Write replica that has the most current information and you wish it to be sent to all other replicas in the ring, highlight it, and click the Send Updates button. All other replicas will then be synchronized to the highlighted one.

WARNING Note that this procedure for rebuilding a replica doesn't work if the DS database is corrupt on the receiving server—the database must be open and available to receive updates. More drastic measures need to be taken if the database is corrupted and won't open or properly receive updates because of time-stamp problems.

Summary

This chapter has explored the NDS concepts of partitioning and replication and has introduced the topic of the synchronization of replicas. We've learned that the implementation of partitions and replicas could improve throughput on the network as well as ensure the reliability and accessibility of the Directory Service.

The chapter has introduced the different types of replicas (Master, Read/ Write, Read-Only, and subordinate reference) and has described the circumstances that give you clues about which to use. It has also looked at the basic rules for partitioning of NDS and the placement of the various replicas.

Finally, we have briefly explored the tool (NDS Manager) used to create, maintain, and remove partitions and replicas within NDS.

CHAPTER

6

Time Synchronization

ime is one of the most important concepts for network administrators (because there's never enough of it). It is equally important to NDS. The directory system places a timestamp on every change made to NDS to ensure that all replicas of the database are changed in the exact same order. It's an excellent method, but it will only work if all of the servers involved in the replication agree on the time. Fortunately, NetWare provides methods to allow the synchronization of time between and among servers. Later in this chapter, we will look at time servers, time groups, and the actual methods used by NetWare to synchronize time, but first we explore the concepts of absolute time and relative time.

Absolute Time versus Relative Time

Absolute time is the actual, correct, to-the-second time according to a mutually recognized time source such as the United States Naval Observatory (USNO). The USNO is charged with the responsibility of determining the precise time and managing time dissemination (that is the distribution of information about the precise time).

A visit to the USNO's Web site will provide you with more information about time and its measurement than you'd ever want—unless you've got too much time on your hands! Point your browser to http://tycho.usno.navy.mil/ to see it all.

Relative time can be defined as the time differential between two time sources. If my watch says its 2:15 P.M. and yours says that its 2:17 P.M., then your time relative to me is +0:02 (plus two minutes), while my time relative to you is –0:02.

An Exercise in Relative Time

In a typical Grade B war movie, you can be sure that at some point a group of the "good guys" will be readying an assault on the "bad guys." At this point in the plot, the leader of the group will tell everyone to "synchronize your watches," so that they can all go busting through the doors on all sides of the building at precisely the same moment. What he's really telling them to do is to adjust their relative time until it is 0:00.

Because relative time is the difference between two—and only two—time sources, the correct way to do this would be for each member of the group to compare their time with that of every other member, determine the relative time, and then adjust their watch by exactly 1/2 the relative time multiplied by –1. If Private Adams claims the time is 2:15 P.M. and Private Bates claims it is 2:17 P.M., then Private Adams' relative time is –0:02, and he would adjust his watch +0:01. Meanwhile, Private Bates would determine that her relative time is +0:02 and adjust her watch –0:01. Both should then go on to compare their time with the other members of the group, adjusting as necessary. Table 6.1 shows each step in this process and its results. Note that 27 comparisons are necessary for these six people to bring their relative time to 0:00!

Starting with six different times on their watches, the group (Privates Adams, Bates, Case, Dawson, Ennis, and Ford) compares by twos and adjusts –1/2 the relative time. The time shown in each column in Table 6.1 is the result of the comparison and adjustment. Note that only whole number adjustments are made: any fractional part is discarded.

Of course, in practice the sergeant simply says, "Synchronize your watches on my mark. 2:15. Mark!" and everyone else adjusts to his time. It doesn't matter what the actual, precise time is as long as everyone's relative time is 0:00. Private A knows that when he breaks through a door at what his watch claims is 2:25, everyone else will also be breaking through a door because their times agree.

T A B L E 6.1: An Exercise in Relative Time

	A	B	C	D	E	F
Time at Start	2:00	2:02	2:04	2:06	2:08	2:10
Compare Adams to Bates	2:01	2:01				
Compare Adams to Case	2:02		2:03			
Compare Adams to Dawson	2:04			2:04		
Compare Adams to Ennis	2:06				2:06	
Compare Adams to Ford	2:08					2:08
Compare Bates to Case		2:02	2:02			
Compare Bates to Dawson		2:03		2:03		
Compare Bates to Ennis		2:04			2:05	
Compare Bates to Ford		2:06				2:06
Compare Case to Dawson			2:02	2:03		
Compare Case to Ennis			2:03		2:04	
Compare Case to Ford			2:04			2:05
Compare Dawson to Ennis				2:03	2:04	
Compare Dawson to Ford				2:04		2:04
Compare Ennis to Ford					2:04	2:04
Compare Adams to Bates	2:07	2:07				
Compare Adams to Case	2:06		2:05			
Compare Adams to Dawson	2:05			2:05		
Compare Adams to Ennis	2:05				2:04	

T A B L E 6.1:   An Exercise in Relative Time *(cont.)*

	A	B	C	D	E	F
Compare Adams to Ford	2:05					2:04
Compare Bates to Case		2:06	2:06			
Compare Bates to Dawson		2:06		2:05		
Compare Bates to Ennis		2:05			2:05	
Compare Bates to Ford		2:05				2:04
Compare Case to Dawson			2:06	2:05		
Compare Case to Ennis			2:06		2:05	
Compare Case to Ford			2:05			2:05
Time at Finish	2:05	2:05	2:05	2:05	2:05	2:05

An Exercise in Absolute Time

Now let's suppose that our group consists of stockbrokers in New York, Chicago, Los Angeles, Tokyo, Cairo, and London. They'd like to simultaneously issue an order to sell stock. They could, as we described above, call each other and—through a series of calls—adjust their relative time to 0:00. Alternatively, they could all adjust their time to agree with that of one of their number. This wouldn't guarantee that their time was accurate, however. Since there is only a 15-minute "window" when all of their stock exchanges are open, it's very important that their time be not only 0:00 relative to that of each other but also as close to 0:00 relative to the stock exchange as possible. But it's hardly likely that the stock exchanges will adjust their clocks in order to synchronize with this group.

In addition, each city is in a different time zone. If New York's time is 2:15 P.M. and Chicago's time is 1:17 P.M., then their relative time is ±0:02, not 0:58, since they both must adjust for the one-hour time zone difference between the two cities.

Fortunately they each have a national time source (such as USNO) available to them, and these national time sources are constantly comparing with each other so that their relative time is 0:00. The time sources also know the adjustments that have to be made because of time zone differences. The comparisons are made in a system called UTC (Universal Time Coordinated). This is still sometimes called *Greenwich Mean Time* or *Zulu Time*. In all cases, it refers to the time at the "prime meridian" (longitude 0'00"), which passes through Greenwich, England. All other time zones can be calculated as plus or minus 1–12 hours from UTC.

Each time zone covers approximately 15' of longitude. Since there are 360' in the circumference of the earth, there are 24 time zones. Those west of Greenwich are plus, while those east of Greenwich are minus up to the 180' mark—also known as the International Date Line.

By agreeing beforehand that the transaction will be initiated at, say, 13:00 UTC (UTC time is kept in a 24-hour system; the hours from 1:00 P.M. to midnight are shown as 13:00 to 24:00), each stockbroker is able to compare their clock to their local time source, reduce their time relative to it to 0:00, and be sure of starting the transaction at the same time everyone else does.

Since the local time source doesn't adjust its setting when the stockbroker compares with it, the actual effect is that the stockbroker's time ends up equaling that of the local source.

At a prearranged time, each stockbroker begins a transaction with their local stock exchange. Later, each will have proof that they complied with the agreement—and didn't start either early or late—because the record of the transaction will be *time stamped*. That is, the electronic and paper records of the transaction will carry an imprint of the date and time the transaction took place.

Relative Time and NDS

NDS relies heavily on time stamps and relative time to ensure that all replicas of a given partition are updated properly. In addition, it can make use of absolute time sources to ease the burden of setting relative time to 0:00, while providing accurate time for users and processes running on the network.

In reality, the servers' relative time is rarely 0:00. The relative time is adjusted until its absolute value is less than a parameter called the *synchronization radius*. This defaults to 2000 milliseconds but is adjustable.

Remember that NDS is defined as a loosely consistent database. This means that changes are not necessarily immediately propagated to other copies of the database. Even if a particular server is down, its replicas will be updated once it's brought back up.

NDS uses time stamping to ensure that changes and additions to and deletions from the database take place in the exact same order for all replicas. Since changes can be made to any Read/Write replica in addition to the Master, without time stamping it would be very easy for the various replicas to quickly become out of synchronization. The time stamp can only be effective, though, if each server storing a replica agrees on the time (that is they have a relative time of 0:00 with each other). For this reason, every NetWare/IntranetWare server runs a time service. In this mode, they are referred to as *time servers*.

Just as the characters in our war movie do, time servers have different ranks or types. Time servers are also organized into groups—called, oddly enough, *time groups*—that use relative time to keep themselves synchronized and can use absolute time to synchronize with other time groups in the NDS tree. Before looking at the details of time servers and time groups, though, let's briefly look at how the time for NetWare servers and NDS is set, changed, and synchronized.

The Time Synchronization Process

Like the stockbroker group in the earlier example, networks can be worldwide. For this reason, NDS keeps time as UTC time, which is also used to timestamp database changes. This way, there's no need to adjust for time zones when figuring in which order to apply changes to the database. The process of synchronization is also similar to the example we used, with one or two very important differences, which we'll get to in a minute. Before the time can be synchronized, though, it needs to be set.

Setting the Time

For the sake of humans, however, time is displayed according to the time zone you set on any particular server using the SET TIME ZONE command. As an example, a server in Chicago would have the following line in its AUTOEXEC.NCF file:

SET TIME ZONE CST6CDT

In this line of code CST is the abbreviation for Central Standard Time, 6 (or +6) is the offset from UTC, and CDT stands for Central Daylight Time.

Four additional parameters control the beginning and end of daylight saving time as this table shows.

SET START OF DAYLIGHT SAVINGS TIME	Used to set the date when DST begins.
SET END OF DAYLIGHT SAVINGS TIME	Used to set the date when DST ends.
SET DAYLIGHT SAVINGS TIME OFFSET	While most of the countries that use daylight saving time offset local standard time by one hour (so this parameter defaults to +1:00:00), there are places that change by 30 minutes, 90 minutes, or possibly by other factors.
SET DAYLIGHT SAVINGS TIME STATUS	Changes DST status from ON to OFF or vice versa. This does not change the local time, but it does force UTC time to be recalculated.
SET NEW TIME WITH DAYLIGHT SAVINGS TIME STATUS	This not only changes the DST status, but also the local time. It does not, however, recalculate UTC time.

WARNING You should never control daylight saving time by changing the server's local time and then using the SET DAYLIGHT SAVINGS TIME STATUS command. This forces a UTC recalculation and could cause disastrous consequences to NDS.

Synchronizing the Time

The NDS server reads its time from the computer's hardware clock at bootup. It then sets up a software clock that it maintains for synchronization purposes. An Intel-based computer updates its hardware clock approximately once every 55 milliseconds; so whenever the hardware clock interrupt is triggered, NDS updates its software clock by 55 milliseconds. Periodically, it will ask other servers for the current *network time*—a term that means the agreed upon, synchronized UTC time for the network, and that may or may not match the absolute time. If the computer finds during synchronization that its relative time is not 0:00, then it will adjust this by either more or less than 55 milliseconds (depending on whether its relative time is plus or minus) until it becomes synchronized.

NDS never subtracts time from its clock. Rather, it slows the clock down as necessary until its synchronization partner (which has meanwhile speeded up its clock) catches up. When that happens, each server will set a flag (called the synchronization flag) to TRUE. Only when this flag is set to TRUE can the server exchange its UTC time as a time stamp with other servers.

Time Servers

NDS recognizes four types of time servers:

- Secondary
- Single reference
- Primary
- Reference

Each type of server has a particular role to play in keeping time synchronized among NDS servers.

Secondary Time Server

A secondary server attempts to remain synchronized with one other server (this is called *following*). This other server is almost always a time provider (in other words, not another secondary server). If there are any other servers on the network during installation, the install program will create the server as a secondary time server. Which server it follows will be determined either through advertising using SAP (Service Advertising Protocol) or through manual configuration. When a secondary time server discovers that its relative time vis-à-vis its time source exceeds the synchronization radius, it attempts to make the correction in one cycle whenever possible, as long as it does not require that the secondary server's time be decreased. Should the secondary's relative time be positive (which means that the time source's time is earlier than that on the secondary) it will *freeze* its time until the difference is within the synchronization radius.

The time source itself must have its synchronization flag set before the secondary time server can set its synchronization flag.

Single Reference Time Server

This type of time server is a special case and should be found only on networks with a single server. Because it has no other server to compare time with, a single reference time server wouldn't know when it was synchronized (or out of synchronization) and would never set the synchronization flag. This special case allows the server to set the flag and tells the server not to bother trying to exchange time information. When a new server is installed, the installation checks for other servers on the network and, if it finds none, sets the server as a single reference time server.

WARNING

There should never be a single reference time server on a network with more than one server. Since it would not participate in time synchronization (neither asking the time nor responding to requests for the time) NDS could very easily and very quickly become hopelessly confused and confusing.

Primary Time Server

Primary time servers participate with reference time servers to set the network time. Additionally, they may act as a time source for secondary servers.

During each polling cycle, a primary time server will contact every other time provider it is aware of. It takes the UTC time provided by each, averages it, and compares it to its UTC time. If the difference is within the synchronization radius, it sets its synchronization flag. If the difference is larger than the synchronization radius, it attempts to adjust its time by exactly one-half of the difference during the next cycle. This is similar to the example shown in Table 6.1. Remember, though, that the time cannot be changed to earlier than the current time.

Reference Time Server

A network with only primary and secondary time servers would seem sufficient at first glance, but on reflection you'll see that under this system you'd never be able to change the network time! Table 6.2 shows the interaction of three primary servers on the network and what happens if you change the time on one of them. Assume that the polling interval is 10 minutes. Once all three have finished synchronizing within the synchronization radius, the 10 minutes you added to Server A has been almost entirely wiped out.

T A B L E 6.2:   Simplified Synchronization of Three Primary Time Servers

Action	Server A	Server B	Server C	Result
Start	2:00	2:00	2:00	
Change A to 2:10	2:10	2:00	2:00	
Server's poll				Average is 2:03:20
Servers adjust by one-half difference	2:10	2:01:40	2:01:40	
Server's poll	2:15	2:11:40	2:11:40	Average is 2:12:47
Servers adjust by one-half difference	2:15	2:12:14	2:12:14	
Server's poll	2:20	2:22:14	2:22:14	Average is 2:21:29
Servers adjust by one-half difference	2:20:44	2:22:14	2:22:14	
Server's poll	2:30:44	2:32:14	2:32:14	Average is 2:31:44

The difference between a reference time server and a primary time server is that the reference server never adjusts its time. This forces the primary time servers (as well as any secondary time servers following them) to adjust their time so that it agrees with the reference server. If we take the same data as in Table 6.2, but make server A a reference time server, the results are very different (see Table 6.3). As a reference time server, Server A never changes its time, so the other two converge with it.

Since a reference time server never adjusts its clock in response to polling, it would seem that you could not have more than one on the network. Fortunately, you can use third-party, precise time sources—such as USNO—to provide time for all of the reference time servers.

T A B L E 6.3:   Simplified Synchronization of Three Servers with One as Reference Time Server

Action	Server A	Server B	Server C	Result
Start	2:00	2:00	2:00	
Change A To 2:10	2:10	2:00	2:00	
Server's poll				Average is 2:03:20
Servers adjust by one-half difference	2:10	2:01:40	2:01:40	
Server's poll	2:20	2:11:40	2:11:40	Average is 2:14:27
Servers adjust by one-half difference	2:20	2:13:04	2:13:04	
Server's poll	2:30	2:23:04	2:23:04	Average is 2:25:23
Servers adjust by one-half difference	2:30	2:24:14	2:24:14	

Marcus Williamson, formerly with Novell Consulting Services, has compiled a list of time synchronization products and solutions. It is available on the Web at http://www.connectotel.com/netware/timesg.html.

Time Groups

A *time group* is simply all of the time providers and secondary servers on a network that exchange time information with each other. While you might conclude that this simply means all servers on the network, that isn't necessarily true. It is possible—and frequently desirable—to configure multiple time groups. Before explaining why and how, let's look at the default configuration.

Default Configuration

As noted earlier, during installation the first server installed on the network is designated a single reference time server. Thereafter, each new server is installed as a secondary server following the single reference server. All servers use SAP to identify time sources.

With only one source of time, the network would appear to be easy to keep synchronized. However, as the network grows, a number of problems can occur:

- The single reference server must be contacted by every other server on the network. This can be a drain on that server's resources as well as on the throughput of slow or overutilized LAN or WAN links.

- Because SAP is used extensively, a single misconfigured server could begin advertising as a time provider, causing some of the secondaries to synchronize with it and bringing mass confusion to the network's time, as well as to NDS.

- If the single reference server is down or unavailable, time synchronization comes to a grinding halt.

Fortunately, it is possible to change this default configuration.

Custom Configuration

The time synchronization process is almost infinitely configurable. By creating a file called TIMESYNC.CFG in the default directory (SYS:SYSTEM on a NetWare 4.*x* server) you can control:

- The type of time server (secondary, primary, or reference)

- The method of synchronization (SAP or *configured sources*)

- Which server to follow (for secondary servers)

- Which servers to poll (for primary servers)

- Optimization parameters for time synchronization

This file is only necessary if you wish to change the default settings of any of the time parameters (see the section called *Configuring Synchronization Parameters* that follows). By issuing the SET TIMESYNC WRITE PARAMETERS command at the file server console, all SET TIMESYNC commands after that are automatically written to the TIMESYNC.CFG file.

If you decide to customize time synchronization, it's important to plan your customization before beginning to implement it. For this purpose, you should map or document all servers on the network—including those planned but not yet installed. It's easiest to perform the customization at the time a server is first installed.

Some of the factors you should determine, or decide on, before instituting customization include:

- The types of time servers and their locations

- Use of SAP, configured sources, or a combination of the two

- Which servers the secondary servers will follow

- Which primary and reference servers will poll each other

- Which servers need external references and their sources

- Which parameters should be changed, for which servers, and to which values

- If there are multiple NDS trees involved, whether each will have an independent time group or all servers be combined for time synchronization

Figure 6.1 shows a network map that serves as a reference in this discussion of time planning. The servers S1–S19 represent secondary servers, while TP1–TP7 represent time providers (primary and reference time servers).

If all the servers are within a building, bandwidth might not seem to be a major consideration, but constructing a TIMESYNC.CFG can improve the use of bandwidth even in such a case. Rather than have each secondary time server connect to time providers at random, configure each with a list of two or three servers to follow. If the first server in the list doesn't respond (if it's busy or down), then the next will be contacted. You should also set up at least one time provider as a reference server that connects to a reliable outside time source. Arbitrarily, let's make TP7 the reference server, with TP1–6 being primary

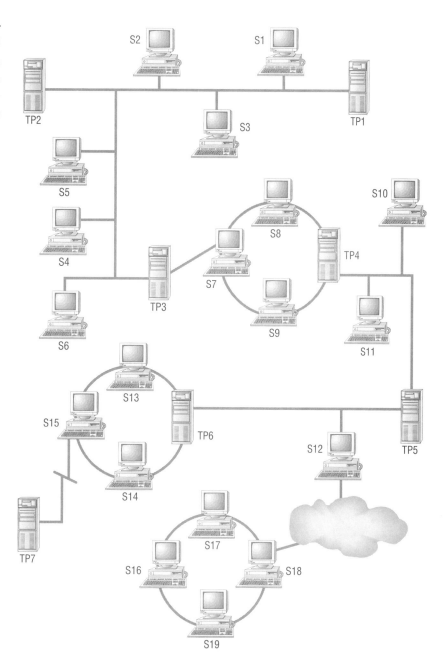

FIGURE 6.1

A network map shows time providers (TP1-TP7) and secondary time servers (S1-S19).

servers. They'll cooperate to ensure that synchronized time is both relatively 0:00 and absolute. Table 6.4 shows a possible arrangement for secondary servers and their time providers, listed in order of contact.

T A B L E 6.4 Possible Arrangement for Secondary Servers and Time Providers	**Secondary Server**	**First Time Provider**	**Second Time Provider**	**Third Time Provider**
	S1	TP1	TP2	TP3
	S2	TP2	TP1	TP3
	S3	TP1	TP2	TP3
	S4	TP2	TP1	TP3
	S5	TP2	TP1	TP3
	S6	TP3	TP2	TP1
	S7	TP3	TP4	TP2
	S8	TP4	TP3	TP5
	S9	TP4	TP3	TP2
	S10	TP5	TP4	TP2
	S11	TP4	TP5	TP6
	S12	TP5	TP6	TP4
	S13	TP6	TP7	TP5
	S14	TP6	TP5	TP7
	S15	TP6	TP5	TP7
	S16	TP6	TP7	TP5
	S17	TP5	TP4	TP6
	S18	TP5	TP6	TP4
	S19	TP6	TP5	TP4

Note that no time provider is the first choice of more than five secondaries, and that TP7—the reference server—is not the first choice of any of the secondaries.

Suppose that the cloud in the lower right of Figure 6.1 shows a slow WAN connection between S18 and S12. Rather than clog this connection with time synchronization packets from servers S16–S19, we could have S16, S17, and S19 configured to follow S18. It's possible for a secondary to follow another secondary, but because this increases the amount of time it takes to fully synchronize (S17 can't be fully synchronized before S18 has synchronized with its time provider), this should be limited to as shallow a depth as possible, usually to no more than one layer (secondary follows secondary, which follows time provider).

Now suppose that the network had a slow link between S10 and TP5. To minimize bandwidth usage, you could make TP1 a reference server (in addition to TP7) as long as both connected to reliable, external absolute time sources. We would also recommend that in this instance the reference servers become first-choice time providers for at least two of the secondary servers. This would ensure that no more than three secondaries would contact any single time provider. Additionally, the time provider servers would be configured to only reference other time providers on their own side of the slow link. You would also turn off SAP broadcasts of time information. This would remove all time traffic across the slow link, while still providing that all servers on the network remained synchronized.

Configuring Synchronization Parameters

Synchronization can be customized in three ways:

- By using a TIMESYNC.CFG file

- By specifying command line parameters when TIMESYNC.NLM is loaded

- By using Console SET commands

All parameters have a default setting. When TIMESYNC.NLM loads, it reads the TIMESYNC.CFG file and applies any parameter settings found there. To temporarily change any of the settings in TIMESYNC.CFG, you can pass parameters on the command line when loading TIMESYNC.NLM that will override any settings in the configuration file. At any time thereafter, you can change parameters by typing them in on the command line.

The following are the parameters that can be changed, their default values, their ranges, and suggestions for their usage. (The part in italics is used after the SET command at the command line, but is not used in a TIMESYNC.CFG file.) Thus, the parameter TIMESYNC ADD TIME SOURCE means type **SET TIMESYNC ADD TIME SOURCE =** if you are using it at the command line, but **TIME SOURCE =** if you are using it in a TIMESYNC.CFG file.

TIMESYNC ADD **TIME SOURCE = <servername>**

Default: None

Range: Up to 48 characters

Usage: To add a time source to a configured list. Normally, you would only use this in a TIMESYNC.CFG file, but it could be used to either temporarily add a time source, or (if TIMESYNC WRITE PARAMETERS has been set to ON) to change a TIMESYNC.CFG file (using Rconsole, for example).

TIMESYNC CONFIGURATION FILE = **<path>**

Default: SYS:SYSTEM\TIMESYNC.CFG

Range: Up to 255 characters

Usage: To change the location or name of the configuration file to use. Obviously, this shouldn't be *in* the configuration file!

TIMESYNC CONFIGURED SOURCES =

Default: OFF

Range: ON or OFF

Set to ON for selected server to use configured servers rather than SAP.

TIMESYNC **DIRECTORY TREE MODE =**

Default: ON

Range: ON or OFF

Usage: Turn off to allow the server to synchronize via SAP with servers that are on the network but outside its directory tree. If you aren't using SAP, don't turn this off.

TIMESYNC **HARDWARE CLOCK =**

Default: ON

Range: ON or OFF

Usage: Single reference and reference servers get their time from the server's hardware clock. If using an external time source, set this to OFF.

TIMESYNC **POLLING COUNT =**

Default: 3

Range: 1 to 1,000

Usage: Specifies the number of packets to exchange during polling. Increase the number only in rare circumstances since this will increase bandwidth use.

TIMESYNC **POLLING INTERVAL =**

Default: 600

Range: 10 to 2,678,400 seconds (equal to 31 days)

Usage: The time between polls. If server time stays synchronized this can be increased to reduce bandwidth requirements.

TIMESYNC REMOVE TIME SOURCE =

Default: None

Range: Up to 48 characters.

Usage: From the command line, temporarily removes a source from the configured list, or (used in conjunction with TIMESYNC WRITE PARAMETERS = ON) permanently changes the configured list.

TIMESYNC RESET =

Default: OFF

Range: ON or OFF

Usage: Resets all parameters to defaults and removes list of time sources (reverting to SAP). Not recommended except in emergency situations.

TIMESYNC RESTART FLAG =

Default: OFF

Range: ON or OFF

Usage: Only from the command line. Forces TIMESYNC.NLM to reload and reread TIMESYNC.CFG.

TIMESYNC **SERVICE ADVERTISING** =

Default: ON

Range: ON or OFF

Usage: Ontime providers, turns off the use of SAP. Be sure that all servers have configured lists before turning this off.

TIMESYNC **SYNCHRONIZATION RADIUS** =

Default: 2000

Range: 0 to 2,147,483,647 milliseconds

Usage: Sets the range in which relative time will be considered synchronized. Setting higher could cause NDS update errors, while setting lower could cause unnecessary (and unresolvable) "out of sync" error messages.

TIMESYNC TIME ADJUSTMENT =

Default: None

Range: Up to 99 characters

Usage: Use only in extreme cases where network time is significantly different from actual time. The parameter takes the form [–] hours:minutes:seconds [at month/day/year]. Set the actual adjustments to make and (optionally) the date to make them. If not specified, the "date" defaults to one hour or six polling intervals from the current time (whichever is longer). This uses the method for daylight saving time adjustment. This command should be used rather than a SET TIME command at a reference, single reference, or primary time server. SET TIME can mess up the time stamps in NDS and cause synthetic time to be issued on the partitions if time is set backward. A time adjustment keeps the consistency of the time stamps intact and still makes the adjustment happen.

TIMESYNC TYPE =

Default: SECONDARY

Range: Secondary, Primary, Reference, Single Reference

Usage: Generally only used within TIMESYNC.CFG, but it could be used to temporarily change a primary to a reference if the only reference server were being taken down.

TIMESYNC WRITE **PARAMETERS** =

Default: OFF

Range: ON or OFF

Usage: If set to ON, parameters typed in at the console using SET are automatically written to the TIMESYNC.CFG file.

Checking Time Synchronization

You use the DSREPAIR utility to check time synchronization on the network (and you should do so before doing anything else in the DSREPAIR utility!). Load DSREPAIR at the console, then choose TIME SYNCHRONIZATION from the menu. This option contacts every server known to the local server and requests information about time synchronization, Directory Services, and server status. The information is written to the log file. When the operation has completed, the log file is opened so you can check the status of time synchronization plus other Directory Services information. Table 6.5 shows the fields in the log.

T A B L E 6.5 DSREPAIR Log File Fields	Field	Meaning
	DS.NLM Version	The version of Directory Services (DS.NLM) running on the responding server. This information is valuable as a quick reference to see the versions of NDS running on the servers of your network.

T A B L E 6.5 *(cont.)*	Field	Meaning
DS REPAIR Log File Fields	Replica Depth	The replica depth indicates how deep in the NDS tree moving away from [ROOT] the first replica is on the responding server. Each server knows which replica is highest in the NDS tree. This value is the number being reported. A positive number indicates how many objects there are from the [ROOT] to the highest replica. A value of –1 indicates that no replicas are stored on the server.
	Time Source ·	The time source is the type of time server the responding server is configured to be.
	Time Is in Sync	This field indicates the time synchronization status of the responding time server. The possible values are Yes and No. The value displayed is the status of the synchronization flag for each server. This means that the server's time is within the time synchronization radius.
	Time Delta	This field reports the time difference, if any, from the time synchronization radius for each server. The time synchronization radius is 2 seconds by default, so you will probably not see a server with more than a 2-second difference. If the value is larger, the Time Is in Sync field is probably set to No. The maximum the field can report is up to 999 minutes and 59 seconds.

Summary

In this chapter we've discussed the importance of time to NDS and looked at why it's vital that time be synchronized among servers in your NDS tree. We explored the concepts of relative and absolute time and applied those concepts to NDS. We then defined NDS time groups and the various types of time servers in a group. Finally, we looked at the NetWare parameters you can set to control the time synchronization process and how to customize them.

CHAPTER

7

Compatibility with the Bindery

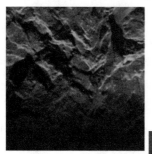

Novell has done an excellent job of maintaining compatibility with client and server applications designed for the bindery-based versions of NetWare (2.*x* and 3.*x*). NDS Bindery Services responds to the NetWare Bindery Application Programming Interface (API) as if it were a NetWare 3 server. The NetSync utility included with NetWare 4 allows the network administrator to manage bindery-based servers using NetWare 4's administrative tools.

In this chapter, we look at all aspects of NDS's backward compatibility, explore the functionality of that compatibility, and mention other possibilities that might make life with a mixed version NetWare network easier.

NetWare 5 does not include the NetSync utility. If there are no NetWare 4.*x* servers in your network you will have to use third party tools, such as Netvision's Synchronicity, to manage NetWare 3.*x* servers' binderies from NetWare 5's NDS.

Bindery Services

When they were first designing NetWare 4 and NDS, Novell's engineers had the foresight to realize that existing networks are rarely updated overnight. Many NetWare sites would upgrade on a server-by-server and client-by-client basis. By including Bindery Services, Novell ensured that existing clients and servers could communicate with and access the new NetWare 4 servers being introduced to the network. NetWare 5 also includes the ability to set a bindery context, so that existing clients and applications can continue to operate.

Bindery Services—What Are They?

In a nutshell, Bindery Services filter the NDS information, presenting only that data which would be present in a NetWare 3 bindery and presenting it exactly as the bindery would. Thus NetWare 3 utilities such as SYSCON, NetWare 3 clients such as NETX, and third-party utilities written for NetWare 3 would all continue to operate just as they had with the earlier version of NetWare.

While it's true that none of the additional functionality of NetWare 4 and 5, or NDS, would be available to these programs or clients, they could be gradually upgraded—to NetWare 4 or 5 versions—without having to make changes at the server or within NDS.

 It's important to note that Bindery Services are *server-based,* not tree-based. Each server that will be accessed by a bindery client or utility must contain a replica of the partition containing the needed bindery context.

Once all of the NetWare 3 server and client software has been upgraded to NetWare 4 or 5, Bindery Services can be removed.

The Mechanics of Bindery Services

Bindery Services are implemented by setting the *bindery context* for a server. This is a pointer to an Organization (O) or Organization Unit (OU) container within your tree. All of the objects within that container that have a bindery counterpart will be exposed as bindery objects by Bindery Services. So all of the users, groups, print queues, and print servers can be viewed using SYSCON or PCONSOLE; but NDS-only objects, such as directory maps or organizational roles, simply do not appear.

In particular, the user's profile is not available to Bindery Services. Bindery Services users needing personal login scripts must have them created in the SYS:MAIL\<userObjectID> directory on the server to which they will log in. The ObjectID for the user can be obtained by using either NWADMIN or SYSCON.

Implementing Bindery Services

Upon installation, every NetWare 4.*x*/5.*x* server contains a *bindery partition* within its database (see Chapter 5 for more information about NDS partitions). However, you must manually implement a bindery context using SET commands before Bindery Services will be offered by that server, unless the server is being upgraded from NetWare 3.

When upgrading from NetWare 3, the upgrade program automatically creates a bindery context on the new NetWare server. It also places a Read/Write replica of the partition containing the container to which the bindery context is set (the container storing the new server) on the newly upgraded server.

Whenever a NetWare 3 server is upgraded, Install creates a bindery context and a Read/Write replica of the partition containing that bindery context to facilitate access by existing clients and applications. This happens on every upgraded server, regardless of the number of replicas that already exist (remember that when installing new servers only the first three replicas are automatically created).

Table 7.1 shows a simple, single partition (<Root>) tree and a network that grows from one to five servers and indicates the action that INSTALL will take as far as automatically creating new replicas. Note that no replica is created on server SRVR-4 because three replicas already exist, and it is a new server. SRVR-5, however, automatically gets a replica because it is an upgrade.

T A B L E 7.1	Server	Method	Replica Created
Install Automatically Creates Replicas for New or Upgraded Servers	SRVR-1	Upgrade	Master
	SRVR-2	New	Read/Write
	SRVR-3	Upgrade	Read/Write
	SRVR-4	New	None
	SRVR-5	Upgrade	Read/Write

To implement Bindery Services on a server that does not currently offer them, you must first install a writable (either Read/Write or Master) replica of the tree partition containing that server. Follow this by setting the server's bindery context at the server console.

The Limitations of Bindery Services

NetWare 4.0*x* allowed only a single bindery context to be set for a server. This meant that all objects that needed to be viewed through Bindery Services had to be within a single O or OU container in your NDS tree. NetWare versions 4.1 and higher allow up to 16 bindery contexts to be set.

Server SET Commands

As we said earlier, you must enable Bindery Services before they can be offered. You do this by setting a bindery context for the server you wish to make available. To begin offering Bindery Services, type the following at the server console:

```
SET SERVER BINDERY CONTEXT = "<container>"
```

Where <container> is the fully qualified name of the container whose objects you wish to be made available via Bindery Services.

With NetWare 4.1 and above, this can be a semicolon-delimited list of up to 16 containers:

```
SET SERVER BINDERY CONTEXT =
"<container>;<container>;<container>;<container>;<container>"
```

WARNING With NetWare 4.0*x,* if you tried to specify an invalid container name, either because it didn't exist or because you mistyped part of the name, you'd immediately receive an error message indicating that an invalid context had been set. With NetWare 4.1 *and above,* if there are multiple containers listed in the SET command and one or more is invalid, no error message is generated (since some are valid). The only way to verify that all contexts have been set is with the CONFIG command.

The validity of the bindery contexts is rechecked every 10 minutes. If a bindery context is no longer valid (for example, if the server is down, the NDS replica has been removed, or the container name has changed) then

Bindery Services are removed from that context and must be reinitialized with the SET command.

SUPERVISOR: A Special Case

Every NetWare 4 and 5 server installed has a user called SUPERVISOR created within its bindery partition. This account is only accessible if a bindery context is set on that server, but the user does not show up anywhere within the NDS tree, because it is not an NDS object. Once a bindery context is set, the SUPERVISOR user has all rights to all objects within the bindery context.

While this object will always have a password associated with it (in NetWare 4.02 and later), you may or may not know what that password is. The password is assigned according to the method used to install the NetWare operating system, based on the following rules:

- If this is a NEW install, the password is the same as that of the user performing the installation (usually ADMIN).

- If this is an in-place upgrade, the SUPERVISOR password from the NetWare 3 bindery is "brought over" and continues to be the SUPERVISOR password in the new version of NetWare, with the following exception.

- If this is an in-place upgrade and the NetWare 3 SUPERVISOR did not have a password assigned, the password of the user performing the upgrade (usually ADMIN) is used.

- If this is an across-the-wire migration, the SUPERVISOR object already exists on the new NetWare server with the password of the user who installed the NetWare operating system. Even if the NetWare 3 SUPERVISOR has a password assigned, it will not be used because passwords cannot be copied using the MIGRATE utility.

While the password may initially be set to the same as that of the ADMIN user, it does not change when ADMIN's password changes. To change the SUPERVISOR's password, you must log in to that server's bindery context, then use the SETPASS utility. Knowing the password for SUPERVISOR allows someone to access a server's console even if locked by MONITOR's lock facility and to unlock it, even if a bindery context is not set.

NetWare 3.*x* Servers in an NDS NetWare LAN

NetWare 3.*x* servers can coexist in an NDS environment in a state of blissful ignorance in that the two environments will operate independently. Early revisions of DS.NLM on NetWare 4.1 servers containing master partition replicas generated an error about not being able to communicate with non-NetWare 4 servers. That error was merely cosmetic and has been fixed in later revisions of DS.NLM for NetWare 4.1 and higher.

NetSync

NetSync was introduced with NetWare 4.1 and provides the ability to manage bindery servers via NDS. The NetSync solution is powerful, albeit a bit awkward, and can provide a means to exploit the power of NDS without needing to upgrade the entire NetWare network right away. NetSync is intended to be a temporary solution to aid you in the process of upgrading your NetWare servers and to ease the integration of NetWare 3.1*x* users into NDS.

NetSync does not ship with NetWare 5. However, networks with a mix of NetWare 3.1*x*, 4.1*x*, and 5 servers can run NetSync on the NetWare 4 platform to administer the NetWare 3.1*x* bindery servers.

Using NetSync requires one NetWare 4.1*x* server (called the *host*). Up to 12 NetWare 3.1*x* servers may participate when grouped into a structure called a *NetSync cluster*.

It is possible for more than 12 3.1*x* servers to participate by creating multiple clusters whose hosts all use the same bindery context. In this situation, every object from every bindery within each of the clusters will be replicated to every 3.1*x* server in any of the clusters.

WARNING All bindery objects in the host's bindery context are copied to the binderies of all 3.1*x* servers in the cluster. This means any user in the bindery context can log in to any 3.1*x* server in the cluster. Access to directories and files are still controlled by trustee rights. (These are not changed by installing NetSync.) It can, however, be disconcerting for users to be able to see and log in to servers on which they have no access rights.

By implementing NetSync, you can:

- Synchronize NetWare 3.1*x* users and groups with objects in a NetWare 4.1*x* server's bindery context. When you update or create a user in the bindery context of the NetWare 4 host, that user is synchronized with all NetWare 3.1*x* servers in the NetSync cluster. The user now exists on all NetWare 3.1*x* servers that are part of the cluster and are actively attached. Consequently, you don't have to update or create this user on each NetWare 3.1*x* server.

- Manage NetWare 3.1*x* users and groups from within the NetWare 4 administrative utilities (NETADMIN or NetWare Administrator).

- Move NetWare 3.1*x* print services to a NetWare 4 server.

- Manage NetWare 3.1*x* printing with the NetWare 4 print utilities (NetWare Administrator or PCONSOLE).

Once you've implemented NetSync, you should no longer use the NetWare 3.1*x* tools (SYSCON, PCONSOLE, etc.) to manipulate bindery objects and print services, but should instead use the NWAdmin program from NetWare 4.*x*. NetSync is a one way street—from NDS to the bindery. Changes made directly to the bindery are not propagated back to NDS or to other servers in the cluster.

Preparing to Install NetSync

The same precautions apply to installing NetSync as apply to migrating multiple servers to NDS or merging directory trees: Strange things may happen if any two objects have the same name. While objects of two different types (such as a print queue and a group) may have the same name in a NetWare 3.1*x* bindery, they cannot have the same name in NDS.

In NetWare 3.1*x*, it is also the case that two users on two different servers may have the same login name: John Doe on the accounting server may be known as JDOE while Jane Doe on the marketing server may also log in as JDOE. If both of these servers are in the cluster, all of the JDOE accounts will be consolidated and a single JDOE account will be propagated to all 3.1*x* servers in the cluster.

The results of synchronizing duplicated objects depend on whether they are the same object type or different object types.

Objects of the Same Type   Let's say there is a user object called JDOE in the bindery on each of two NetWare 3.1x servers that will be part of the same NetSync cluster.

NetSync will merge the two objects in the NetWare 4 bindery context. This is fine so long as the two user objects refer to the same physical user. If, however, they are different (John Doe and Jane Doe, in the example above) the user JDOE (John Doe) on the first NetWare 3.1x server to be synchronized takes precedence—he gets created as an object with all properties intact.

When NetSync encounters the second user JDOE (Jane Doe), it scans her properties for any that did not exist for John Doe. If a property already exists, Jane Doe's property is discarded. If a property does not already exist, Jane Doe's property is added, and the two JDOEs are merged.

If the two JDOEs don't refer to the same user, change one or both login names before running NetSync so that the two JDOEs have distinct names, such as Jane_DOE and John_DOE. Otherwise, the two users will be merged and both users' properties will be corrupted. For example, the merged user JDOE might have John Doe's e-mail address and login restrictions but have Jane Doe's login script.

Objects of Different Types   When multiple 3.1x bindery objects of different object types have identical names and you run NetSync, only the first object to be uploaded will be converted to a Directory object.

For example, if print queue JDOE (so named, perhaps, because it is reserved exclusively for the user Jane Doe) gets uploaded to the NetWare 4 bindery context before user JDOE, the 3.1x print queue JDOE will become an NDS Print Queue object.

Because her object type (user) is different from Print Queue JDOE, the user JDOE will become a different type of object, called a bindery object, and will not show up as a User object. Jane Doe would not be able to access NetWare Directory Services but would be able to access Bindery Services.

Installing NetSync

NetSync must first be installed on the NetWare 4.1x server that will act as host for the cluster. This server must have a bindery context set.

You can then proceed to load NetSync on each of the NetWare 3.1x servers that will be in the cluster. As each server is added, its static bindery objects are moved to NDS and into the container set as the bindery context for the host. Once all affected 3.1x binderies have been moved into NDS and combined, all of the objects are copied to the binderies on each of the 3.1x servers in the cluster. Thus, if user JANE_DOE existed in the bindery of at least one of the 3.1x servers before installing NetSync, she will exist in all of the binderies, on all of the 3.1x servers in the cluster after NetSync synchronizes.

Using NetSync

Once NetSync is installed, there's really nothing the network administrator needs to do actively to keep it working. Any NDS changes made within the bindery context of the host are automatically synchronized to the 3.1x servers' binderies. Should one of the 3.1x servers be taken down, the host will send all bindery data to it once it comes back online.

There is one thing the network administrator should *not* do. They should not use SYSCON to directly manipulate bindery objects on the 3.1x server. After installation, NetSync's synchronization is one way: from the 4.1x host to the 3.1x servers. Changes made at the 3.1x servers are not sent back to the host and are not propagated to the other 3.1x servers.

NetSync and Printing

Optionally, you can move all NetWare 3.1x print servers and merge them into a single print server on the NetWare 4 host server. Print queues in operation before the change appear the same to users, but they are now serviced by the NetWare 4 print server.

Old NetWare 3.1x print utilities are automatically replaced with NetWare 4 print utilities that have been copied to the NetWare 3.1x servers.

What's Synchronized and What's Not

NetSync synchronizes users and all their properties (for example, passwords, login scripts, and login restrictions), groups, NetWare Name Service profiles, print queues created on NetWare 3.1x servers, and changes made to print queues on the NetWare 4 server.

NetSync does not synchronize:

- The SUPERVISOR user (each NetWare 3.1*x* server will have a separate SUPERVISOR and a corresponding password).

- The ADMIN user object (on the NetWare 4 server).

- Print queues created on the NetWare 4 server.

- Accounting charge rates and account balances (this is the only thing you would use SYSCON on the 3.1*x* servers for).

- Object names that include characters that were illegal in bindery names. (Illegal characters for bindery names are $, ?, \, /, ", [,], :, |, <, >, +, and =, but they can vary among different languages.)

- File system rights that NetWare 3.1*x* users and groups have on the NetWare 3.1*x* server. (These rights continue to be server-specific and are only valid for the volumes on those servers.)

- System login scripts.

Monitoring NetSync

NetSync copies all messages that it generates to a log file (SYS:SYSTEM\NETSYNC\NETSYNC.LOG). This is a plain ASCII text file which will grow up to a settable size (default size is .5MB). If this size is reached, the file is copied to NETSYNC.OLD and a new NETSYNC.LOG is created. You can turn off NetSync logging, which might improve network traffic throughput (especially during periods when you expect to change large amounts of NDS information within the bindery context that NetSync is using).

NetVision's Synchronicity for NetWare 3

Because NetSync ships with NetWare 4.1*x*, you might wonder how a company could sell a product that does virtually the same thing. There are three reasons:

- Synchronicity for NetWare 3 is part of a family of NetVision products (including Synchronicity for Windows NT and Synchronicity for Lotus Notes) that integrate other directory systems into NDS and allow single point administration of these systems using snap-in modules for NDS' NWADMIN program.

- Synchronicity for NetWare 3 is both more powerful and more flexible than NetSync.

- Synchronicity for NetWare 3 works with NetWare 5 servers. It does not require a NetWare 4.1x server on your network.

The Benefits of Synchronicity for NetWare 3

The following are among the advantages of Synchronicity over NetSync:

- A single NetWare 4.1 or higher server running Synchronicity for NetWare 3's synchronization agent can synchronize many NetWare 3.1x servers. There is no need for clusters, no limit of 12 3.1x servers per host.

- No NLMs need to be loaded on the NetWare 3 servers. Synchronicity for NetWare 3 has three key components. First, the NetVision Global Event Services (GES) NetWare Loadable Module (NLM) runs on the NetWare 4 or 5 server. Second, a snap-in module for Novell's NetWare Administrator utility adds support for NetWare 3 bindery attributes. The third component is the synchronization agent that runs on one NetWare 4 or 5 server.

- Each user and group object can be mapped across one or more NetWare 3 binderies. Any time a change is made to a user or group account, that information is synchronized across all appropriate NetWare 3.1x servers by Synchronicity for NetWare 3. NetSync requires all bindery information to be synchronized to all NetWare 3.1x servers in the cluster.

- Synchronicity for NetWare 3 provides two password utilities that enable users and help desk support operators to easily change passwords that are then synchronized between NDS and NetWare 3 binderies. NWAdmin can also be used to do password synchronization between the two environments. In order to use the utility, the user or administrator needs to be logged into NDS.

- Synchronicity's NWAdmin snap-in module provides three options for moving objects. The first two provide mass integration of NetWare 3.1x bindery objects into NDS or NDS objects into a NetWare 3.1x bindery. Both provide collision rules, so that administrators can determine how conflicts will be resolved during the integration. The third method supports the mapping of objects on a one-by-one basis so that objects with different names on different servers, or different objects with the same name, can be resolved.

- Synchronicity for NetWare 3 does NDS integration for NetWare 3.1*x* servers. There are no requirements to tie the NetWare 3 servers into the bindery context.

- Any NetWare 3 bindery can be integrated with any part of the NDS tree. This allows departmental NetWare 3 servers to be mapped with the department's NDS organization unit (OU). This also means that a departmental administrator with rights to manage the NDS organization unit can also manage the department's NetWare 3 server through NWAdmin.

- Synchronicity for NetWare 3 provides bidirectional synchronization (NDS-to-bindery and bindery-to-NDS). The NDS changes are made in real time to NetWare 3 servers. A second ability enables NetWare 3 changes to be resynchronized during a scheduled or manually initiated event. This is defined through the NWAdmin snap-in module. Changes made to the NetWare 3 bindery using SYSCON are allowed.

Synchronicity Usage Considerations

One drawback of Synchronicity for NetWare 3 is that (compared to NetSync) it does not synchronize print queues. This is more of an irritation than a major problem, as print queues can be redirected to NDS print servers with the native NetWare 3.1*x* print utilities.

NetSync or Synchronicity?

If you simply need a temporary solution to ease the pace of migration to NetWare 4 or 5's NDS (and there's a NetWare 4.1*x* server on the network), then NetSync is a very good solution, and it's free. If, on the other hand, you foresee that your network will consist of NetWare 5, NetWare 4, and NetWare 3 servers for some time to come (or only NetWare 5 and NetWare 3 servers), Synchronicity's flexibility and completeness will more than repay the investment made to purchase it. NetVision also has available additional Synchronicity modules for Lotus Notes, Windows NT, and Microsoft Exchange Server.

Summary

This chapter has shown how Novell has provided backwards compatibility in NDS for NetWare operating systems and clients prior to version 4. Through the use of bindery contexts on NetWare 4, servers, clients, and applications that have no knowledge of NDS can continue to work just as they did with NetWare 3.1x.

Novell also provides a utility (with NetWare 4.1x) called NetSync, which allows a network administrator to administer NetWare 3 bindery information from within NDS. NetSync is intended as a temporary solution to ease the migration to NetWare 4 or 5 and NDS.

NetVision sells a product, Synchronicity for NetWare 3, which enables the full integration of NetWare 3 servers and users into NDS. While NetSync provides temporary integration of NetWare 3.1x servers into NDS until they can be upgraded to NetWare 4 or 5, Synchronicity is intended for longer-term use.

CHAPTER
8

Directory Design

ovell Directory Services offers a key benefit in the Directory's capability to present users and administrators in an organization with a unified view of objects representing a variety of network resources. Through a single point of access, objects organized in a hierarchy can be located easily for retrieval or maintenance of information associated with the network resources that the objects represent. Planning is required for such benefits to be realized. The amount of planning needed depends on the size and complexity of the networking environment where NDS will be deployed.

This chapter covers the steps and decisions necessary to design a directory that allows an organization to realize the benefits of NDS in an efficient manner.

The planning required for NDS can be broken down into the following phases:

- Planning for the use of NDS logical and physical design elements such as trees, container and leaf objects, partitions, and replicas. The objective of the directory design that results is to provide users with an environment that is easy to use, while enhancing administrative control, availability, performance, and communications efficiency. This is the topic of this chapter.

- Designing time synchronization for the network environment to ensure that all servers on the network keep uniform time while minimizing traffic generated by time synchronization communications. Due to its simplicity, this topic is covered in the general discussion of time synchronization in Chapter 6, "Time Synchronization."

- Specifying guidelines for object naming and property usage to ensure uniformity through an organization's directory implementation. This topic is covered in Chapter 9, "Naming Guidelines."

- Applying NDS security features to provide for the enforcement of organizational security policies that exist either implicitly or explicitly. This topic is covered in Chapter 12, "NDS Security, Audit, and Control."

- Planning for the migration of information from other network directories, such as NetWare's bindery, to NDS. This is often required when NDS systems are replacing systems using other directories. This topic is covered in Chapter 10, "Migration Strategies."

Many of these planning stages can be performed concurrently; they need not be completed in the order in which they are presented. However, key decisions must be made during certain phases, such as the structural design phase, before other phases are completed.

Design Objectives

One of the challenges of Novell Directory Services design is that there may appear to be a limitless range of possibilities for designing a directory. In many cases, the NDS design process requires organizations to address the issue of how they *want* to manage their network resources, which can be a difficult and politically sensitive issue.

The flexibility of the directory services provided by NDS can seem to create these difficulties, because NDS does not necessarily dictate the way organizations should organize their support activities to manage the directory. In other words, the NDS requirements differ from the support requirements that are dictated by directories implemented within other systems. For example, mainframes typically dictate a centralized support structure due to their architecture. Network operating system directories, such as the bindery in early versions of NetWare, on the other hand, were best supported with a decentralized workgroup-based support structure.

The actual NDS design process consists of combining logical and physical design elements into a unified platform for directory services within an organization. Logical design is the organization of containers into one or more hierarchical trees that hold objects representing network resources. Physical design is the specification of how partitioning and replication should be applied within the logical tree structure and the physical network infrastructure. The combination of these design elements should produce a directory possessing structural and operational characteristics that meet the following general objectives:

- Provides a logical structure where objects representing network resources are positioned in the hierarchy so users can locate them easily. This can be achieved by using logic to place objects near users that access them frequently, while allowing users to find other objects elsewhere in the hierarchy because they are located where users might expect them to be.

- Provides a logical structure consistent with the network administration and support philosophy of the organization. This allows administrative responsibilities to be distributed or delegated, when desired, by way of the hierarchy.

- Provides sufficient flexibility so that the directory structure can reflect organizational changes without significant operational disruptions or other inconveniences for users.

- Provides the best possible quality of service to those accessing information in the directory. This can be measured in terms of availability, performance, and efficiency.

The actual NDS design objectives and their relative importance will likely differ across organizations, depending on the specific needs of the organizations. A design decision intended to satisfy a particular objective might increase the difficulty of satisfying other objectives. Such trade-offs require the evaluation of design alternatives in terms of how well the overall objectives are met. Before beginning the actual design process, it is important that the objectives of the directory design be clearly documented so available design alternatives can be evaluated properly.

Design Guidelines

Once the objectives for the directory design have been established, the next step is to plan for the use of the NDS logical and physical design elements to satisfy those objectives in the most effective manner possible. Because a clear delineation exists between the logical and physical design for

NDS, it would seem sensible to consider the two types of designs independently. In this ideal world, NDS design would be simple, since the logical design of the directory would be unconstrained by physical considerations such as geography or the physical layout of the network. Similarly, the physical design would be unconstrained by any organizational considerations introduced with the logical design.

Unfortunately, NDS design is not so simple in most cases. The logical and physical design elements are intimately related and mutually dependent on physical considerations such as geography and the physical layout of the network. Planning for the use of NDS logical and physical design elements to create a directory design that satisfies the defined objectives requires simultaneous consideration of the constraints imposed by design decisions made about all design elements. To deal with this complexity, the design process is best approached in a disciplined manner. Such an approach accounts for mutual dependence on physical considerations while still allowing for separate consideration of logical and physical design elements.

The design guidelines presented in this chapter are organized using just such an approach. Individual design elements are considered separately in five stages, as outlined below:

- Determine the number of NDS trees that will be required. In the event that multiple trees are necessary or desirable, each tree should be considered separately when applying the remaining steps.

- Design the structure of the NDS tree by organizing containers that will hold objects in a hierarchy.

- Divide the tree into partitions to allow for the efficient distribution of information contained in the directory.

- Specify the location of partition replicas to provide for fault tolerance, bindery services, and efficient user access to local resources.

- Establish standards for the use and placement of leaf objects within the directory.

- Devise naming standards to be used throughout the tree. Because of its importance, this topic is covered in its own chapter, Chapter 9.

The order of these design stages reflects the relative rigidity of the design elements. This rigidity can be measured in terms of the difficulty associated with changing decisions about how the design elements should be applied after the directory is constructed. For example, changes to the way containers are organized in a tree would have more of an impact on the other design elements than would changes to partitioning or replication.

The mutual dependencies between the logical and physical design elements that must inform the design decisions made for each design element are considered at each stage. (These mutual dependencies include those that reflect physical network considerations.) These considerations will be clarified as each design element is considered in turn in the relevant sections that follow.

In smaller environments with little complexity caused by wide area network links, such detailed planning probably is not necessary. In those cases, the defaults provided during NDS installation should suffice as the starting point for an NDS implementation.

An important point to consider is that there is usually no single "correct" way that each logical and physical design element should be used in a particular network environment. However, design alternatives will differ in their effect on the ease of use and the operational efficiency of the directory. An additional point to consider is that once a directory design is implemented, it is still possible to make changes to any of the logical and physical design elements, although certain design elements are more difficult to change than others once they are implemented.

The following guidelines explore factors that might influence decisions on how to use the design elements. In all cases, knowledge of the organization, the physical network characteristics, and how the directory is likely to be used will be the most important considerations in the design process.

The guidelines that follow should not be interpreted as definitive but should be thought of as recommendations or rules of thumb that are applicable in general cases. This is true even when actual numbers are used to quantify constraints on the directory design presented by NDS. It is entirely possible that a directory design that strictly adheres to the guidelines as presented might not operate efficiently, whereas a directory design that disobeys a guideline or two could operate efficiently. In most cases, though, using the following guidelines should result in a directory design that will operate efficiently once it is fully implemented.

Determining Tree Requirements

One of the fundamental decisions for Novell Directory Services design is determining how directory trees should be created to support an organization's requirements. In many cases, determining tree requirements can be just as much of a practical issue as a philosophical issue, since the existence of multiple trees in an environment can have a direct impact on interoperability between resources in separate trees.

Although it is conceivable that an NDS tree could extend across organizational boundaries, most NDS trees will encompass one organization at most. This is due to the formidable requirements for agreement between organizations that would be necessary to support such an arrangement. In some cases, it may be desirable to deploy multiple NDS trees within a single organization. Because all other design activities are concerned with arranging design elements within a single tree, an organization's tree requirements should be determined prior to proceeding with subsequent NDS design activities.

An example of a situation where multiple trees would be desirable is a development environment, where there needs to be a "test" environment for NDS changes. At the same time, an organization that has several logical divisions might be better served with a single "production" tree but with several test trees for various development projects.

When multiple trees are present in an organization, the separate trees represent independently operating entities. This is because facilities do not exist at present to relate resources in one tree to resources in another tree. For example, if users want to access resources in separate trees, they must authenticate separately to each tree. In NDS, there is no concept of trust between trees so there is no way that credentials from one tree could be used to gain access to another tree. This situation can be likened to that which existed with bindery-based versions of NetWare. In that case, access to resources on separate servers required that users have accounts on each server. The difference between the two situations is that the scope of resources encompassed by an NDS tree usually extends to multiple servers.

Novell's DirXML technology (see Chapter 18 for more information), due to ship in mid-2000, will allow information from one tree to be made available in another tree. This may make it possible for organizations with multiple trees to allow authentication to one tree as a means of providing access to objects in multiple trees.

A network administrator could use NDS in such a way that it would allow network resources to be managed in a similar manner to bindery-based NetWare servers by defining separate trees for every NetWare server. Some organizations have approached migrations to NDS from previous versions of NetWare in this manner, even going so far as to continue to manage individual servers using bindery-based utilities such as SYSCON.

Novell Technical Support does not recommend that bindery-based user and group management utilities, such as SYSCON, be used for NDS since the continued use of such tools can lead to corruption of an NDS database. If separate trees are defined for individual servers in order to simulate as closely as possible a bindery environment, NDS utilities such as NetWare Administrator should still be used to manage users and groups on those servers.

Operating with multiple trees was more problematic with early versions of NetWare client software. Those versions nearly restricted users to accessing resources in a single tree (although bindery connections could be established to resources in other trees). With the introduction of Novell's Client32 for NetWare, such single tree access restrictions were eliminated and support was provided for full NDS connections to multiple trees. Although Client32 allows attachments to multiple NDS trees, the requirement for authenticating to each individual tree remains.

While Client32 for DOS/Windows and the new Windows-based utilities support multiple trees, the DOS utilities still provide no multiple-tree support. To connect to multiple trees and manage them from DOS requires unsupported utilities, like CHTREE, in order to set the primary tree before launching the utility.

Drawbacks to Single-Tree Directories

The ideal approach to NDS design for most situations is to create a single tree for an entire organization to provide a single repository for network information stored in the directory. However, there are some drawbacks to this approach that might favor the adoption of an alternative approach:

- Merging multiple trees into a single tree is relatively simple with existing tools, but there are no tools available for splitting a tree into multiple trees. Splitting a tree is not impossible, but it is a complex operation that could take a great deal of time.

- Schema extensions that allow for the definition of new object classes or additional properties for existing object classes can only be established for an entire tree. Novell plans to address this issue with federated partitions, which allow the scope of schema extensions to be limited to individual partitions or subtrees instead of the entire tree. Until federated partitions are available, schema management would need to be centralized within an organization sharing a single tree to coordinate the addition of new object classes and new properties to existing object classes. When this level of centralization or alternative methods for coordination is not possible within an organization, then multiple trees will probably need to be created.

- A universally trusted authority is required for administration of the root and the first level of containers in an NDS tree. Agreeing to an administrative authority that can be trusted universally within an organization can be difficult in some cases, in which case multiple trees usually will be necessary.

Advantages of Single-Tree Directories

Despite the potential drawbacks, most organizations likely will conclude that operating with a single tree is the most desirable option because a single tree allows organizations to take full advantage of NDS. In addition to avoiding the operational problems that are often associated with using multiple trees, using a single tree has the following advantages:

- A single NDS tree can present a global view of all network resources within an organization, allowing users to locate resources by navigating a single hierarchy rather than requiring users to attach to multiple trees to do this. Constraints on the types of resources that can be represented in the directory are the only factors that limit this global view.

- When a resource (such as a user) changes its location or function, its position in the tree can be changed to reflect this change simply by moving the object. When multiple trees are being used, if the change were to cross tree boundaries it would not be possible to simply move the object to reflect the change, since separate trees cannot share information. Instead, a new object representing the same resource would need to be created in the target tree, and the old object might need to be deleted.

If the needs of an organization are best served by multiple NDS trees, the remaining stages in the design process will need to be performed separately for each individual tree. Since NDS trees operate independently of each other, it is technically acceptable to proceed independently through the stages without regard for the designs of the other trees. If possible, the design efforts for the individual trees should be coordinated to provide a measure of consistency for users accessing multiple trees. In addition, consistent application of NDS design elements across all trees in an organization will facilitate merging trees into a single tree, if desired in the future.

Organizing Containers

The act of organizing containers into a hierarchy establishes the framework for an NDS tree. The containers will hold objects representing network resources, which should be organized in a logical manner so that users and administrators can easily locate them. In addition, containers could be used to establish default settings or privileges for objects within them and potentially within all subordinate containers, by means of inheritance. This can be accomplished by organizing containers to represent a hierarchical structure that is meaningful to users and administrators. These design objectives are usually constrained by other objectives, such as the following:

- Support for a partitioned directory that distributes directory information to allow for efficient operations.

- A flexible design that allows organizational changes to be reflected in the directory tree without significantly impacting operations.

Organizing containers into an NDS tree framework requires a balancing of these structural design objectives while allowing users and administrators to have easy access to objects in a directory that can be maintained and operated efficiently.

Perhaps the easiest way to define a framework that is likely to be meaningful to users and administrators is to have the directory tree reflect an organizational structure that is commonly known within an organization. Two potentially suitable structural models that could be used as the basis for a hierarchical framework of containers are listed below:

- The *functional model,* which serves to delineate organizational functions by dividing the organization into groups such as divisions, departments, and workgroups. This usually is documented in the organizational chart. A directory design based on this model could define a layer of containers for divisions, another layer for departments, and perhaps an additional layer for workgroups.

- The *geographical model,* which reflects the geographical locations of organizational entities. A directory design based on this model could define containers for each location.

- A third, and more commonly used, model is a hybrid of the two models listed above: geographic at the higher levels (unless multiple Os are needed, when it's geographic inside the highest O level), and functional within a geographic location (usually by department).

These models, along with other similarly meaningful models that may be present within an organization, must be evaluated in terms of how well they can serve as the source for the design of the directory tree within the constraints imposed by other design elements.

Anticipating a Partitioned Directory

The requirement to support partitioning is perhaps the most significant constraint on the design of an NDS tree. Partitions, which allow the directory database to be divided into separate units that can be distributed across the network, use container objects as the boundaries defining the portion of the tree included in a partition. Because partitions are the NDS design elements that contribute most to the efficient operation of the directory in large or complex network environments, it is important that the design of a directory tree allow for effective partitioning.

Partitioning is a physical concept, and its influence on the design of a directory tree requires consideration of the physical network infrastructure when arranging container objects into a hierarchical framework. The physical considerations in this design stage extend only to the point of allowing for effective partitioning without actually specifying how the directory will be partitioned, which occurs in the next stage.

Determining how an NDS tree should be designed to support partitioning requires an understanding of the practical purposes for partitioning and the operational implications of a partitioned directory. Without partitioning, a single server would need to store the entire directory database. In a large network, this database would be vast and the server could be required to respond to a high volume of requests from all users on the network. Even when the most powerful server hardware is used to house the directory, this likely would result in slow performance for users in a geographically dispersed network since a significant portion of the requests and responses would likely travel across wide area network links. Since wide area network links usually are much slower than local network links, fewer requests and responses can travel through wide area network links in a given period of time than is possible over local network links.

Replicating the directory to servers that are closer to users could improve performance for users by decreasing the workload for individual servers. This could also increase efficiency by decreasing the number of requests and responses traveling across slower wide area network links. Any gains in performance and efficiency, however, would likely be negated due to the amount of traffic required to keep the contents of the replicated directory consistent.

The alternative to replicating the entire contents of the directory to servers located close to users is to divide the directory into partitions, storing copies of the partitions on servers located close to the resources represented by objects contained in that portion of the directory. When a user needs information about a nearby resource, the information likely would be contained in a partition copy that is located near the user, so that the request and response would not have to cross wide area network links. When a user needs information about resources that are farther away, the information would still be available, but it would be contained in a partition for which the nearest copy could be farther away, and this could require that the request and response cross slower wide area network links.

Assuming that users most often request information about resources that are located near them, this partitioned directory model increases performance and efficiency by dividing up the workload for servers handling directory requests while reducing the amount of traffic that crosses slower wide area network links.

With NDS, multiple copies of the same partition can be used to provide fault tolerance and to balance the workload for servers handling directory access. The synchronization required to keep the information contained in each of the partition copies up-to-date generates network traffic. The amount of this traffic generated by synchronization for any given partition depends on the size of the partition and the number of copies that exist. In most cases, the level of traffic generated by synchronization can be considered inconsequential unless the traffic travels across slower wide area network links. Consequently, the amount of such traffic crossing wide area network links should be kept as small as possible.

Because container objects are the boundaries of partitions of the directory, the container objects should be organized to reflect the network infrastructure so that partitions can be established in such a way that they do not encompass multiple locations that might be separated by wide area network links. The easiest way to accomplish this is to have at least a portion of the directory design follow the geographical structure of the organization by creating containers for each location.

Establishing a Flexible Design

Organizations are dynamic, and their structures are likely to change in unpredictable ways over time. Basing the design of a directory tree on the structure of an organization requires that the directory tree be capable of changing to reflect changes in the underlying organizational structure, so that the placement of objects within the directory remains meaningful to users and administrators over time. As a result, it is important that the design of the directory tree allow for flexibility. When such organizational changes occur, modifications to the objects within the tree must be limited.

Before determining how to achieve flexibility in the design of the directory tree, it is necessary to understand the changes that occur to objects within the directory when organizational changes must be reflected in the tree. The primary logical design elements are containers that are organized into a hierarchy within a tree. All objects in the tree (including containers) can be uniquely identified by a name that is formed by combining the Relative Distinguished Name of the object itself with the names of all containers that are directly between the object and the tree's [Root] object.

Several types of changes can occur in an organization that will have an impact on the directory tree, but they will all have the same effect when reflected in the directory: they will change the full name of at least one object. Organizational changes reflected in the directory that only require a change to a single object, such as when a user moves to a new department, have a limited impact on the entire directory tree. An organizational change that requires a change to a container object when it is reflected in the directory, such as when an organization's business units are restructured, could result in changes having a much greater impact since the names of all subordinate objects will change when the container's name changes.

Although it is not possible to anticipate all the changes that could occur within an organization that would have a significant impact on the directory, it is possible to identify the changes that are most likely to occur. Perhaps the most common types of change are changes to business units within organizations that might serve as the basis for containers within the directory. Because a directory tree is hierarchical, changes that occur to container objects closest to the top, or root, of the tree will have the greatest impact since all of the container's subordinate objects will experience changes as a result.

Achieving maximum flexibility in the design for a directory tree involves recognizing the structural design elements that are least likely to change and using those to form containers at the top of the tree in order to minimize changes to significant portions of the directory. The inverse of this consideration is that containers representing organizational structures that are most likely to change over time should be placed near the bottom of the tree in order to minimize the impact of changes.

Evaluating Structural Design Alternatives

Despite the constraints imposed on the design of an NDS tree by the requirements for partitioning and flexibility, it is possible to create a framework that achieves a key objective of the directory: providing easy access to information about network resources for users and administrators. As mentioned earlier, one of the easiest ways to achieve this objective is to base the design of the directory tree on an existing structural model that is likely to be meaningful to users and administrators within an organization. The structural models that could serve as the basis for a directory framework are evaluated in this section in terms of how they might be reconciled with the potentially conflicting objectives and constraints.

Of the common organizational structures that were introduced previously (the functional and geographical models), only the geographical model was mentioned as having any significant relevance when considering the requirements for partitioning and flexibility in the formulation of a directory framework. The geographical model is useful because it usually reflects the network architecture. This is important for partitioning purposes because the local networks separated by wide area network links between geographical locations should serve as the basis for partitions so that the directory can perform as efficiently as possible. In addition, because geographical changes usually are not as likely to occur as other types of changes within an organization, basing the design of an NDS tree on an organization's geography should minimize the impact of organizational changes that would need to be reflected in the directory.

A major drawback to basing the design of an NDS tree entirely on an organization's geography is that such a framework is not likely to be meaningful to users and administrators who typically think of an organization in functional, rather than geographical, terms. This would not be a problem in organizations where there is a strict relationship between organizational functions and locations, but functions often are distributed across locations in ways that could make a strict geographical framework for a directory appear unnatural to users. For example, an organization might have resources within a business unit located in offices throughout the world, with a single location potentially housing resources from multiple business units. Users are often interested in resources (such as other users) within their business units, and the location of those resources might not be meaningful or important for them.

Some of the difficulties for users and administrators introduced by the use of the geographical model as the basis for the design of a directory tree can be alleviated through the use of the functional model. Deriving the design for a directory tree from the functional model is a natural approach to directory design because it allows users and administrators to locate network resources using the knowledge of the functional structure of an organization rather than knowledge of how resources are arranged physically within the network. This is possible because a directory framework based on the functional model organizes objects representing network resources along functional lines in a manner that allows users and administrators to predict reliably the location of objects within the hierarchy of the directory tree.

The organizational chart that documents the hierarchical reporting relationships for employees within an organization can be used in the design of a directory tree based on the functional model. Because management within an organization is often defined in terms of functional areas, identifying areas of management via the organizational chart can allow for the identification of functional areas that should be represented in the directory. Such a directory design could include a layer of containers representing the organization's divisions or subsidiaries, along with additional layers of containers representing departments or workgroups.

WARNING   Rendering a strict interpretation of the hierarchical relationships between functional areas—as they are documented in an organizational chart—into a structural design for a directory tree is not necessarily an effective approach to directory design.

Unfortunately, due to the importance of partitioning for the efficient operation of NDS and the system's dependence on the physical network infrastructure and the framework provided by the NDS tree, it usually is not feasible to ignore geography when designing the directory for an organization with a large or complex network. Although it may be possible for the functional units of an organization to be closely aligned with the geographical layout of the organization's locations, such as when business units are segregated by locations, in many cases organizations are geographically dispersed and functional units within the organization are independent of geography.

When functional units of an organization are segregated to specific locations, it is possible to effectively partition a directory based on the functional model. In the other cases, for purposes of effective partitioning, it would be necessary to introduce the geographical structure of the organization into the directory design. This could be accomplished by creating containers based on geographic locations that are subordinate to containers based on functional units. For example, a marketing department that is spread across multiple locations could be represented in a directory tree as a container for the marketing department with subordinate containers for each location where the marketing function is performed. The containers based on geographic locations could hold objects representing marketing network resources for each location, and objects that are common to the marketing function could be held in the functional container at the higher level.

The drawback to the approach of deriving the design of a directory tree from the functional model is the dynamic nature of many organizations' functional structures. When changes occur to an organization's functional structure, perhaps as the result of reorganizations (which may occur routinely many times in a year in some organizations), reflecting the changes in the directory could continuously impact significant portions of the directory.

In most cases, the preferred approach for reconciling these design alternatives with the conflicting advantages and disadvantages is to divide the structural design of a directory tree into discrete physical and functional components. The physical component would be based on the geographical model and the functional component would be based on the functional model. This combination of physical and functional components would result in a directory framework consisting of two groups of container layers where the layers of containers within each group could be of arbitrary depth. The actual depth of the container layers within each group would be dependent on the size of the organization and the constraints on hierarchical container relationships imposed by requirements for effective partitioning. Later in the chapter, we cover these requirements for effective partitioning that result in limits on the number of subordinate partitions.

The highest layer of containers (closest to the root of the tree) would be the physical layer with containers representing geographic locations. The actual arrangement of containers within this layer would depend on the relationships between locations that are created by the network infrastructure. The lowest layer of containers would be the functional layer with containers representing functional units within the organization. The placement of these containers would depend on the locations of the functions they represent.

The advantage of this division of the directory tree into physical and logical components—with physical components placed at the highest level of the tree—is that it usually allows for the reasonable achievement of all of the objectives that were noted earlier. Basing the top portion of the directory tree on the organization's geography and network infrastructure allows for effective partitioning. Basing the lower portion of the directory tree on the organization's functional units provides some measure of ease of use for users and administrators by presenting a natural structure within which objects representing network resources can be located easily.

In addition, administration of security and configuration settings for groups of resources related by a common function is possible with the use of the functional model at the lower portion of the directory tree. Finally, because an organization's geographic location usually is not subject to as much change as the functional structure, the overall directory design is flexible due to the limited impact of changes that are most likely to occur in an organization.

Using Container Object Classes

Arranging container objects into a hierarchical tree structure creates the directory framework. The base NDS schema defines several object classes that can be used for container objects along with rules governing the superior and subordinate relationships that are possible between the container objects. The schema also defines rules governing allowable relationships between leaf objects and various types of containers. This section describes the available container object classes and presents guidelines for their use in creating the framework for a directory.

Root Object   Every NDS tree must possess exactly one root object that serves as the top object in the hierarchy of the inverted tree that forms the structural framework of the directory. The name of the root object serves as the name of the tree, although in most NDS utilities it is displayed simply as [Root]. The [Root] object can serve as a container for a limited range of objects, primarily including other containers such as those derived from the Country or Organization object classes.

Since [Root] is a mandatory object with a fixed location in an NDS tree, it is not of much concern to directory design except for its tree naming characteristics and the restricted range of objects that can be positioned under it. When speaking of the depth of container layers in a directory tree, [Root] is not typically thought of as a layer, although it is an object that participates fully in the directory—for inheritance purposes—in much the same way that inheritance operates for other containers. In a security context, for example, assigning certain privileges to [Root] would allow those rights to be inherited by all subordinate objects except where those rights are filtered.

There is one important difference between the ways that [Root] and other container objects interact with subordinate objects through inheritance, which is covered in Chapter 12, "NDS Security, Audit, and Control."

Country Objects   The Country (C) object class was carried over to NDS from the X.500 specifications, and its use in an NDS tree is strictly optional. The Country object is commonly used in worldwide X.500 Directories as a top-level container allowing national registration authorities to control separate portions of the directory. Public network providers such as AT&T NetWare Connect Services (NCS) have reserved the use of country objects for similar purposes.

Because Country objects are only allowed to be placed directly under [Root] in an NDS tree, their usefulness as part of the physical layer to support partitioning in large worldwide network environments is limited because Organization objects would need to be created under each Country object. The use of Country objects in this manner would be contradictory to the conventions established for X.500 Directories, where Organization objects are placed only under the Country object for the country where the organization was registered in the directory, even when the organization might operate in multiple countries. There are better approaches to using countries to geographically divide the directory structure within the physical layer of an NDS tree, such as the use of Organizational Unit objects under the single Organization object.

Early versions of NDS-based NetWare had another problem with Country objects: some utilities could not operate properly when a Country object was used in the NDS tree. The most notable problem was with the Windows NWUSER utility (that provides a client interface to certain network resources), which could not navigate the hierarchy properly when a Country object was present in the NDS tree. It is recommended that Country objects not be used due to the lack of a clear purpose for them in most network environments and the problems that can occur when they are present in an NDS tree. Because viable alternatives exist for representing countries as containers in an NDS tree, avoiding the use of Country objects likely will not lead to problems with designing an NDS tree.

NDS version 8 introduces a new container object called the Domain (DC) for compatibility with LDAP version 3. A DC can contain C, O, OU, and L containers. Use of the DC is optional, however. It is not installed in the schema with a default installation.

Organization Objects   Every NDS tree must contain at least one Organization (O) object. Organization objects are restricted to being placed only under [Root] or Country objects and typically are used as the topmost containers for all of the objects representing an organization's network resources. It is not possible to nest Organization objects by placing Organization objects under other Organization objects. In most cases, an NDS tree should contain only one Organization object. There are cases, however, when multiple Organization objects should be used instead, such as when a single NDS tree encompasses multiple independent organizations or when units within an organization operate with significant levels of independence.

In all but the smallest networks, Organization objects will serve solely as containers for subordinate Organizational Unit containers and centrally located resources that need to be accessed regularly by all users of the directory. In small network environments with only a single location, a single Organization object can be used as a container to hold all objects representing network resources without requiring the use of Organizational Units.

Organizational Unit Objects   In most cases, Organizational Unit objects will be the most common container objects used to create the structural framework for an NDS tree. Organizational Unit objects are restricted to being placed only under Organization or other Organizational Unit objects. The primary purpose of the Organizational Unit object is to serve as a container for leaf objects, although it is possible to nest Organizational Unit objects by placing Organizational Unit objects under other Organizational Unit objects.

Organizational Unit objects can be used to represent any number of geographical, functional, or other structural entities that can serve as groupings for objects within a directory. These are the design elements that should be used to define the physical and functional layers of containers. For example, the physical layer could consist of Organizational Unit objects representing each of an organization's locations under the Organization object, while the functional layer could consist of subordinate Organizational Unit objects representing functional units for each location.

Other Container Objects   The base NDS schema includes an object class definition for one additional type of container that was carried over from the X.500 specifications: the Locality (L or S) object. This object is commonly used in X.500 Directories as a qualifier or alternative to the Country object. Although the Locality object is defined in the base NDS schema, current versions of NetWare utilities for managing NDS do not support the use of this object class. Consequently, it has no relevance in NDS tree design at present. Attempts to bypass the NetWare utilities and use this object class could render the resulting tree unusable to practically every current NDS client interface and utility.

Due to the extensible nature of the NDS schema, it is possible for authorized individuals or programs to define additional NDS object classes as containers. Since common NDS client software and management utilities are not likely to support such new container objects, it is customary for people defining the new container object classes to restrict the range of objects that can be held in such containers. This restricts the use of the new container object classes so that containers derived from the classes cannot be used to significantly affect the overall directory framework. Some examples of such custom container object classes are those defined for Novell Licensing Services (NLS) and GroupWise, which are restricted so that only related leaf objects can be held in containers derived from the classes.

Partitioning the Tree

With NDS, the physical directory is created when it is initialized on the first server that is installed or migrated into a new directory tree. Assuming that the directory is not divided into partitions at this point, additional servers that are added to the directory will automatically store a copy of the entire directory (a single partition) until there is a total of three replicas, including the copy stored on the first server. As additional servers are added to the directory tree, it would be possible to manually add replicas to each of the new servers. A reason for adding replicas in this manner might be to allow directory information to be stored on servers that are spread across a large and geographically dispersed network, so that directory requests and responses would not need to travel across slower wide area network links.

The problem with this approach is that as replicas are added, there is an increase in the amount of network traffic necessary to keep the directory information stored on each server current. In addition, each server would hold an increasing amount of directory information as the size of the entire directory grows.

It is difficult to imagine that this could be an efficient arrangement, because the amount of network traffic crossing wide area network links for replication could be greater than or equivalent to the amount of network traffic for directory requests and responses traveling over the same wide area network links without replication. Because both options in this scenario have significant drawbacks, these unattractive trade-offs could limit the scalability of NDS were it not for the ability to partition the directory.

The Benefits of Partitioning

Partitioning allows the directory to be physically divided into smaller portions (partitions) that can be located together or separately on systems throughout the network. Strategic placement of these partitions can significantly decrease the amount of network traffic needed for directory requests and responses crossing wide area network links that might otherwise be necessary in a network with a large centralized directory. Decreasing the amount of network traffic is accomplished by placing each portion of the directory closest to the users or systems that will use that information most often. The partitioned directory still appears as a unified whole through the inclusion of mechanisms that allow seamless access to information in other portions of the directory when necessary.

An additional benefit of partitioning is that it can be used to limit the amount of information that any single server needs to manage, since the entire directory can be divided among multiple servers. This allows the directory to grow to an arbitrarily large size while stored on multiple servers, without imposing significant additional resource requirements on the configurations for those servers beyond the normal server requirements. Without partitioning, the only alternative in a network environment with a universal directory would be to use specialized servers to house a large directory.

Partitioning as a Subtractive Process

Partitioning is a physical strategy for optimizing directory operations that involves placing defined portions of the physical directory on servers located throughout the network. Establishment of partitions, though, is dependent on the structural framework of the hierarchical directory tree, since partitions are defined in terms of container objects. Partitioning is best thought of as a subtractive process, which means that the creation of a new partition is accomplished by separating a subtree from the portion of the tree contained within an existing partition. A partition can also be merged with its parent partition at any point in time. These two partition operations are referred to in NDS terminology as *split* and *join* operations, respectively.

Every partition must hold a single root container object (referred to as the *partition root*), and the name of this container object serves as the name of the partition. This container object, acting as the root object of a container, keeps a pointer to its parent container in order to preserve the continuity of the tree's hierarchy. A partition can contain only a single root object as defined by the hierarchy, so it is *not* possible for a partition to be defined in terms of two container objects at the same level in the directory tree. This is demonstrated in Figure 8.1, where a proper partition scheme is displayed on the left and an improper one on the right. When a partition is established, all objects (including containers) that are subordinate to the container object serving as

FIGURE 8.1

Establishing partitions within the directory hierarchy

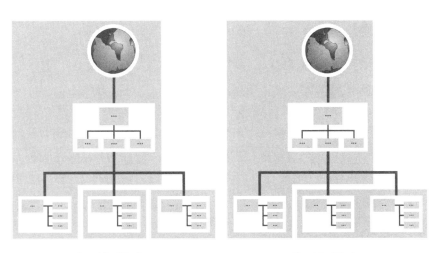

Legal Partitioning   Illegal Partitioning

the root of the partition are contained in the new partition, at least until further partitions are established based on subordinate containers.

If the structural framework for a directory tree is specified in a manner consistent with the recommendations that were outlined in the previous stage, the resulting framework likely will be suitable for effective partitioning due to the influence of partitioning requirements on the structural design process.

At this point, all that remains for partitioning is to determine where the partitions actually need to be established and to fine-tune the structural design to better accommodate partitioning. Geography and object counts are the factors that should contribute most to partitioning decisions within a given directory framework. The requirement for fine-tuning the structural design of the directory tree is the result of practical restrictions on the hierarchical relationships between superior and subordinate partitions that have been identified as contributing to the efficient operation of a partitioned directory.

Planning for Partition Placement

To plan for the placement of partitions in a directory, it is best to work with the directory framework that was designed in the previous stage, beginning with the assumption that a single partition encompasses the entire directory. The specification for the directory framework should include sufficient information so that it is possible to ascertain the following factors that are relevant to partitioning:

- Geographical locations associated with containers
- Planned locations for server objects in the directory tree
- Timetables for the deployment of servers
- Estimates of the number of leaf objects that each container could hold

There are three partition design elements that should be evaluated when deciding whether a container object and its subtree should be separated out into a partition: operational efficiency of the directory, security of information in the physical directory database, and the number of objects contained within a partition. The process for determining the layout of partitions within the structural framework of a directory tree involves evaluating each element to determine the points in the tree where partitions should be established. The best way to approach this is to work through the structural framework of the directory tree, working from the top of the tree in three passes—each addressing one of the design elements.

Efficient Operation   Establish partitions to allow for the most efficient operation of the directory by minimizing the amount of NDS network traffic traveling across wide area network links. Because such traffic will occur due to directory requests and responses as well as replication, determining the most effective layout of partitions within the structural framework requires balancing the competing interests of local access to directory information and traffic minimization. If only a single organization object has been used to reflect the organization, it should not be necessary to separate that container into its own partition. If multiple organization objects were used, each container that reflects a separate geographical location might need to be separated into its own partition. Organizational unit objects that might exist below an organization object should be evaluated in the same way to determine whether they should be separated into their own partitions.

A partition should be established only if doing so would improve the operational efficiency of the directory. Although it is advisable to plan for future partitioning (this is the purpose of this design stage), it is not necessary to actually establish the planned partitions until they are needed.

Security of Information   Establish partitions to allow for the security of directory information in the contents of the physical directory database that makes up a partition. Since the portion of the directory database that is contained in a partition is stored in its entirety on at least one server, all the information in that partition can be accessed or modified by any individual or program with access to that server's console, without any further authentication. This leads to the requirement that directory information be stored only on those servers where access to the server console is controlled adequately. The impact of this requirement on partitioning is that containers representing separate administrative units, or containers that are controlled by separate administrative authorities, should be divided into separate partitions.

Limit Number of Objects   Establish partitions to ensure that the number of objects contained within a partition remains manageable. This allows normal server resources to be employed to house partition replicas. An excessive number of objects within a partition could interfere with replication, while introducing additional resource requirements on servers that will house replicas of large partitions. Any partitions that could contain more than 4,000 to 5,000 objects should be divided into several smaller partitions, if possible. Implementation of NDS version 8, with a new database structure, should make possible the ability to store up to 38,000 objects per partition without impeding replication. Of course, this will require additional resources—memory and disk space—on servers holding replicas of these large partitions.

Finalize Partition Placement

Once these passes are completed, the structural design of the directory tree should be re-evaluated to make sure that the proposed layout of partitions can be implemented within some of the physical constraints that have been identified in the operational behavior of a partitioned and replicated NDS tree. These constraints have led to recommendations by Novell for limits on the number of subordinate partitions of any given partition, as well as limits on the number of objects that should be contained within a partition. The general guidelines call for limits of 10 to 15 subordinate partitions and between 4,000 to 5,000 objects for a partition. In cases where the initial structural design of the directory led to violations of these guidelines as a result of the previous partitioning steps, the following options for modifying the directory framework should be considered:

- When a partition could have more than 10 to 15 subordinate partitions, additional containers and partitions should be added to allow for grouping of subordinate partitions to satisfy the guideline. For example, when separate geographical locations lead to requirements for more than 10 to 15 subordinate partitions below a container, an additional layer of regional containers with associated partitions could be added. This would allow for the grouping of containers for geographical locations so that each regional container would have no more than 10 to 15 subordinate partitions.

- When a container object could have more than 4,000 to 5,000 directly subordinate objects, it should be divided into multiple containers with fewer objects, if possible, to allow for the creation of partitions that satisfy the guideline for the number of objects within a partition. Note that this requirement is lifted with NDS version 8.

Providing for Future Growth

The initial structural design of a directory tree usually provides a framework for growth over a period of time. The layout of partitions established in this design stage is meant merely to ensure that the fully deployed directory can be partitioned to optimize operational efficiency. The tree itself will be constructed as servers are added to the network and as objects are added to the directory. At any point in time during the ongoing construction of the directory, the actual layout of partitions that are established will often differ from the original design.

When determining how to establish partitions, the requirements for current operations—rather than plans for future growth—should be the sole determinant. This partition design step is important, however, because it allows for modeling within a given structure to assess whether it can be partitioned in an effective manner within the constraints that have been identified for NDS.

Replicating Partitions

Novell Directory Services replication is the process by which physical copies of partitions stored on multiple servers are kept in a consistent state. Objects and their properties within partition replicas are updated individually as changes occur. The physical copies of the partitions remain in a loosely consistent state as long as the servers holding replicas are able to communicate. The consistency maintained among partitions via replication is loose in the sense that copies of objects and properties contained within a partition's replicas are identical in most cases, except for transient conditions where updates to objects or properties might not have been propagated to all replicas.

The NDS replication process generates ongoing network traffic due to the communication between servers that is necessary to keep the contents of a distributed partition consistent. The amount of network traffic generated by replication depends on the size of the partition being replicated and the number of changes that occur to objects and their properties within the partition.

As replicas are added for a partition, the overall level of network traffic required in order to maintain consistency increases, because all replicas are generally updated soon after changes to objects and their properties occur. In environments with slower wide area network links between locations, replica placement can have a significant impact on the levels of traffic traveling over these links. For example, the replication traffic required for a partition that has replicas separated by slower wide area network links would have a greater impact on network traffic levels than it would if its replicas were separated by faster network links. This is due to the higher cost of wide area network traffic when compared with traffic over local network links.

NDS replication traffic can be characterized as management traffic that is similar in nature, although typically greater in scope, to traffic required by routing protocols or naming services such as SAP (Service Advertising Protocol). Network managers typically expend a great deal of effort to minimize management traffic that travels over slower wide area network links because excessive levels of such traffic can crowd out normal data communications.

When wide area network links are congested, the quality of the links can deteriorate in a way that causes delays in the propagation of changes. With NDS, this can translate directly into a negative impact on the consistency of information within affected partitions. In some cases, this lack of consistency can become so severe that NDS cannot recover to a sufficiently consistent state.

Types of Replicas

NDS provides three types of full replicas that can be placed on servers: Master, Read/Write, and Read-Only replicas. Another type of replica, the Subordinate Reference replica, is not considered to be a full replica since it does not contain an entire copy of the partition. NDS version 8 introduces another replica type, called a Virtual Replica, used by the dirXML technology. Chapter 5, "Replication and Partitioning," provides more information about this subject.

- The **Master replica** is the first replica created for a partition and is required for every partition. There can only be one Master replica for each partition, and it is possible to access information contained in a Master replica for reading and writing. When split and join operations are initiated for partitions, the servers containing Master replicas are responsible for performing the operations.

- **Read/Write replicas** are similar to Master replicas in the sense that it is possible to access information contained in a Read/Write replica for both reading and writing, but servers holding a Read/Write replica of a partition do not have any responsibility for performing split and join operations. It is possible to have more than one Read/Write replica of a partition. This will be the most common type of replica used in an NDS tree.

- **Read-Only replicas** hold the same directory information as Master and Read/Write replicas, but the information contained in a Read-Only replica is only available to be accessed for reading. Just as with Read/Write replicas, it is possible to have more than one Read-Only replica of a partition, but the usefulness of Read-Only replicas is limited in most cases in NDS. For example, user authentication requires a writable replica, since certain properties need to be updated at authentication time. Consequently, it is likely that Read-Only replicas would not be used in most NDS trees.

- **Subordinate Reference replicas** are created automatically, when necessary, by NDS to ensure namespace continuity to allow for tree walking. Subordinate Reference replicas serve as pointers to replicas for subordinate partitions residing on other servers when replicas of those partitions do not exist on servers where replicas of the parent partitions exist.

- **Virtual replicas** (NDS version 8 and higher) can maintain a filtered subset of information from any directory or application. Using XML (eXtensible Markup Language), LDAP, and XSLT (XML Style Sheets), pointers to data in other directory systems (or even other NDS trees) can be maintained within an NDS partition. See Chapter 18 for more on this exciting new technology.

When determining the servers where replicas will need to be placed, it is necessary to specify the type of replica that should be placed on each server. Each partition needs at least one replica (a Master replica) stored on a server in the NDS tree. All other replica types for partitions need to be either Read/Write or Read-Only.

The Purposes of Replication

Replication of the contents of NDS partitions typically serves three purposes: providing fault tolerance for directory information, improving the quality of service, and supporting bindery services. This is done in the following ways:

- Replication provides fault tolerance for directory information by storing multiple copies of a partition on separate servers, so that if a server containing directory information were to become unavailable due to a server or communications failure, the information would still be available from other servers.

It is important to note that replication of partitions in NDS for fault tolerance has no effect on other information, such as files that might be stored on a server. Only objects and their properties contained in a given partition are replicated.

- The quality of service can be improved through replication by allowing copies of partitions to be strategically located close to users who will be accessing the information within a partition, while also allowing multiple servers containing replicas to share the load of handling user requests. There may be other cases where it is necessary to place a replica on a server to support a directory-intensive service or an application running on a server.

- Support for bindery services requires that writable replicas of partitions holding containers that will be used for bindery services on a server be present on that server. Other applications or services running on a server may impose similar requirements.

Determining How Partitions Are Replicated

The process of determining how partitions should be replicated in an NDS networking environment requires consideration of each of the above purposes for replication. You should also consider the impact of replication on network traffic and partition stability. The following guidelines are useful for such purposes:

- In most cases, partitions should not be replicated across slower wide area network links, so that replication traffic would not be required to travel across such links. Adhering to this guideline has a positive impact on the stability of partitions because it eliminates traffic congestion or communication problems (which are more common with slower wide area network links than with local network links) that can lead to replication problems. This is not an absolute rule, since there are many possible cases where placement of replicas on servers separated by wide area network links could be advisable for fault tolerance, performance, or traffic management reasons.

- The number of full replicas (Master, Read/Write, and Read-Only) for each partition should be minimized so that the total amount of replication traffic necessary to maintain the consistency of the partition can be reduced. A common suggestion is that a partition should have no more than 10 full replicas. The reasoning behind this guideline is that when a change occurs to an object or its property in one replica, the change must eventually be replicated to all other servers. This requires that the server that holds the replica where the change occurred contact all other servers that hold full replicas of that partition to replicate the changes. It is often necessary, as well, to contact all servers holding replicas (including those holding Subordinate Reference replicas) to update timestamps. Each replica that is added for a partition increases the amount of traffic required for maintaining the consistency of the partition. For many partition operations, each server in the replica list needs to contact all of the other servers in the list, which means that the more replicas of a partition there are, the more slowly partition operations will occur.

- Except in cases where a server will be dedicated for the purpose of storing replicas, the number of full replicas held on a server should be minimized. The common suggestion is that a server should hold no more than 15 full replicas, although this number is highly dependent on the processing power, network card performance, and disk controller performance of the server. The number of changes that occur within the partitions for which replicas will be held on the server should also be considered. The reasoning behind this guideline is that since all servers holding replicas of a partition need to be contacted when a change occurs to an object or its properties within the partition, holding replicas for too many partitions could overwhelm a server and keep it from performing other operations. This could also have a negative impact on partition consistency or stability, since a server could be too busy with other activities to keep all of its replicas up-to-date.

- In order to optimize partition operations in cases where a server is dedicated for the purpose of holding replicas, Master replicas should be stored on the dedicated replica server so that the partition operations can be performed as efficiently as possible.

Prioritizing Replication

In order to balance these constraints with the actual purposes for replication, it is advisable that the purposes for replication are considered in prioritized steps based on the relative inflexibility of each of the replica placement requirements. This means that situations requiring a replica, such as bindery services, should be given highest priority, and the other purposes, such as quality of service and fault tolerance, should follow.

- Determine the bindery contexts necessary for each server requiring bindery services. These servers should then be designated to hold either Master or Read/Write replicas for all of the partitions that encompass containers included in the bindery contexts. If bindery services requirements lead to an excessive number of replicas for a partition (based on the suggested guidelines), strong consideration should be given to splitting the partition, if possible, to reduce the number of replicas for each partition. This might require dividing a container encompassed by a partition into multiple containers in order to facilitate splitting a partition to reduce the number of replicas for each partition.

It is important to remember that bindery services are not required for every server. Bindery services were intended to serve a transitional role as organizations migrated from bindery servers to NDS servers.

- Patterns of usage of directory information, as well as the intensity of that usage, should be analyzed to determine whether replicas should be placed on certain servers to improve quality of service for access to directory information.

- For fault tolerance purposes, each partition should have at least three replicas in most cases. Any more than three replicas are superfluous when used strictly for fault tolerance, since three replicas are usually sufficient for such purposes. In cases where considerations for fault tolerance would require placement of replicas on servers separated by slower wide area network links, such as for locations with only a single server, the normal guideline calling for at least three replicas for fault tolerance probably can be ignored. Instead, to minimize the amount of replication traffic traveling across slower wide area network links, only two replicas should be used. In such cases, the second replica should be placed on a server that is close to the primary server.

An additional factor that should be considered when placing replicas on servers is physical security, because physical access to a server holding a replica could allow normal access control mechanisms to be bypassed so that the information contained in any replicas stored on the server could be modified. For example, a user accessing a server console would be able to create (using readily available third-party utilities) administrative accounts in any of the containers encompassed by partitions for which replicas are stored on the server. Replicas should not be placed on any servers that are not protected from unauthorized physical access.

Once full replicas have been assigned to servers, it is possible to forecast the servers where Subordinate Reference replicas will be placed. NDS automatically places Subordinate Reference replicas of partitions on servers that do not hold a full replica of the partition, while holding a full replica of the parent partition. Because Subordinate Reference replicas contain only one object, the root container object of the partition, they are not relevant when considering replica counts for fault tolerance and communications efficiency. The point at which the placement of Subordinate Reference replicas is important is when partition split and join operations are performed or when tree walking needs to occur.

Use of Leaf Object Classes

The final activity required when designing an NDS tree is to develop guidelines for the use of NDS object classes, instances that will populate the containers used to establish the hierarchical structure of the directory tree. The reason for specifying object usage guidelines as part of the directory design process is to allow for uniformity in the ways that network resources are represented and located in the directory.

The following items discuss many of the object classes that are available with the base NDS schema for representing network resources that will be accessed by users of the directory. Other object classes are available in the base NDS schema as well as being available through extensions to the schema—all object types that will be used should be addressed in the guidelines. Discussion of how instances of the object classes should be named, along with recommendations for the usage of the objects' associated properties, is reserved for the next chapter.

User Objects

Often, one of the primary purposes of a directory is to allow human users to access information about other users, as well as to provide information required for the operation of security services. For this reason, the User object is likely to be the most common type of object used in NDS trees. It is important that the many potential roles of the User object in the operations of the directory be recognized at this stage in the design process so as to allow the several requirements for this object class to be documented. The User objects could have any of the following roles:

- Accessing NetWare file and print resources, access to which is controlled at the user level by the NDS security mechanisms

- Accessing electronic mail services, access to which could be controlled at the user level by the NDS security mechanisms

- Holding information about individuals within the organization, such as phone numbers or electronic mail addresses, in a centralized repository

- Providing a single point of user administration for other directories such as Windows NT domains or the UNIX Network Information System (NIS)

It is possible for a given User object to be used for any one or more of these (or other) purposes, and the existence of a User object should not imply any single role. For example, it makes sense that all employees in an organization would be represented as User objects in an organizational NDS tree so as to provide a single point of information about the employees, but all these individuals might not need to access NetWare file and print resources. In this case, the security services provided by NDS for the file and print resources should be used to limit access to the resources by only the authorized subset of User objects.

The definition of the User object in the base NDS schema contains properties that are applicable to many possible roles for the User object. For example, the User object contains phone and fax number properties for informational purposes as well as a variety of NDS security-related properties. Just as with any other NDS object class, it is possible to add additional properties to the User object to serve purposes specific to an organization's requirements.

When an NDS tree is first created, a single user object called Admin is created that has supervisory privileges to the entire NDS tree by means of its supervisory rights to the [Root] object. This User object has no special characteristics beyond its default privileges, and the object can be removed and its rights can be modified or filtered in the same way as is possible for any other User object. In fact, it is possible to modify rights for all User objects in the directory tree in such a way that no object will have sufficient rights to perform administration tasks, so great care must be taken to preserve administrative capabilities for at least one User object when modifying rights.

User objects can be created under any of the base container objects, except for [Root] or Country objects. Using a bit of circular logic, User objects should be placed in containers so that the users they represent can easily access resources that are "close," just as resources should be placed in containers so they are easily accessible by the users that will use them most often. It is also helpful for User objects that are likely to need to be administered in a consistent fashion to be grouped together in containers to allow for use of the directory hierarchy for administrative grouping.

Template Objects

The version of NDS provided with NetWare 4.11 introduced the Template object class as a means of providing a default set of property values and security settings for the creation of User objects. This method replaced the special User object (called USER_TEMPLATE) that played a similar role for previous versions of NDS. The main difference between the Template object class and the USER_TEMPLATE User object is that multiple Template objects can be created to provide different sets of defaults for the creation of User objects that depend on the Template object identified when the User object is created. When using the special USER_TEMPLATE User object, only one set of defaults is available for objects created in a given container. Another limitation of the USER_TEMPLATE object was that it was a normal user object, and as such could present a security hole if it was defined to have excessive rights.

Group Objects

Group objects are used in NDS to allow User objects to be grouped together for administrative purposes in a different manner than is possible by using containers and the hierarchical structure of the NDS tree. A Group object defines multivalued Membership and Security Equivalence properties that can contain the names of User objects identified as members of the group represented by the object. A Group object cannot identify other Group objects as members of the group. Once a group is created it can be used in many of the same situations where User or container objects would be used, with the operations applying to all User objects that are identified as security equivalent to the Group object. For example, assigning a security privilege to a Group object would extend the privilege to all User objects identified as security equivalent to the Group object as long as the privilege is not otherwise overridden in some way.

One of the common uses for Group objects is for determining environmental setup options, such as drive mappings or print queue connections during login script processing under NetWare. Through inclusion of membership tests via the IF MEMBER OF operator in a NetWare login script, certain operations can be performed for any user who is defined as a member of the specified group. Each time such a test occurs, the group membership list is parsed until all members have been tested or until a match occurs. When such membership tests occur, the list is searched sequentially for each item in the list, since only a single member is returned with each query. When large groups used for login script processing are not contained in a local replica, such tests could generate significant network traffic. For this reason, User objects should not be identified as members for Group objects that are contained in other replicas.

Organizational Role Objects

The Organizational Role object is similar to the Group object in that it possesses multivalued Occupant and Security Equivalence properties that can contain the names of User objects identified as occupants of the organizational role represented by the object. The primary use for an Organization Role object is to allow User objects to derive special privileges or status through occupancy of the role. For example, an organizational role could be created with administrator privileges so that occupants of the role can perform administrative functions without requiring that the necessary set of privileges be granted to the User objects themselves. Usage of the Organizational Role object is usually limited to such functions since it cannot be referenced by the IF MEMBER OF operator in NetWare login scripts.

Profile Objects

Profile objects provide an alternative to using group membership and the IF MEMBER OF operator in NetWare login scripts for determining environmental setup options such as drive mappings or print queues for users. The base schema definition for the Profile object class includes a stream Login Script property that can include commands to be executed during login script processing for a user that has been assigned the profile. A Profile object can be assigned to a User object by adding its name to the single-valued Profile property associated with the User object.

A user can be assigned only one profile, although many users can share the same profile. This allows for environmental setup options to be associated with a group of users in a manner similar to what might occur if NetWare clients recognized Login Script properties that could be added to Group or Organizational Role objects. Security equivalence between a User and a Profile object is not established when a profile is assigned to a user. Because of this, the Profile object typically is not used in a similar manner as a Group or Organizational Role object, although it is possible to manually establish a security equivalence between User and Profile objects. If security equivalence were added manually, it would be possible for a User object to derive rights from those granted to a Profile object.

NCP Server Objects

The NCP Server object class in NDS is used for objects representing NCP (NetWare Core Protocol) servers as NDS objects. When an NDS server is installed into an NDS tree, an NCP Server object is created with the name that was given to the server. At server installation time, it is necessary to choose a location in the directory tree where the Server object should be placed. As was mentioned earlier when discussing User objects, a resource such as a file server should have its object placed in the directory tree in a position that is convenient for most of the users that will access its services. Since it is not necessary for a server to hold a replica of the partition that encompasses the container holding its object, partitioning and replication considerations do not need to play a role in determining the location in the directory tree for a Server object.

An interesting property of the NCP Server object class is that it can be used for objects representing any type of NCP server. This allows an administrator to create NCP Server objects for non-NDS NetWare servers, such as those running NetWare 3.12, or machines with NetWare-compatible file services (such as Windows 95 or Windows NT machines running Microsoft's File and Print Services for NetWare). A reason for doing this could be to allow users to locate services running on non-NDS NCP servers by browsing the NDS tree.

Volume Objects

The Volume object class is used to represent volumes that exist on NCP servers as NDS objects. When an NDS server is installed into an NDS tree, Volume objects are created in the same container that holds the associated Server object for each of the volumes mounted on the server. By default, the name given to a Volume object consists of the server name followed by an underscore and the name of the volume. Once created, it is not necessary for a volume object to reside in the same container as its associated Server object, although that is normally the convention. Just like NCP Server objects, Volume objects should be placed in the directory tree in a position that is convenient for most of the users that will access its files.

The Volume object class possesses the same interesting property as NCP Server objects in that it can be used for objects representing any type of volume on an NCP server. This allows an administrator to create Volume objects installed on non-NDS servers such as those running NetWare 3.12 or machines with NetWare-compatible file services. A reason for doing this could be to allow users to locate volumes that are installed on non-NDS NCP servers by browsing the NDS tree.

Directory Map Objects

The Directory Map object class allows objects to be created that point to directories on NCP server volumes. This provides some measure of physical independence for providing access to directories, since users do not need to know the physical server or volume that contains a directory represented by a Directory Map object. If files stored in a directory represented by a Directory Map object are moved to a directory on a different server or volume, only the pointer in the Directory Map object needs to be changed in order to allow users to continue accessing the files through the Directory Map object. When Directory Map objects are not used, it is necessary to inform users and change references in login scripts in order to allow users to continue accessing the files that have been moved.

> A Directory Map object is not intended to provide users with rights to access the files in the directory that the object points to. It is possible to make a Directory Map object a trustee of a directory, but doing so does not provide users with equivalent privileges unless the users are made security equivalent to the Directory Map object.

Due to their usefulness, Directory Map objects should be used liberally to represent directories that users are likely to MAP drives to in login scripts or by browsing through the NDS tree. Just like other objects representing network resources, Directory Map objects should be placed in the Directory tree in a position that is convenient for most of the users that will use them. It is possible for multiple Directory Map objects to point to the same directory, which could allow such objects to be placed in multiple containers to provide easy access for users. In the event that a directory represented by multiple Directory Map objects is moved to another server or volume, all Directory Objects pointing to the directory would need to be updated. In order to eliminate this extra maintenance, aliases (described later) of a single Directory Map object could be used instead of multiple identical objects.

Print Queue Objects

The Print Queue object class is used to represent NDS print queues on NetWare servers as NDS objects. Although a print queue is associated with a server that is represented by a Server object, it is not necessary for the location in the directory tree of a Print Queue object to have any relation to the location of a Server object. As is the case with other objects representing network resources, a Print Queue object should be placed in the directory tree in a position that is convenient for most of the users that will use it for printing.

The NetWare printing model connects print queues to printers, which allows multiple print queues to feed a single printer. The typical reason for creating multiple print queues is to assign different levels of priority to print jobs that are submitted for a printer. This capability, however, could allow for the creation of multiple Print Queue objects, at different locations in a directory tree, that feed a single printer to provide convenient access to Print Queue objects for multiple users. Another option for providing easy access to Print Queue objects for users in different containers is to use aliases.

Printer Objects

The Printer object class in NDS is used for objects representing printers that are capable of accepting print jobs from NDS print queues. It is possible for a printer to be a stand-alone device or to be connected to a NetWare server. In order to print jobs submitted by users, the Printer object must be associated with at least one Print Queue object. There is no need for the Printer object to be associated with a Server object, so a Printer object can be located at any position in a directory tree that would be convenient for the users that will use the printer most often. NetWare users can connect to a Printer object in the same way that they can connect to a Print Queue object, so convenient placement of the Printer object can ease the process of locating printing resources for users.

Print Server Objects

The Print Server object class is used for objects representing the agents that handle the process of monitoring print queues and feeding print jobs to the appropriate printers. A Print Server object will be assigned one or more Printer objects and the print server agent software will determine the print queues that must be monitored from the Printer object definitions. Users will almost never have any need to access Print Server objects, so in determining where such objects should be located in a directory tree you should primarily consider the convenience of those responsible for administering the Print Server object definition.

Alias Objects

Alias objects are not necessarily leaf objects, but then again they are not container objects either. Instead, an Alias object acts as a pointer to another real object, either a container or a leaf object, within a directory tree to allow a single object to be referred to by more than one name. Using Alias objects can increase the effort required to administer objects, so aliases should be used cautiously. A common use for Alias objects is to allow objects representing resources to appear to be located at multiple positions in a directory tree so that users can have convenient access to them.

Some organizations have placed Alias objects associated with User objects in a single container in order to facilitate a contextless login capability. This type of strategy is not recommended, since it increases the effort required to administer accounts and leads to inefficient NDS operation.

Design Scenarios

This section presents examples of how the NDS design guidelines that have been presented in this chapter can be applied in a variety of situations. Several common organizational scenarios are discussed and NDS tree designs that satisfy the objectives for the guidelines are presented. In all cases when discussing design scenarios, it is assumed that the organization has decided to take full advantage of NDS by implementing a single NDS tree encompassing the entire organization.

An Organization with a Single Location

Little or no design is necessary to accommodate small organizations with a single location and no wide area network links. In most cases, the default framework suggested by the "simple" NDS installation routine, shown in Figure 8.2, would be sufficient. This installation routine creates a tree with a single Organization object at the top. At least three objects are created in the O-level container: the Server object for the server where NDS is being installed; Volume objects for each volume that is mounted on the server; and a User object named Admin that has full supervisory rights to the [Root] object.

There is no more than one location, so it is not necessary to expend any design effort for containers at the physical layer because the single Organization object would make up the entire physical layer. Additional containers could be added as Organizational Unit objects that would be subordinate to the Organization object in order to allow for the logical grouping of users with resources. This would be advisable in cases where operational units or workgroups have dedicated resources, such as departments with their own servers that do not need to be accessed regularly by users in other departments. At this point in the design process, containers should be added only

FIGURE 8.2
Default NDS tree
design

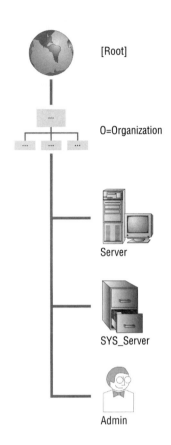

FIGURE 8.3
An organization with a
single location and
multiple departmental
containers

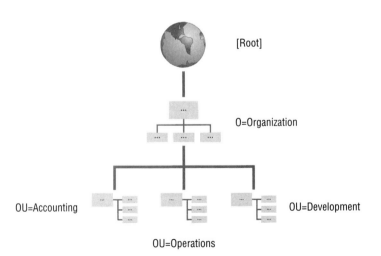

if they will ease administration or access to resources for users. A single layer of OU-level containers could be added beneath the Organization object for this purpose, as illustrated in Figure 8.3.

Determining how the directory should be partitioned will depend on the number of objects in the directory. If the directory will contain fewer than 5,000 objects, partitioning should not be necessary. If it is expected to contain more than 4,000 objects, attempts should be made to separate some containers into separate partitions so that no single partition will contain more than 5,000 objects. Although it is feasible for a partition to contain up to 5,000 objects, partitions should be limited to 4,000 objects at this point in the design process in order to account for the potential of unexpected growth. If you are using NDS version 8 (shipped with NetWare 5.1), you can safely double these numbers.

In order to determine where containers should be separated into partitions, it is necessary to determine the number of objects that each container will hold. Beginning with the assumption that the entire directory is encompassed by a single [Root] partition, the largest containers should be separated into their own partitions until all partitions contain fewer than 4,000 objects (8,000 with NDS v8). If a single container could hold more than 4,000 objects, methods to divide the container into multiple containers at the same level or below the container should be investigated. Expanding on the directory framework from the previous example, a partition could be established as shown in Figure 8.4. Recall that partitioning is a subtractive process and that a partition requires a single container object to act as the partition root.

As long as this process results in no more than 10 subordinate partitions for any partition, no additional modifications should be necessary for the structural framework of the directory. If more than 10 subordinate partitions are specified for a partition, it would be necessary to evaluate alternative designs for the structural framework of the directory, such as the addition of a layer of grouping containers, to limit the number of subordinate partitions for any given partition.

Once partitions with reasonable sizes have been established—even if the directory is not separated into multiple partitions—it is necessary to determine the placement of replicas on servers. The best way to analyze replica placement is to create a matrix in a spreadsheet program that contains a row for each server and columns for the bindery contexts and partitions. An example of an empty matrix based on the previous examples is shown in Table 8.1. Each of the columns under the partitions should be used to list the type of replica that would be held on the server for each given row.

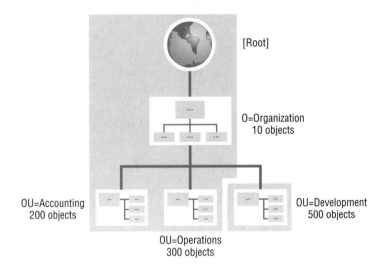

FIGURE 8.4

Separating a large container into a separate partition

[Root]

O=Organization
10 objects

OU=Accounting
200 objects

OU=Operations
300 objects

OU=Development
500 objects

TABLE 8.1: Sample Empty Matrix

Servers	Bindery Context	[Root]	Development.Organization
SERVER1	Accounting.Organization		
SERVER2	Accounting.Organization		
SERVER3			
SERVER4	Operations.Organization		
SERVER5	Operations.Organization		
SERVER6	Development.Organization		
SERVER7	Development.Organization		
SERVER8			
SERVER9	Development.Organization		

Because this scenario covers an organization with a single location, there are no wide area network links that could constrain replication decisions. Requirements for bindery services should be given the highest priority since all servers requiring bindery services must hold replicas of all partitions that encompass containers in the server's bindery context. Recall that bindery services are not required for all servers, so the necessity for bindery services should be carefully considered. The only types of replicas that should normally be used are Master and Read/Write replicas, with the Master replica placed on the most powerful of the servers that will hold replicas for a given partition.

When placing replicas using the matrix, Subordinate References should be tracked as well. An example of replica placement is presented in matrix form in Table 8.2.

T A B L E 8.2: An Example of Replica Placement

Servers	Bindery Context	[Root]	Development.Organization
SERVER1	Accounting.Organization	Master	Subordinate
SERVER2	Accounting.Organization	Read/ Write	Subordinate
SERVER3			
SERVER4	Operations.Organization	Read/ Write	Subordinate
SERVER5	Operations.Organization	Read/ Write	Subordinate
SERVER6	Development.Organization		Read/Write
SERVER7	Development.Organization		Master
SERVER8			
SERVER9	Development.Organization		Read/Write

If satisfying requirements for bindery services results in the placement of more than 10 full replicas on servers for any given partition, the directory should be divided further into partitions, if possible, until all bindery services requirements can be satisfied with fewer than 10 replicas for each partition.

Once bindery services requirements have been satisfied, it may be necessary to place replicas on additional servers for fault tolerance if there are any partitions with fewer than three full replicas. If additional replicas are required for fault tolerance, the additional replicas should be placed on servers in such a way that the quality of service would be improved or the number of Subordinate References would be minimized. One suggestion for placing replicas to improve quality of service could be to place replicas on servers that users are most likely to connect to (such as servers with user home directories) in order to minimize the number of additional connections required for users.

The final step in the design process is to establish organizational guidelines for object usage. There are no special considerations for this step that depend on the type of organization. Once this is completed, the design process is complete, resulting in a graphical diagram of the structural framework for the directory with partitions documented and a matrix of replicas for servers and partitions.

This documentation should then be used to provide guidance for the installation of servers and objects into the directory. While servers and objects are being installed into the directory, the structural framework for the directory should remain consistent, although the actual partitions and replicas should be established to reflect the current operational situation. When requirements change, the design should be modified to reflect the changes.

A Centralized Organization with Multiple Locations

Organizations with multiple locations introduce additional complexity to the NDS design process since it is necessary to consider the effects of wide area network links at most stages of the design process. This section discusses the simplest scenario involving an organization with multiple locations with a single central location that might serve as a hub for network communications. The following two sections discuss more complex scenarios involving organizations that do not have a single central location that could be considered a hub.

In order to provide a consistent example to illustrate the design process for this scenario, we'll use an organization with the following characteristics:

- The organization has six locations scattered throughout the United States. Its headquarters is in Chicago and the other offices supporting regional operations are in Los Angeles, Dallas, Atlanta, New York, and Seattle. All operations are coordinated out of the headquarters office in Chicago.

- All regional offices are connected to headquarters via point-to-point links that are significantly slower than local network links. Other characteristics of the links are not important for this example, as they could consist of leased lines, virtual circuits through a frame relay network, or a Virtual Private Network (VPN) over the public internet.

- Operational functions such as Accounting, Manufacturing, Research, and Development are located in various cities and are not necessarily dedicated to any given location.

The first step in designing the directory for this organization would be to establish the physical layer of containers. Since the organization acts as a single entity, a single Organization object should be created under [Root] to represent the organization. Due to the presence of wide area network links between offices, each office should be represented by its own containers in order to allow for effective partitioning by minimizing the amount of replication traffic required to cross wide area network links. This is best accomplished by creating Organizational Unit objects for each location directly below the Organization object, as illustrated in Figure 8.5.

FIGURE 8.5

The physical layer of containers for an organization with multiple locations

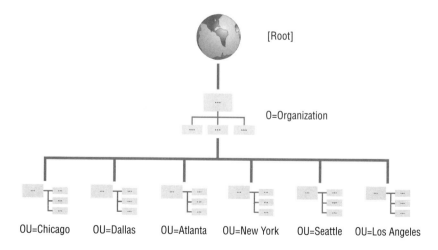

Once the design of the physical layer of containers has been established, the design of the functional layer of containers can proceed. At this point, each location can be analyzed as if it were an independent organization with a single location—similar to the previous scenario with each location's Organizational Unit serving as the root container for the location. Additional containers could be added as Organizational Unit objects that would be subordinate to each location's Organizational Unit object in order to allow for the logical grouping of users with resources. At this point in the design process, containers should be added only if they will ease administration or access to resources for users.

Due to the presence of wide area network links, partitioning likely would be necessary to allow for efficient communications, even when the entire directory will contain fewer than 1,000 objects. The minimum partitioning required would be to separate each location's container into a partition so as to minimize the number of objects that would be replicated across the slower wide area network links. This is illustrated in Figure 8.6.

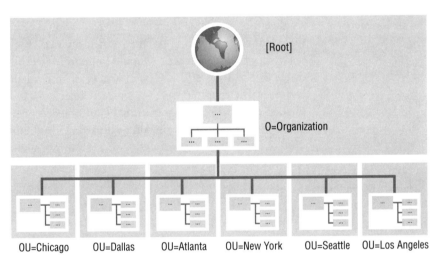

OU=Chicago OU=Dallas OU=Atlanta OU=New York OU=Seattle OU=Los Angeles

Once the containers for locations are separated into partitions, each of these partitions should be analyzed in the manner that was illustrated in the previous scenario. This means ensuring that each partition will contain fewer than 4,000 (for versions of NDS less than version 8) objects and separating subordinate containers into their own partitions when this is not the case.

Notice that the purposes of partitioning differ for the physical and functional layers of the tree—communication drives partitioning of the physical layer, and partition size drives partitioning of the functional layer.

As long as the partitioning process results in no more than 10 subordinate partitions for any partition, no modifications should be necessary for the structural framework of the directory beyond those required for achieving reasonable partition sizes. In the event that more than 10 subordinate partitions are specified for a partition, it would be necessary to evaluate alternative designs for the structural framework of the directory, such as the addition of a layer of grouping containers. At the functional layer, this should proceed as previously illustrated. At the physical layer, this could be accomplished by adding a layer of Organizational Unit objects between the Organization object and the Organizational Unit objects that represent locations. These grouping containers should represent something that is meaningful to users, such as geographical regions or operational divisions, such as the following:

- If the organization possessed additional regional locations that were not dedicated to specific organizational functions, containers could be established along geographic lines, such as West, Central, and East. All Organizational Unit objects representing locations within each of these regions could then be grouped under the Organizational Unit objects representing the regions.

- If the organization possessed additional locations that were dedicated to specific organizational functions, containers could be established along functional lines such as Headquarters, Manufacturing, and Sales. In this case, the Headquarters Organizational Unit could take the place of the Chicago Organizational Unit while the other Organizational Unit objects would hold Organizational Unit objects representing the other locations. In the event that this continued to yield too many subordinate partitions (under the Sales container for example), a layer of Organizational Unit objects representing regions could be added under the Sales Organizational Unit to further segregate location containers.

Achieving a balance of containers based on the number of objects they contain should not be the goal of adding grouping containers at the physical layer of the directory structure. The selection of grouping containers and the placement of geographical containers under them should be based on keeping the number of subordinate partitions within reasonable limits for each partition. However, it is sometimes necessary (in very large organizations) to create grouping containers (or to group business divisions) in order to make individual sites easier to find. An example would be a retail store environment, where thousands of individual stores might be part of several different store chains owned by a parent company. In this environment, it is useful to divide the highest level of the tree by operating division, and then to geographically break the tree up within each business unit, possibly grouping below the highest level by region and then city.

Once partitions with reasonable sizes that do not encompass multiple locations have been established, it is necessary to determine the placement of replicas on servers. The matrix that was illustrated previously should prove to be especially useful in this situation as long as the geographical location of the servers is noted on the matrix.

Again, requirements for bindery services should be given the highest priority when determining replica placement, since all servers requiring bindery services must hold replicas of all partitions that encompass containers in the server's bindery context. The only types of replicas that should normally be used are Master and Read/Write replicas, with the Master replica placed on the most powerful of the servers that will hold replicas for a given partition. When determining replica placement using the matrix, it is important to track Subordinate References.

If satisfying requirements for bindery services results in the placement of replicas for a partition on servers that are separated by a wide area network link, every effort should be made to ensure that the partition is as small as possible so that replication traffic can be minimized. It might also be advisable to reconsider the placement of servers to eliminate such replication across wide area network links. In addition, steps might need to be taken to ensure that the number of replicas for each partition is not more than 10.

Once bindery services requirements have been satisfied, it will probably be necessary to place additional replicas on servers for fault tolerance. The normal requirement for fault tolerance is to maintain at least three replicas per partition, but this should not be considered an absolute requirement if adding a third replica for a partition would require replication across wide area network links. Two replicas for a partition should usually be sufficient to maintain fault tolerance in such cases. In cases where a location has only one server, it would be necessary to replicate partitions across wide area network links. This should be done by placing the replica as close as possible to the location.

Some early NDS design guidelines suggested that all partitions should have replicas placed in multiple locations to allow for easy recovery of NDS information in the event of a site disaster. Due to the amount of replication traffic required to travel across wide area network links that this would cause, such a strategy could lead to partition instability in the event that communication problems occurred. Since effective solutions exist for backing up NDS information for off-site storage, replication across wide area network links should be done only as a last resort when a location has a single server.

One of the important issues to consider when determining the placement of replicas is the handling of the partition (or partitions) encompassing the [Root] and Organization objects. The Organization object, or the [Root] object when multiple Organization objects are present, needs to be reachable at all times in order to allow tree walking when accessing objects in other branches. Both the [Root] and Organization objects normally should be contained in a small partition containing no other objects, so the normal warnings about replicating partitions across wide area network links need not be applicable for this small partition. Placing replicas of this partition on remote servers could speed access to other parts of the tree for users in remote locations, so this aspect of quality of service should be given a high priority for the small [Root] partition.

In this scenario where a centralized organization has multiple locations, placing all replicas of the [Root] partition on servers at the hub location would be the ideal solution. This is because all communications between regional locations would necessarily travel through the hub location. In other cases where there is direct connectivity between regional locations, strategic placement of the [Root] partition on servers at regional locations could eliminate unnecessary communication with the hub location.

WARNING

Great care should be exercised when placing replicas of the [Root] partition on remote servers, due to the security sensitivity of the [Root] and Organization objects. As with other replicas, those for the [Root] partition should be placed only on servers whose consoles are sufficiently protected from unauthorized access. Partitions containing the [Root] and other top-level container objects are especially sensitive since modification of the objects' Access Control Lists (ACLs) could provide a user with supervisory privileges to the object and, through inheritance, the rest of the tree.

The other elements of the design process are equivalent to the scenario for an organization with a single location. The resulting documentation should be used to provide guidance for the installation of servers and objects into the directory. When servers and objects are being installed into the directory, the structural framework for the directory should remain consistent, though the actual partitions and replicas should be established to reflect the current operational situation. Partitions should be established only at a point when doing so would improve the operational efficiency of the directory.

A Decentralized Organization with Multiple Locations

When an organization with multiple locations is decentralized and does not have the luxury of a single centralized location that can act as a communications hub, the NDS design process is somewhat more complex. Such organizations could have multiple locations that could be considered communications hubs, or perhaps no locations clearly play a similar role. The differences between this scenario and the previous one normally could result in the following variations in the design:

- Placement of a second replica for fault tolerance when a location has only a single server should be on the server that is located closest (in terms of communications). Just as in the previous scenario, the goal of minimizing replication traffic over wide area network links should take precedence over the goal of having three replicas for fault tolerance (since two replicas should be sufficient).

- Determination of the placement of replicas of the small [Root] partition should be based on optimizing access to other parts of the tree for users in the various locations. Since there is no centralized hub location, all replicas of the [Root] partition should be placed on servers at various locations determined by the amount of access each location will have to replicas of partitions for other parts of the tree. This requires a more detailed analysis of expected NDS traffic patterns and wide area network design than was required for previous scenarios.

The other elements of the design process are the same as those for the previous scenario for an organization with multiple locations. The resulting documentation should be used to provide guidance for the installation of servers and objects into the directory. While servers and objects are being installed into the directory, the structural framework for the directory should remain consistent, although the actual partitions and replicas should be established to reflect the current operational situation. Partitions should be established only at a point when doing so would improve the operational efficiency of the directory.

Multinational Organizations

The final variation on the scenario where an organization has multiple locations is that of a multinational organization. In this scenario, the organization has operational units in multiple sovereign nations that operate either as relatively separate entities or as an integrated whole. In this case, it is not as likely for an organization to have a single centralized location that could act as a communications hub, but it is entirely possible that several countries could have locations that act as a centralized location for the country.

This scenario might appear to present a situation where the use of Country objects might actually be called for. That is not necessarily the case since Country objects can only be located directly below the [Root] object and using Country objects would require separate Organization objects for each country. This might be appropriate for an organization where operational units in separate countries act as separate entities; but if that is the case, then placing separate Organization objects for each country directly below the [Root] object would serve the same purpose without requiring an extra layer of objects. In cases where the operational units in separate countries act as an integrated whole, it remains advisable to place a single Organization object directly below [Root] and then have Organizational Unit objects representing countries below the Organization object. These alternatives are illustrated in Figures 8.7 and 8.8.

FIGURE 8.7

A multinational organization with relatively independent operations in multiple countries

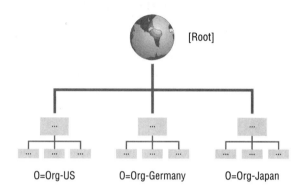

FIGURE 8.8

A multinational organization with operations in multiple countries acting as an integrated whole

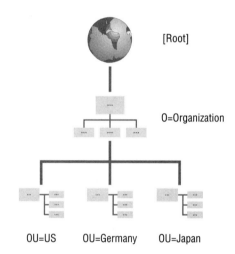

Once objects representing the national operational units are established for the organization, the process of designing the rest of the structural framework for the directory can be considered as equivalent to the previous scenarios that have been discussed. The determination of the most appropriate scenario depends on whether there are multiple locations within each country and whether certain locations can be considered as hubs for communications. It is quite common for different scenarios to be applicable in various countries where an organization operates.

Once the various design scenarios are worked through, the resulting documentation should be used to provide guidance for the installation of servers and objects into the directory tree. While servers and objects are being installed into the directory, the structural framework for the directory should remain consistent, although the actual partitions and replicas should be established to reflect the current operational situation. Partitions should be established only at a point when doing so would improve the operational efficiency of the directory.

Organizations with Special Requirements

Earlier in this chapter, we warned that the NDS design guidelines presented should not be interpreted as concrete rules. Although in most cases application of the guidelines would result in a directory design that will operate efficiently once it is implemented, there are situations where this is not the case. In some situations, it might not even be possible to adhere to the guidelines. This section presents two situations that illustrate this point.

In some cases, organizations might wish to establish containers that are dedicated to holding objects for certain types of network resources other than users or groups. For example, Figure 8.9 shows how an Organizational Unit object could be created to hold Server, Volume, and Print Queue objects at the same level as other Organizational Unit objects that hold User and Group objects.

This approach to tree design would have little impact on the effective operation of NDS in small networks with only a single location, but the value of such an arrangement is limited since it does little to simplify access for users to objects representing network resources. In larger networks with multiple locations, where partitioning likely would be necessary, this design approach could have a negative impact on operational efficiency by making it difficult to effectively partition the directory and optimally place replicas on servers. In the event that a Resource container held objects from multiple locations, its partition would need to be replicated across wide area network links to allow for consistent access to the resources represented by objects in the container. Replication of such an important partition across wide area network links could increase the likelihood that replication problems might occur, leading to a widespread loss of access to important network resources.

Despite the problems identified with the use of such resource containers, there is at least one situation where this design approach is more than likely beneficial. Organizations such as academic institutions typically have large and volatile student populations that access network resources from unpredictable locations on the campus. Due to large changes that occur to the student population at regular intervals as students enter and depart the academic institution, it is desirable to allow for mass updates of user objects. In addition, the relationships between students and network resources often change over time depending on the classes in which the students are registered. Since students are usually registered for classes in multiple departments simultaneously, it is not feasible to locate students in containers near resources they might need to access in a consistent manner at some point in time.

FIGURE 8.9

An NDS tree using a resource container

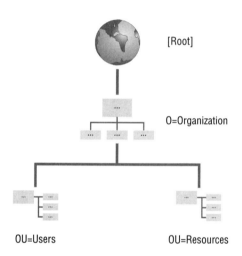

Using separate containers to hold objects representing students and network resources is a natural approach to simplifying administration and access to resources for users, while also allowing for the most efficient operation of the directory that is possible. Due to the large number of objects that could exist in some Directories, this could lead to unreasonably large user and resource containers if a single container is used for each type of object. Since it is necessary for the replicas of a partition to be synchronized when authentication occurs, servers could be overwhelmed by the synchronization requirements and rendered unavailable to service other types of requests. To alleviate this problem, multiple small resource and user containers should be created to allow for smaller partitions that limit the scope of replica synchronization that occurs for authentication. These smaller containers could be based on user last names or the departments where the students are registered, as in Figure 8.10.

FIGURE 8.10

A directory design for an academic institution with multiple containers for students

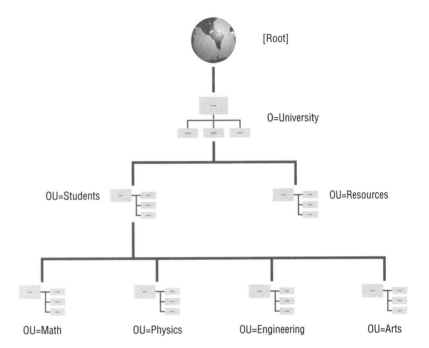

Summary

Based on the design considerations and guidelines presented in this chapter, the process of planning for the deployment of Novell Directory Services in an organization's networking environment can be reduced to the following set of guidelines:

- Decide how NDS trees should be used within the organization. The most important aspect of this decision is whether a single tree or multiple trees should be used. In the event that it is determined that multiple trees are necessary or desirable, each tree should be considered separately when applying the remaining steps.

- Determine how Country and Organization objects should be used within each NDS tree. Country objects probably should not be used unless required for strict adherence to X.500 design guidelines. Most organizations will typically require only a single Organization object at the top of each tree, unless separate operational units that need to be represented in the same tree are independently administered.

- Design the highest portion (the physical layer) of each NDS tree in such a way that the placement of Organizational Unit objects reflects the relationships between the organization's geographical locations as determined by the physical network infrastructure.

- Design the lower portion (the functional layer) of each NDS tree in such a way that containers can be used to simplify administration and access to resources for users. In most cases, the temptation to create separate container objects to exclusively hold frequently accessed objects representing network resources should be avoided since this can result in a design that does not allow for efficient operation of the directory.

- Establish partitions in such a way that all partitions contain no more than between 4,000 and 5,000 objects (twice as many for NDS version 8). Analyze partition relationships to ensure that no partition has more than 10 subordinate partitions. In the event that a partition has more than 10 subordinate partitions, the design of the directory framework should be modified to correct the condition.

- Determine where partition replicas should be placed on servers to satisfy requirements for bindery services. In the event that satisfying requirements for bindery services results in the placement of replicas for any given partition on more than 10 servers or servers separated by wide area network links, the directory should be further divided into partitions. This could require alteration of the structural framework of the directory so that no partition will have more than 10 replicas.

- Additional partition replicas should be placed on servers to ensure that there are sufficient replicas of each partition for fault tolerance purposes. When placing replicas on servers, avoid situations that would result in replication across wide area network links. In most cases, each partition should have at least three replicas for fault tolerance purposes unless this would require placement of replicas for a partition on servers separated by wide area network links. Each partition should have at least two replicas, even if this requires placement of replicas on servers separated by wide area network links.

- Establish guidelines for the use of object types such as User, Group, Organizational Role, Template, Profile, and Directory Map.

In most cases, the previous steps should allow for the implementation of an NDS tree that operates efficiently while achieving the desired objectives of simplifying administration and access to resources for users. There are cases, however, where it might be necessary to ignore or violate some of the guidelines in order to achieve these desired objectives.

CHAPTER

9

Naming Guidelines

O ne of the important elements of a disciplined approach to Novell Directory Services implementation is developing a strategy for establishing naming guidelines. The reason for establishing naming guidelines is to ensure that names and values are assigned to objects and their properties in a consistent fashion throughout an organization. Consistency in assigning names to objects and in assigning values to properties will result in a directory that allows users to access resources easily by choosing from a list or searching on various criteria.

When discussing network directories, some terms are often used interchangeably. Object and entry are usually used as equivalent terms describing the primary data elements or records in a directory, and property and attribute are usually used as equivalent terms describing parameters or fields associated with such records. To minimize the potential for confusion, object and property will be used exclusively in this and subsequent chapters to refer to these particular concepts.

An effective set of naming guidelines will result in a collection of objects within a directory that have the following characteristics:

- Names that are *user-friendly* while allowing users to discern an object's type or purpose without requiring that the user know an object's class.

- Names for certain types of objects that are *unique* not only in the context of the directory but also within other realms, such as flat namespaces, where the object names might be used.

- Names that are *long-lived* so as to allow storage of object references within, or outside, the directory without requiring constant reconciliation processes to ensure referential integrity.

- *Association* of the proper types of data with objects to support all of the intended uses for the directory.

- *Consistent syntax* for values assigned to properties that users might search for in order to find objects.

- *Consistent format* for values assigned to properties that might be used for presentation purposes.

- *Requirements for extensions* to the base schema for various object classes that would allow the directory to maintain additional information related to objects that might be useful to the organization.

These characteristics do not assume any single kind of application for the directory, but are instead appropriate for a number of possible directory applications.

This chapter presents a series of recommendations on object naming and property syntax that should be considered when developing organizational naming guidelines. Differences between organizations can make one naming standard more suitable for one organization than for another, so this chapter discusses the issues that should be considered when developing guidelines, rather than presenting a generic set of naming guidelines. Examples will be provided, however, to illustrate the effects that some of the suggestions could have on an organization's naming guidelines.

The information presented in this chapter should be used to create a customized set of organizational naming guidelines that will result in a directory with the characteristics in the preceding list. Such a development approach can require a great deal of effort, but providing a directory that allows users to easily locate the objects or information they need is a goal worthy of the required investment of time.

Object Naming

Naming an object in Novell Directory Services consists of simply assigning a value to a special property of an object instance, which is called the naming property. For most object classes this naming property is CN, although other properties could be, and are, used. For example, the naming property for the Organization object class is O, and the naming property for the Organizational Unit object class is OU. This is the reason that object names are specified using the notation CN=<*name*> or OU=<*name*>. This name is referred to as the Relative Distinguished Name (RDN) of the object. All RDNs for objects in a container must be unique because NDS implements a flat namespace across all object classes within each container.

Objects can be uniquely identified within a tree by combining the string of RDNs for the object itself and all superior objects. This string of names is referred to as the Fully Qualified Distinguished Name (FQDN) and is presented as a period-separated list of RDNs beginning with the object's RDN, followed by the RDNs of the increasingly superior objects. For example, if a User object with the name BIverson assigned to its CN property is created in a container with an FQDN of OU=Consulting.OU=MSP.O=Organization, the user object's FQDN would be:

CN=Biverson.OU=Consulting.OU=MSP.O=Organization.

The NDS naming system is hierarchical in the sense that an object receives its FQDN by combining its RDN with the FQDN of the container object immediately superior to it. The intention behind implementing a hierarchical naming system for NDS through its tree structure was to provide a globally unified namespace while allowing complete local control over the naming of objects within subtrees. Local control over object naming takes the responsibility away from administrators for ensuring the uniqueness of object names within the network when multiple administrators are required to create objects. As long as an object's name (or RDN) is unique within its container, then its FQDN is guaranteed to be unique due to the uniqueness of each of the FQDN components within their respective containers.

Responsibility for object naming should be assigned for each container so that a single authority can control the unique naming of objects within a given container. Object naming conventions should be documented to provide guidance for each of the assigned naming authorities so that unique and meaningful names are consistently assigned to objects within each container. The following sections discuss suggested object naming practices along with constraints on naming that could be imposed by the environments inhabited by NDS.

General Object Naming Guidelines

Several syntax rules, which are enforced by the directory schema, apply to names that can be assigned to objects. In addition, there are several suggested naming practices that should be followed, although they are not enforced by the directory schema. The following guidelines should be followed when assigning names to objects, regardless of the object types.

Character Limits

NDS imposes a 64-character limit on Relative Distinguished Names and a 256-character limit on Fully Qualified Distinguished Names. Despite the ability to use such long names when naming objects, short names should be used to allow for maximum flexibility. For instance, using short names for container objects could allow for a deeper tree since the names of more container objects would be able to fit within the 256-character limit of an FQDN. Also, users can remember shorter names more easily.

Case Sensitivity

Although object names are not treated as case sensitive by NDS, they are stored internally in the case that was used when the object was created or when the naming property was last updated. The case-sensitive form of the name is also used in most instances when object names are displayed in a list. So, although NetWare interprets the names APPRESOURCE and AppResource identically, users will be more likely to understand the meaning of the latter. Combining both upper- and lowercase characters in the object name may make it easier for the user to understand the name.

Use of Blank Spaces and Underscores

Although blank spaces and underscores are treated interchangeably by NDS, this equivalence is not obvious to users. For example, the names Acct Printer and Acct_Printer are considered to be identical by NDS. The use of blank spaces or underscores should be standardized so that one or the other type of separator is consistently applied. Use of underscores is generally considered to be a better choice than blank spaces since objects with underscores in their names do not require any special considerations when referring to them from a command line. (In some instances, names with spaces need to be enclosed in quotation marks.)

Simplicity and Descriptiveness

The name applied to an object should be simple and descriptive so that users can easily deduce certain characteristics of the resource represented by the object from its name. For example, a printer object called HPLJ_Accounting is usually more meaningful to users than Printer1 (unless all printers are labeled physically with this sort of identifier). As is true with short names, simple and descriptive names are more likely to be remembered by users than cryptic names.

Characters to Avoid

Because of restrictions imposed by NDS, desktop operating systems, some client software, and some applications, the use of nonalphanumeric characters in object names should be restricted. At minimum, use of the following characters should be avoided:

/ (Slash)

\ (Backslash)

: (Colon)

; (Semicolon)

, (Comma)

. (Period)

? (Question mark)

* (Asterisk)

In addition, the use of characters that are not present in most general character sets or codepages should be avoided if it is expected that multiple character sets will be in use. The use of such characters could render presentations of object names for users with different character sets inconsistent and could make searching for object names difficult.

Naming Structural Elements of a Directory

Some of the more important object names are those applied to container objects, which act as structural elements of the directory. Because RDNs assigned to most container objects will act as components of the FQDNs for all objects in the directory, it is especially important that the names of these objects be simple and descriptive so that users are able to remember them easily.

Naming Trees

The name assigned to the [Root] object also serves as the name of the tree, although the [Root] object is still referred to as [Root] in most utilities that operate on only a single tree at a time. Every tree defined on a network must have a unique name because of the way NDS is advertised (see *Accommodating Nonhierarchical Names* later in this chapter).

The behavior of the [Root] object name, when used as the tree name, is different from other object names in that it is normally presented using only uppercase letters. Great care should be exercised when assigning a name to the [Root] object because changing the name later, although easy to do, could be labor-intensive given that it often requires changes to client software configurations or other utilities.

The standard recommendation for forming the name of a tree is to combine some form of the organization's name with a suffix of _TREE. For example, Acme Corporation could use ACME_TREE as the name of its tree. Because users often do not have to deal with the tree name once they are properly attached and authenticated, the normal suggestion for a short name does not necessarily apply in this case.

If an organization will have multiple trees on its network, the names assigned to the trees should provide some form of a description of the purpose or identify the portion of the organization encompassed by the tree. For example, the tree for the test NDS environment at Acme could be given the name ACME_TEST_TREE, while the production tree could continue to be called ACME_TREE. When multiple organizations operating independent trees are sharing a common network infrastructure, it probably will be necessary to designate a common naming authority for trees to ensure that no two trees are given the same name.

Naming Country Objects

According to the specifications for both NDS and X.500, the standard format for the RDN of a Country object is the ISO (International Standards Organization) 3166 country code, which assigns standard two-letter codes to represent all countries. The NDS schema enforces this syntax when naming Country objects, so there is little opportunity for variation. The ISO 3166 country codes are listed in Table 9.1.

T A B L E   9.1:   International Standards Organization 3166 Country Codes

Country Name	Code	Country Name	Code	Country Name	Code
Afghanistan	AF	Albania	AL	Algeria	DZ
Andorra	AD	Angola	AO	Anguilla	AI
Antarctica	AQ	Antigua and Barbuda	AG	Argentina	AR
Armenia	AM	Aruba	AW	Australia	AU
Austria	AT	Azerbaijan	AZ	Bahamas	BS
Bahrain	BH	Bangladesh	BD	Barbados	BB
Belarus	BY	Belgium	BE	Belize	BZ
Benin	BJ	Bermuda	BM	Bhutan	BT
Bolivia	BO	Botswana	BW	Bouvet Island	BV
Brazil	BR	British Indian Ocean Territory	IO	Brunei	BN
Bulgaria	BG	Burkina Faso	BF	Burundi	BI
Cambodia (Kampuchea)	KH	Cameroon	CM	Canada	CA
Cape Verde	CV	Cayman Islands	KY	Central African Republic	CF
Chad	TD	Chile	CL	China	CN
Christmas Island	CX	Cocos (Keeling) Islands	CC	Colombia	CO
Comoro Islands	KM	Congo	CG	Cook Islands	CK
Costa Rica	CR	Croatia	HR	Cuba	CU

T A B L E 9.1:   International Standards Organization 3166 Country Codes *(continued)*

Country Name	Code	Country Name	Code	Country Name	Code
Cyprus	CY	Czech Republic	CZ	Denmark	DK
Djibouti	DJ	Dominica	DM	Dominican Republic	DO
Ecuador	EC	Egypt	EG	El Salvador	SV
Equatorial Guinea	GQ	Estonia	EE	Ethiopia	ET
Falkland Islands (Malvinas)	FK	Faroe Islands	FO	Fiji	FJ
Finland	FI	France	FR	Gabon	GA
Gambia	GM	Georgia	GE	Germany	DE
Ghana	GH	Gibraltar	GI	Greece	GR
Greenland	GL	Grenada	GD	Guadeloupe	GP
Guam	GU	Guatemala	GT	Guiana (French)	GF
Guinea	GN	Guinea Bissau	GW	Guyana	GY
Haiti	HT	Honduras	HN	Hong Kong	HK
Hungary	HU	Iceland	IS	India	IN
Indonesia	ID	Iran	IR	Iraq	IQ
Ireland	IE	Israel	IL	Italy	IT
Ivory Coast	CI	Jamaica	JM	Japan	JP
Johnston Island	JT	Jordan	JO	Kazakhstan	KZ
Kenya	KE	Kiribati	KI	Korea (North)	KP
Korea (South)	KR	Kuwait	KW	Kyrgyzstan	KG

T A B L E 9.1: International Standards Organization 3166 Country Codes *(continued)*

Country Name	Code	Country Name	Code	Country Name	Code
Laos	LA	Latvia	LV	Lebanon	LB
Lesotho	LS	Liberia	LR	Libya	LY
Liechtenstein	LI	Lithuania	LT	Luxembourg	LU
Macau	MO	Madagascar	MG	Malawi	MW
Malaysia	MY	Maldives	MV	Mali	ML
Malta	MT	Marshall Islands	MH	Martinique	MQ
Mauritania	MR	Mauritius	MU	Mexico	MX
Micronesia	FM	Midway Islands	MI	Moldavia	MD
Monaco	MC	Mongolia	MN	Montserrat	MS
Morocco	MA	Mozambique	MZ	Myanmar	MM
Namibia	NA	Nauru	NR	Nepal	NP
Netherlands	NL	Netherlands Antilles	AN	New Caledonia	NC
New Zealand	NZ	Nicaragua	NI	Niger	NE
Nigeria	NG	Niue	NU	Norfolk Island	NF
Norway	NO	Oman	OM	Pacific Islands (U.S.)	PC
Pakistan	PK	Panama	PA	Papua New Guinea	PG
Paraguay	PY	Peru	PE	Philippines	PH
Pitcairn Islands	PN	Poland	PL	Polynesia (French)	PF
Portugal	PT	Puerto Rico	PR	Qatar	QA
Reunion	RE	Romania	RO	Russia	RU

T A B L E 9.1:   International Standards Organization 3166 Country Codes *(continued)*

Country Name	Code	Country Name	Code	Country Name	Code
Rwanda	RW	Sahara (Western)	EH	Saint Helena	SH
Saint Kitts and Nevis	KN	Saint Lucia	LC	Saint Pierre and Miquelon	PM
Saint Vincent and Grenadines	VC	Samoa (American)	AS	Samoa (Western)	WS
San Marino	SM	Sao Tome and Principe	ST	Saudi Arabia	SA
Senegal	SN	Seychelles	SC	Sierra Leone	SL
Singapore	SG	Slovakia	SK	Slovenia	SI
Solomon Islands	SB	Somalia	SO	South Africa	ZA
Spain	ES	Sri Lanka	LK	Sudan	SD
Surinam	SR	Swaziland	SZ	Sweden	SE
Switzerland	CH	Syria	SY	Tadzhikistan	TJ
Taiwan	TW	Tanzania	TZ	Thailand	TH
Timor (East)	TP	Togo	TG	Tokelau	TK
Tonga	TO	Trinidad and Tobago	TT	Tunisia	TN
Turkey	TR	Turkmenistan	TM	Turks and Caicos Islands	TC
Tuvalu	TV	Uganda	UG	Ukraine	UA
United Arab Emirates	AE	United Kingdom	GB	United States of America	US
Uruguay	UY	Uzbekistan	UZ	Vanuatu	VU

T A B L E 9.1:   International Standards Organization 3166 Country Codes *(continued)*

Country Name	Code	Country Name	Code	Country Name	Code
Vatican	VA	Venezuela	VE	Vietnam	VN
Virgin Islands (British)	VG	Virgin Islands (U.S.)	VI	Wake Island	WK
Wallis and Futuna Islands	WF	Yemen	YE	Yugoslavia	YU
Zaire	ZR	Zambia	ZM	Zimbabwe	ZW

Naming Organization and Organizational Unit Objects

When the simple NDS installation method is employed with NetWare, the Organization object is given the same name that was given to the [Root] object and tree. In most cases, when the standard tree naming recommendation is followed (the name of the organization with a suffix of _TREE), the result is not a suitable name for the Organization object.

For a tree with only a single Organization object that is intended to represent the entire organization, a shortened form of the organization's name should be assigned to the object. When multiple Organization objects are used, the names assigned should signify in some way the characteristic used to define the ways that the organization was divided with separate Organization objects. For example, if Organization objects were created for separate subsidiaries, they should be given shortened forms of each subsidiary name.

Similar considerations should apply when naming Organizational Unit objects, except that it is possible to assume the existence of a context in the naming of such objects because they are subordinate to other objects. This means that an Organizational Unit object can be named in such a way that it is meaningful when combined with its parent container objects. For example, Organizational Unit objects named *West* and *East* could be understood by users to represent regional containers when they are subordinate to an Organization object that was given the organization's name.

Due to the absence of support for the Locality object class in most NDS administrative and user applications, Organizational Unit objects will often be used to fulfill a similar role by representing localities such as states, provinces, or cities. When naming objects that represent localities, well-known abbreviations such as the following should be employed when possible:

- Postal authorities in the United States and Canada have assigned two-letter abbreviations for states and provinces. Some examples are MN for Minnesota, TX for Texas, and ON for Ontario.

- Many cities in the United States and around the world can be identified using common two or three-letter abbreviations. Some examples are MSP for Minneapolis/St. Paul, CHI for Chicago, LA for Los Angeles, and NYC for New York City. One additional source for city abbreviations could be codes that were assigned and once used by Western Union for telegram delivery.

Just as when naming trees, great care should be exercised when naming container objects, since changing the name of a single Organization or Organizational Unit object would change the FQDNs for all subordinate objects. Such a change could require changes to the default contexts for all client systems affected by the name change, as well as configuration changes for any applications or utilities that use object references.

When a name change is necessary for a container object, it is possible to create an Alias object with the name of the original container object that points to the new container object's name. Another alternative could be to create a new container object while keeping the original container object. The objects could then be moved into the new container and the See Also property could be used in each container object to point to the other container object. Using an Alias object is the preferred method.

Namespace Continuity with Multiple Trees

There will often be cases when organizations will operate with multiple trees for a variety of reasons. In such cases, it may still be advisable to organize and name container objects within the separate trees in a manner that would allow namespace continuity in the event that trees are merged or accessed as a single unit via some other means, such as Novell's dirXML (see Chapter 18).

When trees are merged, the [Root] object of the source tree is eliminated and all subordinate objects are integrated into a single tree without changing the FQDNs of any of the objects. A prerequisite for the merge to occur is that all objects in each tree should have unique FQDNs, which simply requires that the first-level container objects directly below the [Root] object in each tree have unique names.

Unique names for first-level container objects also allow for some form of directory gateway or other interface to provide a unified view of two or more trees by providing a common replacement root. This type of tree integration could occur simply at the [Root] objects for each tree so that all the first-level container objects would appear at the same level. Another alternative could be to integrate trees into a worldwide directory that might establish Country objects that could be used as replacements for the individual trees' [Root] objects and anchors for their Organization objects.

Accommodating Nonhierarchical Names

If NDS object names were used only within the realm of NDS, guaranteeing the uniqueness of an RDN for objects within each container would be the only consideration necessary to ensure the usefulness of objects. On the other hand, if NDS objects are used in realms outside of a strictly NDS world, additional considerations must be taken into account when naming objects to ensure their usefulness. The following sections discuss situations where additional considerations might be necessary when naming objects, in order to ensure their usefulness for multiple purposes.

Naming User Objects

The User object is almost always the most common object class used in NDS trees, due to the security information that is maintained in User objects and the tight coupling that exists between NDS security facilities and NetWare services. In addition to the role played by User objects in NDS identification and authentication, User objects are often used to maintain other information about individuals within an organization that can be accessed using a variety of methods. Such information can include electronic mail addresses, departments, telephone and fax numbers, and street addresses.

In some cases, these additional informational uses could be the only reasons for creating some User objects to represent individuals in the organization, such as when certain individuals might have no reason for accessing network resources. When this is the case, User objects can be dedicated for informational purposes only by setting security-related properties, such as group memberships or Access Control Lists (ACLs), to disallow access to network resources that are controlled by NDS.

The User object class is best suited for representing human users because it is derived from the Person and Organizational Person base object classes, and the properties maintained with these objects are focused on human users. Neither the Person nor the Organizational Person object classes can be accessed or manipulated directly by standard NDS utilities or applications, so the User object is the only standard means available for representing human users in an NDS tree.

An additional use for User objects is to provide a means for application processes to access resources protected by NDS security facilities. When application processes need to access information in the directory or resources that are controlled by NDS, they usually must impersonate a human user in order to interact with NDS.

Both the human and application roles for User objects should be considered when establishing guidelines for User object naming. Separate naming schemes should be developed for each role so users can discern between User objects representing human users and application processes. One of the conceptual weaknesses in the NDS specification is its lack of ability to distinguish systematically between User objects representing human users and application processes.

The lack of a separate object class to distinguish User objects representing application processes from those representing human users can be addressed by applying a distinct naming scheme to each type of User object. This approach is somewhat limited by the inability to apply naming standards consistently to User objects for application processes, since the names assigned by applications to User objects they create often cannot be controlled by personnel responsible for maintaining the directory.

For User objects representing human users, the CN naming property for the User object serves as the User ID that is typically entered along with a password when users authenticate via NDS. Although it is possible to assign an individual's full name to this property, some form of short User ID typically is used to simplify the login process for users.

Other properties associated with the User object, such as Full Name or Surname (Last Name), can be used to maintain the user's full name as well as the individual components of the name (first name, middle initial, last name, title, etc.). When displaying User objects, an application can use either the object name that serves as the User ID or the contents of one or more of the other properties.

Guidelines for User object naming should establish a systematic method for assigning unique names based on some characteristic associated with the individual that the User object will represent. This characteristic could be an individual's name, an employee number, or an existing User ID from another system. The following conventions are commonly used for assigning names to User objects for human users:

- Three-character name made up of the individual's initials. For example, the User object for Lotte A. Trouble would be named LAT. This naming scheme likely would be susceptible to name collisions due to the short User object name and the common occurrence of individuals with the same initials.

- Name comprising of some combination of the first name (or its initial) and the last name. For example, the User object for Astrid L. Urban could be AUrban, A_Urban, Astrid_Urban, Urban_A, or Urban_Astrid. This naming scheme likely will have a low incidence of name collisions (especially when middle initials are added to the equation), but the length of many of the names could cause difficulties for users or some utilities. For example, the NetWare Login program internally truncates User IDs to eight characters for some operations.

- Name with a maximum of eight characters made up of the initial of the first name and the last name. For example, the User object for Brenda J. Radinsky could be BRadinsk or RadinskB. When the length of the last name would result in a name that is longer than eight characters, it would need to be truncated to allow the object name to fit within the limit. This naming scheme is a popular compromise between the two naming schemes described previously, since the longer User IDs decrease the potential for name collisions, while the eight-character maximum ensures predictable behavior with utilities.

- Name comprised of an identification number, such as an employee number or student ID (but not a Social Security Number, because of its length and the desire to keep it hidden), that is often combined with one or more alphabetic characters as a prefix. Prefixes can be assigned either arbitrarily or systematically, and often are used to differentiate the identification numbers from other numbers. For example, the User object for Bob S. Gallagher (employee number 12345) could be

Z12345 (arbitrary prefix), G12345 (last name's initial as prefix), or BSG12345 (initials as prefix). Using such identification numbers for User object names (especially when combined with initials) provides a systematic way to avoid name collisions, although procedures could be necessary for assigning names for individuals who have not been assigned identification numbers.

- Name based on a user account from an existing system. Organizations with mainframes often have procedures for assigning unique IDs to users. Using these names for NDS User objects would be a simple matter, since users might only need to remember their RACF, ACF2, or Top Secret names for both mainframes and NDS. Using procedures and User IDs that already exist for naming User objects can improve efficiency while also easing some aspects of system access for users.

The security implications of sharing User IDs between systems are nearly insignificant and should be contemplated only by the most paranoid security officers or administrators. The risks associated with users having the same passwords on multiple types of systems, on the other hand, should be a major concern. Users should be instructed to use unique passwords on all systems—especially those that are vulnerable to password harvesting attacks, such as mainframes or UNIX systems. Use of Novell's Single Sign-on solution (see Chapter 15) can mitigate these problems, though.

The choice of a User object naming scheme will depend on the organization. Any of the previous schemes, as well as other possible schemes, would be perfectly acceptable as long as they are accepted by users and used consistently throughout a tree.

The hierarchical namespace of NDS allows multiple User objects to be assigned the same RDN if the objects are located in different containers (giving each User object a unique FQDN). Nevertheless, it is desirable in most cases to ensure that all User objects representing human users have unique RDNs. There are several reasons for doing this:

- Most users are aware only of the CN naming property that makes up a User object's RDN and are unaware of the FQDN. This is because most users have their workstation context preset, and they need to enter only their User ID when authenticating to NDS. In the event that users need to log in to NDS from a location without a properly set context, a contextless login utility could allow them to continue using only the RDN as their User ID, since a unique RDN could be unambiguously associated with a specific User object.

- Unique RDNs for all User objects for human users would allow a User object to be moved from one container to another without the risk of encountering a duplicate RDN. In the event that a duplicate RDN were encountered when moving a User object, one of the objects would need to have its RDN changed.

- Applications such as electronic mail would be able to map User objects into a flat namespace using only RDNs, instead of requiring the use of the more complex FQDNs or the assignment of some other electronic mail ID. This would be useful for providing easy-to-remember Internet mail addresses associated with specific User objects, without requiring the maintenance of separate names for electronic mail addresses.

The only drawback associated with requiring universal uniqueness for User object names is the requirement for centralized control over the assignment of names to ensure uniqueness of the RDN.

Facilitating Bindery Services

Bindery services are provided by NDS for compatibility with utilities and applications that were written to access NetWare resources for versions of NetWare available before NDS was introduced. Because the bindery is a server-centric directory, bindery services provided by NDS servers are established at the server level and the settings affect only a single server. Bindery services present a flattened view of a subset of objects available to users in the NDS directory tree. Information accessible through bindery services is limited to NDS objects and properties for which there are bindery equivalents. The subset of properties associated with each object class that is accessible through bindery services is limited to properties with bindery equivalents.

Bindery services are established on an NDS server by setting a bindery context for the server that consists of an ordered list of one or more container objects. The only restriction on containers available for inclusion in a bindery context is that Master or Read/Write replicas of all partitions encompassing all containers in the bindery context be present on the server.

The ordered list of containers that makes up the bindery context always implicitly contains an additional component, the bindery partition, as the first element in the list. The bindery partition, which is maintained on every NDS server regardless of whether bindery services are being provided, holds dynamic bindery objects to provide persistence for advertised resources such as servers and stand-alone print servers.

When an NDS server that provides bindery services receives a bindery-style request, it searches through all containers in the bindery context in order, starting with the bindery partition. If the request is for an object name, the search concludes when the first object with the particular name is located in one of the bindery context containers or when all bindery context containers have been searched (which results in an Entry Not Found error). If the request is for a list of a certain object type, all names for objects of that type are listed.

When a name is used for the same type of object in more than one container included in a bindery context, the name will not be duplicated and will only refer to the object that occurs earliest in the ordered search of containers in the bindery context. All other objects of the same type with identical names in containers included in the bindery context will be inaccessible through bindery services.

Due to the potential for name clashes when multiple containers are included in a bindery context on an NDS server, special care should be taken when naming instances of NDS object classes with bindery equivalents such as User, Group, Printer, Print Queue, and Profile objects. The objective should be that no object in a container included in a bindery context would have an RDN that is the same as the RDN for an object of the same type in a container that could be included in the same bindery context. For example, the RDN JBanks should not be used for User objects in two different containers if there is a possibility that the two containers could be included in the same bindery context. Following the earlier recommendation for ensuring the uniqueness of RDNs for all User objects within the entire tree would prevent this problem from affecting User objects. It might be desirable to establish similar guidelines for other NDS object classes for which there are bindery equivalents.

Use of the name SUPERVISOR should be avoided for any NDS User object since this is a reserved name in the bindery context. NDS objects that are named SUPERVISOR will behave inconsistently when bindery services are present, because different objects will be accessed depending on whether the access occurs in a bindery or NDS context.

The use of bindery services also introduces some restrictions on the names that can be assigned to objects where the object classes have equivalent bindery object types:

- The bindery imposes a 47-character limit on names of objects, compared with the 64-character limit on NDS object RDNs. Any NDS object with a name longer than 47 characters will not be accessible via bindery services.

- Certain characters that can be used in NDS object names cannot be used in bindery object names. Any NDS object that uses one of the illegal characters in its name will not be accessible via bindery services. The converse of this is also true: There are some characters that could be used in the names of bindery objects that cannot be used in NDS object names; use of these characters should be limited as well.

Naming Servers and Advertising Services

Bindery NetWare servers and other IPX/SPX or NCP services advertise their availability on a network using Service Advertising Protocol (SAP) type 0x0004 broadcasts. NetWare 4 and 5 servers providing bindery services also advertise their availability via SAP in the same manner, using the RDN of the Server object as the name that is advertised. Because bindery NetWare servers exist in a realm that transcends Novell Directory Services, there are special requirements for server names that go beyond the standard NDS requirement for uniqueness within the container that holds the server object.

All NetWare servers must have unique internal IPX network numbers within the entire network, and all bindery NetWare servers (including NetWare 4 and 5 servers providing bindery services) should have unique names as well. Server names should contain 47 characters or less (since they could act as bindery objects) and should contain only alphanumeric characters, dashes, or underscores. Duplicate server names or internal IPX network addresses will cause communications problems since at any point in time an advertised server name could be associated with different internal IPX network numbers.

The names that are broadcast via SAP are independent of the version of NetWare and any NDS information that might be associated with the server. For example, it is not feasible to have one NetWare 3.12 server named SERVER1 on the same network with a NetWare 4 server that provides bindery services and is also named SERVER1. Similarly, it is not feasible to have two servers that provide bindery services named SERVER1 in separate trees (or in separate containers within the same tree).

The requirement for uniqueness of names for bindery NetWare servers is not absolute for the entire network when filtering effectively blocks the propagation of SAP broadcasts between certain segments of the network, but requirements for uniqueness remain within the boundaries set by the filters. It is generally easiest, though, to require uniqueness of server names for the entire network.

If possible, server names should be centrally administered. It is possible, however, to systematically maintain the uniqueness of server names by establishing a multipart naming scheme for servers in environments where centralized control over server names is not feasible. In a geographically dispersed network, such a naming scheme could require a site identifier as part of the server name while allowing local administers to assign the rest of the name in a manner that ensures local uniqueness of the name.

Other services that advertise their availability via SAP often require the same considerations. Fortunately, most services that advertise using SAP are running on a NetWare server and therefore advertise under the server's name with different SAP types that identify the type of service.

In cases where services will advertise using names other than those assigned to NetWare servers (with the exception of printers, which should generally have their SAP broadcasts blocked by filters as soon as possible), the same naming scheme should be applied to the services. One special service that is advertised via SAP and that requires similar treatment is NDS itself. Each NDS server holding a replica advertises its availability via SAP type 0x0278 using a name that combines the tree name with a byte form of the server's address. These broadcasts of NDS services via SAP illustrate the reason for ensuring that all trees on the network have unique names.

Resource Naming

The main goal of resource naming is to allow for easy identification of the type of resource represented by an object without necessarily knowing the object's class. In most cases, this can be done effectively by using type identifiers as prefixes to the object names. For example, an organization's naming guidelines could specify that directory Map objects include a prefix of DM_ and that Profile objects contain a prefix of Profile_. Suffixes can work just as well in some cases. Consistency should be the main objective in establishing guidelines for the naming of objects representing resources, just as it should be with guidelines applicable to other object classes.

Naming Print Resource Objects

Printing is an essential service in most networking environments where users demand the flexibility to select printers on their own without the intervention of administrators. NDS object naming provides an opportunity to simplify the process of selecting printers for users. This can be accomplished by naming objects representing print resources in such a way that the type and location of the printer associated with each object is included in the name. Because print resources are usually selected by users from a list, the normal recommendations for using short object names do not necessarily apply— although the shortest possible descriptive names should be used to avoid unnecessary complications with desktop operating systems.

The basic NetWare queue printing services require three components to operate correctly: a print queue that collects print jobs, a printer definition that serves to associate a physical printer with a queue, and a print server that spools print jobs from print queues to a printer. In NDS, all three components are represented by different object classes: Print Queue, Printer, and Print Server objects. Only Printer and Print Queue objects are relevant to users in most cases, because accessing either type of object allows a user to send print jobs to a printer that is associated with the chosen object.

In most current network environments, where printers often contain their own network cards and print server capabilities, each printer normally will be associated with individual Print Server, Printer, and Print Queue objects that are dedicated to the printer. In other cases, a single Print Server object will represent a program running on a NetWare server that spools print jobs from multiple print queues to multiple printers.

A common naming convention for objects representing print resources is to use prefixes to distinguish the different object types, such as PS_ for Print Server objects, P_ for Printer objects, and Q_ for Print Queue objects. When print resource objects represent a printer connected to the network with a self-contained print server agent, the names assigned to the three objects that represent the printer should differ only in the prefixes that differentiate the object types. When a print server resides on a NetWare server (or in a stand-alone box) and controls multiple printers, the Print Server object's name should reflect the server where it is located (or some other server-style name). The Printer and Print Queue objects that represent each printer should differ only in the prefixes that differentiate the object types.

The object names that will be important to users are those for Printer and Print Queue objects, because those are the objects users can select for sending print jobs to the printers that are represented by the objects. In most cases, users will not have any need to access Print Server objects, so names assigned to these objects do not need to be meaningful to users. They should instead be meaningful to administrators.

Both Printer and Print Queue object names should provide information to users about the type of printer and its location. One possible approach for this is to provide in the naming guidelines a menu of standard printer type and location identifiers that can be combined to form names. For cases where several printers of the same type will be located close to one another, an additional component, such as a number that is physically posted on the printer, could be used to allow users to distinguish between the printers.

Printer type identifiers should be sufficiently descriptive to allow users to select the proper driver when they connect with a printer. Location identifiers should be descriptive as well, but most of the time these identifiers can assume a geographic location due to their relationships with container objects that will hold the Printer and Print Queue objects. When users are required to infer some of the information about a printer's location from its position in the directory, the location component of the name could simply be a floor or an office number. The following lists contain some possible identifiers that could be included in the naming guidelines as a menu for print resource object names.

Printer Identifiers

HPLaserJetIIISi

HPLaserJet4Si

HPLaserJet4SiMX

QMS3825PrintSystem

CompaqPageMarq20

Location Identifiers

Chicago Headquarters (1stFloor, 2ndFloor, 3rdFloor, etc.)

Dallas Manufacturing (Office, ShopStation1, ShopStation2, ShopStation3, etc.)

Sales Offices (Office)

When constructing names for print resource object names, blank spaces or underscores can be used to separate the identifier components. Notice that neither blank spaces nor underscores were used in the suggestions for individual components. For example, a HP LaserJet 4Si MX with a JetDirect interface located on the second floor at the Chicago headquarters (OU=CHI.O=Organizaton) could be assigned Printer, Print Queue, and Print Server objects with the names shown in Table 9.2.

T A B L E 9.2: A Print Resource Naming Scheme

Object Type	Object Name (FQDN)
Printer	CN=P_HPLaserJet4SiMX_2ndFloor.OU=CHI.O=Organization
Print Queue	CN=Q_HPLaserJet4SiMX_2ndFloor.OU=CHI.O=Organization
Print Server	CN=PS_HPLaserJet4SiMX_2ndFloor.OU=CHI.O=Organization

This type of naming scheme, which uses the entire hierarchical naming system for object names, would provide users with all the information they need to choose the correct printers.

Providing Standard Role-based Objects

In a human-oriented directory, users can benefit from the ability to identify certain User objects based on functions that are frequently performed by individuals rather than only by the name of the individual. The Organization and Organizational Role object classes do not contain properties that could be used to identify contacts. This can be facilitated by NDS using either Organizational Role or Alias objects that point to User objects for individuals that perform the named functions. Some of the role-based objects that could be created to represent some functions are:

- CN=Administrator
- CN=Directory Manager
- CN=Postmaster
- CN=Secretary

As an example of how such a role-based object could be used, objects called CN=Secretary could be created in each container with each of these objects pointing to User objects for the individuals that perform the secretarial function for each location encompassed by a container. When other users need information about a location, they could look up the CN=Secretary object for the location to identify the individual they would need to contact. The decision whether to use Organizational Role or Alias objects for this purpose would be determined by the ways that users would access the role-based objects.

The Organizational Role object class is the standard object type provided for this purpose, with roles represented by Organizational Role objects associated with one or more User objects through the Occupant property. One of the advantages of using the Organizational Role object is that it is possible to have an Organizational Role unoccupied occasionally, just as it is possible to have more than one User object identified as an occupant. Unfortunately, NDS does not automatically dereference User objects that are identified in the Occupant property, so accessing an Organizational Role only provides users with the names of the objects identified in the Occupant property. To obtain information about the objects that are identified in the Occupant property, it would be necessary to access each object individually.

Using Alias objects for the same purpose has the disadvantages of not allowing roles to be unoccupied for any period of time and not allowing more than one object to be identified with any given role represented by an Alias object. In addition, it is necessary to delete and re-create the Alias object in order to assign the role to a different User object. The advantage of using Alias objects, on the other hand, is that when they are accessed, the object that is pointed to is automatically dereferenced and the Alias object behaves just as it would if the object were accessed directly.

Assigning Values to Properties

The properties associated with objects serve a number of purposes, some of which are determined in advance by NDS, while others are left to the discretion of designers and administrators of the directory. The naming properties, such as CN, O, and OU, which have been the focus of our discussion up to this point, have well-defined roles that in most cases are determined for them in advance by NDS. Other properties, such as Description or See Also, do not have such well-defined roles, and it is perfectly acceptable in some cases to avoid assigning values to them.

One of the purposes for naming guidelines should be to identify situations where properties associated with various objects should be used. In addition, naming guidelines should specify acceptable formats and content for values assigned to properties. The following sections describe how properties are implemented in the NDS architecture and provide suggestions on the ways that properties should be addressed in an organization's naming guidelines.

Managing Mandatory and Optional Properties

In NDS, properties are defined independently of object classes in the schema as data types that can hold certain types of information. The definition of a property includes a name, such as CN or Description, and an allowable syntax, such as Distinguished Object Name or Case Insensitive String. Object classes that are defined in the schema contain a list of properties, each of which must also be defined in the schema.

It is possible for a given property to be associated with more than one object class. The property will behave identically across every object class that it is associated with, although the given property could be used for different purposes. For example, the OU property is used as the naming property for the Organizational Unit object class and as the departmental property for the User object class. In each case, regardless of the object type it is associated with, the property is restricted to containing case-insensitive strings up to 64 bytes long. The only exception is the Locality object, which can be 128 bytes. Since the Locality object is rarely used, you should adhere to the 64-character limitation for all objects.

Each object class, other than Top, is defined with one or more immediate super classes and a list of directly associated properties. The properties associated with an object class are all the properties that are directly associated with the object class itself along with those that are associated with all super classes. Certain properties that are associated with an object class will be flagged as mandatory, meaning that the object (and all objects for which the object class acts as a super class) cannot be considered valid unless the mandatory property contains a valid value.

In cases where an object class has more than one mandatory property, all mandatory properties must contain valid values. Optional properties do not need to contain values in order for the object to be valid, although in many cases certain optional properties will need to contain values in order for the object to be useful. For example, Group objects are valid but of limited usefulness if the multivalued "Member" property (an optional property) does not contain any User object names.

Naming guidelines need to identify the mandatory properties for all object classes that are to be used in the directory and provide guidelines for the values that are to be assigned to the properties. Certain optional properties should be identified in the naming standards as well, with guidelines covering the format that should be used for values assigned to the properties.

Property Usage Guidelines

The goal of naming guidelines for both mandatory and optional properties should be consistency of formats so that users can define queries based on properties in order to obtain lists of all objects that satisfy the query conditions. If the format for a property is not standardized in the naming guidelines, the likelihood of a successful query based on the property is decreased. For example, the naming guidelines could define a list of acceptable values for the L (Locality) property so users can define searches for all User objects that are associated with a location. The following sections provide suggestions for naming guidelines that can be applied to the values for properties associated with various object classes.

Organization and Organizational Unit Object Properties

The various informational properties associated with the Organization and Organizational Unit objects, such as SA (Street Address), Physical Delivery Office Name (City), S (State), or Telephone Number, should contain the information necessary for someone to contact the organization or the area represented by the particular container object. This information could be of limited use for a small organization or for a directory that is not accessible via networks outside of the organization, but even in such cases the properties could serve as source fields for other applications.

NOTE   In cases where nonauthenticated users might have an interest in such organizational information, the standard [Public] trustee should be given Read and Compare privileges to the relevant properties.

User Object Properties

As was discussed previously, User objects can be used to represent both human users and application processes, though in most cases, the naming guidelines should allow users to distinguish between the two types of User objects. Additional naming guidelines should be applied to certain properties to allow for a systematic selection of either type of User object in the event that object naming guidelines cannot be applied uniformly. One option could be to use the L (Locality) property to hold a value of Application for objects representing application processes and a different set of values for objects representing human users. This would allow a query, defined to exclude all User objects for which L=Application, to return a list of all human users.

The naming guidelines should cover all properties that would be used to search for and to obtain information about User objects. Properties most likely to be used for searches would be the Surname (Last Name), L (Locality), and OU (Department). Properties most likely to be used for informational purposes with human users would be Full Name, Surname (Last Name), Given Name (First Name), Initials (Middle Initial), EMail Address, Telephone Number, and Facsimile Telephone Number.

Server Object Properties

In many cases with NDS, users will have little interest in servers because they will interact most often with Volume, directory Map, and Print Queue objects that are presented to users by NDS as being independent of any particular servers. There are situations, though, where users might wish to obtain information about particular services, such as when searching for a service or for the location of certain files or directories. Properties associated with Server objects supply a method for providing information about servers that users might find useful for search purposes.

The security implications of providing information about data or services available on a server should be considered when developing naming guidelines for this purpose. In the wrong hands, such information could be used to compromise system security. One reasonable security precaution could be to allow only authenticated users to access such information by ensuring that the [Public] trustee does not have Read and Compare privileges to the relevant properties.

The Description property could be used to provide a general description of the purpose of the server as well as of the types of data that might be stored on the server. The multivalued Supported Services property could be used to hold the names of services that are supported on the servers. The names used to describe services should be standardized in the naming guidelines so that users can create searches that would provide a list of all Server objects that are identified with a particular service. Finally, the See Also property could be used to reference objects that are associated with the Server object, such as Volume or Print Queue objects.

One of the reasons for using the Server object to store information about the types of files that are stored on a server's volumes is that Volume objects do not contain Description fields.

Print Resource Object Properties

Printer and Print Queue objects are likely to be the most common resource types that users will need to search for and connect to on a regular basis. The naming standards that were discussed previously are intended to provide information about printers that are represented by each type of object. Such information could include a printer's type (sufficient information for selecting a printer driver) and its location. In some cases, users might want additional information about a printer that is represented by Printer and Print Queue objects. To support this need for information, additional information about printer capabilities could be associated with print resource objects. Printer objects would need to be the focal point of such information about printer capabilities, since the Printer object class is associated with properties intended for this purpose.

Both Printer and Print Queue objects should provide information about the printers that they are associated with in their Description properties. In some cases, additional information regarding purpose might be necessary in the Description property for Print Queue objects when multiple print queues are used to feed a single printer. The multivalued Page Description Language property that is associated with Printer objects should be used to hold standard identifiers for page description languages that are supported by printers, such as PCL or PostScript.

A standard list of allowable values for page description languages should be provided in the naming guidelines so users can create successful queries for printers that support their desired capabilities. The Memory property should also be used to hold a value for the amount of memory (in KB) that the printer supports so users can create queries for all printers with a minimum amount of memory if desired.

Other Object Properties

Naming guidelines should be established for the properties associated with other object classes where necessary. In most cases, where it is available for an object class, the Description field should be used to store information about the purpose and use of objects. Other properties that are shared by many object classes, such as O (Organization), L (Locality), and OU (Department), should also be considered for usage standards in the naming guidelines. The purpose for including properties in the naming standards should be to make it easier for users to construct successful queries to select objects that might share some characteristics.

Schema Extensions

One of the most powerful features of Novell Directory Services is the capability it provides to organizations and application vendors to extend the schema to provide custom object classes and properties. Object classes can be added to the schema to provide data entities that represent resources that were not envisioned by the designers of NDS. Properties can be added to the schema to support data elements that can be associated with base object classes or with custom object classes.

Many NDS-aware applications extend the schema with their own custom properties and associate these new properties with base object classes. For example, Novell Web Server introduces the Home Page and Photo properties to the User object class so that individual user home pages and photographs can be displayed when browsing NDS using a Web browser such as Netscape Navigator or Microsoft Internet Explorer. Naming guidelines should address such custom properties when known in advance, so that naming guidelines do not only cover base properties. For properties such as Home Page and Photo that store binary stream data, guidelines could also address allowable file sizes for home pages or required dimensions for photographs. Similar considerations should be applied to other custom properties that are added by applications.

In cases where organizations plan to make extensive use of the directory to provide information to users, a similar approach should be considered to provide information that is not provided for in the base object class definitions within the NDS schema. When creating custom properties as schema extensions, it is not only necessary to define the syntax for the new properties and to associate them with object classes, but it is necessary to create snap-ins for NetWare Administrator (or other administrative interfaces) to allow for the management of the custom properties. The creation of custom snap-ins (or other administrative interfaces) provides a great opportunity to enforce naming guidelines for values that can be assigned to the new properties. For example, the size of the data elements could be restricted or pick-lists of allowable values could be provided.

Summary

This chapter discussed many of the reasons for developing naming guidelines for NDS objects and properties. The overall goal of any naming guideline should be to allow users to discern the purpose for objects from their names or from the values assigned to certain key properties. By standardizing the format of values assigned to properties, the likelihood of success can be increased when users conduct queries for objects that they might wish to use.

Several suggestions for applying naming guidelines to various object classes and properties have been presented in this chapter. Because the environment where NDS will be operating will most often determine how naming guidelines actually should be developed and applied, many of the examples might not be appropriate for some organizations. Due to the site-specific nature of many naming guidelines, the considerations and suggestions presented in this chapter should be used merely as input to the development process for an organization's naming guidelines.

Further information about the naming of objects and the syntax for property values in similar directory environments can be found in RFC 1617 *Naming and Structural Guidelines for X.500 Directory Pilots* and RFC 1781 *Using the OSI Directory to Achieve User Friendly Naming*.

C H A P T E R

10

Migration Strategies

Rolling out a new directory service on an existing network can present formidable problems, among them the migration of user accounts and file system permissions from the old operating system. To avoid the onerous task of manually recreating all of your users and groups in the NDS database, Novell provides tools that automate the migration of accounts from NetWare bindery servers, as well as from other operating systems, such as Windows NT and Banyan VINES. This chapter examines the procedures for safely migrating directory information into NDS and the use of the various migration tools that are provided with NetWare and that are available from Novell's online services.

Migration Principles

While there are certainly a large number of NetWare networks that are built from scratch—cases in which administrators create a new NDS tree and manually populate it with users and other objects—many more are upgraded from previous versions of NetWare or migrated from another operating system. The upgrade and migration processes both present unique sets of problems to the network administrator, making it necessary to carefully formulate a plan of action, so that user services are not interrupted.

These problems can be summarized as follows:

- Creating new user and group objects in the NDS database that are equivalent to those in the old directory.

- Migrating the information contained in the old directory entries to the new NDS objects.

- Copying data files from the old server to the new while preserving the access rights granted to users and groups.

The following sections examine each of these problems in turn.

Creating New Objects

Because nearly all directory services use a unique object name for each network user, the process of reading the user names from the old directory and creating user objects with the same names in the NDS database is not difficult. However, the procedure can be complicated by the need to combine the contents of several directories into a single NDS tree.

The fundamental difference between the bindery-based directories of NetWare 2.*x* and 3.*x* and Novell Directory Services is that bindery servers each maintain their own directory, while NDS is a shared network resource. When you migrate a bindery network to NDS, you must combine the directories of the existing servers into a single NDS database. This naturally leads to the problem of combining duplicate bindery accounts into a single NDS user object.

On most bindery-based NetWare networks, administrators create identical accounts on multiple servers, so that users can always log in with the same name and password. If you migrate the binderies from multiple servers to a single NDS container, duplicate user names are combined into a single object. However, migrating bindery servers to different containers causes the creation of duplicate user objects, as shown in Figure 10.1.

The NDS tree design is a crucial element in any multiserver bindery migration strategy, so much so that we've devoted Chapter 8 to NDS design principles. Since NDS permits the creation of objects with the same name in different containers, you must decide beforehand whether you will migrate all of your binderies to a single container, or distribute them around the tree. If your network has thousands of users, it is obviously not practical to store them all in a single container. This can degrade NDS performance and defeat the purpose of having a hierarchical directory service. However, an equally fundamental premise for building an NDS tree is to create only one object for each user.

The Novell Upgrade Wizard program included with NetWare 5 enables network administrators to import the bindery information from NetWare 3.*x* servers, and then model the data into the desired NDS tree configuration by adding, moving, and deleting objects in different containers. NetWare 4.*x* includes the Windows based DSMigrate utility and the DOS-based `MIGRATE.EXE` program to handle this migration.

FIGURE 10.1

When migrating bindery servers to NDS, the tree layout determines whether duplicate user names are combined.

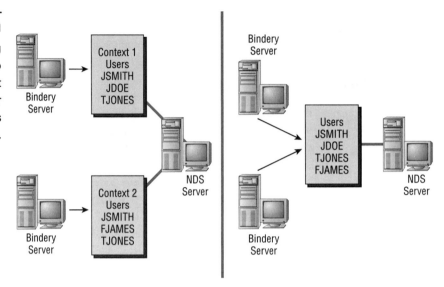

If you have users that log in to various bindery servers with different names, we recommend that you combine the properties of the various bindery accounts into a single NDS user object. Unfortunately, this is a manual operation.

The NetWare migration tools can copy group objects, as well as users, to the NDS database. However, groups are not as commonly used in NDS as they are in the NetWare bindery and other directory services. The hierarchical structure of the NDS tree naturally lends itself to the use of container objects as a means of grouping users instead. Group objects are typically employed only when users in different containers must be addressed as a single entity.

Assigning rights to NDS group objects is less efficient than using container rights because groups can contain objects located anywhere in the tree. Group rights processing therefore requires communication with all of the tree's partitions, while processing container rights involves only the partition in which the container is located. As a result, while you may migrate the groups from your bindery or other directory servers, you should develop an NDS tree design in which inherited container rights are used instead of groups wherever possible. Reserve the use of groups to situations where it is impractical to put all of the affected users into a single container.

Migrating Object Information

Aside from creating new user objects in the NDS database, the migration process must also copy the user account information from the source directory to NDS. The basic structure of a directory service, to use NDS terminology, calls for objects, which are composed of a collection of *properties*, each of which has a particular *value*. The user object JSMITH, for example, has a Surname property with the value Smith. Different directory services may use other terms for these elements, but the structure is basically the same.

The migration of data from an existing user account to an NDS object requires a program that can map the properties of the old directory object to those of the new one. In the case of a bindery server migration, many of the properties are the same. Elements such as login scripts, security equivalences, and group memberships exist in both the bindery accounts and the NDS objects, so the transfer of data is uncomplicated.

Migrating from other directory services, however, may involve properties with different names and functions. In some cases, certain properties of the old directory objects may be incompatible with NDS or may have to be mapped to a different NDS property, as shown in Figure 10.2. Most of the Novell migration tools handle the migration of property values internally, with no interaction from the user. However, certain properties cannot be migrated at all (such as passwords, when migrating to NetWare 4.*x*), and the migration of others may be complicated by the combination of users (for example, different users with the same login name) from different servers into a single NDS object.

FIGURE 10.2

During the account migration process, values from the old directory service may be transferred to different properties in the NDS database.

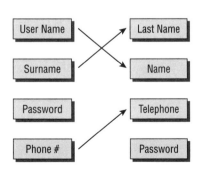

For directory services that are not directly supported by the Novell migration tools, there is a program called `UIMPORT.EXE`, that enables network administrators to import directory data into the NDS database from a text file. With NDS version 8, an improved importing tool called BULKLOAD can be used. With these tools, any directory that can export its database in a comma-delimited ASCII format can be migrated. However, with UIMPORT the mapping of property names must be performed manually through the creation of a control file. This is a second ASCII file that specifies the fields of the database that are to correspond to specific NDS object properties. BULKLOAD uses the LDIF (LDAP Data Interchange Format) version 1 file format, obviating the need for a control file.

Copying Data Files

Rolling out NDS on an existing network involves more than just migrating directory service information. The data files stored on the old servers' volumes must also be migrated. While this may at first appear to be a matter of simply copying the files from one volume to another, this is not the case. The access control lists that specify which users and groups have rights to files and directories are stored in the directory entry table (DET) found on each NetWare volume, not in the directory service database.

NDS utilities like NetWare Administrator and NETADMIN are capable of granting users trustee rights to specific parts of the file system, but when they do this they are actually modifying the DET entry for each file or directory by adding the trustee to the access control list. When you migrate a bindery server to NDS, the trustees listed in the access control list for each file and directory on the server's volumes must be converted from a bindery reference to an NDS object reference (see Figure 10.3).

FIGURE 10.3

To effectively migrate files, DET entries must be modified to reflect the trustees' NDS user objects.

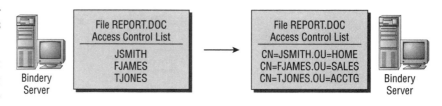

Transferring trustee rights is arguably a more important element of the migration process than the creation of NDS user objects, because trustee rights are usually much more difficult to reproduce. Remember, however, that the user object must exist in the tree before trustee rights can be transferred. In the event of a disaster, in which your network's directory service information is lost, the user objects could be re-created from company personnel records or other resources. However, trustee rights to network resources are often manually assigned to individual users as needed over the course of time. For all but the most fastidious network administrators, the only record of these assignments are in the DETs themselves. If the trustee assignments are lost during the migration process, administrators can look forward to a long line of user access requests.

Because the creation of trustee assignments on NetWare volumes requires that the referenced user objects exist in the NDS database, file migration always occurs after user migration. NetWare 4.*x* includes a GUI-based File Migration utility that is designed to work with DS Migrate to form a complete NetWare 3.*x* migration solution. MIGRATE.EXE also migrates trustee rights and the LMIGRATE.EXE program does the same for volume migrations from Windows NT drives. With NetWare 5, the Upgrade Wizard performs this task in addition to migrating directory objects.

Only NetWare 4.11/4.2 includes the DS Migrate and File Migration utilities. Earlier versions of NetWare must use the MIGRATE.EXE program for all bindery and file migration tasks.

Before You Migrate

Migrating an existing network to NDS is a major task, not to be undertaken lightly. When performing it as part of an upgrade to NetWare 4.11/4.2 or NetWare 5, you have the choice of performing an *inplace* or an *across-the-wire* upgrade. In other words, you can take an existing NetWare server and upgrade it to the new version, creating an NDS database out of the existing bindery and converting the existing volumes, or you can build a new NetWare server and transfer the bindery and volume data over the network.

The across-the-wire method is the safer of the two, because the bindery servers remain unchanged during the migration process. If a severe problem arises, you can abort the procedure and your users can continue to use the old servers. In either case, however, you should take the precautions on the following checklist before beginning any migration process:

- **Back up your servers**   Before you perform any major procedure like an NDS migration, be sure that you have complete and current backups of all of the servers involved. Be sure that the backups include directory services such as binderies, existing NDS databases, and Windows NT domains. Don't trust your software when it tells you that a backup was successfully completed; perform a series of test restores to verify your backups.

- **Test the health of your servers**   Run BINDFIX.EXE twice to ensure that your binderies are functioning properly, and to update the *.OLD files that serve as a backup. Run DSREPAIR.NLM if you are migrating to an existing NDS tree, and check for problems on your volumes with VREPAIR.NLM. If you are migrating from non-NetWare servers, use the appropriate utilities for the operating system. Resolve any problems detected by these utilities before you begin the migration process.

- **Synchronize NDS versions**   If you are migrating directory service information to an existing NDS database, be sure that all of the servers hosting NDS partitions and replicas are running the same version of the DS.NLM module, and that it is the most recent version for that platform.

- **Prune your directory services**   To maximize the efficiency of the NDS database, remove any obsolete or unused accounts from your binderies or other directory services before migration.

- **Check for duplicate user names**   If you are combining multiple binderies into a single NDS tree, make sure that your users log into all of the bindery servers using the same name, so that the properties of the accounts can be combined into a single NDS user object. Conversely, check to see that you do not have different people using the same name on different bindery servers. If John Smith in Accounting and Jane Smith in Sales both log into their respective servers as JSMITH, these accounts will be (incorrectly) combined into a single user object in the NDS. Finally, make sure that no bindery contains objects of different types with the same name. For example, a group and a print queue that are both named SALES will conflict when you migrate them to NDS.

- **Check file and directory names** If you are migrating NetWare 2.*x* volumes to NetWare 4.*x* or 5.*x* servers, be aware that NetWare 2.*x* allows file and directory names to be up to 14 characters in length. If your new server volumes use only the default DOS name space, files and directories that do not conform to the 8.3 naming convention will not be migrated.

- **Log off all users** Make sure that there are not any users logged into the network during the migration process. Files that are locked open by an application cannot be migrated.

- **Leave sufficient disk space** Make sure that your new NetWare volumes have sufficient disk space to hold the migrated data, and that the SYS volume on all servers containing NDS partitions have sufficient space for the new objects.

Migrating Multiple Servers

The migration of directory service and volume data can be a relatively simple procedure, such as when a single-server NetWare 3.12 network is upgraded to NetWare 4.*x*/5.*x* and NDS. On larger networks, however, the migration can be one part of an enterprise network upgrade strategy that requires careful planning and execution. If you plan on migrating a network with a large number of servers to NDS, you must consider the impact of the change on the network's users and its administrators.

The object of the migration process is to leave the network in a usable state when the procedure is completed, meaning that network clients can log in and access all of the resources that they are accustomed to using. Depending on the size and configuration of the network, this may involve the migration of a great many bindery objects and large amounts of data. In addition, you can expect your new NDS database to require a certain amount of manual adjustment.

No migration process is perfect. Novell's migration tools do a good job of creating the required user objects, but you will almost certainly have to perform some tasks manually. Some of this may include the configuration of print objects, the adjustment of login scripts to the new environment, and the reorganization of trustee rights to take advantage of NDS' hierarchical structure.

To lessen the shock of a sudden migration to NDS, you can develop a plan that proceeds in stages by creating an NDS tree on one NetWare server and migrating your bindery servers into it a few at a time. As the bindery servers are assimilated into NDS, you can upgrade them to the new version of NetWare as well, partitioning the tree and creating replicas as you go. This type of plan allows you to create a realistic schedule for the migration process, giving you time to deal with unforeseen occurrences. Servers that remain unmigrated can still be accessed by users in the traditional manner.

For any introduction of NDS onto a large network, the most important part of the implementation is that the development of an NDS tree design is suitable for the size and operational characteristics of your organization. Included in this design should be the partition and replication strategy that will provide fault tolerance and increased performance. Chapter 8 is devoted to NDS design principles and should be consulted before your first migration.

Client Migration

Another important consideration when migrating a network to NDS is the impact on clients, in the sense both of the workstations and of the people that use them. While it may be practical to plan for the migration of 10 servers in a weekend, upgrading the 1,000 client workstations that use those servers is an entirely different problem. In addition, you can expect a flood of support calls on Monday morning when your users are faced with new login procedures.

Even if your workstations are already running an NDS-capable client, the migration process requires that they be reconfigured to perform an NDS instead of a bindery login. You must supply the clients with the tree name, the appropriate default contexts for their user objects, and instructions for changing their passwords (because passwords from bindery accounts may not be migrated, depending on the new version of Netware and the migration method chosen).

The problems involved with acclimating your clients to the new environment are one of the chief reasons for performing a gradual migration. Even if you migrate all of your server binderies at once in order to build your NDS tree, you can still leave your bindery servers active and convert your clients one department at a time. This way, you can also ramp up the usage of the

NDS database gradually and make adjustments to your partitioning and replication strategy as needed.

 For more information on NetWare's NDS-capable clients, see Chapter 14.

Migrating from Bindery to NDS

The most common NDS migration scenario is when a network based on NetWare 3.11 or 3.12 is upgraded to NetWare 5. On a single server network, the INSTALL.NLM program included with NetWare 5 installs the operating system, creates a simple NDS tree, and migrates the contents of the bindery into a single context. The server volumes remain in place and their directory entry tables are updated to use NDS object references instead of bindery references.

Multiserver Migration Scenarios

In a multiserver environment, the existing binderies are combined into one NDS tree, either simultaneously or one at a time. The overall process usually proceeds in stages like the following:

1. One NetWare 3.1*x* server is upgraded to NetWare 5, or a new NetWare 5 server is installed on the network.

2. An NDS tree is created as part of the NetWare 5 installation process.

3. The binderies of the NetWare 3.1*x* servers are migrated to the NDS database.

4. The remaining NetWare 3.*x* servers are upgraded to NetWare 5, with their volumes either remaining in place or migrated to a newly installed server.

5. The NDS tree is partitioned, with replicas distributed on servers around the network.

The steps in the migration process largely depend on the hardware available and the migration tools that you use. If you intend to upgrade all of your servers in place, then one bindery (that of the first server you upgrade) must be migrated to the new NDS tree during the NetWare 5 installation. The primary limitation to this method is that all of the new NDS objects created from the bindery are placed into the same context as the server object.

Once the first server is upgraded to NetWare 5, you can use the Upgrade Wizard (DS Migrate in NetWare 4.11/4.2) to migrate the binderies from the other servers, as shown in Figure 10.4. Then, when you upgrade the operating system on the other servers, the objects representing the servers and their volumes can be inserted into the existing NDS tree by the INSTALL.NLM program.

F I G U R E   10.4

When upgrading servers in place, the bindery of the first server is migrated to NDS during the NetWare installation process.

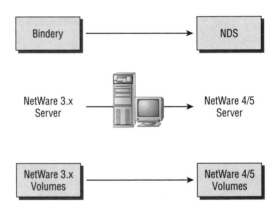

In many NetWare shops, an upgrade to version 5 requires the installation of new servers as well. The Pentium 100Mhz-based systems that were cutting edge servers only a few years ago are now barely suitable for use as workstations. When you deploy one or more new servers as part of your network upgrade, you can install NetWare 5 from scratch and create a new NDS tree containing a single server object. Then you can use the Upgrade Wizard to read the binderies from all of your existing servers, and model the data by building a custom tree design and placing the migrated objects in any container you wish, as shown in Figure 10.5. Once you have created the NDS database, the Upgrade Wizard utility continues to migrate some or all of your NetWare 3.*x* volumes to the new NetWare 5 servers.

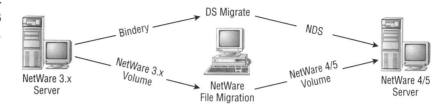

The Upgrade Wizard runs on a 32-bit Windows (Windows 95/98 or
Windows NT/2000) workstation that is logged into the network using a
standard NetWare client. The programs do not transfer the bindery
directly to the NDS database. Instead, they read the bindery information
into a database created on the workstation's local drive and then copy the
information from the database to NDS in a separate operation. You can
manipulate the information in the database with the program's graphical
interface while it is on the workstation, and write it to NDS when you are
finished.

Migrating Bindery Properties

Many of the properties found in bindery objects perform the same functions in NDS, and the Upgrade Wizard transfers them smoothly to the new
database. However, some bindery properties do not translate easily and
are modified during the migration process, while others are not migrated
at all. In addition, when you migrate the contents of multiple binderies
into a single NDS database, it is important to understand what happens to
the properties when duplicate accounts are combined into one NDS
object.

Most of the nonconflicting properties in bindery users and groups are
migrated to the NDS database intact and combined into a single object. For
example, when a bindery account on one server with a security equivalence
to user A is combined with an account on another server with equivalence
to user B, the resulting NDS object has security equivalence to both A and B (see
Figure 10.6).

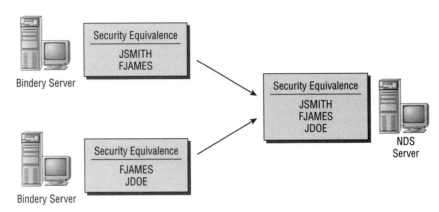

FIGURE 10.6

Bindery properties with values that do not conflict are combined during the migration to NDS.

The values for the following bindery properties can be migrated to NDS user and group objects without alteration and combined with the values of the same properties from other migrated binderies:

- Security equivalences (except Supervisor equivalences)

- Managed users and groups

- Group memberships

- Group member lists

- Trustee rights to directories and files

- Print server operators and users

- Print queue operators and users

There are also a number of bindery properties that can be migrated to NDS, but which cannot be effectively combined with the same properties in other binderies because the values conflict. For example, when a bindery account containing a login restriction that requires the use of a 6-character password is combined with an account for the same user on another server that requires an 8-character password, the values contradict each other. In cases like this, the new NDS object is usually assigned the value from the first bindery to be migrated, as shown in Figure 10.7. When bindery accounts for the same user are migrated to the same NDS object, values for these properties are ignored. Because of this behavior, the order in which you migrate binderies into the NDS tree can be very important.

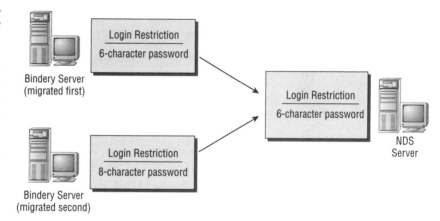

FIGURE 10.7

When bindery
properties with
conflicting values are
migrated, the value
found in the bindery
migrated first is used
in the NDS object.

In the following properties, the value migrated to the new NDS object is taken from the first bindery processed:

- User login script
- System login script
- Login restrictions
- Accounting balances and settings

Passwords

NetWare 5's Upgrade Wizard, unlike the upgrade facilities available in Net-Ware 4.*x*, preserves the passwords of objects that are migrated.

NetWare 4.11's DS Migrate replaces the password in the user objects that it reads from bindery servers with a default password that is the same for all users. You can specify a default password of your own or use DS Migrate's default, which is Defaultpw. You can also modify the passwords of your user objects during the tree modeling process, either by having DS Migrate assign a random password for each user or by manually specifying your own.

The passwords provided by DS Migrate are modified to conform to the limitations imposed by the minimum password length property. If, for example, the password specified for assignment to all new objects is five characters and a user is required to have a password of at least seven characters, the assigned password is padded out with Xs to achieve the required length.

NetWare 4.*x*'s `MIGRATE.EXE`, instead of assigning a single default password to all of the user objects it creates, assigns a different random password to each user. The passwords are stored in a text file that you can supply to users as needed.

Both DS Migrate and `MIGRATE.EXE` automatically set the property that forces users to change their passwords during their first NDS login. This places the responsibility for password maintenance back into the hands of the user without seriously compromising security.

The one NetWare 4.*x* migration method that does preserve user passwords is an in-place server migration using the `INSTALL.NLM` program. You can use this technique to migrate accounts from another server's bindery with their passwords intact by copying the bindery to a NetWare 4.*x* server. Run the `BINDFIX.EXE` program and copy the backup files it creates (`NET$OBJ.OLD`, `NET$PROP.OLD`, and `NET$VAL.OLD`) from the `SYS:SYSTEM` directory on the bindery server to the same directory on the NetWare 4.*x* server. Then load `INSTALL.NLM` on the NetWare 4.*x* server and, from the Directory Options screen, select Upgrade NetWare 3.*x* Bindery Information to the Directory.

Supervisors

Because NDS is intended as a resource for enterprise networks, it does not use the Supervisor user account in the same way as a bindery-based NetWare server. The Supervisor user in NetWare version 3.12 and earlier has full access to the entire operating system that cannot be rescinded. On large enterprise networks, it may not be practical to have a single user with this type of power. In large corporations, the ultimate responsibility for different parts of the network is often distributed among various administrators.

Instead of Supervisor, NetWare 4.*x*/5.*x* uses the Admin user, which has full access to the entire NDS tree by default, but you can modify by revoking certain rights. When you migrate a bindery into the NDS database, the Supervisor user is not migrated. Bindery users that have Supervisor equivalence are granted Supervisor object rights in NDS, but only to the objects that were migrated from that particular bindery. Users are also granted Supervisor object rights to any managed users and groups listed in their bindery accounts. A migrated user is never granted full rights to the entire NDS tree.

Every NetWare 4.*x*/5.*x* server has a user called SUPERVISOR automatically created in its bindery context. See Chapter 7 for more information about this special case.

Login Scripts

The login scripts associated with bindery objects are migrated to NDS by the Upgrade Wizard, DS Migrate and `MIGRATE.EXE`. In `MIGRATE.EXE`, scripts from duplicate objects in multiple binderies cannot be combined into a single NDS object, so it is the order in which you migrate the servers that determines that script is used. In DS Migrate and the Upgrade Wizard, you can specify whether the login scripts of merged objects are to be combined or whether an existing script should be replaced during subsequent merges.

User login scripts are migrated from the first bindery where the user appears. The system login script in a bindery becomes the container script for the context to which you are migrating the bindery, as long as a script does not already exist for that container.

Many of the property values found in binderies, such as security equivalences, are altered during migration to reflect the names of the new NDS objects they reference rather than the old bindery accounts. Login scripts, however, are migrated without modifications of any kind. References to servers, volumes, and other bindery elements may not function in the NDS environment, and they must be changed manually.

Print Objects

Print objects can be migrated from NetWare binderies by the Upgrade Wizard or DS Migrate. During an in-place server upgrade, you must run the

PUPGRADE.NLM module to migrate bindery print queues, print servers, and printers to NDS. For a DOS workstation-based migration, NetWare includes a separate utility called MIGPRINT.EXE.

One of the most common problems that occurs during the migration of print objects is name conflicts. Administrators frequently give print queues or printers the same name as other objects, especially groups. Having the users in the Sales group access a printer also called Sales can be convenient to administrators and users, but it causes problems in NDS. Be sure to check for duplicate names before beginning the migration process.

NetWare versions 4.0 through 4.02 permitted the creation of identically named objects in the same container, as long as the objects were of different types. Thus, a printer object called Sales could coexist with a group object called Sales in the same context. With the release of NetWare 4.1, however, this practice was proscribed.

If you use direct-attach printing devices, like Intel NetPorts or HP JetDirect cards, you need to make sure the firmware supports NDS attachments. If it doesn't, the bindery queues need to exist as bindery queues within NDS.

Migrating with INSTALL.NLM

The simplest form of bindery migration occurs during an in-place upgrade of a NetWare 3.1*x* server to NetWare 4.1*x*/5.*x*. As part of the operating system installation process, the INSTALL.NLM program creates objects representing the new NetWare server, the server's volumes, and the Admin user. You have a choice of placing these objects into an existing NDS tree by specifying the tree name and a context, or you can create an entirely new tree.

INSTALL.NLM can only create a simple NDS tree with a single branch. You can specify the name of a country or organization object at the tree's top level, and up to three layers of organizational units in the fields beneath. The server objects and any objects that you may migrate from the bindery are placed in the bottom layer container. When you are adding objects to an existing tree, you can use these same fields to specify the names of existing containers or new ones to be created.

As you specify the names of organizational units in the fields provided, the Server Context field displays the NDS name of the context in which the server object will be created. You can specify a context that is more than four layers deep by directly modifying the contents of the Server Context field to include up to 25 container layers.

You must create the server, volume, and Admin user objects during the installation process, but the migration of the server's bindery and its volumes is optional, and occurs after the NetWare installation has been completed. INSTALL.NLM's migration process places all of the converted bindery objects into the same container as the server object. If you want to place the objects into different containers or build a more complex tree by combining the binderies of multiple servers, then you can skip the INSTALL.NLM migration process and use DS Migrate to populate your tree at a later time.

If you plan to use DS Migrate or the Upgrade Wizard to combine multiple binderies into one NDS tree, it is recommended that you skip the bindery migration process during the server installation. Neither DS Migrate nor the Upgrade Wizard can read the contents of an existing NDS database. The process of modeling a complex tree is easier if all of the objects are available for manipulation.

If you do want to use INSTALL.NLM to migrate the server's bindery or volumes, you must first complete the NetWare 4.1*x*/5.*x* installation procedure. Once this is done, you can select Directory Options from INSTALL.NLM's Installation Options box to display the screen shown in Figure 10.8. Selecting Upgrade NetWare 3.*x* Bindery Information to the Directory causes the program to scan the server's SYS volume for the bindery files and convert its users and groups into NDS objects. Selecting Upgrade Mounted Volumes into the Directory converts the directory entry tables of the server volumes to use NDS instead of bindery references.

F I G U R E   10.8

You can migrate the bindery and volumes of an upgraded NetWare server to NDS at any time after the NetWare 4.1*x* installation process has been completed.

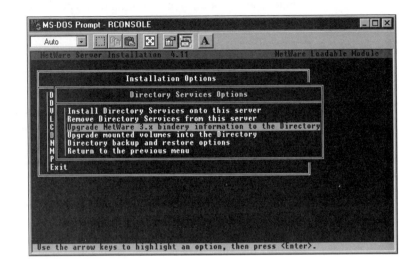

Using PUPGRADE.NLM

The bindery migration performed by INSTALL.NLM ignores the printer and print server objects used by the NetWare 3.1*x* server. To migrate these objects to the NDS database, you must load the PUPGRADE utility at the server console after the NetWare 4.*x* installation has been completed. You can also launch the program by selecting Upgrade 3.1*x* Print Services from INSTALL.NLM 's Product Options screen.

PUPGRADE is only used when upgrading to NetWare 4.*x*. NetWare 5's INSTALL utility and the Upgrade Wizard handle print servers and printers along with other objects.

Like INSTALL.NLM, PUPGRADE automatically scans the server for the NetWare 3.1*x* bindery files and locates the print-related objects like print servers and printers. After logging in to the NDS tree, you can migrate the print objects to the NDS tree by selecting Available Options ➤ Upgrade Print Server and Printers. The program presents a list of the print servers found in the bindery, from which you can select the one to be migrated.

PUPGRADE reads the properties of the selected print server and creates NDS objects for the server itself, as well as any printers and print queues with which it is associated. As with the user and group migration process, new NDS objects are created in the same container as the NetWare server object.

You can also use PUPGRADE to convert databases that you have created with the PRINTCON and PRINTDEF utilities.

PUPGRADE can create NDS objects for the print queues associated with a selected print server, but it does not migrate the queue itself, that is, the directory on the NetWare volume where queued print jobs are temporarily stored. The queue directory is migrated as part of the volume migration process performed by INSTALL.NLM.

Migrating with DS Migrate

Novell has licensed DS Migrate, a Windows application, from Preferred Systems, Inc. for inclusion with NetWare 4.11 and 4.2. Preferred Systems has since been acquired by Cheyenne Software, Inc., which has in turn been acquired by Computer Associates International. DS Migrate is a subset of Cheyenne's full-featured NDS management product: DS Standard NDS Manager, which can be purchased separately. Designed specifically for migrating bindery information to NDS, DS Migrate can read the binderies from all of the NetWare 3.1*x* servers on your network. You can then model the data to build a customized NDS tree, create new objects, and modify the properties of existing ones.

DS Migrate is a NetWare 4.*x* utility. It is replaced by the Upgrade Wizard in NetWare 5.

The primary difference between DS Migrate and DS Standard is that DS Migrate can only import data from NetWare binderies. The DS Standard product can also read the contents of an existing NDS database, enabling you to integrate migrated bindery data into an existing tree. DS Standard also includes more elaborate object management tools, including the ability to merge like objects and perform complex, global search-and-replace operations.

> If you think you require the additional capabilities of DS Standard to perform your bindery migration, you can preview the program's capabilities by downloading a 30-day live trial version of the product from Computer Associates' Web site at `http://www.cai.com/evaluate/download/ds_standard.htm`.

DS Migrate is installed to the NetWare 4.*x* server's `SYS:SYSTEM\DSMIGRAT` directory during the operating system installation. You can run the `DSMIGRAT.EXE` program in that directory from any Windows workstation, or launch it from the Tools menu of the NetWare Administrator utility.

The bindery migration procedure as performed by DS Migrate proceeds in three stages:

- **Discovery**   The process by which DS Migrate reads information from the binderies on the network and adds it to its own database.

- **Modeling**   The process by which the user manipulates DS Migrate's database to create a customized NDS tree design.

- **Configuration**   The process by which DS Migrate replicates the tree created in its own database to the actual NDS database.

The following sections examine each of these processes in detail.

The Discovery Process

DS Migrate begins the migration process by accessing the data in your NetWare binderies and adding it to its own internal database. During the discovery process, DS Migrate reads the bindery objects and properties and creates a view on the workstation. A *view* is a facsimile of an NDS tree built from the data now stored on the workstation. To NetWare servers, discovery is strictly a read-only process; users can continue to access the binderies during and after the process.

To perform a bindery discovery, the workstation running DS Migrate must be logged into a NetWare 2.*x* or 3.*x* server or to a NetWare 4.*x* server in bindery emulation mode. You can use any standard NetWare client, but your user account must have the appropriate rights to access the objects and properties that you intend to migrate.

While you can perform a discovery of a NetWare 4.x server, only the container specified as the server's bindery context is read by DS Migrate. In addition, the discovery process only recognizes the properties found in a standard NetWare bindery. Properties unique to NDS are not read into the DS Migrate database. As a result, performing a bindery discover on a NetWare 4.x server is not a substitute for an NDS discovery, which can only be performed by the DS Standard product.

DS Migrate can perform a discovery of all of your network's binderies in one process. When you create a new bindery view, you are prompted to enter a name for the view and are then presented with the dialog box, shown in Figure 10.9, that lists the bindery servers to which you are attached.

FIGURE 10.9

For a bindery discovery, you select the servers and the bindery elements that you want to discover.

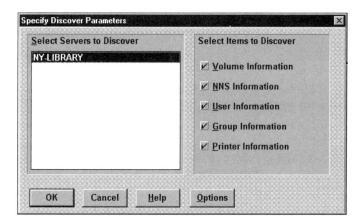

For each server you select, DS Migrate discovers the following properties:

- System login script
- Default time restrictions
- Default volume restrictions

- Default account restrictions

- Console operators

You also have the option of including any or all of the following information in the discovery:

- Volume information

- NNS (NetWare Name Server) information

- User information

- Group information

- Printer information

By default, all of the discovered bindery information is placed in an organization object that you name before the process begins. For each server discovered, DS Migrate creates an organizational unit object in the organization, and places the new objects from each bindery into the organizational unit named for its server. Thus, a discovery of the binderies on three servers would result in a view that would look something like that shown in Figure 10.10.

F I G U R E   10.10

Each discovered bindery is placed in an organizational unit named for its server.

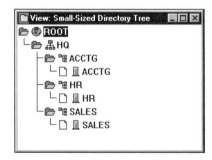

Each object found during the discovery process is logged to a file that you specify in the Bindery Discover Options page of DS Migrate's Options dialog box (see Figure 10.11), which you access from the Tools menu. On this page, you also specify the name of the organization object in which the discovered binderies should be located and the password that should be applied to all user objects.

FIGURE 10.11

On the Bindery
Discovery Options
page, you set the log,
organization name,
and password options
for the discovery
process.

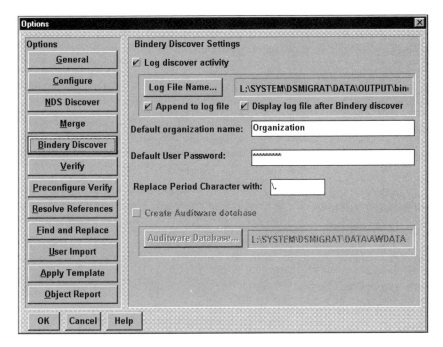

Bindery object names can contain periods, but NDS objects cannot, because the period is used as a separator in compound object names. DS Migrate therefore provides a field on the Bindery Discover Options page in which you can specify a replacement character for any periods found in bindery names during the discovery process.

The default organization of the bindery view is designed primarily to facilitate the location and differentiation of objects; it is not intended to be a final NDS tree design. Although you can elect to use this arrangement for your actual NDS tree if you wish, you will have ample opportunity to redesign the view during the modeling phase of the migration procedure.

The Modeling Process

Once you have discovered all of the information in your network's binderies, you are ready to begin modeling the data. At this point, you are working only with the resources stored on the workstation. This is one of DS Migrate's greatest strengths. You can now manipulate the data in any way you wish, without endangering the operability of your bindery servers or your NDS tree. In fact, you can use DS Migrate to design your NDS tree before you have even installed a NetWare 4.*x* server.

At its simplest, DS Migrate's data modeling capabilities enable you to alter the default tree design by creating new objects, dragging and dropping objects to different containers, and manually changing property values. Because you are not writing data to different NDS partitions and replicas located on other servers, these processes are much faster and easier than when working with live NDS data. Each object in the tree has a property dialog box that looks a lot like those in the NetWare Administrator utility (see Figure 10.12), but they are not so much alike as to cause confusion.

F I G U R E   10.12

DS Migrate enables you to modify any of an object's properties using a dialog box similar to those found in NetWare Administrator.

While DS Migrate can create logical objects, such as users and containers, it cannot create objects that reference actual physical hardware, such as servers. The relationship between a server object and the server hardware itself must be established during the NetWare installation process by the `INSTALL.NLM` utility. Thus, you can create references to a server object during the modeling process, but that server must exist in the live NDS tree before the objects with those references can be configured.

DS Migrate's tree display and dialog boxes are also similar to those of NetWare Administrator in that they do not let you perform operations that would not be possible on a real NDS tree. For example, you cannot create an organization object subordinate to an organizational unit or assign to a user a membership in anything other than a group object. The program also tries to prevent mistakes that can severely affect the design process. You cannot delete a container object without first deleting all of the objects it contains.

Merging Objects

Because DS Migrate places each discovered bindery in a different container, objects with the same name are not automatically merged. You can merge objects together in several different ways, and control the rules by which DS Migrate handles the properties of the merged objects. Merging two objects with the same name is as easy as dragging one object and dropping it on the other or on the container in which the other object is located. You can drag and drop objects between views or within the same view. To operate on a larger scale, you can drag one container onto another, causing all identically named objects in the two containers to be merged.

On the Merge Options page (see Figure 10.13), you specify the actions that DS Migrate should take when merging objects. For properties that can have multiple values (such as security equivalences), you can have the values for the merged objects combined, or you can replace the values in the old object with those of the new one. A single value property can be left as is or replaced by the new value. Container merges can proceed automatically, or DS Migrate can generate a confirmation dialog box each time it encounters objects with the same name.

FIGURE 10.13

DS Migrate enables
you to control what
happens to property
values when objects
are merged.

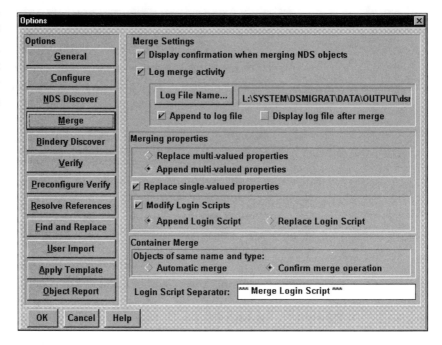

You can also control how DS Migrate handles login scripts during an object merge. You can have the existing script replaced by the new one or combine the two by appending the commands from the new script to the old. While this technique may not eliminate the need to manually adjust the scripts for use with NDS, it does place all of the script commands in one place for easier editing.

Find and Replace

One of the most powerful tools provided by DS Migrate is the ability to perform global find and replace operations on user and group object properties. You can, for example, replace the default password assigned to user objects during the discovery process with a different global password, a randomly generated password, or a password equivalent to the user's login name. You can also modify the trustee rights granted to users and groups on NetWare 2.x servers by searching objects for a particular path and replacing or deleting the volume reference and rights assignments.

The find and replace capabilities provided by DS Migrate are limited to certain basic properties of user and group objects only. DS Standard includes support for many more properties and for different objects, as well as the ability to find and replace object names and object references.

Importing User Information

Another way to add user objects to a DS Migrate view is to import the data from text files generated by an external database application. As with the bindery discover process, imported users are merged into objects in the same context with identical names. Like NetWare's UIMPORT.EXE, you must create a properly formatted data file and a control file in order to import user information. The format of the ASCII files is the same as that for UIMPORT, except that DS Migrate supports object types that UIMPORT does not.

For more information on creating data and import control files, see Migrating with UIMPORT.EXE, later in this chapter.

The Configuration Process

The final stage of the migration process is the configuration, in which the tree that you have created in the DS Migrate database is written to the actual NDS tree. However, before you commit your changes to a live environment, DS Migrate provides several tools with which you can check your tree for problems. These tools are as follows:

- **Resolve References for Selected Objects**   Verifies that the objects referenced in the properties of other objects actually exist at the appropriate location. If, for example, you move a server object to another container and fail to move its volume objects, this function will point out the possible discrepancy.

- **Verify Tree Metrics**   Verifies that the tree conforms to the metrics defined in the Verify page of the Options dialog box. Tree metrics are design limitations, such as the maximum number of objects allowed in a container, the maximum number of levels in a tree, and the maximum length for a fully distinguished NDS name.

- **Verify Object Dependencies**   Checks to see that all mutually dependent object references are properly configured. For example, verifying the dependencies for a user checks to see that every group object listed in the user's group membership property also lists the user object as one of its members. Each object must reference the other in order for the relationship to operate.

Before you can configure your tree design, you must log into NDS using an account that has the rights needed to create and modify objects in the tree. Before DS Migrate actually writes any data to NDS, it performs a final check in which it compares the proposed changes to the existing environment. This final verification is performed by DS Migrate:

- Checks to see that all hardware objects (such as servers and volumes) referenced by other objects in the proposed tree design actually exist at the specified location in the live NDS tree.

- Checks all references to objects not selected for configuration to see if they can be found in the existing NDS tree.

- Verifies that all print server and print queue objects to be configured have at least one operator. If not, DS Migrate adds the user currently logged into the workstation to the operator list.

Once the configuration process actually begins, objects added to NDS are merged with existing objects of the same name. The properties of the merged objects can be combined or replaced, according to the settings found on the Configure page of the Options dialog box (see Figure 10.14).

Using the NetWare File Migration Utility

Once you have migrated the binderies of your NetWare server to NDS, you can migrate the contents of your volumes with the NetWare File Migration utility. This is a graphical, wizard-based utility that intelligently copies the contents of NetWare 3.1x volumes to NetWare 4.x servers, updating the directory entry tables to use NDS references in its trustee lists instead of bindery references.

F I G U R E   10.14

The configure process can merge objects with those in an existing NDS database, just as you can merge objects in the DS Migrate database.

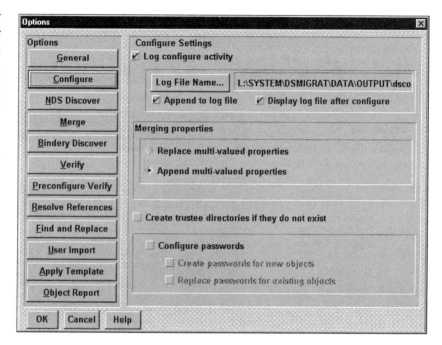

 The File Migration utility is only available in NetWare 4.11 and 4.2. Its capabilities have been incorporated in the Upgrade Wizard with NetWare 5.

 The NetWare File Migration utility can only migrate NetWare 3.1x volumes. To migrate files from NetWare 2.x servers, you must use MIGRATE.EXE.

It is only necessary to migrate volumes if you are building new NetWare 4.x servers on your network and you want to move the data from your old servers to the new ones. If you plan to upgrade your NetWare 3.1x servers to Net-Ware 4.x, then you can leave your volumes in place and upgrade them during the operating system installation process.

To use the file migration utility, you must be logged into both your NetWare 3.1x servers, using a bindery connection, and to your NDS tree before you launch the program. Like DS Migrate, you run the file migration utility from the Tools menu of NetWare Administrator or by running MIGWIN3X.EXE from the SYS:PUBLIC directory. The wizard screens guide you through the selection of the source and destination servers (see Figure 10.15).

F I G U R E 10.15

The NetWare File Migration utility copies the contents of NetWare 3.1*x* volumes to NetWare 4.*x* servers while updating the access control list of each file and directory with the names of the NDS objects that have replaced the bindery users and groups.

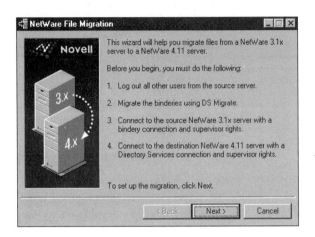

Before Migrating Files

Before you begin the file migration process, observe the following prerequisites:

- Be sure that there is sufficient disk space on the destination volume to accommodate the new files.

- Be sure that the same namespace modules loaded on the source volume are also loaded on the destination volume. The OS/2 name space in NetWare 3.*x* and NetWare 4.0–4.10 is replaced in NetWare 4.11 and 4.2 by the *long* (LONG.NAM) namespace.

- Log into both servers with an account that has appropriate rights to the source and destination volumes.

- Unload any third-party programs on the source server that may lock files open, preventing their migration.

- Because objects may have been moved to other tree locations during the modeling process, you must run NetWare File Migration from the same workstation where you ran DS Migrate. The file migration utility accesses DS Migrate's name mapping file to determine the new locations of the objects referenced in the volumes' directory entry tables.

- NetWare File Migration accesses the volumes on the source server(s) using NetWare's SMS (Storage Management Services) modules. Before beginning the migration process, you must upgrade the modules on the NetWare 3.1*x* server(s) by copying the following files from the \PRODUCTS\NW3X directory of the NetWare 4.11/4.2 CD-ROM to the SYS:SYSTEM directory of each source server:

    - TSA311.NLM or TSA312.NLM

    - SPXS.NLM

    - TLI.NLM

    - CLIB.NLM

    - AFTER311.NLM

    - A3112.NLM

    - SMDR.NLM

    - STREAMS.NLM

WARNING   It's possible that a more recent patch applied to the NetWare 3.1*x* server contains more recent versions of these files. Only copy the files from the CD-ROM that have file dates that are later than those of your existing files.

- Load the updated TSA311.NLM or TSA312.NLM module (whichever is appropriate for your NetWare version) on each source server.

- If the volumes on your source servers have the MAC namespace installed, check to see if the MAC.NAM module is version 3.12 or later. If not, perform the following procedure:

    1. Dismount the volumes using the outdated MAC namespace module.

2. Copy the `MAC.NAM` module from the `\PRODUCTS\NW3X` directory of the NetWare 4.11/4.2 CD-ROM to the `SYS:SYSTEM` directory of your source servers. If MAC namespace has been added to the SYS volume, then copy `MAC.NAM` to your server's DOS partition.

3. Run a VREPAIR on each volume using the new module.

4. Remount the volumes. If the SYS volume had the old MAC namespace, then load `MAC.NAM` from the DOS partition before mounting the SYS volume.

File Migration Behavior

During the file migration process, the contents of directories with the same name are combined on the destination volume. However, duplicate files are not overwritten; they are instead renamed with numerical extensions starting with .001.

When migrating a NetWare 3.1x server's SYS volume, the file migration utility omits the files in the system directories that are not needed on the Net-Ware 4.x server. These directories are as follows:

- `SYS:SYSTEM`
- `SYS:SYSTEM\NLS`
- `SYS:PUBLIC`
- `SYS:/PUBLIC/OS2`
- `SYS:PUBLIC/UNIX`
- `SYS:PUBLIC/NLS`
- `SYS:PUBLIC/CLIENT`
- `SYS:LOGIN`
- `SYS:ETC`

The utility also skips the `TTS$LOG.ERR` and `VOL$LOG.ERR` files on each volume, as well as any files that are left open during the migration process.

Migrating with MIGRATE.EXE

MIGRATE.EXE is a DOS-based utility that can migrate both bindery information and data volumes to a NetWare 4.*x* server. MIGRATE lacks many of the advanced functions provided by the combination of DS Migrate and NetWare File Migration, such as data modeling and intelligent file migration. You can use MIGRATE to perform across-the-wire or in-place migrations; but except under certain circumstances, the use of INSTALL.NLM for in-place migrations and DS Migrate/NetWare File Migration for across-the-wire migrations is recommended.

In addition to NetWare 2.*x* and 3.1*x* bindery servers, MIGRATE.EXE can also migrate user information from the following operating systems: IBM PCLP (PC LAN Program) 1.3 Extended Services, IBM LAN Server versions 1.0 through 1.3, and Microsoft LAN Manager 2.0.

The MIGRATE.EXE utility is not copied to a NetWare 4.*x* server during the default installation process. You can run the program directly from the \PRODUCTS\MIGRATE directory of the NetWare 4.11 CD-ROM, or use the DOWNLOAD.BAT file in that same directory to copy the necessary files to your local workstation.

If you run MIGRATE.EXE from the CD-ROM, be sure to change the value of the Working Directory field to point to a directory on a writeable drive.

Inplace Migrations

When you are upgrading a bindery server to NetWare 4.*x*, the INSTALL.NLM program is typically used to migrate the bindery to an NDS tree and update the volumes. INSTALL can perform these tasks solely within the server itself; a workstation is not required. INSTALL can also migrate the print objects from a bindery to NDS, something MIGRATE cannot do. If, however, your bindery server lacks a large enough DOS partition (15MB of free space) or does not have sufficient free disk space (at least 100MB) available on the SYS volume for INSTALL to perform the migration, then you can use MIGRATE.EXE instead.

Across-the-Wire Migrations

When you use MIGRATE.EXE to perform an across-the-wire migration, the limitations are more severe. Like DS Migrate, MIGRATE.EXE functions by reading the information from a bindery, converting the objects to NDS format, and storing them on the local workstation drive. The program then adds the new objects to the NDS tree on a NetWare 4.x server. However, unlike DS Migrate, MIGRATE.EXE can process only one bindery at a time, and can access the NetWare 4.x server only in bindery emulation mode (see Figure 10.16).

F I G U R E 10.16

MIGRATE.EXE
connects to a NetWare
4.x server only in
bindery emulation
mode and can create
objects only in the
server's bindery
context.

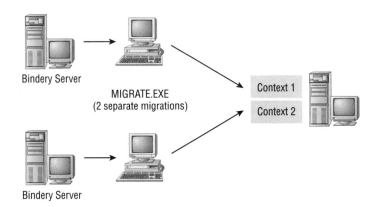

Bindery Server

MIGRATE.EXE
(2 separate migrations)

Context 1

Context 2

Bindery Server

This means that the contents of each bindery must be migrated to a single container, which is identified by the SET BINDERY CONTEXT command on the NetWare 4.x server. If you want to migrate multiple binderies into different containers, you must perform a separate migration for each one, logging into the server with a different bindery context each time. There is also no way to modify the properties of the objects after they have been read from the bindery and before they are written to NDS.

If multiple bindery contexts are set on the destination NetWare 4.x server, then only the first context is used.

When it comes to migrating files, MIGRATE.EXE can process NetWare 2.x volumes, which NetWare File Migration cannot, but lacks the intelligence with which the GUI utility filters out the system files during the migration process. There is no danger of damaging a NetWare 4.*x* installation during the migration of an SYS volume, because MIGRATE never overwrites existing files on a destination volume. However, the migration of an SYS volume can place a large number of useless files in NetWare 4.*x*'s system directories. It is recommended that you migrate SYS volumes to a subdirectory on the target server, so that you can manually delete the unneeded files.

The bindery migration capabilities of `MIGRATE.EXE` are largely the same as the default settings of DS Migrate. You cannot configure MIGRATE's object merging behavior. Multivalued properties are always combined, while single value properties use the value from the first bindery migrated. You can, however, select the information in the bindery that you want to migrate, as shown in Figure 10.17.

F I G U R E   10.17

MIGRATE.EXE lacks the modeling capabilities of DS Migrate, but it does let you selectively migrate specific objects from a bindery.

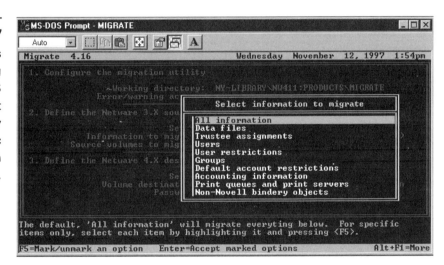

Using **MIGPRINT.EXE**

`MIGRATE.EXE` cannot migrate the print objects from a NetWare bindery. To do this, you must use a separate DOS workstation utility called `MIGPRINT.EXE`. `MIGPRINT.EXE` migrates print server, print queues, printers, and print job configurations, creating the appropriate NDS objects and associations in the destination tree.

To use MIGPRINT, you must log into the destination NDS tree as well as the source bindery server. The program is located in the same directory on the NetWare 4.11 CD-ROM as `MIGRATE.EXE`, and is copied to the local workstation when you run the `DOWNLOAD.BAT` file. To run `MIGPRINT.EXE`, use the following syntax from the command line:

`MIGPRINT /d=destination /s=source [vol=volume o=filename]`

where *destination* is the name of the destination NetWare 4.*x* server, *source* is the name of the source bindery server, *volume* is the name of an alternate destination volume (the default is SYS), and *filename* is the location of the log file created during the migration process.

Migrating with UIMPORT.EXE

UIMPORT.EXE is a DOS workstation utility that you can use to create large numbers of user objects in your NDS tree from the information stored in an external database application. Any database that can export its data in a delimited ASCII format can be used with UIMPORT. You can also update existing NDS user objects with new information by re-importing the data as your database changes.

To use UIMPORT, you must create two ASCII text files, as follows:

- **The data file** Contains the information about your users as produced by your database application, using punctuation marks (usually commas and quotes) to separate the fields.

- **The import control file** Identifies the NDS user property where the value in each data field should be written.

DS Migrate can also import database information to create user objects in its own database, which can later be written to the NDS tree. Once the objects are created in the DS Migrate database, you can modify their properties and model the tree structure just as you would with objects created during the bindery discover process. The structure of the data and import control files are the same as for UIMPORT, with the exception that DS Migrate supports a larger set of object properties into which data can be written. Using DS Migrate also provides a safety buffer, so that if there are problems with your text files, you don't end up creating hundreds of incorrectly formatted objects in your live NDS tree.

NDS version 8 (which ships with NetWare 5.1 and is available for earlier versions) includes a new utility called the bulkloader. This utility provides the capability of adding millions of objects to NDS using the LDIF (LDAP Data Interchange Format) version 1 file format that is in draft form in the Internet Engineering Task Force. LDIF is the standard format for exporting and importing information into directories that support LDAP v3. Bulkloader is an NLM that runs on the server.

Creating a Data File

Most database applications can export their data to an ASCII file, using punctuation marks to separate the fields that comprise each record. Because you will create an import control file that maps the data fields to the NDS object properties, the order of the fields in each record is not important. It is important, however, to make sure that that the data file is punctuated correctly. A typical ASCII export format places quotation marks around each field and separates the fields with commas, as follows:

```
"Smith","John","123 Broadway","New York","NY","10019"
```

Another factor to consider when creating a data file is the nature of your data itself and its usability in NDS. The only properties that are required to create an NDS user are the object name and the user's last name. While your database will certainly include the full name of each user, it might not contain the last name in a separate field, or an abbreviation suitable for use as an object name, such as JSMITH for John Smith. You may find it necessary to manipulate your data file using a text editor or other tool (such as an AWK or Perl script) before you import it into NDS.

Creating an Import Control File

The import control file consists of two sections: the control parameters and the field definitions. Each section is comprised of a heading, which must be flush with the left margin, and a series of entries, which must each be preceded by at least one space, as follows:

```
Import Control
    Separator=;
    Name context=".CorpNet.US"
    Create home directory=Y
    Home directory path="users"
    Home directory volume=".vol1.CorpNet.US"
Fields
    Last name
    Name
    Mailing label information
    City
    State or province
    Postal (ZIP) Code
    Skip
    Telephone
```

The control parameters define the characters used in the data file, as well as how and where the user objects should be created in the NDS tree. If you omit all control parameters, UIMPORT uses the comma as its default separator and creates the objects in the workstation's current context. Other control parameters specify whether you want to create a home directory for each user and, if so, where it should be created.

The field definitions section consists of a list of object properties that correspond to the order of the fields as found in the data file. The value in each field of a data file record is inserted into the user object property specified in this section. The sample file shown above contains field definitions for a data file with records like the following:

```
"Smith";"John";"123 Broadway";"New York";"NY";"10019";
"123-45-6789";"212-555-1212"
```

When the record is imported with this import control file, the value "Smith" is inserted into the new object's last name field and "John" becomes the user's login name. The next four fields are inserted into the object's various address fields. The seventh field, containing the user's social security number, is skipped as this information is not desired in the NDS object. The eighth and last field is written to the object's telephone property. Each field must be accounted for, even if it is not to be added to the user object.

A complete listing of the control parameters and field definitions supported by UIMPORT.EXE can be found in the NetWare 4.11/4.2/5.0 Upgrade manual.

Running UIMPORT.EXE

Once you have created the two files, you log into NDS from a DOS workstation and run the UIMPORT.EXE program, which is found in your NetWare 4.*x*/5.*x* server's SYS:PUBLIC directory, using the following syntax:

UIMPORT control data [/C]

Where *control* specifies the name and location of the import control file and *data* the name and location of the data file. The /C switch causes the program to execute without stopping each time the display is full.

Adding large numbers of users with UIMPORT can take a very long time and can noticeably degrade the performance of the NDS tree, so it is recommended that you perform the operation after working hours.

Summary

This chapter has presented an overview of the various methods of migrating NetWare 2.*x* and 3.*x* servers to NDS-based servers, principally NetWare 4.11/4.2 and 5. The options of in-place upgrade versus across-the-wire migration have been discussed, as well as the effect each has on the NDS objects imported. Similarly, the use of different tools—the Upgrade Wizard, DS Migrate and MIGRATE.EXE—was explored, along with the limitations and specific requirements of each.

Special reference has been given to the migration of passwords and login scripts, which may require manual intervention depending on the migration method and tool used.

CHAPTER

11

NDS Maintenance

ovell Directory Services is designed to be a crucial element of an enterprise network, and when it performs poorly, all of the network's users can suffer a loss of productivity. Creating an effective NDS tree is not only a matter of design and deployment. It is also essential to have an ongoing program of maintenance and adjustment in order to keep the NDS database healthy and to modify the tree design as your network evolves. This chapter covers some of the tools and techniques that you can use to make sure that your NDS tree continues to perform efficiently and that it adequately supports your users.

While the emphasis in this chapter is NDS running on NetWare servers, the same principles apply (as do many of the utilities) to NDS running on other platforms such as Windows NT, Solaris, Linux, and Windows 2000 utilizing NDS eDirectory and NDS Corporate Edition. See Chapter 17 for more information on these other platforms.

Creating an NDS Maintenance Plan

The distributed nature of the NDS database on most networks makes replication and convergence the most critical aspects of directory communications. *Convergence* is the process by which a change made to one replica is propagated to all of the other replicas on the network. NDS is a *multiple master* database, meaning that changes can be made to any one of several replicas, all of which then apply those changes to the others (see Figure 11.1). This is in contrast to a *single master* database (such as Windows NT 's domain structure), in which all changes must be made to one Master replica that then updates the other replicas.

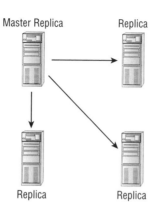

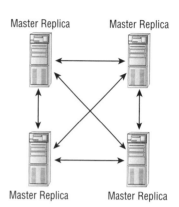

The advantage of a multiple master database is that administrators all over the enterprise network can make modifications to the nearest Read/ Write replica, rather than having to address a single Master replica that may be located in another building or even another city. However, the inherent problem in multiple master updating is that administrators at different locations can conceivably make database modifications that conflict.

There is a time lag inherent in any database convergence process. It may take several seconds or minutes for the changes made to one replica to be applied to all of the database's other replicas. If two administrators modify the same property of the same NDS object on two different replicas, it is essential that their changes be propagated to the other replicas in the correct order, so that they all contain the same correct information. To make this possible, all NDS communications contain a timestamp that is used to apply the changes to each replica accurately. This is why all NetWare servers hosting NDS replicas must be synchronized to a common time signal.

Classifying NDS Volatility

The network communications involved in maintaining a multiple master database are quite complex, and the complexity increases with the number of modifications made by administrators at different locations. Even more complicated are the communications processes involved in the manipulation of an NDS database's partitions and replicas. Creating, moving, and deleting partitions and replicas require even more intensive communications and longer convergence times. In short, the more modifications that you make to your NDS database, the more care you must take to maintain its health.

To keep your NDS tree healthy, you should devise a schedule of regular maintenance, the timing of which depends on the frequency and complexity of your database modifications. During the process of upgrading a large network to use NDS, you may have to make major modifications to the NDS database at frequent intervals. During this time, you should perform daily checks on your NDS time and replica synchronization and make frequent backups of your database.

For a fully deployed NDS tree with multiple administrators making regular modifications to different replicas of the same partitions, weekly checks should be sufficient. For a small network, an NDS database with only a few partitions and replicas, or a database that is not often modified, regular monthly maintenance would be in order, as you can see from the list that follows. The list shows the conditions under which daily, weekly, or monthly NDS maintenance is recommended.

Daily Maintenance

Mass migration of objects from other directories to NDS

Installation of new or upgraded NetWare servers

Creation of multiple new partitions and replicas on remote servers

Weekly Maintenance

Occasional creation of new partitions or replicas

Partitions and replicas in remote locations connected by WAN links

Creation of large numbers of new objects

Frequent modification of existing objects on different replicas by multiple administrators

Monthly Maintenance

Small NDS trees

A small number of partitions and replicas, all on the same LAN

Occasional modification of existing objects

NDS Maintenance Tasks

When one person is responsible for building and maintaining an NDS database, it is relatively easy to make sure that the structure of the tree remains within the limitations recommended by Novell. However, on many enterprise networks, there are many different people working to maintain the tree, sometimes at distant locations. Communications between the network administrators at various branch offices may not be as frequent as they should be, and not all of the administrators may have the NDS knowledge and experience needed to maintain a healthy tree.

Regular NDS maintenance procedures not only check to see that the NDS inter-server communications processes are proceeding normally, they also monitor the database's growth and configuration to determine whether the tree structure is growing in such a way as to jeopardize performance. The same principles that you use to design an NDS tree should also be used to control its growth. In addition to diagnosing and correcting communications problems, the NDS maintenance tools can help you to decide when to create new partitions, when a container holds too many objects, and when to modify your replication strategy.

The primary NDS maintenance procedures are as follows:

- **DS.NLM version check**   When an NDS database is distributed among two or more NetWare servers, it is important that all of the systems be running the same version of DS.NLM, the core NDS module. This check is particularly important when the servers are at different locations or are being maintained by different people. Other NDS platforms, such as Windows NT or Solaris, will not run the NLM (NetWare Loadable Module) of course, but their version numbers should still be checked and kept up to date with the version running on your NetWare servers.

- **Time synchronization check**   Proper time synchronization is crucial to a healthy NDS tree, especially when different administrators are making changes to different replicas of the same partition.

- **Replica synchronization check**   Accurate and timely synchronization of replicas is one of the most important elements of NDS functionality. This check examines the replication patterns for the entire tree and reports on errors and delays.

- **Replica continuity check** Novell publishes guidelines for the proper placement and configuration of replicas. This check examines the replica ring and calls for the timing of the replica synchronization process.

- **Partition design check** As a network evolves, new objects added to a tree can cause partitions and containers to grow too large. This check enables you to determine when it is time to split a partition or move some objects to a different container.

NDS Maintenance Tools

Novell provides some tools for the maintenance and repair of NDS databases with the NetWare product, and also makes others available from their online services. The following sections describe the basic functions of these tools; their use is discussed later in this chapter.

NDS Manager

NDS Manager is the graphical NDS administration application, first introduced in NetWare 4.11, that supplanted the DOS-based Partition Manager program of earlier NetWare 4 versions (see Figure 11.2). It is installed in 16- and 32-bit Windows versions to the server's SYS:PUBLIC and SYS:PUBLIC\WIN95 directories during the operating system installation. You can run NDS Manager as a stand-alone program, or launch it from NetWare Administrator's Tools menu.

Configuring NDS Manager under NWADMIN's Tools menu requires manipulating the Windows (95/98 or NT) registry. This is not for the faint of heart, but if you wish to make the attempt I suggest you visit the Novell Knowledgebase (http://support.novell.com/servlet/Knowledgebase) and search using the keywords "NDS", "manager", and "registry". This will turn up a group of documents, at least one of which can be used for your particular situation.

With NDS Manager, you can view and manipulate your partitions and replicas, update the DS.NLM module on all of your servers, check the synchronization of your replicas, and start database repair operations. NDS Manager includes Schema Manager, which enables network administrators to modify the schema that define the properties making up specific NDS object types.

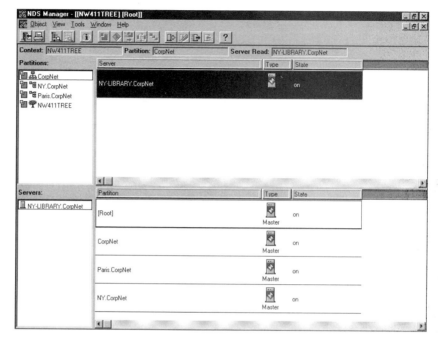

F I G U R E   11.2

NDS Manager uses a graphical interface to display the NDS tree and its partitions and replicas.

Partition Manager

Partition Manager is the DOS-based utility that was the only means of creating, removing, and administering partitions and replicas in NetWare versions 4.0 through 4.10 (see Figure 11.3). Still included with NetWare 4.11 (but not in NetWare 5.*x*), Partition Manager is installed to the SYS:PUBLIC directory on every NetWare 4.*x* server.

DSREPAIR.NLM

DSREPAIR is a server-based utility that diagnoses and repairs problems in the NDS database (see Figure 11.4). Once it is installed with the operating system to the SYS:SYSTEM directory, you can load DSREPAIR from the console prompt of any NetWare server, but the program can only address the partitions and replicas stored on that server. You can also launch DSREPAIR operations from the Partition Continuity screen of the NDS Manager utility, which automatically loads the module on the appropriate server for a selected partition. You can use DSREPAIR to perform a comprehensive unattended repair procedure, or select individual repair processes from a wide variety of options.

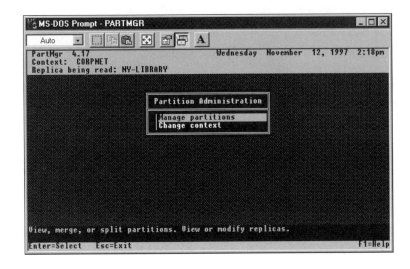

FIGURE 11.3

Partition Manager is the DOS-based predecessor to the NDS Manager utility.

FIGURE 11.4

DSREPAIR.NLM runs on the NetWare server and it is used to repair the NDS partitions and replicas stored on that server.

DSTRACE

DSTRACE is an optional screen on the NetWare server console (see Figure 11.5) that displays your network's ongoing NDS communications activities in real time. Activated by issuing SET commands from the console prompt, DSTRACE has a multitude of command options and filters that can control the amount and type of information displayed.

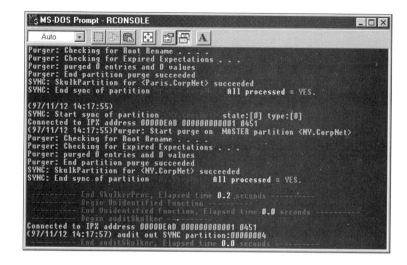

FIGURE 11.5

DSTRACE is a server
console screen that
displays NDS' ongoing
communications
processes.

DSDIAG.NLM

DSDIAG.NLM is a server-based utility (see Figure 11.6) that collects diagnostic
information for an entire NDS tree, not just the partitions and replicas stored on
the server running the program. DSDIAG.NLM is included with NetWare 5.*x*
servers. For NetWare 4.*x* servers it is available from the Novell Support Connection Web site by searching for the archive name, DSDIAG.EXE, in the file finder.

FIGURE 11.6

DSDIAG.NLM gathers
diagnostic information
for an entire NDS tree,
not just a single server.

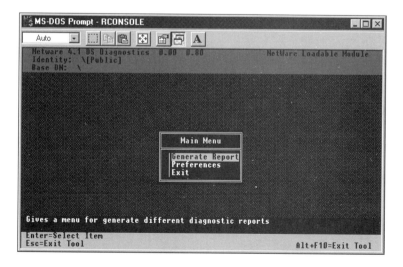

SCANTREE.EXE

SCANTREE.EXE is a DOS command line NDS treewalker utility—that is, a program that scans the entire NDS database and produces an inventory containing the number of objects of each type. The program is available from the Novell Support Connection Web site by scanning for the archive name, SCANDS.EXE, in the file finder.

Backup/Restore Applications

NDS' first line of defense in the area of fault tolerance is its ability to store multiple replicas of each partition on various servers around the network. Novell recommends that each partition have at least three replicas, so that even the failure of two servers cannot cause a loss of NDS data. However, disasters such as fire or theft can cause the loss of three, or even all of your servers, and your NDS tree along with them. For this reason, server backups are still a necessity, and you must be sure that NDS is backed up with the other data from the server.

It is not necessary to back up NDS on each server. Rather, back it up from one server, and the entire tree will be backed up (as long as [Root] is the base it is backed up from—some backup programs have an option to back up a partial tree).

NetWare includes a rudimentary backup program called SBACKUP that is capable of backing up the NDS database to tape and restoring it, but which lacks the features that make it suitable for use on an enterprise network. There are several third-party products available that can back up and restore the NDS database, and that also include the advanced scheduling and tape rotation features that you can use to automate your network backup processes.

Maintaining NDS

Many NDS maintenance procedures generate a significant amount of additional network traffic, and can have a noticeable effect on user performance. This is particularly true for operations that involve writing to the database, such as the creation or merging of partitions or replicas. Tasks like these are inherently more dangerous when performed while other users are accessing the NDS database. It is therefore recommended that NDS maintenance procedures be performed after working hours, whenever possible.

NDS maintenance can also be a test of an administrator's patience. A procedure that at first seems to be completed in an application like NDS Manager may actually require a long period of convergence before all of the replicas have been synchronized. Depending on the number of replicas you have on your network and the speed of the connections between your servers, the convergence process may take as long as 30 minutes. You should always wait until the current operation has been fully completed and the tree synchronized before beginning the next task.

To check the current synchronization status of your NDS database, you can use the DSTRACE screen on the NetWare server console, or the Check Synchronization command on NDS Manager's Object menu. Another place to check sync status is in DSREPAIR. The Report Synchronization Status option from either the main menu or the Advanced menu's Replica and Partition Operations menu gives one of the most comprehensive synchronization reports available.

The following sections describe the common maintenance tasks that you can perform with the various NDS tools supplied by Novell.

Using NDS Manager

The primary function of the NDS Manager utility is to display and manipulate the partitions into which your tree is divided and the replicas of those partitions that are stored throughout the network. In Chapter 5, you learned about the concepts involved in creating partitions and replicas in order to realize your NDS tree design. Once the tree is operational, though, the partitioning and replication strategy may have to evolve along with your network.

As your network changes over time, you may find it necessary to create new partitions or replicas, or remove existing ones. Opening or closing a branch office, for example, can require significant changes to the NDS database. In addition to manipulating partitions and replicas, NDS Manager is capable of performing many other maintenance tasks, making it NetWare's primary NDS administration utility.

Creating and Merging Partitions

As your network grows, you may find it necessary to move a branch of the NDS tree to its own partition. There can be several reasons for doing this. An existing partition may grow too large, or a department may move to a different location and be given its own server. Conversely, there are also reasons why an existing partition may have to be merged back into its parent. You may find that a server hosting a particular partition is being overburdened by other tasks, or that your network is growing smaller due to corporate downsizing.

In any case, the creation and merging of partitions are among the most complex and time-consuming of NDS maintenance procedures, and major database modifications like these should not be undertaken lightly. A utility like NDS Manager makes operations like these appear to be simple, but the activities that occur behind the scenes after you have ostensibly completed the task in the user interface are intensive.

Before you create a new partition or merge an existing one, make sure that NDS is operating properly, and is ready for the operation, by performing the following checks:

- Log in to the NDS tree using an account that has the object and property rights needed to manipulate the partitions.

- Make sure that the database is not in the midst of a replica synchronization process.

- Make sure that there are no users logged on to the network.

- Perform the operation after working hours, when network traffic is light.

- If you have replicas at other locations, make sure that all of the WAN links and remote servers are operational.

- Make sure there are no sync problems of any kind in the partition affected by the operation. If there are corrupt objects, it is possible that the operation will never be fully completed.

To create a new partition with NDS Manager, you select the container object in the program's tree view that is to become the root of the new subtree, and select Object ➤ Create Partition. Once you confirm the decision to create the new partition, the effect on the NDS Manager display is almost immediate. The icon for the selected container object changes to represent a partition, as shown for the CorpNet container in Figure 11.7. However, the actual process of creating the partition continues at the server and may take some time, depending on the number of objects involved.

FIGURE 11.7

NDS Manager's tree view displays each container object that functions as the root of a subtree with a special icon.

Partition icon

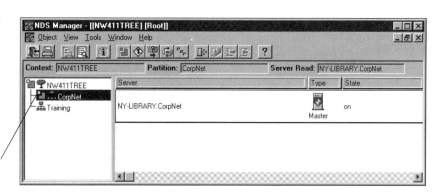

When you are performing a multistep procedure, be sure that each step is completely finished before you begin the next. For example, you may be planning to create a new partition and then replicate it to several servers at different locations. Each step of the process can involve the creation of hundreds or thousands of new objects, each with its own set of properties. Make sure that each replica that you create is completely synchronized before you create the next one. After you complete the last step of the procedure, let the replicas synchronize again before you allow users access to the network.

You can also use the Partition Manager utility to create and merge partitions by browsing to the desired container object and pressing the F10 key. The precautions you should observe are the same as those for using NDS Manager.

Monitoring Synchronization Status

In order to determine when it is safe to perform a new task, NDS Manager provides a feature that enables you to check the synchronization status of any partition in the tree. By selecting Object ➣ Check Synchronization, you display the Partitions Synchronization Check dialog box shown in Figure 11.8. When you select a partition from NDS Manager's tree view display, you can check only that single partition. From the partitions and servers view, you can check the synchronization status of all of the tree's partitions at the same time.

F I G U R E   11.8

With NDS Manager, you can check the synchronization status of any partition in the tree.

 You can also check the NDS synchronization status using the DSTRACE screen at the NetWare server console. To activate the screen and display synchronization information, type the commands SET DSTRACE=ON and SET DSTRACE=+SYNC.

Upgrading DS.NLM

Because every server that contains a partition or a replica participates in the synchronization process, it is important that they all be running the same software. Novell periodically releases updates of DS.NLM, the primary NDS module, and if you install an updated version to one of your servers, you should install it to all of them. Any new features incorporated into the release will not be available unless you update all of the servers participating in the replica ring.

WARNING   NDS running on different platforms will rarely be at the same revision level. Before upgrading any single version of NDS, it is important to understand its implications for other versions running on other platforms. Always read the supporting documentation before installing a new version of NDS.

NDS Manager includes a feature that enables you to view the version number of the DS.NLM module on any of your servers and update them all from a single source, without having to access the console of each server individually. When you select a container object in either the tree or the partitions and servers view of NDS Manager and then select Objects ➤ NDS Version/View, a dialog box like that shown in Figure 11.9 appears, displaying the DS.NLM versions installed on the servers in that container.

FIGURE 11.9

NDS Manager can display the DS.NLM versions for all of the servers in a selected container or subtree.

When you select a server object from either view, the Object menu's NDS Version/Update command is activated, displaying the dialog box shown in Figure 11.10. You have to manually install the new DS.NLM version on one server, so that it can act as the source for all of the others. The NDS Version Update dialog box then lists all of the NDS servers on your network and enables you to select those that you want to update, or have the program scan the servers and automatically select those running older DS.NLM versions.

F I G U R E   11.10

NDS Manager can automatically update all of your NDS servers with a new version of DS.NLM.

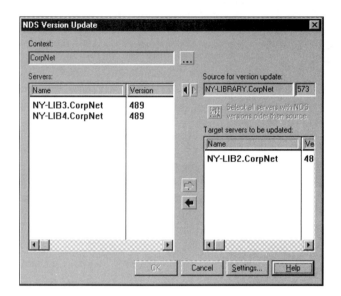

Novell releases separate DS.NLM updates for different NetWare versions. It is strongly recommended that you run the same operating system version on all of your network's NDS servers, but if you have (for example) NetWare 4.10 servers on your NetWare 5.1 network, NDS Manager will not install the 5.1 upgrade to a 4.10 server.

Using the Partition Continuity Screen

Before the release of NetWare 4.11, the only way to repair the NDS database was to run the DSREPAIR.NLM program from the server console, either by traveling to the server or using RCONSOLE. DSREPAIR can address only problems with replicas stored in the server where it is running, and it could at times be difficult to isolate the exact location of the problem. NDS Manager includes a Partition Continuity screen that displays the locations of a selected partition's replicas and indicates whether there is a synchronization problem with any one of them (see Figure 11.11). From this same screen, you can select a replica and trigger a synchronization process or perform any one of several different repair options on it.

Launching any repair process from NDS Manager actually launches DSRE-PAIR on the server. For that reason, DSREPAIR needs to be available and current on that server.

FIGURE 11.11

NDS Manager can display all of the replicas of a partition, and it uses icons to identify those that need repair.

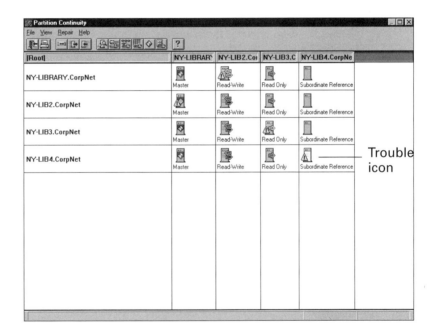

To synchronize or repair replicas, you highlight a partition either in the NDS Manager tree or in partitions and servers view, and then select Objects ➤ Partition Continuity. The Partition Continuity screen contains a row of icons for each server containing a replica of the selected partition. The icons represent each server's view of the replica ring for that partition. In Figure 11.11, for example, the partition has a total of four replicas, all of which are visible to the four servers listed.

It may seem as though this information is redundant, but certain database problems can prevent a server from seeing all of the replicas. If one of the servers showed only three replicas, for example, you would know that that server needs attention. The other obvious sign of a problem is when an icon representing a replica is modified to contain an exclamation point in a yellow triangle. This indicates the existence of a synchronization error, meaning that the replica may not contain an updated image of the partition. In either case, the replica is experiencing a problem that should be addressed immediately. Another status that is shown is a blue jagged line indicating that the server in question is down or cannot be read.

Triggering Replica Synchronization   The NDS database normally synchronizes itself, without the need for administrative attention. However, it is possible to manually trigger the replica synchronization process from the Partition Continuity screen. After highlighting a replica, you can select one of three commands from the Repair menu (you can also use your mouse to right-click the replica), as follows:

- **Synchronize Immediately**   The Synchronize Immediately command triggers a full synchronization process for the selected partition, in which every replica attempts to synchronize its information with the replicas on the other servers.

- **Receive Updates**   The Receive Updates command causes the selected replica (and only the selected replica) to be overwritten with the information contained in the Master replica for the partition. You can use this option when the Partition Continuity screen indicates that a replica other than the Master is out of synchronization and when you are certain that the master replica contains the authoritative information for the partition. Because this option overwrites all of the data, the target replica is marked as being a new replica for a brief period. This operation cannot be performed on the Master replica itself. Because this command is, in essence, the same as the creation of a new replica, the process can create a large amount of network traffic. You should observe the same precautions as when creating a new partition or replica.

- **Send Updates**   The Send Updates command causes the data from the selected replica to be transmitted to all of the partition's other replicas, including the master. Unlike the action triggered by the Receive Updates command, the data from the selected replica does not over-write the existing data; it is instead combined with the information that already exists in the target replicas. Any objects in the target replicas that are not in the selected replica are left in place.

Manually triggering a replica synchronization process can be a convenient method of preparing the NDS database for another operation, but it may address a symptom of database corruption without providing a cure. If you repeatedly find that a replica is left in an unsynchronized state, it may be a sign of a more serious problem. If the replica itself has become corrupted, the Receive Updates operation may remedy the problem by overwriting the entire replica. However, continued synchronization problems usually indicate that a database repair process is needed.

Repairing the NDS Database   From the same Partition Continuity screen, you can trigger NDS database repair processes on a selected server or replica. NDS Manager does not perform the repair operations itself. Instead, it functions as a front end for DSREPAIR.NLM by running the program with specific options on the server containing the selected replica and returning the results to the workstation. In this respect, therefore, NDS Manager is a tool of convenience. It does not provide all of the options available when you run the DSREPAIR program on the server yourself, but it does save you from having to access each server individually.

After highlighting a replica on the Partition Continuity screen, you can select one of the procedures from the Repair menu. Some of the procedures address only the selected replica, while others address all of the databases found on the server hosting the selected replica. The NDS repair options provided by NDS Manager are as follows:

- **Verify Remote Server IDs**   Every NDS object in a replica is assigned a unique ID number. Different replicas have different object IDs for the same objects. Each replica assigns an ID number to the server that hosts it. It also maintains a list of remote server IDs, that is, the ID numbers that the other replicas use to refer to that same server. Incorrect server IDs can prevent the replica from communicating with the other servers in the ring. The Verify Remote Server IDs procedure examines these server IDs to ensure that they all refer to the correct server name, and corrects those that do not. This process is relatively noninvasive. It does not lock the NDS database, allowing network users to work normally. Use this option as the first step in repairing an NDS communications problem, and proceed to more rigorous procedures if it fails to remedy the situation.

- **Repair Replica**   The Repair Replica procedure performs a more extensive check of the remote server ID information than the Verify Remote Server IDs option, by examining the IDs on all of the servers in the replica ring. However, as with any DSREPAIR operation, repairs can only be made to the server hosting the selected replica. This procedure should only be performed after running the Repair Local Database process.

- **Repair Network Addresses**   The Repair Network Addresses procedure scans the server's SAP table for the hardware addresses broadcast by every server on the network. It then compares these addresses with the IPX network address property of every server object and the replica property of the partition root object in the local NDS database files. As with remote server IDs, a discrepancy in this information can prevent NDS servers from communicating properly. If the NDS properties do not contain the same addresses as the SAP table, then they are updated. This procedure, too, can be used as a preliminary repair process while users are working on the network, as it does not lock the NDS database.

- **Repair Local Database**   The Repair Local Database procedure attempts to repair corruption that is preventing access to the database files on the server hosting the selected partition. This procedure is more resource-intensive than the network address or remote server ID checks, and it can noticeably affect users' access to the server. While this procedure can often repair the local database to the point at which it is accessible by users, there is no guarantee that all of the objects will remain intact. If some of the objects are adversely affected, you can restore the replicas to their original state by using NDS Manager's Receive Updates command, or by deleting and recreating the replicas.

- **Assign New Master**   The Assign New Master command causes a selected Read/Write or Read-Only replica to be converted into the Master replica for the partition. This procedure is different from that performed by the Change Type command in the Replica menu of NDS

Manager's main views. You should only use Assign New Master when the existing Master replica for a partition is unavailable, either because it has been irretrievably damaged or the server hosting it is offline. A partition must have a Master replica in order to perform many NDS maintenance procedures.

- **Remove Server**   The Remove Server operation is a drastic procedure that should only be performed when replicas are trying to synchronize with a server that no longer hosts a replica in the partition's ring. Remove Server is not the same as the Delete Server operation, which deletes the server object from the NDS database and allows the replica ring to update itself. You should only perform a Remove Server when the database is damaged to the point at which the references to the servers hosting the other replicas cannot be updated. When you initiate a Remove Server procedure, NDS Manager always attempts to perform a Delete Server first. Only if the Delete Server operation fails does the program prompt you for confirmation to perform the Remove Server process.

- **Repair Volume Objects**   The Repair Volume Objects process checks the associations between the NetWare volumes mounted on the server and the volume objects in the NDS database. If the mounted volume corresponding to a volume object is not found, then NDS Manager searches the context in which the server is located for the appropriate volume. If the search fails to locate the volume, the program attempts to create one.

Using DSREPAIR.NLM

DSREPAIR.NLM runs at the NetWare server console and can perform a large number of NDS diagnostic and repair procedures. DSREPAIR is capable of reading information and reporting status data from the other servers hosting NDS partitions and replicas, but it can write only to the server on which it is running. If DSREPAIR detects a problem with the replicas on another server, you must run the program on that server or use NDS Manager to launch a repair procedure there.

Remote repair operations can only be performed on NetWare servers. Remote repair operations for servers other than NetWare (Windows NT, Solaris, Linux, etc.) can be performed by running DSREPAIR at that server's console, using the DSREPAIR utility for that platform.

DSREPAIR is a menu-driven utility that can perform a comprehensive NDS repair procedure or let you select individual diagnostic and repair processes. All test and repair results are saved to a log file called SYS:SYSTEM\DSREPAIR.LOG that you can view with DSREPAIR or from a workstation using any ASCII text viewer or editor.

The following sections examine the operations that you can perform from the DSREPAIR menus.

Unattended Full Repair

DSREPAIR's Unattended Full Repair procedure is the program's most complete and most commonly used option. The program examines the NDS database files on the local server and performs all possible repairs that do not require user interaction. These repairs include the following:

- Local database repair
- Schema check
- Replica ring repair
- Remote server ID check
- Network address check of all servers known to the local database
- Volume object and trustee check

Any problems that DSREPAIR finds are immediately corrected, and the results of the procedure are displayed on screen and saved to the log file.

Time Synchronization Check

The Time Synchronization Check causes DSREPAIR to contact all of the servers referenced in the local database files and request that they return NDS status and time synchronization information. Whether or not information is reported for every NDS server on the network depends on the replicas stored on the local server. If the server contains a replica of the root partition, then the time synchronization report will list all of the network's NDS servers.

The time synchronization report lists the following information for each server that is contacted:

- **DS.NLM Version** Specifies the version of the DS.NLM module running on the listed server.

- **Replica Depth** A value of 0 indicates that the server contains a replica of the root partition. A value of −1 indicates that the server contains no replicas. A positive value specifies the distance (in terms of the number of objects) of the server's highest replica from the [Root] of the NDS tree.

- **Time Source** Specifies the type of time reference server used to synchronize the replicas on this server. An improper time reference configuration (such as two servers using a single reference time server) can be the source of a time synchronization problem.

- **Time Is in Sync** Specifies the state of the time synchronization flag maintained by every NDS server. A value of "Yes" indicates that the server has been able to successfully communicate with its configured time reference server.

- **Time +/−** Specifies the time difference between the listed server and the local server, using the format MINUTES:SECONDS, up to a maximum of 999:59 (values over 999:59 register as −999:59). On a properly functioning network, the time on all NDS servers should be synchronized to within one minute.

This function only reports on the time synchronization status of your network's servers. It takes no action to remedy any problems that it finds. It is important to understand that the accuracy of the time maintained by your servers is not nearly as important as their synchronization. In nearly all cases, time synchronization problems are caused by improperly configured time options or by a failure to contact the designated time reference servers.

Synchronization Status Report

This option causes DSREPAIR to contact all of the servers referenced in its local database files and compile a report on the replica synchronization status of each partition with a replica on the local server. The report lists the replicas found in the local databases, specifies whether or not each replica is synchronized with the partition's other replicas, and displays the time of the last successful synchronization process. If any partition has not been synchronized within the last 12-hour period, DSREPAIR displays a warning message in the report.

Like the time synchronization check, this process is noninvasive; it simply reads the synchronization status property from the replica root object of each server contacted. DSREPAIR makes no attempt to initiate replica synchronization processes.

Advanced Options

DSREPAIR's Advanced Options screen (see Figure 11.12) provides access to the program's individual repair procedures with a greater degree of configurability than is available anywhere else. In most cases, this precision is not needed. Unless you are certain that you know the exact nature of the problem affecting your NDS database, or you are being directed by a technical support engineer, running an unattended full repair is usually preferable.

FIGURE 11.12

From the Advanced Options screen, you can execute repairs on specific elements of the NDS database.

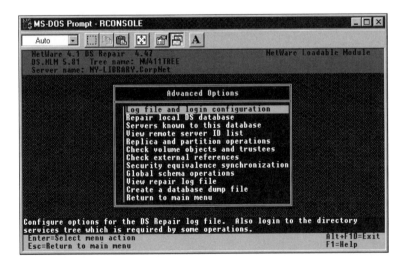

The functions available from the Advanced Options screen are as follows:

- **Log File and Login Configuration**   Enables you to reset (erase) the current log file, provide an alternate location for the file, and specify how new information should be logged. From this screen, you can also log in to the NDS database to grant the DSREPAIR program the access that it needs to perform certain operations.

- **Repair Local DS Database**   Performs the same repair process on the server's local database files as NDS Manager's Repair Local Database function. However, you can also set a number of options controlling certain elements of the repair process, such as whether mail directories should be validated and whether the program should pause when it encounters an error.

- **Servers Known to This Database**   Displays a list of the servers referenced in the replicas stored on the local server. For each server listed, you can perform individual processes such as repair network addresses, update schema, and check time synchronization.

- **View Remote Server ID List**   Displays the current server's object ID in the local databases and the object IDs for the current server as found in the databases of the other NDS servers referenced in the locally stored replicas.

- **Replica and Partition Operations**   Displays a list of the replicas stored on the local server. For each replica listed, you can trigger synchronization procedures, modify the replica type, and repair the replica, among many other procedures.

- **Check Volume Objects and Trustees**   Checks the associations between the volumes mounted on the server and the volume objects in the NDS database, just like the Repair Volume Objects function in the NDS Manager.

- **Check External References**   Scans the server's NDS databases for references to objects stored in partitions on other servers and checks to see if the referenced objects are accessible.

- **Security Equivalence Synchronization**   Adds the "equivalent to me" property introduced in NetWare 4.10 to servers running NetWare 4.0x.

- **Global Schema Operations** Examines the schema of all servers in the NDS database and updates those that are not running the current operational schema.

- **View Repair Log File** Displays the DSREPAIR log file.

- **Create a Database Dump File** Copies the contents of the NDS database files on the server to a compressed file called SYS:SYSTEM\DSREPAIR.DIB, by default. This feature is intended to be a mechanism for transporting the NDS database to a technical support engineer for study. It cannot be used as a substitute for system backups.

Using DSDIAG.NLM

DSDIAG.NLM is a server-based NDS diagnostics program that performs checks and displays information about your entire NDS tree, not just the databases on the server where it is running. DSDIAG is a read-only utility. It does not attempt to correct the problems that it finds, but it does issue warnings when dangerous conditions exist.

By selecting Generate Reports from DSDIAG's Main Menu, you display the screen shown in Figure 11.13, where you can create reports about the status of your NDS tree, based on your own formatting and database access preferences.

FIGURE 11.13

DSDIAG.NLM generates reports about the condition of your entire NDS tree.

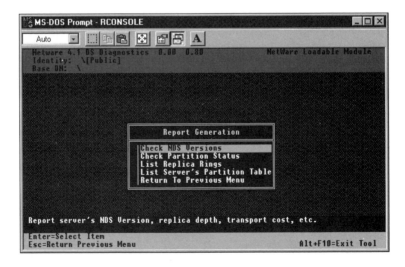

From a screen like that shown in Figure 11.14, you can specify the following options for each report type:

- The means by which DSDIAG should locate your servers

- The type of replicas that DSDIAG should use to gather information

- How much of the NDS tree should be included in the report

- The location where the report file should be created

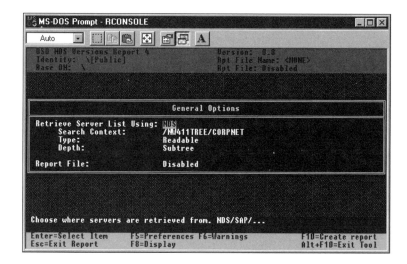

The following sections examine the four report types and the information that DSDIAG provides.

Check NDS Versions

The NDS version check locates the servers on your network by scanning the NDS databases, the server's SAP table, or IPX addresses and creates a report like the following:

```
Report Title: DSD NDS Versions Report
Report Version: 0.8
Base DN: \NW411TREE\CorpNet
Retrieved Servers From: NDS
Search Context:  .
     Type: Readable
     Depth:  Subtree
Status Address        Repl Obje Serv Server's NDS Name
                      Dept Vers Vers
     0 0101001C          0  581  581 \NW411TREE\O=CorpNet\CN=NY-LIBRARY
     0 0101001D          2  581  581 \NW411TREE\O=CorpNet\CN=NY-LIB2
     0 01010161          1  581  581 \NW411TREE\O=CorpNet\CN=NY-LIB3
  -663 --------------   -1  573  573 \NW411TREE\O=CorpNet\CN=NY-TEST
  -625 0101017A              573     \NW411TREE\O=CorpNet\CN=NY-TEST2
Contacted 3 server(s) out of 5 attempted.
Count Error Numbers       Message
    1  -663  FFFFFD69  ds locked
    7  -625  FFFFFD8F  transport failure
Count Warning             Message
    1     C               Container/Context Information
    3     S               The Originating and Server names are not the same.
```

For each report entry, the status field indicates the program's success or failure in contacting the server. A value of 0 means that the server was contacted successfully; a negative value specifies an NDS error code, which is explained in a separate table after the server listing. The remaining fields for each entry in the server list provide the following information:

- Internal IPX address
- Replica depth
- NDS object version

- NDS server version

- NDS server object name

After the list of error codes, the report includes a table of warnings that reference specific problems encountered while communicating with the servers. The possible warnings are as follows:

- **C**   Container/context information

- **E**   Server is equal to requested version

- **H**   Server is above requested version

- **L**   Server is below requested version

- **N**   Name expansion information

- **S**   The originating and server names are not the same

- **W**   Server is not in specified tree

Check Partition Status

The partition status report contains a separate table for each partition, listing the servers that contain replicas of that partition, as follows:

```
Report Title: DSD Partition Sync. Status
Report Version: 0.8
Base DN: \NW411TREE\CorpNet
Identity: \[Public]
Retrieved Partition Roots Form: NDS
     Search Context:  CorpNet
     Type: Readable
     Depth:  Subtree
Retrieved replica ring from:  Ring
Partition Name: OU=CorpNet
Server Name: \NW411TREE\OU=CorpNet\CN=NY-LIBRARY
Outbound Synchronization Status:
 Status Warni Syn Synchr Last Attempted                   Destination                       Entry
           Dir Status Synchronization                     Server Name                       Name
     0          Ok        0 Oct 24, 1997 10:23:32 am EST \NW411TREE\O=CorpNet\CN=NY-LIBRARY
     0          Ok        0 Oct 24, 1997 10:23:32 am EST \NW411TREE\O=CorpNet\CN=NY-LIB2
     0          Ok        0 Oct 24, 1997 10:23:32 am EST \NW411TREE\O=CorpNet\CN=NY-LIB3
     0       H  RE     -684 Oct 24, 1997 10:23:32 am EST \NW411TREE\O=CorpNet\CN=NY-TEST OU=CorpNet
     0          Ok        0 Oct 24, 1997 10:23:32 am EST \NW411TREE\O=CorpNet\CN=NY-LIB4
Partition Name: OU=Paris
Server Name: \NW411TREE\OU=CorpNet\OU=Paris\CN=NY-LIB2
```

```
Outbound Synchronization Status:
Status Warni Syn Synchr Last Attempted            Destination                Entry
           Dir Status Synchronization            Server Name                Name
      0        Ok       0 Oct 24, 1997 10:22:55 am EST \NW411TREE\O=CorpNet\CN=NY-LIB2
      0        Ok       0 Oct 24, 1997 10:22:55 am EST \NW411TREE\O=CorpNet\CN=NY-LIBRARY
      0        Ok       0 Oct 24, 1997 10:22:55 am EST \NW411TREE\O=CorpNet\CN=NY-LIB3
      0        Ok       0 Oct 24, 1997 10:22:55 am EST \NW411TREE\O=CorpNet\CN=NY-LIB4
Replica Synchronization Summary:
Status Warni Tota OK   Acce Repl Repl Most-Recent Complete       Partition
           Repl Repl Erro Erro Unkn Synchronization Time        Name
      0    H    2    1    0    1    0 Oct 24, 1997 3:39:37 pm EST OU=CorpNet
Replicas found: 4
Partitions found: 2
Servers contacted with Partitions and Replicas: 4
Count Error Numbers    Message
    1   -684  FFFFFD54 secure ncp violation
Count Warning          Message
    2     H             Completed sync. has not occurred in the hours.
```

For each replica entry, the report specifies the synchronization status, the time of the last synchronization attempt, and any error and warning codes that may have occurred during the information-gathering process. Summary tables at the end of the report list all of the errors and warnings found during the information gathering process, as well as text messages for the error and warning codes. DSDIAG's possible warning messages are as follows:

- **A**   Replica attribute not found on entry.

- **B**   Duplicate replica numbers found in ring.

- **C**   Container/context information.

- **D**   Duplicate servers found in the ring.

- **E**   Additional servers found that were not on the original server.

- **I**   Entry ID is not contained in the replica ring.

- **L**   An illegal replica type was found.

- **M**   No master was found in the replica ring.

- **N**   Name expansion information.

- **O**   Replica has not been on for more than given time.

- **P**   Partition name being searched; entry does not match.

- **Q**   More than the maximum number of readable replicas were found.

- **R**   Fewer than the minimum number of readable replicas were found.

- **S**   Originating server was not found in the replica ring.

- **T**   Replica type of entry does not match the replica ring.

- **V**   More than the maximum number of subordinates were found.

- **2**   Multiple masters were found in the replica ring.

List Replica Rings

The List Replica Rings report examines each of the partitions in your NDS tree and inventories the replicas found for each one. Each entry specifies the replica's number, type, and state, as well as the server on which the replica is located, as follows:

```
Report Title: DSD List Replica Rings
Report Version: 0.8
Base DN: \NW411TREE\CorpNet
Retrieved Partition Roots Form: NDS
     Search Context:  .
     Type: Readable
     Depth:  Subtree
Retrieved replica ring from:  Single
Partition Name: .
Server Name: \NW411TREE\CorpNet\CN=NY-LIBRARY
Server's Address: 0101001D
Entry:
  Status Entry ID Repl Entry
               Type Name
      0 010000B7 RW    .
Replica:
  Status Repl Repl Replica Replica  Server                                   Address
         Numb Type State   Root ID  Name
      0    1 M    On       010000B7 \NW411TREE\CorpNet\CN=NY-LIBRARY 0101001D
      0    6 RW   On       010000B7 \NW411TREE\CorpNet\CN=NY-LIB2    0101001C
      0    7 RW   On       010000B7 \NW411TREE\CorpNet\CN=NY-LIB3    0101001B
      0    2 SR   On       0100045C \NW411TREE\CorpNet\CN=NY-TEST2   01017B05
      0    3 SR   On       0100096C \NW411TREE\CorpNet\CN=NY-TEST3   010159B9
      0    4 SR   On       010009D9 \NW411TREE\CorpNet\CN=NY-TEST4   010159B0
```

```
Partition Name: OU=Paris
Server Name: \NW411TREE\CorpNet\CN=NY-LIB2
Server's Address: 0101001C
Entry:
  Status Entry ID Repl Entry
                  Type Name
      0 2000097C RW   OU=Paris
Replica:
  Status Repl Repl Replica Replica  Server                        Address
         Numb Type State   Root ID  Name
      0    1 RW   On       240009E4 \NW411TREE\CorpNet\CN=NY-LIBRARY 0101001D
      0    2 M    On       2000097C \NW411TREE\CorpNet\CN=NY-LIB2    0101001C
Replicas found: 8
Partitions found: 2
Servers contacted with Partitions and Replicas: 6
Count  Warning  Message
    3        R  Fewer than the minimum readable replicas found.
```

DSDIAG also examines the replica rings that it finds and issues warnings when they do not conform to Novell's NDS design specifications. For example, DSDIAG detects when there are fewer than the recommended minimum of three replicas for each partition or more than the maximum of 10. Other warnings are issued when an OU is detected that has more than 15 subordinate OUs, and when a partition has no Master replica or more than one. The possible warning messages for the List Replica Rings report are as follows:

- **A** Replica attribute not found on entry.

- **B** Duplicate replica numbers found in ring.

- **C** Container/context information.

- **D** Duplicate servers found in the ring.

- **E** Additional servers found that were not on the original server.

- **I** Entry ID is not contained in the replica ring.

- **L** An illegal replica type was found.

- **M** No master was found in the replica ring.

- **N**   Name expansion information.

- **O**   Replica has not been on for more than given time.

- **P**   Partition name being searched; entry does not match.

- **Q**   More than the maximum number of readable replicas were found.

- **R**   Fewer than the minimum number of readable replicas were found.

- **S**   Originating server was not found in the replica ring.

- **T**   Replica type of entry does not match the replica ring.

- **V**   More than the maximum number of subordinates were found.

- **2**   Multiple masters were found in the replica ring.

List Server's Partition Table

DSDIAG's partition table report lists the partitions found on each of your NDS servers, providing the name of the partition and the type of replica, as follows:

```
Report Title: DSD Server Partition Table
Report Version: 0.8
Base DN: \NW411TREE\CorpNet
Retrieved Servers From: NDS
  Search Context:  .
  Type: Readable
  Depth:  Subtree
  Status Entry ID Repl Replica Repl Part Partition Name
                  Type State   Numb Busy
      0                         .
Server Name: \NW411TREE\OU=CorpNet\CN=NY-LIBRARY
Server's Address: 0101001D
        0 010000B7 RW   On       6   No \NW411TREE
        0 01001096 RW   On       6   No \NW411TREE\OU=CorpNet
        0 CA00018F RW   On       6   No \NW411TREE\OU=CorpNet\OU=NY
        0 2C001090 RW   On       6   No \NW411TREE\OU=CorpNet\OU=Paris
4 Replica(s) Found
```

```
Server Name: \NW411TREE\OU=CorpNet\CN=NY-TEST2
Server's Address: --------------
      -663
Contacted 4 server(s) out of 5 attempted.
Count Error Numbers     Message
   1   -663  FFFFFD69  ds locked
Count Warning           Message
   1        C              Container/Context Information
```

As with the other DSDIAG reports, the partition table list includes NDS errors and warnings that are encountered during the information-gathering process. The possible warning messages for the server partition list are as follows:

- **B** Replica indicates that the partition is busy.

- **C** Container/context information.

- **F** Modification or purge time was found in the future.

- **L** An illegal replica type was found.

- **N** Name expansion information.

- **P** Subref was found without its parent.

- **O** Replica was not turned on.

- **U** Purge time for replica had expired.

Using SCANTREE.EXE

SCANTREE.EXE is a read-only DOS command-line utility, available with NetWare 4.1*x*, that takes a snapshot of an NDS tree and produces an inventory of the objects found in the database and their attributes. The syntax for using SCANTREE is as follows:

```
SCANTREE [context] [/d] [/users] [>filename]
context - Causes the program to scan the specified context
/d - Causes the program to display the object hierarchy of the NDS tree
/users - Causes the program to report on user objects only
>filename - Redirects the program's output from the screen to the specified file
```

With no parameters, executing SCANTREE produces a report like the following:

```
========= SUMMARY STATISTICS =========
Test duration was 00:00:23
Alias                        3
App:Application              5
Application (Windows 3.x)    2
Audit:File Object            2
Directory Map                1
Group                        9
Organization                 2
Organizational Role          1
Organizational Unit          16
Print Server                 2
Printer                      1
Profile                      2
Queue                        3
Template                     2
Top                          1
User                         26
Volume                       4
{ Attributes - # }           1049
{ Attributes - size }        90880
{ Errors - NWDSRead }        1
{ Group memberships }        7
{ Largest container }        59
{ Objects }                  122
{ Partitions }               4
{ Replicas - Master }        4
{ Streams - # }              28
{ Streams - size }           47287
{ Tree depth }               5
```

The SCANTREE display first lists the number of objects of each type found in the database. Then, the program provides a series of summary statistics (enclosed in curly brackets) that show combined totals for all of the objects listed. By scanning specific contexts, you can keep track of the rate at which your tree is growing (or shrinking) and determine when it is time to create or remove partitions.

When you run SCANTREE with the /d parameter, the report lists all of the NDS objects in the tree, arranged to create a view of the NDS tree hierarchy, as follows:

```
========= TREE HIERARCHY =========
OBJECT NAME (SUBORDINATES, ATTRIBUTES, ATTRIBUTE SIZE)
[ROOT] (3, 14, 1120)
O=CorpNet. (59, 18, 2622)
  CN=NY-LIBRARY (0, 12, 1651)
  CN=Admin (0, 13, 1535)
  CN=NY-LIBRARY_SYS (0, 8, 485)
  CN=NY-LIBRARY_VOL1 (0, 6, 547)
  CN=CraigZ (0, 37, 3575)
  OU=NY.O=CorpNet (7, 14, 1927)
    OU=East Wing.OU=NY.O=CorpNet (2, 5, 686)
      CN=SmithJ (0, 7, 1186)
      CN=GaltJ (0, 7, 1168)
    OU=North Wing (0, 5, 690)
    OU=West Wing (0, 5, 686)
    OU=South Wing.OU=NY.O=CorpNet (2, 5, 886)
      CN=HerbertG (0, 7, 1214)
      CN=BlochJ (0, 7, 1256)
    OU=Accounting.OU=NY.O=CorpNet (8, 6, 698)
      OU=East Wing.OU=Accounting.OU=NY.O=CorpNet (5, 5, 798)
        CN=Everyone (0, 6, 539)
        CN=HerbertB (0, 9, 1574)
        CN=users (0, 4, 89)
        CN=CorbinG (0, 9, 1556)
        CN=NT Users (0, 7, 114)
      OU=West Wing (0, 5, 798)
      OU=North Wing (0, 5, 802)
      OU=South Wing (0, 5, 802)
      CN=DoeJ (0, 10, 1328)
```

```
        CN=Admin(Alias) (0, 13, 1535)
        CN=GrantG (0, 7, 1190)
        CN=Francis2 (0, 21, 1486)
    CN=JonesB (0, 12, 1215)
    CN=RamnarS (0, 12, 1272)
```

Using DSTRACE

DSTRACE is an NDS debugging and monitoring tool that is incorporated into the NetWare DS.NLM module. DSTRACE is not a program in itself; it is activated through the use of SET commands at the NetWare server console. Issuing the command SET DSTRACE=ON causes an extra screen to appear on the console that displays real-time messages concerning the server's ongoing NDS communications activities.

When DSTRACE is configured to display all possible NDS information, a great many cryptic and repetitious messages can appear on the screen. For this reason, there are a great many DSTRACE filter commands that you can use to display only the information you need. You can also capture the DSTRACE screen's output to a file for later examination. Finally, for testing purposes, you can manually trigger specific NDS processes with other SET commands, so that you can observe the results on the DSTRACE screen.

DSTRACE Commands

The following basic DSTRACE commands must all be preceded by SET DSTRACE= on the NetWare server command line:

- **ALL** Displays all debugging information.

- **AGENT** Enables the display of the same error messages as when the following filters are activated: ON, JANITOR, BACKLINK, RESNAME, DSAGENT, and VCLIENT.

- **CHECKSUM** Enables the use of checksums for error detection during NDS communications.

- **DEBUG** Enables the display of the same error messages as when the following filters are activated: ON, INIT, FRAGGER, MISC,

STREAMS, LIMBER, JANITOR, BACKLINK, SKULKER, SCHEMA, INSPECTOR, ERRORS, PART, EMU, VCLIENT, RECMAN, and REPAIR.

- **NOCHECKSUM** Disables the use of checksums during NDS communications.

- **NODEBUG** Resets DSTRACE to display no messages at all.

- **ON** Enables the DSTRACE screen.

- **OFF** Disables the DSTRACE screen without resetting the display filters.

- **MIN** Disables the DSTRACE screen and resets the display filters.

To capture DSTRACE information to a file, you should first issue the SET NDS TRACE FILENAME = <filename> command at the server console prompt, substituting the name of the file you wish to use to capture the output. Then, when you issue the command SET NDS TRACE TO FILE, all further information is captured to the file you specified. To prevent the file from growing too large, use the SET TTF=OFF command to disable the capture process.

DSTRACE Filters

DSTRACE filters enable you to select the types of messages that are displayed on the console screen and captured to the DSTRACE.DBG file. The filters function as toggles that can be turned on and off using SET commands. Each of the filters is activated or deactivated by the use of a plus or minus sign with the SET DSTRACE= command. For example, to display the error messages generated by the replica synchronization process, issue the command SET DSTRACE=+SYNC at the server console prompt.

Some filters can also use abbreviations for the filter name (supplied in parentheses). Thus, you can also use the command SET DSTRACE=+S. To deactivate the displays of synchronization error messages, use the command SET DSTRACE=-SYNC or SET DSTRACE=-S.

Displaying DSTRACE information on the server console, and especially replica synchronization (such as SYNC) information, can negatively affect the server's performance. DSTRACE is intended for occasional use as a debugging and troubleshooting tool, and should not be left running for extended periods of time.

The DSTRACE filters are as follows:

- **AUTHEN** Displays error messages produced during authentication processes.

- **BACKLINK (BLINK)** Displays messages produced by the back-linking process (the process by which an NDS server validates the references to external objects found in its databases).

- **COLLISION (COLL)** Displays error messages caused by collisions (two changes made to the same object).

- **DSAGENT (DSA)** Displays "normal" error messages related to DS agent common requests.

- **ERRORS (E)** Displays all error messages (both common and problem errors).

- **EMU** Displays error messages by bindery emulation processes.

- **FRAG/FRAGGER (FRAG)** Displays error messages generated by the NCP fragmentation process.

- **IN** Displays error messages resulting from inbound replica synchronization traffic.

- **INIT** Displays error messages generated during the directory services initialization process.

- **INSPECTOR (I)** Displays error messages generated by the inspector (the NDS process that checks objects for adherence to the schema, in preparation for the janitor process).

- **JANITOR (J)** Displays error messages generated by the janitor process (that removes deleted entries, checks NDS server connectivity, and performs miscellaneous database management chores).

- **LIMBER** Displays error messages generated by the limber process (that verifies the names, IPX addresses, and connectivity of all servers referenced in the local databases).

- **MERGE** Displays error messages generated during the merging of objects.

- **MISC** Displays error messages generated by miscellaneous processes.

- **OUT** Displays error messages resulting from outbound replica synchronization traffic.

- **PART** Displays error messages generated by partitioning operations

- **RECMAN** Displays error messages generated by database manager processes.

- **REPAIR** Displays error messages generated by database repair processes.

- **RESNAME (RN)** Displays error messages generated by resolve name requests (tree walking).

- **SAP** Displays error messages generated by SAP transmissions.

- **SCHEMA** Displays error messages generated by schema modification and synchronization processes.

- **SYNC (S)** Displays error messages generated by the replica synchronization process.

- **STREAMS** Displays error messages concerning streams (attributes that exist as a file stored in the server, such as login scripts).

- **TIMEVECTOR (TV)** Displays error messages involving local and remote "Sync Up To" time vectors.

- **VCLIENT (VC)** Displays error messages generated by server-to-server communications.

DSTRACE messages frequently contain references to NDS errors, but not all of these errors require administrative attention. For example, errors caused by failed authentications or by collisions, in which two people try to modify the properties of the same object, are normal occurrences that are dealt with by NDS' automated processes.

DSTRACE Process Commands

To trigger specific NDS processes on a server, you use DSTRACE process commands that consist of an asterisk, a single or double letter, and occasionally another variable. For example, to trigger the replica synchronization (heartbeat) process, you would issue the command SET DSTRACE=*H.

DSTRACE process commands are intended for use in testing, debugging, and other investigative situations, not for everyday NDS maintenance. If, for example, you must synchronize a replica, it is better to use the NDS Manager or DSREPAIR.NLM utility than the SET DSTRACE=*H process command.

The DSTRACE process commands are as follows:

- *. Reloads DS.NLM from the SYS:SYSTEM directory, renaming the version in memory to DS.OLD.

- *B Triggers the backlink process, in which the server creates a pointer to the external objects referenced in the local databases.

- *D Aborts the synchronization process triggered by a "send all objects" or *I command when the process cannot be completed due to the unavailability of a server.

- *E Verifies that the entry cache is viable.

- *F Triggers the flatcleaner (or janitor) process that purges unneeded objects from the database.

- *G Causes a server to give up and change its status to "down" because there are too many requests currently in process and the server ID cannot be specified.

- *H Triggers the heartbeat (or skulker, or synchronization) process, causing all of the servers in the replica ring to exchange timestamps and begin synchronizing their data.

- *I Causes the server to copy all of the objects in the local replica to all of the other replicas in the ring, just as in DSREPAIR's "send all objects" function.

- *L Triggers the limber process, in which the name, ID, and location in the tree are verified.

- *M*bytes* Sets the maximum size of the DSTRACE.DBG file to the number specified by the *bytes* variable.

- ***P** Displays the current settings of the NDS parameters that can be modified with other SET commands or the SERVMAN utility.

- ***R** Deletes the current contents of the DSTRACE.DBG file.

- ***S** Causes the server to see if any of its replicas require synchronization and, if so, schedules the skulker to run early.

- ***SS** Triggers the schema synchronization process.

- ***U** Changes a server's status to "up" and resets its communications status list.

Replica Synchronization Time

One of the most useful functions of the DSTRACE screen is the ability to view the server's ongoing replica synchronization activities. One of Novell's recommendations for an NDS installation is that the replication process take no longer than 30 minutes to complete. You can check the duration of the replication process using DSTRACE by displaying the server's synchronization activity and triggering an immediate synchronization procedure. To do this, activate the DSTRACE screen with the following command:

    SET DSTRACE=ON

Then enable the synchronization filter with this command:

    SET DSTRACE=+SYNC

To trigger a synchronization procedure, type:

    SET DSTRACE=*H

Begin timing the process as you hit ⏎. When all of the partitions on the server have been fully synchronized, stop the clock. This is your replica synchronization time. If the process takes more than 30 minutes, you should examine your NDS tree for structural faults, mis-configurations, or hardware problems.

WARNING There are some conditions under which an "All Processed=Yes" will be reported even when sync hasn't been completed. For example, when creating a new replica Sync will be temporarily suspended but an "All Processed=Yes" message will be displayed on the DSTRACE screen.

NDS Backups and Restores

On an enterprise network with servers at many remote locations, administrators may be tempted to create replicas of all of the NDS tree's partitions at every site, both for fault tolerance and to facilitate local access to the entire tree. However, if this practice is taken too far, it can drastically reduce NDS performance. Communications between replicas over slow WAN links can slow down the entire network and may not offset their value in protecting the NDS tree.

Whenever possible, you should restore lost NDS database files by accessing replicas on other servers, but it is still very important to perform regular backups either to tape or to another removable storage medium, in case of a catastrophic loss of data. NetWare's Storage Management Services (SMS) provides the means by which you can fully protect your network data, including the NDS tree and all file system trustee rights.

SMS is a modular system consisting of components that you can use selectively for performing system backups. NetWare's SBACKUP.NLM is an SMS-based backup solution that is capable of protecting your network, but which lacks the convenience features that make many of the third-party products preferable solutions.

SBACKUP.NLM is a *storage management engine* (SME), an SMS component that forms the core of the backup system. Other components called *target service agents* (TSAs) read the data from the source, package it, and send it to the SME (see Figure 11.15). The SME then uses the *storage management services device interface* (SMSDI) to transmit the data to the tape drive or other device. The TSA used to read the data from the NDS database is called TSANDS.NLM. The TSAs are the most essential part of any full-featured NetWare backup system. You can use a third-party product that supplies its own SME, but you'll need the TSAs to properly back up NDS.

Target Service Agents

The TSAs included with Novell's NetWare 5.*x* releases contain significant improvements over the earlier versions. If you are running NetWare 4.2 or earlier, you can download the new TSAs as part of an SMSUPx.EXE upgrade, in which *x* is replaced by a number representing the latest SMS release. As of this writing, the latest release for NetWare 4.*x* is SMSUP6.EXE, dated 1/31/97.

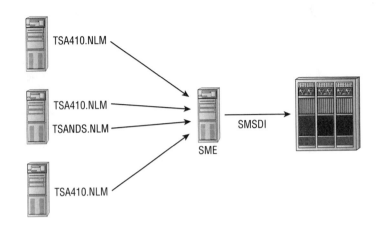

TSA500.NLM is the file system TSA included with the NetWare 5 product. This TSA is needed to back up and restore the trustee rights of the files and directories on your NetWare volumes. This new version of the file system TSA provides an additional resource to SMS-compliant SMEs, called *server specific info,* that aids in the protection of NetWare networks by creating the following files and sending them to the SME as a single entity:

- SERVDATA.NDS   Contains information about how NDS is deployed on a particular server, facilitating the recovery from a disaster in which the entire SYS volume of a server is lost using INSTALL.NLM.

- DSMISC.LOG   Contains a list of the replicas stored on the local NetWare server, as well as the other servers that are participants in the replica rings.

- VOLSINFO.TXT   Contains information about the volumes on the local NetWare server, including the namespaces used, compression, and data migration status.

- STARTUP.NCF   The NetWare server file that contains references to the disk drivers and other modules needed to boot the system.

- AUTOEXEC.NCF   The NetWare server file that loads required modules and configures the system for use during the boot process.

TSANDS.NLM, the module that reads the NDS information and packages it for backup to tape, has also been improved in the new release. While

TSA410 (for NetWare 4.1x) only processes information about the server on which it is running, TSANDS reads the data from the entire NDS tree and sends it to the SME. Unlike previous versions, TSANDS.NLM can now back up all of the schema extensions and new object types that third-party products may have created in your NDS database. Previously, the module backed up the objects themselves, but not the schema that defines the object types. You no longer have to manually extend the schema by reinstalling the product before you restore the objects.

While the TSA410.NLM module must be loaded on every NetWare 4.1x server whose volumes are to be backed up, you only have to load TSANDS.NLM on one server, because it is capable of reading data from the entire tree. To minimize the network traffic incurred by the backup process, it is recommended that you load TSANDS.NLM on the server where the largest partition is located.

TSANDS.NLM also includes improved error recovery capabilities. When earlier versions of the module were not able to process the entire NDS database because one or more servers were not available, the backup process would cease, generating an error. The TSA now packages and sends all of the NDS data that it can find, so that all of the available data is successfully backed up.

When you use a third-party backup product that includes its own SME, check with the manufacturer to determine whether the improvements in the latest TSA releases are supported by the product. The TSAs are responsible for reading data from the network and transmitting it to the SME, but the manufacturer is responsible for processing the information and writing it to the backup device.

NDS Backup Issues

Backing up and restoring NDS servers is a complicated task because of the interactions between the enterprise components (NDS) and the local server resources, such as the data stored on the volumes. The following sections discuss some of the issues that you should consider when developing a network backup strategy.

Partitions and Replicas

When TSANDS.NLM collects NDS data and transmits it to the SME, it does not consider the distribution of the database among various servers and the replicas scattered around the network. The module walks the tree like any other NDS-aware application and assembles a composite of the entire database before backing it up. The result that is written to tape, therefore, consists of the entire tree as though it were stored in a single partition.

If you have to restore only a part of the NDS database, such as when all the replicas of one partition are lost, the restoration process is mindful of the tree's existing partitions, making it possible to restore only the missing parts. If you must restore the entire NDS database, however, there is no partitioning information stored on the tape, and the entire tree is restored as a single partition. You must then manually re-create your partitions and replicas. For this reason, it is a good idea to maintain a paper record that details how your tree is partitioned and where the replicas of each partition are stored.

Trustee Rights

NetWare uses object IDs, the unique numbers that are assigned to every object in the NDS database, to create trustee assignments in its file system. The access control lists that are a part of every volume's directory entry table (DET) are actually lists of object ID numbers. If you delete an NDS object and then re-create it, it is assigned a new object ID, and the DET references to the old ID are rendered useless. The same is true if your NDS database is lost and you must restore it from a backup tape. As the restoration process creates the objects in the tree, they are assigned new object IDs. Volumes with references to the old ID numbers would no longer be able to process user and group trustee rights.

To make it possible to back up the NDS database and NetWare volumes and retain the trustee rights assignments, the TSA410.NLM module converts the object IDs in the directory entry tables to fully distinguished NDS names. Thus, the access control lists found in a volume's DET on a backup tape are actually lists of the trustees' object names themselves, not their object ID numbers. This makes it possible to restore files and directories from tape with their trustee rights intact, even if you restore them to a different volume than that from which they were backed up.

However, it is crucial that the objects referenced in the directory entry tables be restored to the NDS database before the files and directories that use those tables. When restoring from tape, you should always restore the NDS database first and make sure that it is fully operational before you restore the data in the NetWare volumes.

Summary

This chapter has explored the tools and procedures used to perform regular maintenance on your NDS database. These same tools can also be used to repair NDS problems. Some of the tools discussed are new with NetWare 5, but those tools shipped in both 4.11 and 4.10 have been identified and details of their operation have been given.

Many maintenance tasks are either server intensive, network intensive, or both. It has been reiterated that these tasks should be performed in off hours to minimize the impact on users.

A maintenance schedule, based on network size and level of NDS activity, has been suggested. This should be modified to fit your own circumstances.

Finally, the importance of NDS backup has been stressed. While NetWare provides a rudimentary backup application, it is recommended that third-party NDS-aware applications be used because of their greater flexibility and ease of use.

CHAPTER

12

NDS Security, Audit, and Control

Directories are often interesting merely for the ways they can be used to organize and access information for a variety of purposes. Directories based on Novell Directory Services, in particular, are capable of organizing and providing access to a broad range of information related to items and concepts that are present in an organization's entire operating environment.

Because the scope of information accessible via NDS is so large within the context of an organization, it is usually critical that access to the information be controlled. Without control over access to NDS information, all individuals or systems could be able to access or modify all information in the directory. To address the requirement for directory security, Novell has incorporated a rich set of security, audit, and control capabilities in NDS.

This chapter describes the security, audit, and control features available with NDS. These features are made available by NDS not only to control access to information within the directory, but also to allow for control of access to external systems and any information that might reside on these systems.

First is a brief overview of the fundamental security principles that should typically form the basis of information security plans for organizations. Next, the three distinct features of NDS that provide for security, audit, and control are described: authentication, access control, and auditing. Finally, tips for implementing the NDS security, audit, and control features to achieve specific control objectives are presented at the end of the chapter.

Fundamental Security Principles

Security of an information system is best defined as the combination of features and practices that protect an asset—either the system itself or information stored on the system—from unauthorized access or modification.

Security is usually implemented to achieve one or more of the following objectives based on the content or nature of the system or information:

- Confidentiality, which is the protection of sensitive information from disclosure.

- Integrity, which is related to the accuracy and completeness of information in terms of its intended use.

- Availability, which is related to systems or information being available when necessary.

Some or all of these objectives will be applicable in their own ways for any particular asset at different points in time. The applicability of an objective for an asset is determined by combining the value of the asset itself with the accumulated value of the processes with which the asset is involved.

For example, confidentiality and integrity would likely be critical for a payroll file at all times, but availability might be critical only at certain times (when paychecks are generated). On the other hand, confidentiality might not be necessary for a payroll system configuration file, but both integrity and availability would be critical at any time when the payroll system would run.

A key component of this concept of security in the realm of information systems is that there are individuals or systems that are authorized to perform certain functions at certain times. For example, certain individuals within an organization could be authorized to read or modify confidential information that is critical to the organization while everyone else would not have any such authorization. An effective implementation of security for the information system would establish controls that would systematically allow access to this confidential information only to those authorized individuals, while denying access to all others.

There usually are many choices available when determining how to implement security controls. In most cases, a combination of controls will be put in place to protect a particular asset. Each control choice has costs and benefits, and determining the best controls for a situation involves an optimization of the ratio of benefits to costs.

Benefits are measured in terms of the protection that the control provides to the asset, while costs are measured in terms of the cost of maintaining the control and any barriers that the control presents to legitimate use of the asset. In these terms, a control that presents excessive impediments to the legitimate use of an asset would have a high cost. The overall goal of establishing security controls should be to minimize the cost of the controls while increasing the cost of gaining unauthorized access to the asset to a point that this cost is higher than the value of the asset.

An axiom of information security asserts that when the value of the asset is greater than the cost of gaining unauthorized access to it, it is likely that the controls will be breached and the asset will be compromised.

Typically, three types of controls are available to those implementing security for information systems: preventive, detective, and corrective controls. *Preventive controls* are controls that are employed to prevent activities that might endanger any of the objectives stated on the previous page. *Detective controls* are controls that are employed to detect activities that might endanger the security of a system. *Corrective controls* are controls that are employed to correct situations that might have resulted from activities that could have endangered any of these objectives, such as locking accounts after a certain number of invalid passwords have been entered.

Preventive controls, which are controls established to prevent unauthorized activities, typically are the least expensive to implement. In cases where preventive controls are not available, identical objectives often can be achieved using detective controls by logging access to confidential information by individuals and systems and then reviewing the logs on a regular basis. Such detective controls typically are more expensive to implement than comparable preventive controls since reviewing security logs to detect unauthorized access is an ongoing process that consumes resources.

Additionally, detective controls do not provide the same immediate benefits that are provided by preventive controls, because they only allow policies to be enforced after a security breach occurs and is detected. Implementing a combination of preventive and detective controls is often the most effective method for controlling access to sensitive systems or information. Corrective controls are less common than preventive and detective controls in a security context simply because it's usually impossible to reverse the act of reading sensitive information.

When authorization is required for individuals or systems to access or modify information, the access control mechanism must be capable of unambiguously identifying the individual or system so that it can reliably determine whether an activity is authorized. This process is called *identification and authentication* since it involves discovering the identity of an individual or system and then authenticating that identity.

In the case of human users, this process of authentication is usually accomplished by having the individual provide some unique knowledge, such as a password, or a physical characteristic, such as a fingerprint. In the case of systems, this process of authentication could be as simple as verification of a network address or as difficult as an encrypted sequence involving a complex key exchange and validation process. The strength of this authentication can be measured in terms of the ease with which this unique knowledge or characteristic can be misappropriated by someone who wishes to impersonate an authorized individual or system. If addresses can be spoofed easily for system authentication, or if passwords can be guessed easily for user authentication, then the authentication is not sufficiently strong.

The final important component of this security concept in the realm of information systems is *granularity,* which is the degree to which access can be controlled. In a system that lacks granularity for security controls, it might be possible to limit access to the system itself, but any control beyond that—such as limiting access to particular bits of information within the system—might not be available. In a system with highly granular security controls, it could be possible not only to restrict access to specific bits of information but also to control the activities that can be performed with that information. In most cases, increased granularity allows for greater levels of security control within an information system.

Security Policies, Standards, and Procedures

The first—and perhaps most important—aspect of an organization's security plan should be the establishment of security policies, standards, and procedures that document the expectations, responsibilities, available methods, and instructions for establishing security within an organization. In order for policies, standards, and procedures to be effective, support from the organization's upper management is critical. In addition, it is necessary to monitor compliance with the security policies, standards, and procedures in order to ensure that the organization's security goals are adequate and are being achieved.

Security services should not be provided if there are no established policies, standards, and procedures for security. Security services provided by an information system serve as little more than a mechanism for enforcing the security policies to which users of a particular system are subject. Even when security policies, standards, and procedures are not documented, they exist in implicit form through the implementation of security features and the application of operational procedures to systems. The absence of documented security policies, standards, and procedures, though, can lead to confusion and inconsistent implementation of security services.

An important topic that should be addressed in security policies and standards is the organization's stance, or the standard approach to security within the organization. Many organizations implement a stance of "that which is not expressly permitted is prohibited" while some organizations might be more comfortable with the opposite approach of "that which is not expressly prohibited is permitted."

The popularity of the first approach in organizations has led to the axiomatic information security principle of least rights: Users should be given only the rights they need to do their jobs and nothing more. The actual stance that is documented in policies and standards will have much to do with the culture and basic philosophy of the organization. Another issue that should be covered in policies, standards, and procedures is separation of duties so that those responsible for implementing and operating systems will know to avoid assigning conflicting duties (such as system administration and data entry) to a single person or function.

In some cases, control features might not be present in a system to allow for adequate achievement of security policy goals. It is also possible that control features, although present in a system, might be too difficult to implement without introducing an unacceptable burden for users. In these cases, diligent attempts should be made to introduce compensating controls in order to achieve policy goals. In such situations, even when compensating controls are not possible or feasible, it is necessary to document the exceptions in the policies, standards, and procedures so that management can acknowledge the risks and decide whether to accept them. When this occurs, user control considerations should be documented so users can be educated about their role in maintaining security in the absence of automated controls.

Responsibility for establishing policies, standards, and procedures within an organization should be clearly defined. Network and system administrators should not be responsible for setting policies, but should instead be responsible for implementing systems that allow for the enforcement of policies. Network and system administrators should, however, play an important role in consulting with the organization's management during the development of policies, standards, and procedures since they are often the professionals most likely to understand how policy goals can be translated into automated controls for information systems.

Simply developing and publishing policies, standards, and procedures is not sufficient to provide for a secure information systems environment. The published policies, standards, and procedures should be accessible to and understood by those responsible for implementing and using systems. Documenting the policies, standards, and procedures for an organization should not be a one-time event. Instead, they should be adapted over time to reflect changes in organizational requirements, technology, and identified threats. User responsibilities for adhering to published policies, standards, and procedures should be clearly documented along with management responsibilities for enforcing them.

One of the reasons for noting policies, standards, and procedures as separate items within the documentation of an organization's security plan is to emphasize the hierarchical relationship that exists between the items. Although it is not necessary for the items to be separated in an effective security plan, recognizing the hierarchical relationship could be of assistance when developing a plan. The sections below describe the role that each item plays within a comprehensive security plan.

Policies

Policies should state the principles for the organization in general terms that can be applied to a variety of situations in a similar manner. For instance, a policy covering access to or use of company property could just as easily cover logical access to computer systems as it would cover access to physical buildings. From this policy, requirements for identification and authentication to information systems could be inferred when establishing standards for system implementation.

Standards

Standards govern the approved ways in which business is conducted within the organization while satisfying the policy goals. Using the policy example mentioned in the previous section, a set of standards supporting this policy would describe the ways that control features within a system should be enabled or configured. A standard should not be approved if it is not consistent with the goals of the organization unless the business requirements it satisfies are so compelling that they merit an exception. In such cases the exceptions should be documented and it should be recognized that any exception could serve as a precedent.

Procedures

Procedures document the steps that, when followed, will ensure that policy goals are achieved using approved standards. Using the policy example mentioned previously, the procedures could document necessary steps and forms required to become authorized to access an information system. In addition, procedures could be created to provide guidance for reporting or dealing with policy violations.

Sample Security Policies

The organization is committed to maintaining security with regard to all assets, including those that are tangible, intangible, material, or information-oriented.

The organization's policies establish goals and responsibilities for the protection of the organization's information assets as they relate to data (magnetic, image, text, and/or voice) and computer software within internal systems. This includes the prevention of misuse or loss of information assets, establishing the basis for audits and self-assessments, and preserving the organization's options and legal remedies in the event of information asset loss or misuse.

All employees or authorized agents of the organization are responsible for ensuring the integrity and accuracy of the organization's data; providing for the privacy of proprietary, trade secret, personal, privileged, or otherwise sensitive data; and protecting and preserving corporate assets from misappropriation, misapplication, and conversion.

Managers are responsible for identifying, classifying, and protecting information and computer assets within their respective areas. The security officer should be notified immediately of any security breaches.

- Access to the organization's information assets is restricted to authorized individuals and should be used only for authorized purposes. All data and applications stored on the organization's systems shall be considered the property of the organization unless specifically noted otherwise.

- Access to systems shared by multiple users shall be controlled through unambiguous identification of the individual or machine accessing the system. For example, unique user IDs and passwords should be assigned to individuals.

- All individuals shall employ reasonable measures to protect the integrity of their communication sessions with other systems. For example, individuals should not disclose passwords to others and users should not leave active communication sessions unattended.

- Classification of information stored on the organization's systems shall comply with the organization's Document Protection standards.

- Computing installations (mainframe, midrange, and microcomputer systems) and supporting facilities shall be controlled in areas of restricted physical access when operation is considered essential or when storing confidential or proprietary information.

- Installation of proprietary and vendor software must be authorized through the information systems department to prevent system or licensing violations.

- Controls for restricted software programs shall be established and enforced to prevent unauthorized use, reproduction, and modification. Disk files and hard drives are subject to inspection to ascertain that original documentation, system diskettes, and required licensing material exist for each copy of software products found. Federal copyright restrictions shall be complied with.

- The organization's applications under development or modification, whether the organization or others do the work, must be reviewed and approved by the organization's security officer for information asset security compliance prior to becoming operational.

- Access to the organization's systems through remote connectivity is restricted and requires authorization by the organization's security officer or other appropriate management.

- Computers or equipment that connect to the organization's computers or terminals must be used only for management-approved purposes. Interconnection controls shall include nondisclosure agreements and other contracts as appropriate, and must be reviewed annually by appropriate levels of management. Nondisclosure agreements also apply to employees' use of hardware and software when used for processing of the organization's information, regardless of the environment.

- A self-assessment program, consisting of a review of controls and classification of information assets, shall be conducted periodically. If exposures are identified, a risk assessment must be conducted resulting in either a compliance plan being established or acceptance of the risk. Compliance plans and risk acceptance must be documented, approved by appropriate management, and maintained on file.

- Auditability is fundamental to all requirements established in this document. An auditable application is one whose performance according to specifications and compliance with control requirements can be demonstrated to, or formally tested by, an independent reviewer.

Industry Security Classifications

Unlike most other areas of networking and information systems, there are no clear industry standards for security. In the absence of such standards, it might be difficult for organizations to make comparisons of security and control features of systems from different vendors. To address this issue, organizations have occasionally developed their own standards or adopted "best practices" standards from other organizations. One such standard is the *Trusted Computer System Evaluation Criteria*, which has served as the basis for classifying security features and practices in systems for the degrees of trust that can be placed on them. This standard is known as the *Orange Book* because it was published with an orange binding as part of the *Rainbow Books* series of information protection standards that are published for the Department of Defense by the National Computer Security Center (NCSC).

Because the Orange Book presents evaluation criteria for security features and the NCSC performs evaluations based on these criteria to assign rating classes to systems, many view certification of a rating by the NCSC to be the ultimate statement of the security capabilities of a system. The ratings defined in the Orange Book consist of seven classes, which are meant to rank security capabilities of systems for relative degrees of trust that can be placed in them. Each increasing class level in this rating system builds on the previous level. The system consists of the following classes (listed from the lowest rating class to the highest):

- **D—Minimal Protection** This class is reserved by the NCSC for those systems that have been evaluated but that fail to meet the requirements for a higher evaluation class.

- **C1—Discretionary Security Protection** This type of system nominally satisfies discretionary security requirements by providing separation of users and data. It incorporates some form of credible controls capable of enforcing access limitations on an individual basis, such as allowing users to protect project or private information and to keep other users from accidentally reading or destroying their data. This type of system is intended for environments where users cooperate to process data at the same level of sensitivity.

- **C2—Controlled Access Protection** This class builds on the control capabilities documented for class C1 with a more finely grained discretionary access control facility, making users individually accountable for their actions through login procedures, auditing of security-relevant events, and resource isolation. This is actually the lowest security rating that is granted by the NCSC through its evaluation process since it no longer evaluates products at the C1 rating class.

- **B1—Labeled Security Protection** This class builds on the control capabilities documented for class C2 by requiring an informal statement of the security policy model, data labeling, and mandatory access control over named subjects and objects. The capability must exist for accurately labeling exported information. Any flaws identified by testing must be removed.

- **B2—Structured Protection** This class builds on the control capabilities documented for class B1 by requiring a clearly defined and documented formal security policy model that requires that the discretionary and mandatory access control enforcement found in class B1 systems be extended to all subjects and objects in the system. In addition, covert channels are addressed. The system must be carefully structured into protection-critical and non-protection-critical elements. The system interface should be well defined and the design and implementation should enable it to be subjected to more thorough testing and a more complete review. Authentication mechanisms are strengthened, trusted facility management is provided in the form of support for system administrator and operator functions, and stringent configuration management controls are imposed.

- **B3—Security Domains** This class adds little to the control capabilities documented for class B2, but introduces the requirement that a reference monitor should mediate all accesses of subjects to objects, be tamperproof, and be small enough to be subjected to analysis and tests. The system should be structured to exclude code not essential to security policy enforcement, with significant system engineering during system design and implementation directed toward minimizing its complexity. A security administrator is supported, audit mechanisms are expanded to signal security-relevant events, and system recovery procedures are required.

- **A1—Verified Design** Systems in this class are functionally equivalent to those in class B3 in that no additional architectural features or policy requirements are added. The distinguishing feature of systems in this class is the analysis derived from formal design specification and verification techniques and the resulting high degree of assurance that the system is correctly implemented. This assurance is developmental in nature, starting with a formal model of the security policy and a formal top-level specification (FTLS) of the design. In keeping with the extensive design and development analysis required of systems in class A1, more stringent configuration management is required and procedures must be established for securely distributing the system to sites. A system security administrator is supported.

The process of submitting a system configuration for evaluation by the NCSC is long and expensive, so there are relatively few systems that have actually endeavored to navigate through the entire evaluation process to receive certification of a rating class. One classification described in the Orange Book, C2, has been generally accepted as the *de facto* industry standard for security capabilities of commercial information systems. The majority of systems intended for commercial use that are submitted to the NCSC for evaluation are seeking a class C2 rating. Many other systems that are not eventually submitted for evaluation still attempt to implement class C2 security principles in their designs. The most important technical principles from the C2 classification are listed below:

- The system must enforce a security policy.

- The system must maintain a security kernel, or reference monitor, and must protect it from tampering.

- The system must maintain an audit log and must protect that audit log from tampering.

- The system must force identification and authentication of all user objects to the granularity of a single object and must protect the identification and authentication mechanism from tampering.

- The system must require stringent identification and authentication for access to security-relevant objects such as audit logs, security information, and the security software.

Some of these principles are not directly applicable to networks. For this reason, another book in the Rainbow Books series, the *Red Book*, was produced to provide guidelines for implementing security in a network to achieve equivalent Orange Book classifications. The official title of the Red Book is the *Trusted Network Interpretation of the Trusted Computer*

System Evaluation Criteria, and it serves as a guide to interpreting the Orange Book evaluation criteria for network environments. Since the evaluation criteria presented in the Orange Book and Red Book vary because of the differences between stand-alone and network systems, a certification at a particular rating using Orange Book evaluation criteria does not imply that a system would achieve a similar rating using Red Book evaluation criteria.

Another point to consider with regard to Orange Book and Red Book security classifications is that when a system is certified with a particular rating class, there is no guarantee that the level of protection associated with the rating class will be provided by the system once it is implemented. One reason is that the evaluation and certification process deals only with a particular version and configuration of a product. Consequently, any previous or subsequent versions or alternate configurations should not be considered certified at the same class unless a similar evaluation and certification process has been completed. Another reason is that the principles that are documented for the various security classifications include many issues that are related to policy and operation rather than just technology. When it comes to implementing proper security, it's not only what you use but also how you use it. Finally, it is impossible to detect all software flaws that could lead to security problems during even the most rigorous testing regimens, so it is possible that flaws could be detected and exploited even in systems that have received certification for a security classification.

NDS Identification and Authentication

Security controls for information systems are usually supplied by a system so that subjects (machines or individuals) are authorized to perform certain operations on objects (such as files or services) based on rules that are associated with either the subjects or the objects. In order for this type of security to be effective, it is necessary for the system's security facilities to know the identity of the subject with a high degree of certainty. Identification and authentication is the process by which a system verifies the identity of a machine or individual that wishes to access resources that are controlled by the system's security facilities. This process usually involves the machine or individual providing its identity to the system, along with some proof that the assertion of the identity is genuine. When dealing with human users asserting their identity, three types of proof could potentially be accepted by the system:

- What the user knows

- What the user has

- What the user is

Passwords and pass phrases fall into the category of what a user knows. Smart cards or keys would fall into the category of what a user has, although devices such as smart cards usually require additional proof in the form of what a user knows. Fingerprints, retina scans, or voiceprints that are fed into biometric measurement devices would fall into the category of what a user is.

The standard identification and authentication facilities for human users that are provided by Novell Directory Services use a combination of what the user knows and what the user has. In many cases, the same facilities are used to authenticate systems performing automated tasks (such as mail or database servers) as well, since the NDS access control facilities require that systems must impersonate users in order to gain access to resources that are controlled by NDS. The standard NDS identification and authentication process involves two phases that are performed with NDS-aware client software: an initial authentication and subsequent background authentications. With NDS, authentication is a network service, so it is possible for other applications to use NDS authentication services to set up authenticated sessions between their own services and clients. In addition, other authentication methods occasionally are made available so those clients that do not support NDS can be authenticated via NDS.

The following sections describe the types of authentication that can occur with NDS as well as the control features that are available for user accounts. The first two sections describe the initial and background authentication phases that make up the standard NDS identification and authentication facilities. The following section describes the ways in which support for other authentication methods typically is implemented with NDS. The final section describes the control features that are available for user accounts.

Initial Authentication

Initial authentication occurs only once during a network session—when a user first logs into the network. At that time, a user asserts their identity by providing a login name and attempts to prove their identity with something they know (a password). The initial authentication is successful if the server handling the login process is able to determine that the login name corresponds to the name of a User object in the directory and that the password is correct. Once the initial authentication is successful, the user is ready to use background authentication to actually gain access to network resources.

The actual initial authentication process is much more complex than it might seem to be from the previous basic description. The added complexity is necessary in order to protect the integrity of the initial authentication process so that others who might be listening in on the authentication would not be able to use any information from the isolated authentication process to masquerade as the user in the future. Most of the complexity is added by the use of a randomized handshake and cryptography to virtually eliminate the possibility that a third party could observe the authentication sequence and learn secret information or replay the sequence in the future.

When a workstation is first started and the network software is initialized, it attempts to establish a connection with a server that can provide some network information that is needed before the authentication process can occur. The workstation establishes an unauthenticated service connection with this server so that it can learn the name and location of the nearest NDS server. NetWare clients use SAP (Service Advertising Protocol) Get Nearest Directory Server requests to learn the tree names and addresses of nearby servers. With this information, the workstation will choose the desired tree name and attach (via an unauthenticated connection) to a server in the tree with the appropriate address. The server that the workstation attaches to for initial authentication must contain a writable replica (a Master or Read/Write replica) since the authentication process involves updates to some properties.

Once an unauthenticated connection to the NDS server is established, the initial user identification can take place. Actually, the user enters both the login name and the password at this point, but the password is not used until authentication begins. The login name (combined with a directory context that could be preset on the workstation) is sent by the workstation to the server within a Get Directory Information request to determine whether there is a User object with the same name in the directory. If the server can resolve the user name to a User object in the directory, the server returns the entry ID of the User object and the initial authentication process can proceed.

The workstation initiates the authentication process by sending a Begin Login request to the server with the entry ID that was received in the previous name resolution step. The server uses the entry ID that it receives to determine that the workstation is attempting to authenticate using a valid User object, and if that is the case, the server retrieves the security information, shown in Figure 12.1, that is stored as properties of that User object. The password hash that is stored with the User object is actually based on a combination of the user's password, its length, and a *salt value* (see the definition later in this chapter) that is based on the User object's entry ID. The private key that is stored with the User object is encrypted using the password hash as the encryption key.

F I G U R E 12.1

Security information maintained by the directory for each object

User object

The server responds to the Begin Login request with a message containing the salt value and a *nonce*. The nonce, which is a random number, serves as the challenge allowing the workstation to prove its knowledge of the password provided by the user. The workstation takes the salt and nonce that it receives from the server and computes two values: a hash of the password combined with the salt, and then another hash based on the first hash combined with the nonce that was provided by the server. The first hash that is computed by the workstation would be identical to the password hash stored on the server if the user entered the correct password. This hash is never actually sent across the wire, but the salt and nonce that the workstation received from the server allow the workstation to prove that it calculated a hash value identical to the password hash that the directory stored with the User object.

The workstation then retrieves the server's public key (if it was not already cached at the workstation) and uses this key to encrypt a nonce key that is randomly generated by the workstation. This nonce key is then used to encrypt the second hash that was calculated by the workstation combined with a random string that is provided to help the server conceal its final response. The encryption of the nonce key is accomplished using public key encryption while the encryption of the combined hash and random string is accomplished using secret key encryption. A Finish Login request containing the two encrypted quantities is sent to the server.

Meanwhile, the server independently computes its own hash of the original password hash that it retrieved from the directory, combined with the nonce that the server generated and sent to the workstation. This hash should be identical to the second hash that was computed by the workstation. The server then decrypts the nonce key contained in the Finish Login request that it received from the workstation using its RSA private key—it is able to do this because the nonce key was encrypted using the server's RSA public key. This nonce key is then used to decrypt the hash and random string from the rest of the Finish Login request. The hash is compared with the hash that the server calculated independently and, if the two hashes are identical, the server is convinced that the workstation is in possession of the proper password.

Once the user's identity is verified based on the demonstration of the workstation's knowledge of the correct password, the server prepares to send the user's RSA private key back to the workstation with a Finish Login reply. The RSA private key is encrypted through secret key encryption using the password hash as the key. An exclusive OR operation with the random string that was received from the workstation is used to obfuscate the RSA private key. This obfuscated key value is combined with the nonce that was provided by the workstation and the combined quantity is encrypted with the hash that was used for password verification. This Finish Login reply is then sent to the workstation to close the authentication conversation. Figure 12.2 illustrates this process.

The workstation obtains the user's private key from the Finish Login reply by performing the following operations:

- It decrypts the message with its version of the hash that was used by the server for password verification.

- It reverses the key obfuscation by performing an exclusive OR operation on the obfuscated RSA private key with the nonce that it generated.

- It then decrypts the private key using the first password hash (based on the user-entered and salt value) as the decryption key.

The workstation verifies the server's identity by determining that the nonce included in the Finish Login reply is identical to the nonce that it generated. This works because the only way that the server could have provided the nonce in the Finish Login reply was to successfully decrypt the nonce in the Finish Login request.

FIGURE 12.2

NDS initial
authentication
sequence

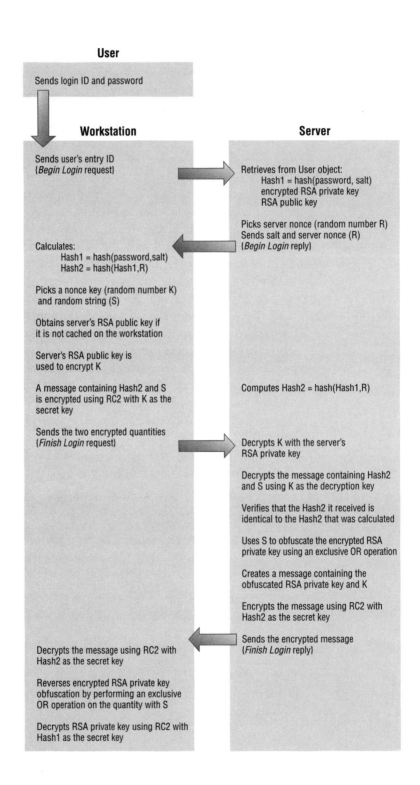

User

Sends login ID and password

Workstation

Sends user's entry ID
{*Begin Login* request}

Calculates:
  Hash1 = hash(password,salt)
  Hash2 = hash(Hash1,R)

Picks a nonce key (random number K)
 and random string (S)

Obtains server's RSA public key if
it is not cached on the workstation

Server's RSA public key is
used to encrypt K

A message containing Hash2 and S
is encrypted using RC2 with K as the
secret key

Sends the two encrypted quantities
{*Finish Login* request}

Decrypts the message using RC2 with
Hash2 as the secret key

Reverses encrypted RSA private key
obfuscation by performing an exclusive
OR operation on the quantity with S

Decrypts RSA private key using RC2 with
Hash1 as the secret key

Server

Retrieves from User object:
  Hash1 = hash(password, salt)
  encrypted RSA private key
  RSA public key

Picks server nonce (random number R)
Sends salt and server nonce (R)
{*Begin Login* reply}

Computes Hash2 = hash(Hash1,R)

Decrypts K with the server's
RSA private key

Decrypts the message containing Hash2
and S using K as the decryption key

Verifies that the Hash2 it received is
identical to the Hash2 that was calculated

Uses S to obfuscate the encrypted RSA
private key using an exclusive OR operation

Creates a message containing the
obfuscated RSA private key and K

Encrypts the message using RC2 with
Hash2 as the secret key

Sends the encrypted message
{*Finish Login* reply}

Once the workstation is in possession of the private key, it is able to begin preparations for background authentication. NDS background authentication is not based on RSA data encryption but is instead based on a variant of the Gillou-Quisquater zero-knowledge proof system.

This process begins with the creation of a message that includes a validity interval for the key that is about to be created. This message is then signed with the user's RSA private key that was retrieved in the previous authentication process. The signed value will serve as a form of private key that the workstation will not divulge but will instead use to sign future authentication requests. The workstation then discards the user's password and private key since they are no longer needed. At this point, the initial authentication process is completed and the workstation is now ready to participate in background authentication as necessary when the user needs to access resources.

Encryption Glossary

Novell Directory Services authentication is heavily dependent on cryptography. Because the terminology used to discuss cryptography may be unfamiliar to many readers, the following short glossary defines some common cryptography terms.

Challenge   A number given to something so that it can be cryptographically processed using a secret quantity it knows and then can return the result (called the response). The purpose of the exercise is to prove knowledge of the secret quantity without revealing it to an eavesdropper. This is known as *challenge/response authentication.*

Cryptography   Mathematical manipulation of data for the purpose of reversible or irreversible transformation.

Hash   A cryptographic one-way function that takes an arbitrarily-sized input and yields a fixed-size output. NDS uses both the MD2 and MD5 message digest functions to generate hashes.

Nonce   A number used in a cryptographic protocol that must (with extremely high probability) be different each time the protocol is run with a given set of participants in order to ensure that an attacker can't usefully inject messages recorded from a previous running of the protocol. There are many ways of generating nonces, including suitably large random numbers, sequence numbers, and timestamps.

Private Key   The quantity in public key cryptography that must be kept secret.

Public Key   The quantity in public key cryptography that is safely divulged to as large an extent as is necessary or convenient.

Public Key Cryptography   Also known as *asymmetric cryptography.* A cryptographic system where encryption and decryption are performed using different keys. The public key encryption system used by NDS is based on RSA's BSAFE encryption library.

RSA   A public key cryptographic algorithm, named for its inventors (Rivest, Shamir, and Adleman), that does encryption. The security of this system depends on the difficulty of factoring extremely large numbers.

Salt   A user-specific value cryptographically combined with that user's password to obtain the hash of that user's password. Salt serves several purposes. It makes the hash of two users' passwords different even if their passwords are the same. It also means that an intruder can't precompute hashes of a few thousand guessed passwords and then compare that list against a stolen database of hashed passwords. The salt can be a random number that is stored, in the clear, along with the hash of the user's password, or it can consist of the user's name or some other user-specific information.

Secret Key   The shared secret quantity in secret key cryptography that is used to encrypt and decrypt data.

Secret Key Cryptography   Also known as *symmetric cryptography,* a scheme in which the same key is used for encryption and decryption. The secret key cryptographic system used by NDS is RC2.

Sign   To use your private key to generate a digital signature as a means of providing a guarantee that you generated, or approved of, some message.

Signature   A quantity associated with a message which only someone with knowledge of your private key could have generated, but which can be verified through knowledge of your public key.

Zero Knowledge Proof   A scheme in which you can convince someone you know a secret without actually divulging the secret. You know a secret; they know something equivalent to a public key. You answer questions, and the answers convince the other that you know the secret without giving them any information that will help them find the secret. NDS uses a variant of the Guillou-Quisquater zero-knowledge proof system for background authentication.

Background Authentication

Background authentication refers to authentication that occurs to additional services after the initial authentication. This authentication occurs transparently to the user since it is performed in the background, so the user is not required to enter a login name and password each time a new resource is accessed. Background authentication is based on the Gillou-Quisquater authentication method using the key that was generated during initial authentication. Background authentication occurs when a server receives a new connection request from a user that is already authenticated to NDS. The server sends a challenge to the workstation, and the workstation feeds this challenge, the Gillou-Quisquater key, and the user's RSA public key into a function that creates a signature. This signature serves as the response from the workstation, and the server verifies the signature using the following information that it possesses:

- The challenge that was sent to the workstation

- The signature on the challenge that was received in response from the workstation

- The message that includes the validity interval for the Gillou-Quisquater key that was also received in response from the workstation

- The user's RSA public key

If the comparison function performed by the server validates the response, the authentication is successful and the user is allowed to access resources with permissions determined by the user's identity.

This authentication scheme is secure because the challenge presented by the server is sufficiently random and the signed response proves that the workstation had knowledge of the user's private key.

Alternative Authentication Methods

Although the standard NDS identification and authentication facilities provide an extremely reliable way for systems or individuals to prove their identity to the directory, many useful applications and services exist that use different authentication schemes. In order for these applications and services to allow authentication via NDS, some form of accommodation needs to be provided. This accommodation can take one of two forms:

- A *passthrough authentication service* can be provided to adapt the non-NDS authentication to NDS.

- A *proxy authentication service* can be provided to accept the non-NDS authentication and perform its own authentication on behalf of the user.

The bindery services option to allow non-encrypted passwords on NetWare servers is an example of a passthrough authentication service, while FTP and HTTP services provided by NetWare are examples of proxy authentication services.

With a passthrough authentication service, the NDS server providing the authentication service acts as an intermediary between NDS and the client that wishes to be authenticated. The NDS server interprets requests and responses generated by the client, and NDS then reformulates them so that the authentication occurs as expected—assuming that the information provided by the client is correct. Once the authentication is completed, the passthrough authentication service steps aside and both the client and NDS are allowed to proceed as if an NDS authentication had occurred. Using bindery services as an example, if a bindery client attempts a NetWare Version 3 authentication with an unencrypted password, the bindery services passthrough authentication service assists in the authentication process so that it appears to the client as a normal bindery authentication. Since background authentication is not available for bindery clients in the same way that it is for NDS clients, if a user needs to access resources on another server, it needs to initiate a new bindery authentication sequence using bindery services passthrough authentication once again.

With a proxy authentication service, the system providing the authentication service acts as an independent agent when it interacts with NDS. When a client attempts to authenticate to the proxy, the proxy collects the authentication information (such as a login name and password) and then proceeds to perform a normal authentication via NDS on behalf of the client. If the authentication is successful, the system providing the proxy authentication service possesses an authenticated NDS connection on behalf of the client. Any operations that the client wishes to initiate could be performed by the proxy service—using the credentials it obtained on behalf of the client or using its own credentials. Since the proxy service possesses the authenticated connection with NDS, the client is not able to use the session to perform actions without the assistance of the proxy service.

We can use the FTP Server service provided with NetWare as an example. A normal FTP client can connect with the FTP server and be authenticated using the normal FTP authentication mechanisms. The FTP server is actually authenticated to NDS on behalf of the client, and all actions that are possible with FTP are initiated by the client but performed by the FTP server on behalf of the user. Access to files on NetWare servers is based on the identity of the user on whose behalf the FTP server is acting.

Although alternative authentication services provide a valuable function by allowing non-NDS clients to be authenticated for services or applications via NDS, there is a danger inherent in providing such methods. Since such alternative authentication services rarely provide for authentication as strong as that provided by the standard NDS authentication services, the services could weaken authentication for the NDS environment. For example, the standard FTP authentication protocol involves the transmission of passwords over the network in cleartext form. This is never done with standard NDS authentication, so providing this service could allow attackers to capture NDS passwords that would normally not be able to be captured if only standard NDS authentication were allowed.

When evaluating whether to implement services that use alternative authentication services, the needs of users must be balanced with the overall security requirements to ensure that the organization's security goals are not compromised.

User Account Restrictions

In addition to the security information that NDS maintains as properties with each User object, several properties are provided that, when properly used, allow organizations to enforce policies and standards to decrease the possibility of unauthorized access to systems via User accounts. Additionally, NDS provides security controls that can be implemented for multiple accounts at the container level to further decrease the possibility of unauthorized access to systems via User accounts. The following sections describe the security controls that are available for individual User objects and container objects.

Individual Security Controls for User Accounts

User objects that are created without using a user template do not have any restrictions placed on their use since none of the account restriction properties are assigned any values by default. This unrestricted condition can be addressed by modifying the properties for existing User objects and by creating user templates with default account restrictions that can be used when creating new User objects.

NDS management utilities included with early versions of NetWare 4.*x* allowed for the creation of one User object in each container to serve as a template for creating new User objects. This User object had to be given the special name User Template or User_Template in order to be recognized as a template. With NetWare 4.11 and subsequent versions, a User Template object class was added to the default NDS schema so that multiple user templates could be created in each container or shared between containers. The graphical NDS management utilities included with NetWare 4.11 and later do not recognize the old style of user templates, although the DOS-based utilities UIMPORT and NETADMIN still do.

The following are the User object properties that are available to provide account restrictions for User objects:

- **Account Disabled**   When this Boolean value is True, the User object cannot be used for authentication, although it can continue to be associated with other objects for security purposes. Disabling User objects for terminated employees allows file ownership and trustee assignments to remain until they can be analyzed and transferred to other User objects if necessary.

- **Account Expiration Date**   When a date and time are assigned to this property, the User object will be available for authentication up until the noted date and time, unless it is explicitly disabled. This provides an automated way to maintain control over temporary user accounts (for visitors or contractors) without requiring manual follow-up when access privileges are supposed to be terminated.

- **Limit Concurrent Connections**   By default, a User object can be used to authenticate from an unlimited number of workstations at the same time. This could be considered a security vulnerability, since it could allow attackers to use legitimate User accounts during regular hours of operation. In addition, allowing unlimited connections could make sharing passwords painless for users. When this Boolean value is True, concurrent connections are limited to the maximum number of connections allowed for the User object.

- **Maximum Connections**   When concurrent connections are limited, the numeric value for this property represents the maximum number of workstations from which the User object can be authenticated concurrently.

- **Allow User to Change Password**   When this Boolean value is True, a user authenticated with this User object can change the object's password.

- **Require a Password**   When this Boolean value is True, the User object cannot be assigned a null password during password changes. If this property is enabled while a user does not have a password, the user will be required to create a password after logging in, if the password has expired.

- **Minimum Password Length**   When passwords are required, this numeric value represents the minimum length for any password that is assigned to the User object. This property has no effect for existing passwords that might be shorter than the minimum, although any new password will need to conform to the minimum length if the old password expires.

- **Force Periodic Password Changes**   When this Boolean value is True, the password assigned to the User object will expire after a certain period of time. When the password expires, the user is required to assign a new password to the User object.

- **Days between Forced Changes**   When periodic password changes are required, this value represents the length of time that any given password can be used. Once a password expires, it can still be used for most forms of NDS authentication, but it must be changed within a certain number of uses (determined by grace logins).

- **Date Password Expires** When a date and time are assigned to this property, the current password will expire at the date and time specified. When password changes are required, this property is automatically modified when the password is changed. Once a password expires, it can still be used for most forms of NDS authentication, but it must be changed within a certain number of uses (determined by grace logins).

- **Require Unique Passwords** When this Boolean value is True, users are not allowed to use passwords that they used previously within a range of time determined by multiplying the days between forced changes by the number nine. For example, if a User object were forced to change its password every 40 days, enabling this property would restrict a user from assigning a password to this User object that they had used within the last 360 days.

- **Limit Grace Logins** When this Boolean value is True, the number of times that an expired password can be used without requiring a change is limited for most forms of NDS authentication.

- **Grace Logins Allowed** When grace logins are limited, this numeric value represents the maximum number of times that an expired password can be used without changing it for most forms of NDS authentication.

- **Grace Logins Remaining** When grace logins are limited, this numeric value represents the maximum number of times that the current password can be used without changing it for most forms of NDS authentication. Once the password is changed, this value is automatically reset to the value assigned to Grace Logins Allowed.

- **Login Time Restrictions** This grid-style property limits the days of the week and times that a User object will be available for authentication. When this property value is empty, the User object is available for authentication at all times every day of the week. The actual times that are recorded for this property could depend on the utility used to modify this property, since the times are stored in NDS using UTC (Universal Time Coordinate) but are translated differently by utilities to reflect local time (with or without daylight savings time offsets).

NDS security administrators are often baffled by the ways that time restriction settings are stored in NDS and then applied to users during authentication. NDS stores time restrictions in UTC (Universal Time Coordinate, a fancy name for Greenwich Mean Time) format and then adjusts the times when the property is accessed by utilities or during authentication. This can make the time restrictions appear to drift depending on the utility used to edit the time restrictions, local workstation time zone settings, and changes in daylight savings time. Another point to consider when using time restrictions is that they are global in nature, that is, they cannot be used to restrict access for a User object to specific services based on time while leaving access to other services unrestricted.

- **Network Address Restrictions** This multivalued property can be used to limit the workstations from which the User object will be available for authentication. Multiple network address types can be used, including IPX/SPX, TCP/IP, or AppleTalk. Partial addresses, such as subnetworks, are allowed. A match can occur only on addresses for protocols that are being used to carry the authentication process. When this property is empty, the User object is available for authentication from any workstation.

- **Account Locked** When this Boolean value is True, the User object cannot be used for authentication because an intruder event has been noted for the User object. The lockout condition can be reversed either by setting this property to False or by allowing the intruder lockout reset interval to expire.

Container Security Controls for User Accounts

Properties that can control how invalid login attempts are handled for directly subordinate User objects are available for Organization and Organizational Unit objects. Based on the values assigned to these properties, it is possible to automatically lock out a User object for a period of time after a certain number of invalid login attempts. This is an important compensating control that preemptively protects User objects from attacks where an intruder tries to guess passwords. Another control that is provided by NDS is a three-second delay after invalid login attempts, which dramatically decreases the number of passwords that can be guessed in a given period of time. The Intruder Detection and Lockout features that are available for container objects are described here:

- **Detect Intruders**   When this Boolean value is True, NDS will increment a counter for every invalid login attempt that occurs for each User object. The length of time that this information is retained is determined by the Intruder attempt reset interval.

- **Incorrect Login Attempts**   When Intruder Detection is enabled, the numeric value for this property represents the number of invalid login attempts that must occur within the intruder attempt reset interval for a given User object before an intrusion event will be noted.

- **Intruder Attempt Reset Interval**   This property sets the amount of time in days, hours, and minutes that the counter that tracks invalid login attempts for each User object will be retained. At the point where this time period expires without any new invalid login attempts being recorded for a User object, the counter will be reset to zero.

- **Lock Account After Detection**   When this Boolean value is True, NDS will automatically lock out a User object from being able to authenticate if an intrusion event is noted. Once a User object has a lockout condition, a user with the proper authority can either manually reverse it or it will be automatically reversed when the intruder lockout reset interval expires.

- **Intruder Lockout Reset Interval**   This property sets the amount of time in days, hours, and minutes that a User object will be unavailable for authentication once an intrusion event is noted.

WARNING   It might seem reasonable that the apparently normal rules of inheritance would apply to Intruder Detection and Lockout settings for Organization and Organizational Unit objects, but this is not the case. In order for the feature to be enabled for the User objects in a container, the container object itself must have the proper settings, because the settings from any superior containers are not inherited. A common mistake in NDS security implementations is to establish Intruder Detection and Lockout settings for the top container only while ignoring the settings for subordinate container objects.

NDS Access Control

Novell Directory Services possesses a highly scalable and granular access control model for protecting information in the directory from unauthorized access or modification. This model allows rights assignments (called *trustee assignments*) to be established for objects or individual properties within objects. The model also takes advantage of the concepts of equivalence and inheritance to allow single strategically placed trustee assignments on objects to affect hundreds and even thousands of other objects.

These NDS object rights and NDS property rights govern access to the objects within the directory tree based on the identity of the subject that is attempting to gain access to the object. Object and property rights are assigned separately to provide enhanced security and better access control over the objects themselves and the information (properties) associated with NDS objects.

Security decisions made by NDS occur in real time and are based on a somewhat complex form of security arithmetic. This security arithmetic takes into account the combination of direct trustee assignments, security equivalence, inheritance, and filters to calculate effective rights every time a subject attempts to access an object. The following sections provide an overview of these concepts and their roles in controlling access to information in the directory.

Object Rights

Each object in the directory has rights that can be assigned explicitly to it via its Object Trustees, or Access Control List (ACL), property. Every object class is defined with this ACL (Access Control List) property, and object trustee assignments within this property control what a subject can do to the object. The ACL is a multivalued property, which means that the property can accept any number of different trustee assignment entries. Each entry consists of three fields:

- **Subject**   The Relative Distinguished Name of the object to which rights are being given. This name is given relative to the location of the object.

- **Property**   For all object trustee assignments, this field is given a value of [Object Rights].

- **Entry Rights**   The list of rights that are being assigned.

The available object rights are:

- **Browse**   The right to see the object in the directory tree.

- **Create**   The right to create a new object below this specified object in the directory tree. This right applies only to container objects.

- **Delete**   The right to delete the object from the directory tree. Leaf objects and empty container objects are the only objects that can be deleted.

- **Rename**   The right to change the name of the object.

- **Supervisor**   Equivalent to selecting every object right as well as all rights to all of the object's properties.

As an example, if a user has the Browse right to an object, they would be able to see that object in a list of objects from the tree. As another example, if a user has the Supervisor right to an object, they could do the following:

- See the object in the tree (the Browse right).

- Create subordinate objects if the object is a container (the Create right).

- Delete the object if it's a leaf object or an empty container (the Delete right).

- Change the object's name (the Rename right).

- Access and manipulate the values of any of the properties associated with the object (implied supervisory rights to all properties).

Any object can be a trustee of any other object, including itself, within its own directory tree. When NDS is first installed, some default object trustee assignments are created to allow for immediate usage and management of the new directory tree:

- The first User object (Admin) that is created is given Supervisory rights to the [Root] object. Because of inheritance (explained later) this gives the Admin user all rights to every object in the tree.

- The special [Public] trustee, which is not an actual object, is given Browse rights to the [Root] object. Again, because of inheritance, this gives all users—including those who are not yet authenticated—the right to view the name and type of every object in the tree.

Property Rights

Each property associated with an object in the directory has rights that can be assigned explicitly to it via the Object Trustees (ACL) property. Every object class is defined with this ACL property (this is the same property that is used for object trustee assignments), and these property trustee assignments within this property control what a subject can do to the property's value.

As is the case with object trustee assignments, entries within the ACL property for property rights assignments consist of three fields:

- **Subject**   The Relative Distinguished Name of the object to which rights are being given. This name is given relative to the location of the object.

- **Property**   The name of the property when the property rights assignment is applicable to a single property or [All Properties Rights] when the property rights assignment is applicable to all properties.

- **Property Rights**   The list of rights that are being assigned.

The available property rights are:

- **Compare**   The right to compare a given value to the value of the property. This does not allow the subject to see the object's property value.

- **Read**   The right to read the values of the property. If the Read right is given, the Compare right is implied even if it is not explicitly granted.

- **Write**   The rights to add, remove, or change any values of the property.

- **Add or Delete Self**   The right of the subject to add or remove itself as a value of the property. The subject cannot affect any other values of the property, so this can be useful for membership list properties within objects such as mailing lists or groups.

- **Supervisor**   All rights to the property.

For example, if a user has the Compare right to another User object's Password Expiration property, the only way to figure out if the user was currently due to change passwords would be to compare likely values with the property until one matches. Another example would be if a user has Write rights to another user's Object Trustees (ACL) property. The user would be able to add, change, or delete any entry in this ACL property or even add himself (or herself) as a trustee with Supervisor object rights, if desired.

Rights are assigned to properties individually, so it is possible for a subject to have Read and Write rights to one property while having only Read rights to another property within the same object. The special [All Properties Rights] trustee assignment affects all properties for an object. It is still possible to use individual property trustee assignments when an [All Properties Rights] trustee assignment is used on an object, and in such a case the individual property trustee assignment will take precedence over the [All Properties] trustee assignment.

WARNING Of particular importance is the ACL property itself. Giving specific rights to that property makes it possible to do things like change passwords and reset intruder lockouts, but it also opens up security holes if not applied appropriately to objects with higher levels of security (like administrative accounts). Imagine what would happen if a helpdesk person could go in and change an admin's password, or grant themselves security equivalent to that of the administrator by modifying the ACL to allow them to do it!

Default Rights Templates

When an NDS tree is first created, templates are created that provide default trustee assignments for Server, Volume, and User object classes so that all objects that are created from these classes have similar characteristics beyond the property associations that they gain from the NDS schema. The following sections describe how these default rights templates influence the generation of explicit trustee assignments for newly created Server, Volume, and User objects.

Server and Volume Objects

When a NetWare server is installed in a directory tree, one Server object and one or more Volume objects are created in a container that is designated to hold the server's objects. When these objects are created, the default rights templates cause several trustee assignments to be created to facilitate connectivity with these resources:

- The new Server object is given Supervisor object rights to itself.

- The special [Public] trustee is given Read property rights to the Messaging Server property for the new Server object. This gives all users—including those who are not yet authenticated—the right to read this property for these objects.

- The [Root] object is given Read property rights to the Host Server Name and Host Volume Name properties of the Volume objects that are created with the Server object. Because of inheritance this gives all authenticated users the right to read this property for these objects.

User Objects

When a new User object is created, the default rights templates cause several trustee assignments to be created:

- The new User object is given the Browse object right. This allows the user to see its own object in lists of objects from the tree—even if the user would normally be denied this right for some reason.

- The new User object is given the Read all properties right to itself so that it can read the contents of its own properties. It is also given Read and Write property rights to the Login Script and Print Job Configuration properties of itself so that the user can modify the contents of these properties to change the login script or print job configurations.

- The [Root] object is given Read property rights to the Network Address and Group Membership properties of the User object. Because of security equivalence, this gives all authenticated users the right to read this property for these objects.

- The special [Public] trustee is given [Read] property rights to the Default Server property of the User object. This is done since the Default Server often serves as a Messaging Server property and it might be useful for nonauthenticated users. Because of inheritance, this gives all users—including those who are not yet authenticated—the right to read this property for these objects.

NetWare File System Security

NetWare file system security, the model for which was created long before NDS appeared on the scene, is conceptually similar to the security model that was developed for NDS access control. Because of this, it uses many of the same concepts of direct trustee assignments and security equivalence to calculate the rights that are effective for any given file.

 The NetWare file system also includes some additional concepts of inheritance of trustee assignments within the file system, but that is outside the scope of this chapter and this book.

NDS influences NetWare file system security in two ways:

- Any type of object can be assigned as a trustee of a directory or file on a NetWare volume. This allows for a great deal of flexibility in assigning file system rights, since security equivalence can be leveraged through the use of container objects or the [Root] object as directory or file trustees.

- Any object that possesses effective Write privileges to the Server object's Object Trustees (ACL) property gains supervisory access to every volume connected to the server. For example, if an object is given supervisory object rights to a Server object, that object would have supervisory rights to every volume connected to that server since the object would have effective Write privileges to the Server object's ACL. This is the only place within the NDS security model where object or property rights directly influence or override file system trustee assignments.

Equivalence, Inheritance, and Filtering

Up to this point, NDS object and property rights have been discussed only in terms of direct trustee assignments. The concept is simple to understand: If a subject is directly assigned rights to an object or property, then the subject can be expected to perform the operations on the object or property that are allowed by the trustee assignment.

Direct trustee assignments, however, are only one part of the security model for NDS. The additional concepts of equivalence, inheritance, and filtering combine with direct trustee assignments to determine the effective rights that a subject would possess for any given object. The following sections describe each of these additional concepts in turn, finishing with a description of how all the NDS security concepts interact to determine the effective rights to an object that a subject would possess.

Security Equivalence

Security equivalence allows an object to acquire the rights that are granted directly to another object. For example, if an object (A) is security equivalent to another object (B), object A will acquire all rights that object B possesses through direct assignment. In other words, object A will acquire all trustee assignments that name object B as the subject.

Security equivalence is not transitive, so it is not possible for an object to gain rights to some other object via a chain of security equivalences. Security equivalence is a one-way relationship between objects, with one object designated as equivalent to the other object. In the example where object A is security equivalent to object B, object A acquires all rights that object B possesses through direct assignment but object B does not acquire any rights that object A possesses (unless object B is security equivalent to object A).

With NDS, security equivalence is established both explicitly and implicitly. *Explicit security equivalence* is the type of equivalence that is established when a user is made security equivalent to another user, when a user is made a member of a group, or when a user occupies an organizational role. This security equivalence is granted through the Equivalent To Me and Security Equals properties that are associated with many object classes. When an object (A) is security equivalent to another object (B), the name of object A is added to object B's Equivalent To Me property and the name of object B is added to object A's Security Equals property. Although only the Equivalent To Me property is needed to establish security equivalence, both properties are used for purposes of referential integrity.

Implicit security equivalence is a form of automatic security equivalence that is established for all objects in a tree. As is the case with explicit security equivalence, implicit security equivalence cannot be overridden. The following security equivalences are implicitly established:

- All objects are security equivalent to the [Public] trustee. This includes users that have not yet authenticated to the directory.

- All objects are security equivalent to the [Root] object.

- An object is security equivalent to all superior container objects.

For example, an object named CN=User.OU=Department.O=Organization will be security equivalent to the [Public] trustee, the [Root] object, the OU=Department.O=Organization object, and the O=Organization object.

Inheritance

With inheritance, an object inherits portions of the ACLs of superior container objects and the [Root] object. Only object trustee assignments and all properties trustee assignments can be inherited, so it is not possible to establish a trustee assignment for an individual property with the expectation that it will be inherited. Inheritance flows down through the hierarchy to an object from the [Root] object and can be overridden either by filters (described below) or by direct trustee assignments along the path all the way to the object itself. Creating an object trustee assignment with a given subject for a container has the same effect as creating the same trustee assignment for all subordinate objects that do not already have object trustee assignments of their own for the same subject.

Inheritance is the way that the Admin object, which is created when NDS is first installed, gains supervisory rights to all objects in the tree. An object trustee assignment is created for the [Root] object that gives Supervisor rights to the Admin object. These supervisory rights could be overridden for a given object by creating a trustee assignment for the object that gives some other right to the Admin object.

Inherited Rights Filters

The Inherited Rights Filter (IRF) blocks the normal progress of inherited trustee assignments from traveling down through the hierarchy to objects. The IRF should be thought of as a shield that can be placed in front of an object to keep it from inheriting trustee assignments that contain certain types of object or property rights, regardless of the subject. For example, placing an IRF for the Supervisor object right on a container object would not allow the container's subordinate objects to inherit the object trustee assignment for the [Root] object that contains the Supervisor object right for the Admin object.

This would effectively keep the Admin object from gaining supervisory rights to these subordinate objects unless explicit trustee assignments were used. But if the object trustee assignment for the [Root] object also contained the Browse, Create, Rename, and Delete rights, the same IRF would only block the Supervisor right so that all the subordinate objects would inherit trustee assignments containing all rights except the Supervisor object right.

WARNING

Great care should be exercised when using Inherited Rights Filters since it is possible to inadvertently block all legitimate access to an object through their use. Before creating an Inherited Rights Filter, make sure that some object in the directory has sufficient explicit rights to the object to allow it to be modified in the future. The minimum explicit rights are those that would allow the Inherited Rights Filter to be removed in the future if necessary. Usually, explicit Write rights to the object's Object Trustees (ACL) property would be sufficient since Inherited Rights Filters are stored in this property.

Calculating Effective Rights

Each attempted interaction between a subject and an object causes a security calculation to take place to determine whether the subject possesses adequate rights to perform the desired operation. This security calculation results in a quantity known as the effective rights that the subject has to the object. Effective rights are calculated by adding the applicable direct trustee assignments, rights gained from security equivalence, and rights gained from inheritance (see Figure 12.3).

Inherited Rights Filters modify the rights gained from inheritance before they are added to the calculation of effective rights. Since the calculation of effective rights is additive, the highest rights prevail regardless of whether they are obtained from direct trustee assignment, security equivalence, or inheritance. So, for example, if a subject has a direct Browse object trustee assignment to an object but is equivalent to an object that has a direct Supervisor object trustee assignment, the subject will have effective Supervisor object rights to the object.

F I G U R E   12.3

Calculating effective rights

Effective Rights = Direct Trustee Assignments

+ Equivalent Rights

+ Inherited Rights

− Inherited Rights Filter

Security Monitoring

Security monitoring is the process by which the controls of a system are evaluated to determine whether they are configured properly and operating as expected. This typically consists of two separate activities:

- Reviewing the implementation and configuration of control features. This can be done in a number of ways, but the process usually involves some combination of the following: interviews with personnel responsible for maintaining security, independent observation, and the use of automated tools. Organizations often use outside consultants for this important task in order to ensure independence and to benefit from the valuable expertise that consultants can offer. Tools that can be used to review the implementation and configuration of NDS security controls are discussed at the end of this section.

- Auditing of security events, which is usually implemented in the form of security logs that are reviewed regularly—either to detect potential security problems or to investigate suspected security incidents. NDS provides rich auditing capabilities that can be used to record almost any type of security event related to the directory. This capability is described next.

Directory Auditing

Auditing is a process by which designated users examine an organization's records to ensure that confidential data is secure and that transactions are handled correctly. Organizations normally call on independent auditors to ensure that the audit process will be unbiased and accurate.

For NDS, directory auditing serves the purpose of gathering historical information about significant security events related to objects in the directory. This information can allow for the detection of possible intrusions or for the detection of unauthorized access. Auditing is often a necessity when preventive controls are not possible or feasible to support the desired separation of duties. In such a case, the detective controls represented by auditing must suffice. When such security monitoring is a critical component of a security plan, the logs that are generated become assets that must be secured to protect their integrity and confidentiality.

NetWare provides a rich set of auditing capabilities for monitoring NDS security events. The AUDITCON utility is provided to audit server events (involving access to the file system) and Directory Services events. Records concerning server and directory events are stored in an audit log file in the SYS volume of the server being audited.

Only an authorized auditor has access to the audit file. This auditor should not be the network administrator, in order to ensure independence in the monitoring process.

Two methods exist for controlling access to audit information: trustee assignments to Audit File objects and audit passwords. Novell recommends the use of trustee assignments to Audit File objects, which is a capability that was first made available with NetWare 4.11. When this method is used, the ability to view audit logs or change the audit configuration is controlled by rights to properties of the Audit File objects. Audit File objects are created when auditing is enabled for an audit source such as a directory container or a file system volume.

The audit password method allows any auditor with knowledge of the proper password to access audit logs and to change the audit configuration. This was the only access control method available for NetWare 4.10 and earlier.

When Audit File objects are used to control access to audit logs, effective rights to two properties control the actions that an auditor is able to perform:

- The Audit Policy property controls access to the audit policy for the audit log that is controlled by the Audit File object. An auditor with Read and Write rights to this property can add, change, or remove events that are logged.

- The Audit Contents property controls access to the audit log itself that is controlled by the Audit File object. An auditor with Read rights to this property can view the contents of the audit log. The Write right has no effect on this property since the NetWare audit mechanism only allows audit sources to append records to the audit logs.

The object that is responsible for enabling auditing for a particular audit source is granted Supervisory object rights to the Audit File object that is created, and these rights provide effective Read and Write rights to the Audit

Policy property and Read rights to the Audit Contents property. Any object that has Write all properties rights to the Audit File object can create trustee assignments for these properties to allow other objects either to modify the audit policy or to access the audit logs.

Since Audit File objects are normal objects in the directory tree, the normal processes of security equivalence and inheritance could have an effect on effective rights for these objects. Although this could allow for the creation of Group or Organization Role objects to provide an easy method for granting access to audit logs, it could also allow excessive access to this sensitive information.

Security Evaluation Tools

Evaluating the way that security controls are implemented in an NDS tree is an important activity that should be performed on a regular basis. Although it is possible to observe the implementation of security controls using the standard NDS administrative utilities, this process can be tedious and prone to errors and omissions. Several tools and utilities are available for automating the process of monitoring the NDS security configuration for compliance with standards.

NetWare Utilities

NetWare includes several utilities that can be used to extract information from NDS. These utilities are provided strictly for information purposes and do not make any attempt to assess the implementation of security controls. The utilities are useful, however, for extracting information related to security from the directory for purposes of evaluation.

NLIST This is a DOS command line program that provides access to a wealth of information about NDS objects and their properties. The program has many options that control how information is displayed as well as allowing for searches and filtering of results. Using NLIST, it is possible to do the following:

- List all objects in the directory within a container or within the entire directory. The list of objects can be limited to specific object types and can include a specified set of properties or all properties for each object.

- Search for objects that have properties with a certain value or range of values. For example, it is possible to use NLIST to display all User objects that have never logged in or that have not logged in for a specified period of time.

The results of the NLIST command can be saved to a file for offline analysis using normal DOS redirection. A common use of this technique is to create a list of objects and their properties and then use a separate program (like a Perl script) to analyze the information.

RIGHTS   This is a DOS command line program that provides access to file system trustee assignments for NetWare volumes. The program has many options that control how information is displayed, as well as allowing for results to be filtered. Using RIGHTS, it is possible to do the following:

- Display the effective rights that an object has to a file or directory.

- List the trustee assignments (including object and rights) for a selection of files and directories.

- Provide an overview of how an object received rights to a file or directory.

The results of the RIGHTS command can be saved to a file for offline analysis using normal DOS redirection. A common use of this technique is to create a list of trustee assignments for a volume and then use a separate program (like a Perl script) to analyze the information.

Third-Party Tools

Several third-party tools are available that can extract information from NDS and provide a richer set of reporting capabilities than is available with the utilities that are provided with NetWare. Some of the tools that are useful for evaluating the implementation of security controls for NDS trees are described briefly below.

BindView EMS   BindView Development's BindView EMS (Enterprise Management System) with its NOSAdmin component is a data extraction tool that provides flexible access to virtually every bit of information related to NetWare servers and NDS trees. The main strength of BindView is *ad hoc* reporting capabilities that allow individuals to generate reports. The reports can be used to list security-related information or to provide answers to specific questions about security configuration.

AuditWare   Computer Associates AuditWare for NDS is an offline reporting tool for NDS. AuditWare uses the discovery engine component of the popular DS Standard tool to generate an offline model of an NDS tree that can be used to generate reports. The reports can be used to list directory security-related information or to provide answers to specific questions about security configuration.

Kane Security Analyst   Intrusion Detection's Kane Security Analyst for NDS is a security analysis tool that generates a series of reports that can be used to assess the security of NetWare servers and NDS trees.

Implementing Effective NDS Security

So far in this chapter, the important concepts of NDS security have been discussed. These have included the fundamental security principles that should drive a security implementation and the mechanical aspects of identification and authentication, access control, and security monitoring. Implementing effective NDS security requires additional considerations, some of which are discussed in the following sections.

User Accounts and Account Restrictions

One of the driving principles of information security is the requirement that users be individually accountable for their actions. Individual accountability requires that users identify themselves to the system in a reliable way so that access controls can operate effectively and so that the logging of security events, when present, can be linked with individuals.

In practice, this requires the assignment of individual user accounts to users so that only one user is associated with any given user account. Enforcement of this requirement can be accomplished by disallowing the use of shared accounts (such as Guest) and by enforcing strict controls over access to user accounts to decrease the possibility that the identity of a user could be misappropriated.

Two types of user accounts are typically implemented for systems that are controlled by NDS. The first type of user account is used for human users who need to gain access to network resources such as the directory, network file systems, services, or printers. The second type of user account is used for machines or automated processes that also need to gain access to network resources such as the directory, network file systems, services, or printers. Since NDS requires machines or automated processes to impersonate human users to gain access to network resources, the same types of user accounts are used for human users, machines, and automated processes.

Access to user accounts, which are represented by User objects in NDS, is controlled by the NDS identification and authentication facilities. The configuration of these facilities is controlled by properties associated with the User and container object classes. Authentication controls available for User objects can be set differently for each individual User object.

Authentication controls available for container objects can be set differently for each individual container, but they affect every directly subordinate User object in the same way.

Although the same type of user account is used for human users, machines, and automated processes, the controls governing access to these user accounts usually are implemented quite differently. For example, machines are able to remember high quality secrets, whereas human users are restricted to remembering secrets of limited quality (typically passwords that are relatively short). In addition, user accounts that are used for impersonation purposes by machines or automated processes rarely move from one system to another, so it is possible to restrict access to accounts used for these purposes to only allow access from selected network addresses.

Only user accounts that are actually in use on a regular basis should be available for authentication at all times. User accounts that are used infrequently or those associated with terminated individuals or inactive services should be disabled so that they cannot be exploited to gain unauthorized access to the system. In order to accomplish this, procedures should be established to inform security administrators of individuals that will no longer be allowed to access the system so that the associated User objects can be disabled and eventually deleted.

Compensating controls should be established as well. These controls should detect accounts that have not been used for a certain period of time so that these dormant accounts can be disabled or deleted. The length of time required for an account to be considered to be dormant will depend on the organization, but a reasonable guideline is to use the length of time between forced password changes, when users are required to change passwords. For example, if users are required to change their passwords every 45 days, then procedures should be established to disable any User objects that have not been used for authentication for a period of 45 days.

The following is a list of recommendations for the configuration of authentication controls for user objects that are used for human users, machines, and automated processes:

- Intruder Detection and Lockout features should be enabled for every container object that will hold User objects. These features compensate for the lower quality secrets employed by human users (relatively short passwords) by decreasing the likelihood of success and increasing the likelihood of detection for password-guessing attacks. A reasonable starting point for the configuration of this feature is to allow only three invalid login attempts in a one-hour period with a two-hour lockout reset interval.

- All user accounts should be required to have passwords of a substantial length. Since human users are limited in the quality of the secrets they can remember, the minimum length of passwords for human users can be less than the length of passwords for machines. A minimum length of six to eight characters for passwords for human users is typically considered sufficient.

- Human users should be required to change their passwords on a regular basis. The actual number of days between required password changes should be between 30 and 90. A password change interval that is too short could encourage users to choose low-quality passwords or to write their passwords down. In addition, users should be required to use unique passwords every time they change their passwords. Since user accounts for machines should have longer passwords than user accounts for human users, password change requirements for these accounts can be less frequent or completely ignored.

- All user accounts should have the maximum number of concurrent connections limited to the actual number of connections they will actually use. Typically, this number is one, but occasionally it could be as high as three. Failure to restrict the maximum number of concurrent connections could encourage users to share user accounts since the users would not suffer an immediate loss of functionality as a result of this behavior.

- The maximum number of grace logins allowed should be limited so that users will change their passwords in a timely manner once they expire. The actual number of grace logins allowed should be limited to three.

- If users are allowed to work only during set times of the day or on certain days of the week, login time restrictions should be established to reflect these requirements.

- User accounts that are used for systems or automated processes should be assigned station restrictions whenever possible.

- Human Resources or Payroll departments should be required to provide security administrators with lists of terminated employees so that the accounts assigned to these employees can be disabled in a timely fashion.

- Expiration dates should be set for user accounts that are created for use by temporary employees or contractors. The reason for this is that organizations often do not have established procedures for dealing with the departure of temporary employees or contractors, so there is an increased possibility that security administrators might not be notified upon their departure.

Securing the Bindery Supervisor User Account

One NDS security consideration that is often overlooked is the security of the bindery Supervisor user account contained in the bindery partition of every NDS server. When bindery services are enabled on a server, logging in to the server as Supervisor in bindery mode provides supervisor-level access to the file system as well as to objects visible through bindery services. This access could be used to change the password of an NDS user object with rights extending beyond the bindery context, which would then allow access to a wider scope of directory or network resources. The password for a server's bindery Supervisor user can also be used to unlock the server console if it was locked using Monitor.

The bindery Supervisor user is created in the bindery partition when NDS is installed on a server. A password is usually assigned to the bindery

Supervisor user when it is created, although it is possible that under certain circumstances a password might not be assigned. With NetWare 4.0 and 4.01, which did not provide for the creation of a password for the Admin user that was created when the first NDS server was installed in a tree, the bindery Supervisor user was often created without a password. With current versions of NetWare, the initial password assigned to the bindery Supervisor user depends on the following conditions:

- If the server is new or does not contain an existing bindery database, the bindery Supervisor user will be assigned the password of the user that logs into the directory to install NDS on the server.

- If bindery information in a database residing on the server where NDS is being installed is migrated to NDS (as in a NetWare inplace upgrade using INSTALL.NLM), the bindery Supervisor user will be assigned the same password as the SUPERVISOR object that exists in the local bindery database.

- If bindery information is migrated to the server where NDS is being installed from a database residing on a different system (as in a NetWare across-the-wire migration), the bindery Supervisor user will be assigned the password of the user that logs into the directory to install NDS on the server.

The third case is identical to the first case since migration of bindery information from a different system can occur only when an established NDS database is present to receive the information. Even though the bindery Supervisor user is assigned the same password as the user installing NDS on the server, the bindery Supervisor user has no further association with this user. Any subsequent changes to the user's password will not be synchronized with the password for the bindery Supervisor user. The second case differs from the others since the NDS database is created concurrently with the migration of information from the bindery.

The bindery Supervisor users' passwords should be changed for servers even where bindery services are not enabled (such as for servers that don't hold any Master or Read/Write replicas). Unfortunately, there is no easy way to do this at present. In such cases, it would be necessary to enable bindery services temporarily on the server (placing a replica on the server if necessary) to allow the password to be changed.

The bindery Supervisor users on all servers should be maintained in the same manner used to maintain NDS user accounts that have powerful privileges. This includes requirements for selecting strong passwords and changing the passwords frequently. Since the bindery Supervisor user on any given server will rarely be used, reminders to change passwords generated by setting the password change interval will not likely be effective. A regular routine for changing the bindery Supervisor users' passwords on all servers should be documented as a security procedure and performed by the security administrators responsible for the servers containing bindery partitions.

Extra care should be taken to select strong passwords for bindery Supervisor users since invalid login attempts are not recorded in the audit log even when NDS auditing of login failures is enabled. Fortunately, the risk of intruders gaining access to a server using brute-force password guessing against the bindery Supervisor account can be decreased because the bindery Supervisor user is subject to intruder detection and lockout settings established for the first container of a server's bindery context.

Physical Security

Since the physical NDS directory database is divided into partitions with replicas of the partitions stored on servers scattered throughout the network, the physical security of servers holding partition replicas is critical. This is because an individual with access to the console of a server holding a partition replica could bypass NDS authentication controls and modify the contents of the partition. Such modifications could consist of creating User objects or adding ACLs to objects that exist within the partition. This ability could allow an intruder with physical access to a server console to create a User object and grant supervisory rights for the partition's root container to the new User object.

An additional risk associated with physical access to a server is that an intruder could obtain a copy of a replica stored on the server and subject the replica to offline password cracking. Since NDS passwords are stored in the replica (along with salt) in hashed form, password cracking would be computationally intensive and could require several hours or days to complete, even when using computers with the fastest processors. Due to the difficulty of this kind of offline password cracking attack and the ease with which NDS authentication controls can be bypassed with physical access to the server console, the offline password cracking scenario is much less likely to occur.

To reduce the risks associated with physical access to server consoles, all servers containing NDS partition replicas should be secured sufficiently to prevent all types of unauthorized access to their consoles. This should include protecting against both physical and remote access to the server's console.

To protect against physical access to servers' consoles, servers should be housed in locked rooms to which only authorized personnel are allowed access. Automated card key locks are usually the most effective way to secure such rooms since these systems typically include logging capabilities that allow tracking of who enters the secured room. In addition, when partition replicas are stored on NetWare servers, the NetWare console locking facilities should be employed to require entry of a valid password to gain access to the server's console.

To protect against remote access to a NetWare server's console, unique passwords should be used for every server running REMOTE.NLM. If the same password were used for multiple servers, gaining unauthorized access to one server's console would allow access to other servers' consoles. These passwords should be changed on a regular basis. Knowledge of the passwords should be severely restricted because there is no way to enforce individual accountability for remote access to the server console. The REMOTE ENCRYPT command should be used to translate the password to an encrypted form so that it is not possible to find out the remote console password by looking at server startup files, either directly or in documentation.

WARNING   Novell's INETCFG utility should not be used to initialize the remote console password because this utility stores the password in clear text form in the `SYS:ETC\NETINFO.CFG` file. That file is too often accessible by many non-administrative users of the system.

Authentication Controls

Due to the cryptographic strength of the standard NDS identification and authentication process, it is possible to place a high degree of faith in the integrity of user authentications as long as they adhere to the standard NDS authentication process. If users are allowed to use NDS for authentication with alternative authentication facilities, it is not always possible to place the same level of faith in user authentications that occur with these alternative authentication facilities. For example, the NetWare 3 authentication method that is supported to provide backward compatibility for bindery clients when bindery services are available is not as cryptographically strong as the standard NDS authentication method when the option to allow unencrypted passwords is used.

When a client uses the NetWare 3 unencrypted password authentication method, there is a greater possibility than with the standard NDS authentication method that an eavesdropper could use the communications that occur during the authentication process to gain unauthorized access to NDS. The extent to which this is possible with an alternative authentication method that is made available for NDS means that an organization should have less faith in these user authentications.

When a system administrator chooses to provide alternative authentication methods for authentication via NDS, the problems that can be caused could have a much greater impact than the slightly diminished faith that results from the subtle cryptographic differences between bindery and NDS authentication. Any form of alternative authentication that is allowed to be performed via NDS, and that does not provide the same level of cryptographic controls that are provided by the standard NDS authentication process, serves to devalue the strong encryption provided by NDS. The most severe damage is done by those alternative authentication methods that allow NDS passwords to be transmitted across the network in weakly encrypted or cleartext forms. When this occurs, it is relatively easy for an eavesdropper to obtain NDS passwords that can be used to gain unauthorized access to the directory or to systems that are protected by NDS authentication.

To take advantage of the strength of NDS authentication, alternative authentication methods that do not possess cryptographic controls comparable to those provided by standard NDS authentication should be used as little as possible. In those cases where weak authentication methods must be implemented in order to allow some measure of secure access to valuable services, attempts should be made to limit the use of these services so that the resulting exposure can be limited. In other cases, weak authentication methods might be used, even though it might be possible to use a stronger authentication method.

For example, the bindery services provided by NetWare provide a parameter that can be set to allow unencrypted passwords. This is provided for backward compatibility with old client software that did not support encrypted authentication. Today, this is mostly used for print servers with out-of-date firmware, but it is also possible that the capability could allow some normal clients to use unencrypted passwords. In many cases, it is possible to upgrade the firmware or software of clients using unencrypted passwords so that they can support encrypted authentication. Doing so would mean that support for unencrypted passwords could be disabled.

Directory Audit Configuration

The directory auditing capability provided by NetWare for NDS is an important but underutilized detective control feature that supplements the preventive controls that are provided through account restrictions. Enabling directory auditing for containers with User objects and selecting certain events for logging can enhance the overall security of the system by providing a means to evaluate the effectiveness of controls on an ongoing basis. It is also possible to select certain User objects for auditing so that the activities of sensitive user accounts can be logged.

In order for directory auditing to be implemented in a useful manner, the important security events should be selected for logging and the logs should be reviewed on a regular basis. Among the useful security events that should be logged are changes to objects or properties that might require authorization prior to being executed. Logging these events and reconciling the recorded events with authorized requests could allow for the evaluation of the effectiveness of request procedures.

Some of the more important NDS security events that should be selected for logging when directory auditing is enabled are described below:

- **Add Entry**   This event is triggered whenever an object is created.

- **Add Member to Group Property**   This event is triggered when a User object is added as a member of a group.

- **Change ACL**   This event is triggered whenever a trustee assignment for an object is added, modified, or deleted. This could be useful for detecting dangerous trustee assignments that might be established either intentionally or accidentally.

- **Change Security Equivalence**   This event is triggered when security equivalences are added or removed. This could be useful for detecting unauthorized changes to security equivalence.

- **Change Station Restriction**   This event is triggered when a station restriction is added, modified, or removed. This could be useful for detecting unauthorized modifications to station restrictions that might be necessary in order to restrict accounts with otherwise weak account restrictions.

- **Disable User Account**   This event is triggered when a User object is disabled. Logging this event could allow for a review of the timeliness with which user accounts are disabled when requested.

- **Enable User Account**   This event is triggered when a User object is enabled. This could be useful for detecting the unauthorized activation of disabled User objects that could be used for unauthorized access to the system.

- **Intruder Lockout Change**   This event is triggered when intervention of an administrator results in a change to the intruder lockout status for a User object.

- **Log In User**   This event is triggered when a User object is used for authentication to the directory. This could be used to detect user activity that might occur outside the normal pattern.

- **Log Out User**   This event is triggered when a User logs out. This could be used in combination with login records to determine the period of time when a user was authenticated to the system.

- **Modify Entry**   This event is triggered when a change is made to an object.

- **Remove Entry**   This event is triggered when an object is removed from the directory.

- **Remove Member from Group Property**   This event is triggered when a User object is deleted as a member of the group.

- **Rename Object**   This event is triggered when an object is renamed.

- **User Locked**   This event is triggered when a User object is locked due to excessive invalid login attempts. This could be useful for detecting attempts to gain unauthorized access to the system since a concerted effort could result in several accounts becoming locked out in a short period of time.

- **User Unlocked**   This event is triggered when a User object is unlocked after intruder detection and lockout has locked it.

Maintaining Separation of Duties

Separation of duties is a standard control principle asserting that individuals should not be responsible for performing conflicting duties. Separation of duties is usually established in an organization by assigning conflicting duties—such as purchasing and disbursing payments—to different employees so that the separation of these duties introduces a control to a process that could be abused easily if it were controlled by an individual. This concept could be extended to the implementation of NDS security by identifying activities that could be considered conflicting and then assigning responsibility for these conflicting activities to different people.

The most important activities that could be considered as conflicting are those involving the configuration and review of security controls. Different people should perform these duties, and security controls should be established when possible to enforce this separation of duties. For example, an individual who is responsible for configuring security controls should not be allowed to modify the audit configuration. That could destroy the integrity of the audit logs. Conversely, someone who is responsible for configuring and reviewing audit logs should not be allowed to configure security controls. That would create a conflict by requiring that the person review their own activities.

The following steps would provide for reasonable enforcement of this separation of duties via NDS access control mechanisms when Audit File objects are used to restrict access to audit logs.

- Explicit trustee assignments should be established for all Audit File objects, giving Supervisor object rights to the individual responsible for configuring and reviewing the audit logs.

- An IRF (Inherited Rights Filter) should be added to the Audit File objects to block the inheritance of all rights so that no objects would be allowed to inherit access rights to the audit logs.

- Only objects authorized to configure or review the audit logs should be allowed to be security equivalent to User objects for people with similar responsibilities.

Other instances of conflicting duties are typically found in information systems environments. For example, responsibilities for configuring security controls and performance of data entry tasks usually are considered to be conflicting. Another example involves responsibilities for programming, staging, testing, and placing programs into production. In this case, someone responsible for programming should not be allowed to certify test results and place programs into production. In addition, employees responsible for programming should not be allowed to have the direct update authority to data that is used by production programs.

All of the security controls that are required to enforce these separations of duties can be accomplished with procedures and a combination of preventive and detective controls. When access to objects in the directory needs to be restricted in order to enforce a separation of duties, the concepts of equivalence, inheritance, and filtering can be used to implement preventive controls. Auditing can be used to implement detective controls.

Delegating Authority

The Admin object that is created when NDS is first installed is granted Supervisor object rights to the [Root] object, which provides Supervisor rights to every object in the directory through inheritance. When organizations have large NDS trees, there are typically many different people responsible for performing various administrative activities. This could be handled by making these users equivalent to the Admin object so that all of them would possess Supervisor rights to all objects in the directory. Such a broad scope of authority, however, is neither desirable nor necessary in most cases.

The NDS access control model provides several means by which the scope of administrative authority for individual users can be limited through the delegation of authority. The Organizational Role object is a perfect means by which the various types of delegation can be established within the directory.

The principle of least rights asserts that individuals should have only the rights that are necessary for them to do their jobs. Any additional rights are unnecessary and could lead to problems at some point in time, as the result of either deliberate acts or accidents. Implementing this principle in an NDS environment requires a clear definition of functions and the use of NDS access control features to restrict possible activities to allow only the defined functions. In some cases, a user might need to perform restricted activities only occasionally, and this should be facilitated through temporary rights assignments rather than permanent rights assignments. This can be done by granting access to special administrative accounts (often called "fire-call IDs") that are provided for this purpose, or by temporarily making the user an occupant of an Organizational Role object that provides the necessary rights.

Although NDS provides sufficient granularity to allow for the delegation of almost any level of administrative authority, it is still desirable to provide certain privileged users with Supervisor rights to the entire directory, similar to those provided to the Admin object that is created when NDS is first installed. Such privileged accounts allow for the ongoing management of delegated administrative privileges and also allow these individuals to serve as backups in the event that individuals to whom administrative privileges have been delegated are unavailable.

No more than two or three privileged accounts should be granted Supervisor rights to the entire directory. These rights should be granted explicitly to the [Root] object instead of using equivalence to the Admin object, so that the privileges would continue to be in effect in the event that the Admin object was accidentally deleted.

Beyond the User objects that are granted Supervisory rights to the entire directory, all other administrative privileges should be granted through role-based delegation of authority. The following sections describe some of the common roles that can be established through delegation of authority.

Container Administrator

One of the most common ways that authority is delegated within NDS is through the creation of container administrators that have authority to manage objects within a given container. This can be accomplished by granting supervisory object rights for the container object to an Organizational Role object that can be occupied by the User objects for container administrators. Users that have supervisory object rights to a container also have the ability to create Inherited Rights Filters that could be used to block other objects from inheriting rights to objects within the container. This can be avoided by doing the following:

- Give a directory administrator explicit Supervisor rights to the Organizational Role object that is assigned Supervisor rights to the container object.

- To prevent modification of the ACL, place an Inherited Rights Filter that blocks the inheritance of Write and Supervisor rights on the User or Organizational Role object that is assigned Supervisor rights to the container object.

User Manager

The responsibility for creating User objects for new users is often delegated to users that are not required to perform other security functions within the directory. This can be facilitated by creating Organizational Role objects with Create, Rename, and Delete privileges to the portions of the directory tree that will be separately managed. User objects for those responsible for creating and deleting objects can then be added as occupants of these Organizational Role objects for the areas of the directory tree that they are responsible for.

Server Installer

Technicians that perform installation of servers often do not have any daily responsibility for security administration. Since installing servers into a particular container is not an activity that occurs on a regular basis, granting the privilege for this activity is best done using a temporary rights assignment. This can be accomplished using Organizational Role objects within each container that have Supervisor rights to the container. When an individual needs to install a server into a container, the individual's User object can be made an occupant of that container's Organizational Role, which was created for the purpose of installing servers into the container. Once the server is properly installed, the User object can be removed from the Organizational Role.

Server Manager

Separate people are occasionally given the responsibility for installing applications or assigning rights on servers without being required to perform other management activities within the directory. Creating Organizational Role objects with supervisory object rights to Server objects for servers that will be managed by such individuals can facilitate this function. These individuals can then be added as occupants to these Organizational Role objects.

One of the problems with this approach is that granting supervisory object rights to a Server object allows the user with such rights to access and change any data that is stored on the server's volumes. If particularly sensitive information is stored on the server, file system auditing can be used to track access to this sensitive information so that unauthorized access can be detected.

Partition Operator

Some organizations wish to restrict the ability of establishing partitions and placing replicas on servers to certain people. This requires that all other administrative roles be restricted from acquiring supervisory rights to container ACLs since such rights allow for the performance of partition operations. These other administrators should be granted Read and Compare rights to the Object Trustees (ACL) property of the container objects so that they are restricted from adding, modifying, or removing trustee assignments for the container objects. Since property assignments for individual properties are not inherited, occupants of the container administrator Organizational Role objects with Supervisor object rights to the container will inherit complete Supervisor object rights to all subordinate objects.

In order to allow certain other individuals to perform partition operations, an Organizational Role object should be created with Supervisory rights to the container objects that are similar to the Organizational Role objects for the container administrators. They should not have the restrictive property rights to the container's ACL.

Helpdesk Administrator

Many organizations have helpdesks that users can call for assistance with simple technical problems. Among the activities that organizations often want helpdesks to perform are reversing account lockout conditions and resetting passwords for users that forget their passwords.

To reverse a lockout condition in NDS, it is only necessary for a subject to have Write rights to the object's Account Locked property. This type of privilege can be difficult to administer since individual property trustee assignments cannot be inherited. This means it would be necessary to establish the required trustee assignments for each managed object.

For a subject to change another object's password it is necessary for a subject to have Write rights to the object's ACL property. Since Write rights to the ACL property allow the subject to add any trustee assignment to the object's ACL, this is usually thought to be too much authority for the staff of helpdesks.

This is one area where NDS itself is not capable of providing sufficient granularity to achieve a desired level of delegation. In order to provide helpdesk personnel with an efficient means to reverse lockout conditions and reset users' passwords, it is necessary to provide a proxy service that performs password resets on behalf of helpdesk personnel. One such proxy service is the Change Password Service that was developed by Novell Consulting Services.

Summary

This chapter has presented some basic information on security concepts and an overview of the security, audit, and control features of Novell Directory Services. Because the overview of NDS security, audit, and control features was presented in mechanical terms, it would be useful to review the security roles played by NDS within the framework of fundamental information security principles. The following list summarizes how the objectives of confidentiality, integrity, and availability can be achieved with NDS:

- Confidentiality is achievable through the proper implementation of NDS identification, authentication, and access control facilities to control access to objects in the directory or to services that use NDS authentication facilities.

- Integrity of the standard NDS authentication process is achieved through the use of cryptographic controls and mutual authentication. Integrity of sessions is achieved through continual authentication based on a session-specific token that the workstation possesses.

- Availability is integral to NDS due to the partitioned and replicated directory database that allows NDS services to remain available even when a single server becomes unavailable.

C H A P T E R

13

Printing and NDS

Most of the objects in an NDS database are logical representations of organizational concepts, such as container objects, or of human resources, such as users. Only a few object types, such as servers and volumes, are actually representative of physical network components. The objects that comprise NetWare's printing subsystem, however, are all associated with actual hardware and software elements that existed before the advent of NDS.

If you are upgrading your network to NDS from a previous version of NetWare, migrating your bindery print objects to NDS requires no changes to the actual printing architecture. The new NDS objects are simply representations of your existing printers, print queues, and print servers. This chapter examines the NDS objects that are associated with the printing hardware and software installed on your network, the relationships between the objects, and how to use tools like NetWare Administrator to manage your network printers.

Although many networks will, no doubt, continue to use the traditional NetWare print architecture, Novell encourages you to use its next generation network printer control technology, Novell Distributed Print Services (or NDPS). NDPS is designed to improve the communications between users and printers, and to simplify the printer setup process.

The NetWare Printing Architecture

The traditional NetWare printing architecture consists of three physical elements, each of which is represented by an NDS object type. The primary function of the NDS objects is to establish the relationships between the elements and control access to them. The three object types are as follows:

- **Printer** The printer object represents a physical printer itself that is connected either to a server, to a workstation, or directly to the network. The properties of the printer object specify the print queues that are to be serviced by the printer, and the type of network connection.

- **Print queue** The print queue is a directory on a NetWare volume where print jobs are temporarily stored while they wait for a print server to send them to a printer. The print queue lets multiple clients share a single printer by acting as a buffer that is always ready to receive print output from a workstation. The print queue object is associated with printers that are to receive the jobs from the queue and is configured to allow specific users to access and manage the contents of the queue.

- **Print server** The print server is a hardware or software product that controls the network printing process by transmitting print jobs from print queues to printers. A print server can be a software product (like NetWare's PSERVER.NLM) that controls many different printers, or a dedicated hardware device that is installed in a network printer. The print server object also maintains a list of the users that are granted access and management rights to the server.

Both printers and print servers (whether hardware or software) require an installation process that is wholly separate from their related objects in the NDS database. You must physically connect the printer to the network using an interface card, a server, or a workstation as a host. The print server is either a software product that is loaded and configured on a NetWare server, or a physical device that connects a printer to the network. Once you have installed the physical printer and print server, you create NDS objects that represent those physical entities.

Print queues are different from print servers and printers in that the process of creating the NDS object actually creates the directory that is the queue itself. To the network client, the print queue is the entry point to the printing subsystem. When you configure a client operating system to use a network printer, you select a queue object from an NDS display. The network administrator, by configuring the print objects, specifies the printer that is to service the queue and the print server that is to control the printing process.

The NetWare Printing Process

Network printing is intended to solve two perennial problems: how to let multiple users share printers and how to avoid conflicts and delays when multiple users try to access a single printer at the same time. NetWare solves these problems by using a directory on a shared volume as a temporary holding area for the print output generated by clients. An application on a client workstation generates a print job just as if a printer were attached to the system. Instead of sending the print job out the parallel port, however, it is intercepted by the NetWare client and transmitted to a print queue on a server.

A printer can only process one job at a time, and it only contains a limited amount of memory for storing data. If network workstations transmitted print jobs directly to shared printers, then users would be forced to wait for a job to finish printing before theirs could be processed. Since a print queue is actually just a directory, it can accept print jobs from many different users simultaneously, storing them as files on the NetWare volume.

Once the print job is queued, the printing process is completed, as far as the client is concerned. All of the subsequent actions are performed by other systems, and the client can continue working. In fact, a print queue can accept print jobs from clients even when the printer is switched off, out of paper, or out for repairs. The jobs can remain in the queue indefinitely, until a printer is available to service them. Network administrators can also manipulate the print jobs while they are queued, by changing the print order, placing them on hold, or deleting them altogether.

Print queues are associated with specific printers. A print server functions as the arbiter of the printing process, taking jobs from queues and sending them to the appropriate printers, one at a time, as shown in Figure 13.1. The print server receives rudimentary signals from the printer, so that it knows when to send the next job or when the printer cannot accept jobs because it is offline or out of paper.

The relationships of the three print elements are not necessarily one to one. A single print server can control the activities of many different printers. You can configure a single print queue to be serviced by multiple printers, or you can have one printer service multiple queues. This enables the network administrator to devise a printing strategy that suits the organization's working environment.

FIGURE 13.1

The NetWare print sub-system uses a print server to feed jobs from a print queue to an actual printer.

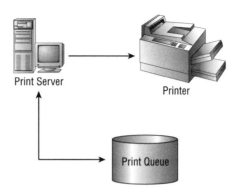

For example, you can have dozens or hundreds of users send their print jobs to a single queue, and configure the print server to send the jobs to any one of a dozen printers that are currently available (see Figure 13.2). Other sites use printers with internal print servers that control only that one printer, retrieving jobs from a dedicated queue.

FIGURE 13.2

A single print queue can be configured to send its jobs to a fleet of printers.

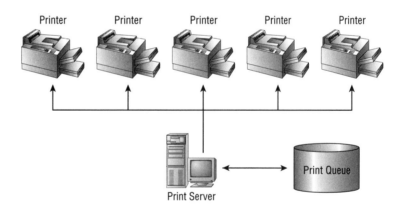

Print Communications

The proximity of NetWare print elements has no bearing on their associations. You can create a print queue on one server, install a print server on another, and connect a printer to a client workstation. As long as the elements are connected to the same network, the network printing process can be made to function. However, it is worthwhile to consider the effect that your printing strategy will have on network traffic.

Print jobs can consist of enormous amounts of data. A 100KB word processor document can generate several megabytes of print data. Depending on how you organize the print objects, this data may have to be transmitted over your network several times. For example, the scenario described in the previous paragraph would require that the print job data be transmitted three times: from the client workstation to the server containing the print queue, from the queue to the print server, and from the print server to the workstation hosting the printer.

If, on the other hand, you have hosted all three print elements on a single NetWare server, you reduce the required bandwidth to one single transmission: from the client workstation to the server. In most cases, the ideal solution falls somewhere between these two extremes. It is not worth running PSERVER.NLM on all of your NetWare servers just to save a few megabytes of network traffic but, on the other hand, you should avoid sending print traffic over relatively slow WAN links.

Creating NDS Print Objects

Because objects like printers and print servers must reference external resources, their configuration depends on the type of print server you are using or the means by which the printer is connected to the network. You can create print objects using either the NetWare Administrator or PCONSOLE.EXE utility. Both programs provide the same basic functionality, including a Print Services Quick Setup feature that can create all three of the objects needed to operate a network printer from a single dialog box.

The Quick Setup feature is a simple method for creating a basic network printing environment, as the program places all of the objects in the same context and creates the associations between them automatically. If, however, you intend to create more complex print architectures, it is a good idea to create the individual objects manually, so that you can learn about the properties that establish the relationships between the three object types and between each object and the physical element it represents.

The following sections examine the process of creating and configuring each of the three print objects in the NDS tree.

PCONSOLE.EXE is a DOS-based printer control program that can operate in both bindery and NDS modes. After launching the program, you use the F4 key to switch between the two modes. Be sure that the program is operating in NDS mode before you perform the procedures outlined in the following sections.

Creating Print Queue Objects

When you create a print queue object in the NDS tree with PCONSOLE or NetWare Administrator, you specify the name of the object and the NetWare volume where the queue should be created. NetWare Administrator then creates a subdirectory on that volume, beneath a directory call \QUEUES, in which print jobs are temporarily stored. You can create the queue on any volume, as long as it has sufficient disk space to hold the print files, which can be quite large. Remember that if a printer should malfunction or run out of paper, jobs will continue to build up in the queue until the situation is resolved.

If queues are created in bindery mode using PCONSOLE, the volume choice is not optional. SYS: is used for all bindery queues.

If you are running NetWare's print server software, it is also recommended that you create your print queues on the same server that is running PSERVER.NLM. This eliminates the network traffic generated by an additional transmission of print job data from the queue to the print server.

You can also create a print queue object in the NDS tree to represent an existing bindery queue, by selecting Reference a Bindery Queue when creating the object and specifying the name of the server and the queue, using the form SERVER\QUEUE.

Of the three print objects, the location of the print queue object in the NDS tree hierarchy is the most important. When network clients configure their applications or operating systems to use a network printer, they select a print queue object from the tree, not a printer. Creating the print queue in the same context as its users will therefore simplify the client configuration process.

You can also use alias objects to provide users in other contexts with easy access to the queue. The server that hosts the queue is also significant, since a licensed and authenticated connection is created to the queue's host server.

If disk space is an issue, do not create the queue on the SYS volume of a server containing NDS replicas. Running out of space can cause NDS to malfunction, preventing users from accessing network resources.

Once you have created the print queue object, you use NetWare Administrator or PCONSOLE to configure the object's properties, such as the lists of queue users and operators. You also use the screens of the Print Queue Details dialog box to manage print jobs after the queue is operational. The following sections examine the screens and the options they contain.

The Identification Dialog Box

Most of the properties found on the Identification dialog box (see Figure 13.3) are purely informational. You can use them to specify the location of the server hosting the print queue or to identify the type of print jobs for which it is intended, so that users can employ the values as keywords when searching the NDS database.

F I G U R E   13.3

You can use the operator flags in the Identification dialog box to control the general function of the print queue.

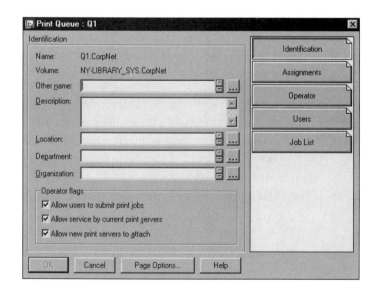

In the Operator Flags box, there are three checkboxes that control the functionality of the print queue.

WARNING The Operator Flags box is only available to those listed as operators. Having S rights to the object does not make these properties available.

You can use the checkboxes to temporarily prevent users from sending jobs to the queue or to prevent print servers from processing queued jobs. The Operator Flags checkboxes are as follows:

- **Allow Users to Submit Print Jobs** When this option is deactivated (by clearing the checkbox), users cannot submit jobs to the print queue. Client workstations return an error message to the user indicating that the queue is unavailable. This option is typically used to temporarily remove a print queue from service while the printer is being repaired or maintained.

- **Allow Service by Current Print Servers** When this option is deactivated, users are permitted to submit jobs to the queue in the normal manner, but the print server cannot send the jobs to printers. The print data remains queued until the checkbox is reactivated and the print server can resume processing the jobs. This option suspends the processing of print jobs without affecting the printing functionality of client workstations.

- **Allow New Print Servers to Attach** When this option is activated, a new print server can be configured to process the existing jobs in a queue, even when processing by the currently configured print server is suspended. This option enables administrators to use an alternative print server to process queued jobs, such as when the queue's regularly configured print server is offline.

The Assignments Dialog Box

In the Print Queue Details dialog box, the Assignments dialog box (see Figure 13.4) is purely informational. The screen displays the objects representing the print servers that are configured to manage the queue and the printers that are configured to service the queue, but you cannot create new assignments or modify existing ones. You can only do this by modifying the properties of the printer and print server objects themselves.

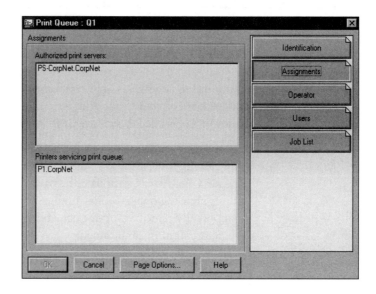

The Operators Dialog Box

In the Operators dialog box (see Figure 13.5), you select the user objects of the people who are to be allowed to manipulate the print jobs waiting in the queue. A print queue operator can pause specific print jobs, change their order in the queue, or delete them entirely. In many cases, users near the printers are delegated print queue operator privileges, so that they can tend to printing problems as they arise.

The Users Dialog Box

A print queue user is a person who has been granted the right to submit print jobs to the queue. In most cases, administrators add container or group objects to the user list, so as to allow all users access to the queue. However, you may have a printer to which you want to restrict access, such as a color or letterhead printer that uses more expensive consumables. In this case, you can create a queue that has only a selected few users, and only those users are granted access to the printer.

In the Operator dialog box, you designate specific users as print queue operators.

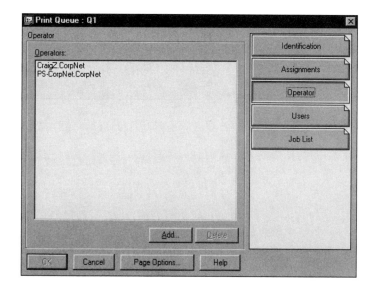

The Job List Dialog Box

The Job List dialog box (see Figure 13.6) displays the print jobs that are currently in the queue and enables a print queue operator to manipulate their print order and status. Print queue operators can manage any of the jobs in the queue, while queue users can only manage the jobs that they submitted themselves.

For each of the jobs in the list, NetWare Administrator displays the following information:

- **Seq** Specifies the order in which the queued jobs will be processed by the print server.

- **Job Name** Specifies the source of the print job, depending on how the job was submitted to the queue. Jobs redirected from a local printer port using the CAPTURE utility are named for the port (such as LPT1); jobs submitted with the NPRINT utility are named for the file being printed; jobs submitted by a Windows printer driver are named for the user's login name.

- **Description** Specifies the origin of the print job by showing the name of the application or document that was its source.

F I G U R E   13.6

From the Job List
dialog box, print
queue operators can
pause, delete, and
reorder print jobs.

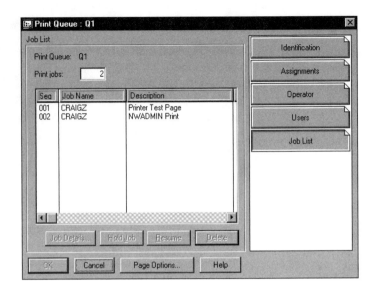

- **Form** Specifies the name of the predefined printer form used for the job, when there is one.

- **Status**   Specifies the current status of the print job. Possible values are Printing, Ready, Paused, or Held.

- **Job ID**   Specifies the unique ID number assigned to the print job by NetWare.

From the Job List screen, you can place a specific job on hold, resume it, or delete it entirely from the queue. When you select a job and click the Job Details button, you are presented with a dialog box, like the one shown in Figure 13.7, that enables you to exercise greater control over the processing of the job.

The Print Job Detail dialog box contains the following settings:

- **Print Job**   Specifies the job ID number, also displayed on the Job List screen.

- **File Size**   Specifies the size of the print job file (in bytes) as stored in the queue.

- **Client**   Identifies the user who submitted the job to the queue.

F I G U R E 13.7

The Print Job Detail dialog box enables queue operators to modify a job's print properties.

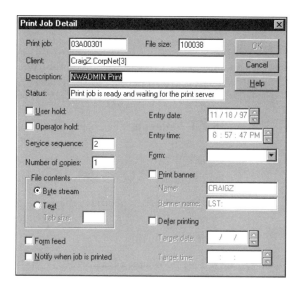

- **Description** Specifies the origin of the print job, as in the Job List screen.

- **Status** Specifies the current status of the print job. Possible values are as follows:

  - Print job is being serviced.

  - Print job has operator hold.

  - Print job is ready and waiting for the print server.

  - Print job is being added to the print queue.

  - Print job will be serviced at the target date and time.

- **User Hold** Specifies whether or not the job has been put on hold by its owner (the user who submitted it). The owner can modify the status of this checkbox at will.

- **Operator Hold** Specifies whether or not the job has been put on hold by a print queue operator. An authorized operator can modify the status of this checkbox at will.

- **Service Sequence**   Specifies the print job's place in the order of jobs to be serviced. A print queue operator can modify this value to change the print job's place in the sequence.

- **Number of Copies**   Specifies the number of copies of the print job file that are to be sent to the printer. Print queue operators and the job owner can modify this value.

- **File Contents**   Specifies whether the print job file consists of page description language (such as PCL or PostScript) or plain ASCII text, in which case a queue operator or the job's owner can specify the number of spaces to be used for tab stops.

- **Form Feed**   Specifies whether a form feed command is to be appended to the print job. Queue operators and the job's owner can modify this field.

- **Notify When Job Is Printed**   Indicates whether the job's owner should be notified when the printing is completed.

- **Entry Date**   Records the date that the print job was submitted to the queue.

- **Entry Time**   Records the time that the print job was submitted to the queue.

- **Form**   Specifies the predefined printer form that should be used when printing the job (if any). Queue operators and the job's owner can modify this field.

- **Print Banner**   Specifies whether a banner page should be printed with the job and if so, what information should appear on the page. Queue operators and the job's owner can modify these fields.

- **Defer Printing**   Enables a print queue operator or the job's owner to defer the printing of the job until a specified date and time.

Creating Printer Objects

The primary functions of the NDS printer object are to define the way in which the printer is connected to the network and to specify which queues the printer is to service. The print server that is assigned control of the printer needs this information to establish the communications link that will enable it to retrieve jobs from the chosen queue and send them to the printer. The printer object also supplies the name that other objects will use to uniquely identify that printer on the network.

Connecting a Printer

You can connect a printer to a NetWare network in one of three ways:

- By connecting it to a NetWare server using a parallel or serial port.

- By connecting it to a NetWare client workstation using a parallel or serial port.

- By connecting it directly to the Network medium (usually a cable) using a specially designed network interface card that is installed in or connected to the printer.

The last option in this list has become the most popular network printing solution. Many printers intended for network use are now equipped with a built-in network interface or an expansion bus that accommodates an interface card like those in the Hewlett-Packard line of JetDirect adapters. These network interface adapters include an onboard print server, so that no other software is required except for the print queue on a NetWare server.

Connecting the printer to a server or a workstation requires a port driver such as NetWare's NPRINTER, a software program that is supplied both as an NLM for server use, and an EXE for DOS and Windows 3.1 workstations. A GUI-based Windows 95/98 version of the program, called NPTWIN95.EXE, is also included. The NPRINTER program functions as the link between the printer hardware and the print server, enabling network communications between the two.

When you create a printer object in the NDS tree, you must specify the type of connection that the printer uses to access the network as well as the print server that will control it. However, unlike print queue and print server objects, the printer object is not intrinsically associated with the physical entity that it represents.

You can create printer objects for printers that don't actually exist; NDS won't stop you. It is only when the first job is actually sent to the printer that the existence of the hardware and its operational status are tested.

Printer Object Configuration

You create printer objects for Windows users using the NetWare Administrator utility, just as you would any other type of NDS object. The location of the printer object in the NDS tree is not particularly important from an operational standpoint, since it is only the network administrator, when configuring the print server object, who selects the printer object from the NDS tree.

Like any other NDS object, the NetWare Administrator program has a Details dialog box for the printer object, and the dialog box has multiple screens that you use to configure the object's properties. The following sections examine the screens that you use to configure the printer object.

Many NDS objects contain properties that are strictly informational and that have no function other than to hold reference data for the benefit of network administrators and users searching the NDS database. In the Printer Details dialog box, these properties are found on the Identification Features and See Also screens, which require no alterations during the printer configuration process.

The Assignments Dialog Box   In the Assignments dialog box (see Figure 13.8), the administrator specifies the names of the queues that the printer is to service. By clicking the Add button, you display an NDS tree from which you can select existing queue objects. A printer can receive jobs from multiple queues, and this dialog box enables you to set the priority for each selected queue.

When more than one queue contains a job that is ready to print, the queue with the lowest priority number is serviced first. You can also designate one print queue as the default, which will be serviced first when two queues with the same priority are contending for the use of the printer.

The Configuration Dialog Box   On the Configuration dialog box (see Figure 13.9), you specify how the printer is connected to the network, or how it is connected to the system through which it accesses the network.

F I G U R E 13.8

In the Assignments dialog box, you select the print queues that are to be serviced by this printer.

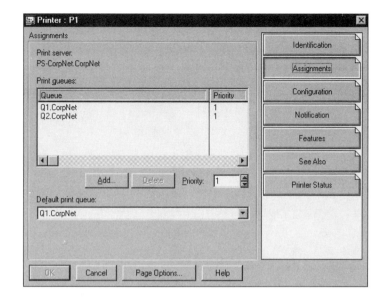

F I G U R E 13.9

In the Configuration dialog box, you specify the type of network connection used by the printer.

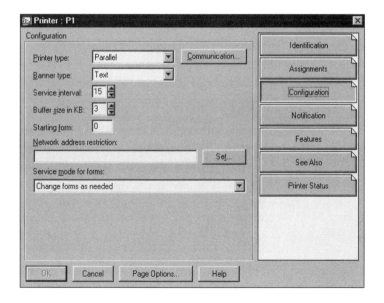

The properties in the Configuration dialog box are as follows:

- **Printer Type**   Specifies the type of network connection used by the printer. Possible values are as follows:

  - **Parallel**   The printer is connected to a server or workstation through a parallel port.

  - **Serial**   The printer is connected to a server or workstation through a serial port.

  - **Other/Unknown**   Usually indicates that the printer is directly connected to the network medium using an internal network interface adapter. This setting can also indicate that the printer is connected to an OS/2 workstation.

  - **XNP**   The printer uses the Extended Network Printing protocol.

  - **AppleTalk**   The printer is connected to a Macintosh workstation using the AppleTalk protocol to communicate with NetWare servers.

  - **UNIX**   The printer is connected to a UNIX workstation.

  - **AIO**   The printer is connected to the network through an asynchronous communications server.

- **Banner Type**   Specifies whether the printer should print NetWare banner pages using ASCII text or PostScript.

- **Service Interval**   Specifies how often the print server should check the print queues for jobs that are destined for this printer. The default value is every 5 seconds; possible values range from 1 to 255 seconds.

- **Buffer Size in KB**   Specifies the largest amount of data that can be sent to the printer at one time. The default value is 3KB; possible values range from 3 to 20KB.

- **Starting Form**   Specifies the number of the initial form to be used by the printer, if any. Possible values range from 0 to 255.

- **Network Address Restriction**   Specifies the network and node address of the only interface that can be used to connect the printer to the network. This can be a network adapter installed in the printer or the adapter installed in the computer to which the printer is attached.

- **Service Mode for Forms** Specifies how the print server will process jobs intended for this printer that require different forms. Possible values are as follows:

    - Change forms as needed.

    - Minimize form changes across print queues.

    - Minimize form changes within print queues.

    - Service only currently mounted form.

After selecting a printer type, click the Communications button to display a dialog box in which you configure the properties specific to the chosen printer type. For example, you select an LPT port for a parallel printer, or a COM port for a serial printer.

The Notification Dialog Box In the Notification dialog box, you select the users who are to receive pop-up messages when the printer needs attention, such as when it is offline or out of paper. Click the Add button to select user or container objects from an NDS tree display. You can also activate the Notify Print Job Owner checkbox to send messages to the user who submitted the job that was interrupted. This option also notifies the print job owner when the job has been serviced by the queue.

By default, the users in the list are notified one minute after the printer fault occurs and every five minutes thereafter. You can modify these intervals by changing the values in the Notification Settings box.

The Printer Status Dialog Box The Printer Status dialog box is only visible to users who have been designated as operators of the print server in control of the printer. From this screen, you can find out the general status of the printer, as well as information about the job currently being printed. Print queue operators can pause, start, or abort the current print job, as well as eject the current page by sending a form feed command to the printer.

Creating Print Server Objects

Whether you choose to use PSERVER.NLM, NetWare's software-only print server, or a third-party hardware or software product, you must create an NDS object to represent the print server and advertise its presence to the rest of the network. When creating the print server object, you must use the same name that you assigned to the print server itself. For example, when you load

PSERVER.NLM on a NetWare server, you specify the print server name on the command line, as follows:

```
LOAD PSERVER PS-CORPNET
```

The following sections examine the options in the Print Server Details dialog box that you use to configure the properties of the print server object.

The Identification Dialog Box

The Identification dialog box (see Figure 13.10) contains fields for purely informational properties (like the same dialog box in the printer and print queue sections), but it also displays important data. The Advertising Name field displays the name used in NetWare's SAP transmissions to announce the availability of the print server to the network. This name is the same as the one you used to create the print server object, unless the object name contains any characters other than the letters A to Z, the numbers 0 to 9, hyphens, underscores, and periods, which are not permitted in SAP names and are omitted.

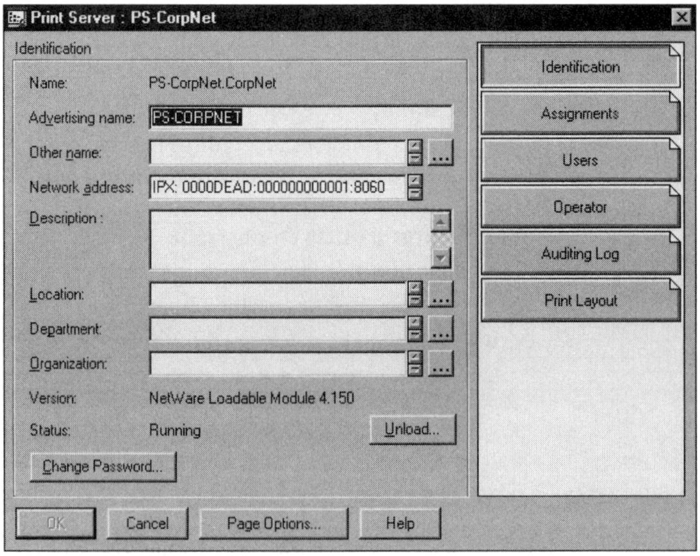

F I G U R E   13.10

The Identification dialog box displays information about the print server and enables you to control its function.

The dialog box also displays the network and node address of the network interface connecting the print server to the network, and the version of the printer server software, if applicable. The Status indicator shows the current condition of the print server, either Running, Going Down, or Down. If you are a print server operator or the ADMIN user, you can use the Change Password button to secure the print server, or the Unload button to remove the PSERVER software from memory.

The Assignments Dialog Box

In the Assignments dialog box (see Figure 13.11), you specify the names of the printers that the print server is to control. The printer objects, in turn, reference the queues that they are to service, completing the link between the three object types.

FIGURE 13.11

From the Assignments dialog box, you select the printers to which the print server will send jobs.

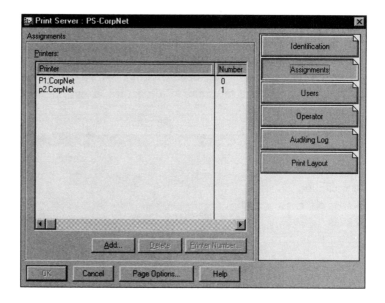

Print servers built into network interface cards like the JetDirect are designed to control only the printer in which they are installed. There are other external hardware devices available that function as print servers for several printers, which connect to the device using parallel ports. NetWare's PSERVER.NLM print server can control up to 256 printers located all over the network.

The Users Dialog Box

Print servers have users and operators, just like print queues. A print server user is able to view the operational status of a print server. In the Users dialog box, you select the objects from an NDS tree display that are to be granted user privileges. Network clients do not need print server user privileges in order to submit print jobs.

The Operators Dialog Box

A user with print server operator privileges can start and stop the print server, view its status, and specify the printers that the server is to manage. In the Operators dialog box, you select users from the NDS tree who are to be designated as operators of the print server.

The Auditing Log Dialog Box

PSERVER.NLM can maintain a log of all of the print jobs that it processes, including the time that the job was submitted, the size of the job, and the user who submitted it. From the Auditing Log dialog box (see Figure 13.12), you can enable the logging feature (which is disabled by default), view the current log, and set limits to restrict the growth of the log file.

FIGURE 13.12

NetWare's PSERVER.NLM can log its activities to a file called PSERVER.LOG.

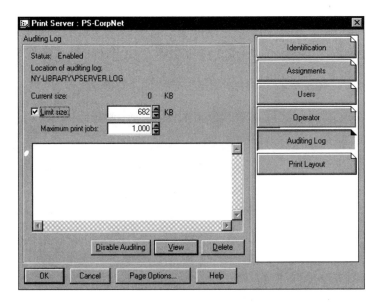

You can limit the size of the print server log by specifying a maximum size or a maximum number of entries. In either case, the logging process stops when the maximum is reached, and it does not continue until you manually delete or rename the current log file.

The Print Layout Dialog Box

The Print Layout dialog box (see Figure 13.13) contains a graphical display of the relationships that you have established between print server, print queue, and printer objects. You can highlight any object in the display and click the Status button to view its current operational state. An icon with an exclamation point on the left side of the display indicates that there is a problem with that element, and appears in cases such as if you create a printer object for a printer that does not exist, or if a print queue directory is accidentally deleted.

FIGURE 13.13

The Print Layout screen displays the associations between the three print-related NDS object types.

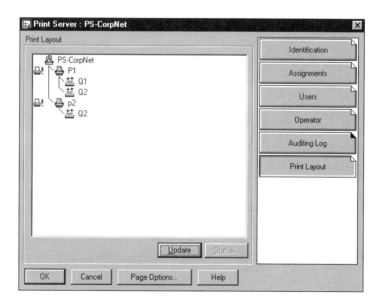

Using NetWare Distributed Print Services

NetWare Distributed Print Services is Novell's latest revision of the NetWare print architecture. NDPS is intended to simplify the process of network printing, both for administrators and clients. By consolidating the functions of the three traditional NetWare printing elements into a single object, NDPS provides a single point of administration from which you can access more detailed information about a printer's capabilities, configuration parameters, and current status.

Instead of managing the print server from the NetWare server console and the print queue from PCONSOLE or NetWare Administrator, with NDPS you perform all of the maintenance tasks for a given printer by manipulating a single NDS printer object. Users can check the capabilities and the status of a printer before they commit a job to it, enabling them to find a color printer when they need it or to avoid delays by sending their jobs to the printer with the shortest queue.

Novell has also taken great pains to ensure that NDPS is completely backwards compatible. The product includes new NetWare clients for Windows 3.1*x* and Windows 95/98 that include NDPS client capabilities, but any NDS client can print to an NDPS printer. Eventually, the full range of NDPS services will be supported by printers with embedded NDPS controllers, but you can use any legacy printer with NDPS. Migrating to the new service does not require that you sacrifice any of your existing functionality.

NDPS enhances NetWare's printing capabilities in the following areas:

- **Communication** NDPS can support any communication capabilities provided by a print output device. The introduction of more complex devices, such as printer/copiers and full-featured publishing systems, has created a need for more elaborate control communications traveling to and from the printer.

- **Notification** NDPS provides extensive user notification features that provide information about the actual condition of the printer, not a print server. Notifications can be sent using the traditional pop-up window, e-mail, or other options developed by third parties.

- **Scheduling** NDPS can schedule jobs to print at times when printer use is low, or when specific resources become available.

- **Installation**   Administrators can configure controlled access printers to be automatically installed on the workstations of selected users. NDPS also provides Windows 3.1 and Windows 95/98 users with Drag and Print capabilities. Simply selecting a printer from the NDS tree causes the correct driver to be downloaded from the server and installed on the client workstation. No other configuration is needed.

- **Customization**   NDPS uses an open architecture that facilitates the development of customized modules by third-party print device manufacturers that are designed to take full advantage of the hardware's capabilities.

NDPS Architecture

NDPS introduces an entirely new collection of print-related programs and NDS objects to the NetWare environment. The following sections examine the various elements of the NDPS architecture.

Printer Agents

NDPS eliminates the need for three different print objects in the NDS tree and the associations that you must establish between them. Instead, all of the three objects' functionality is combined into a single server module called a *printer agent*. The printer agent is the conduit for communications between an NDPS client and a printer, enabling you to take advantage of the increased capabilities provided by NDPS and today's printers.

For most of the printers in use today, the printer agent takes the form of an NLM running on a NetWare server (see Figure 13.14). As always, the printer can be physically connected to a server, to a workstation, or directly to the network. Future printers will be manufactured with a hardware-based NDPS printer agent incorporated into the device itself, eliminating the need for the software component.

The NDPS printer agent combines the functionality of the NDS printer, print queue, and print server objects.

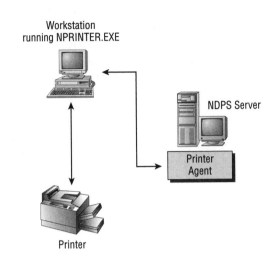

Workstation running NPRINTER.EXE

NDPS Server

Printer Agent

Printer

Novell is positioning NDPS as a enterprise network printing solution, a strategy that is already being aided by hardware manufacturers Hewlett-Packard and Xerox, who are incorporating NDPS printer agents in their output devices. Cooperation from other vendors is expected, largely because NDPS is not a wholly proprietary system, as many of Novell's earlier products were. NDPS is based on the ISO Document Printing Application (DPA) standard.

In the traditional queue-based NetWare printing arrangement, the print server is able to receive basic communications from a printer, such as messages indicating that it is offline or out of paper, but little else. However, many of the new printers have more elaborate bidirectional communications capabilities, and the printer agent can pass this information from the printer to the network administrator or client.

NDPS communications are not just involved in the ongoing operations of the printer. Printer agents can provide clients with information about a printer's capabilities and identify the driver that the workstation operating system needs to access the printer, which simplifies the client's printer installation process. NDPS also maintains a database of printer drivers on the network, so that the correct driver can be downloaded to a client system automatically. The agent performs these notification and installation tasks by accessing the new services provided by the NDPS Broker.

NDPS Manager

The NDPS Manager is the server module (called NDPSM.NLM) that ties all of the NDPS elements together, and that you use to create and configure software-based printer agents. Every server running printer agent modules must also have the manager module running to coordinate their efforts. The NDPS Manager exists in the NDS tree as an object that you must create before you can install printers to an NDPS server. During the object creation process, you associate the manager with a specific server and volume. You can then access the manager interface through the NetWare Administrator utility or from the NetWare server console.

The NDPS Manager program is needed only on servers running printer agents. If your network uses printers that have internal printer agents, then you do not have to run NDPSM.NLM.

Printer Types

You can configure any NDPS printer to function in one of two ways, depending on the needs of your users. These two configurations are as follows:

- **Public Access Printers**   A public access printer is one that is freely available to all network users without limitation or authentication. Public access printers do not exist as objects in the NDS tree and cannot take advantage of NDPS features like event notification and secured access. Instead, they are added to the NDPS registry that clients see as a separate list of available network resources.

- **Controlled Access Printers**   A controlled access printer does exist as an NDS object and takes full advantage of NDPS' advanced capabilities. Clients can browse the NDS tree to locate this type of printer, or can perform a search to find specific printer attributes and capabilities. The use of features like event notification, automatic print driver installation, and secured access is possible only with controlled access printers.

Although public access printers cannot take advantage of advanced NDPS features, they have the advantage of not requiring that a user be authenticated to the NDS tree in order to use them. Public access printers also do not cause their users to occupy a connection on their host server. Thus, the public access printers that you install on a server can be used by more clients than the server's user license allows.

Gateways

An NDPS gateway is a server-based software module that enables non-NDPS printers to communicate with NDPS (see Figure 13.15). Novell provides NPRINTER gateways that support legacy printers attached to NetWare servers and workstations. A gateway for Hewlett-Packard printers using JetDirect network adapters is also included with the NDPS product. HP's gateway is an NLM that can detect the JetDirect printers on the network by scanning for SAP transmissions. The module then creates printer agents for each of the printers it finds and disables any further use of SAP. The gateway also includes a snap-in module for NetWare Administrator that provides access to a printer-specific control utility from the Tools menu. NetWare 5's NDPS also includes a gateway for Xerox printers.

FIGURE 13.15

NDPS gateways provide the backwards compatibility to operate legacy printers with NDPS.

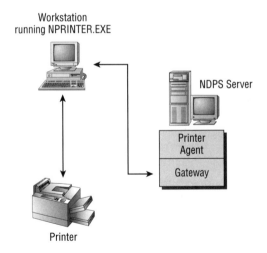

Manufacturers of printers and network interface adapters for printers are developing their own gateways for printers that are attached directly to the network medium. A printer that is made fully NDPS-capable by the inclusion of an internal printer agent does not require the use of a gateway.

Novell's NPRINTER gateway consists of two elements: a print device subsystem (PDS) and a port handler (PH).

Print Device Subsystem   A print device subsystem enables the printer agent to communicate with a printer using a specific page description language, such as PostScript or PCL. You configure the PDS along with the printer agent by selecting the drivers used to address the printer and then specifying a printer type.

Port Handler   The port handler works with the PDS to establish a communications link between the printer hardware itself and the printer agent, by specifying the type of connection that the printer uses to attach to the network. Port handlers support the standard printer interfaces, such as serial and parallel ports, as well as the direct network connections provided by network interface adapters.

NDPS Broker

The NDPS broker is a software module and NDS object that is automatically installed and loaded on the first server where you install NDPS, and on every additional server that is more than three hops away from another NDPS server. The broker provides three new network services that are used by NDPS, as follows:

- **Service Registry Service (SRS)**   The service registry is a centralized source of information about devices and services found on the network. Information about public access printers is added to the registry, so that users all over the network can locate them easily by accessing a single database.

- **Event Notification Service (ENS)**   The notification service is responsible for dispatching status information received from printer agents to the appropriate users or administrators using any one of several media. The service functions as an interface to (GroupWise and MHS) e-mail systems and log files, and can also be extended by third-party developers to access other media, such as pagers.

- ▪ **Resource Management Service (RMS)** The resource management service maintains a centralized storage area for drivers, fonts, and other software elements that may be accessed as needed by network clients and printers. The service enables administrators to perform software updates to a single location and make the new modules available to the entire network.

All three of these services are intended for use by other modules besides NDPS. Their functions are general enough to be useful to many other NetWare programs, developed either by Novell or third parties. For example, SRS is the intended replacement for the SAP transmissions that NetWare currently uses to advertise network resources. The network traffic generated by repeated SAP broadcasts for the same devices has long been a cause for complaint by network administrators. SRS provides the information that network systems need by advertising the existence of the registry using SAP and preempting all of the transmissions advertising individual objects like printers and servers.

Novell Printer Manager

The Novell Printer Manager is a graphical utility for Windows 3.1 or Windows 95/98 that NDPS clients use to install preconfigured network printers into the workstation environment, view a printer's status and its currently queued jobs, and create print job configurations. The manager lists all of the NDPS printers available to the client, both the controlled access printers found in the user's NDS context and the public access printers registered in the SRS. Simply selecting a printer from the list installs it on the client workstation. There is no need to manually capture printer ports or select a driver. With NDPS, the user does not even need to know the make and model number of the printer.

When the user double-clicks a printer icon, the program displays a Printer Information dialog box that describes the printer's characteristics and lists all of the jobs currently waiting to be printed. The status of each job is also listed, so that users can avoid sending their print jobs to printers that are too busy, offline, or out of paper.

Printer Manager also enables users to locate printers with the specific capabilities that they need. Using keywords for printer mechanisms, descriptions, and locations, the manager can display just the color inkjet printers on the third floor, for example, or just the duplex laser printers. Users can also create print job configurations and save them in Printer Manager for use at a later time. A configuration consists of a set of print job options, such as paper size and number of copies, that are commonly used to print a specific type of document.

Deploying NDPS

Whether you use NDPS or queue-based printing, the first step in network printer deployment is to decide where your printers will be most beneficial to your network's users. The criteria for making these decisions is the same for NDPS and traditional NetWare printing. NDPS supports all of the standard NetWare printer location and connection options. You can upgrade your existing printers to use NDPS without making any modifications to the hardware.

Adding NDPS to your network requires the installation of new software on the NetWare server, modifications to the NDS schema, the creation of NDS objects, and an enhanced Windows (95/98 or 3.1) client. A utility for migrating your existing print objects to NDPS is included with the product— or you can choose to configure your printers from scratch.

Migrating your queue-based printers to NDPS does not require that you immediately disassemble your existing print subsystem. You can leave the existing software and the NDS objects in place, and reactivate them later if problems inhibit the deployment of NDPS.

Installing NDPS

To install NDPS, you use NetWare's `INSTALL.NLM` utility from a server console prompt. The installation procedure copies the appropriate files to the server and modifies the NDS schema to allow the creation of three new object types: NDPS brokers, NDPS managers, and NDPS printers. Only the broker object is created by the installation program, assuming that another NetWare server running the broker NLM is not located less than three hops away.

The creation of NDPS manager and printer objects is not automatic, because they may not be needed. As more printer manufacturers support NDPS and include internal printer agents in their devices, these objects will be needed less and less. When you purchase an NDPS-equipped printer, installing it on the network is simply a matter of plugging it in. The device immediately becomes a public access printer, available to all network users. To convert it to a controlled access printer, you create a single NDPS printer object and configure it by selecting users and modifying notification parameters.

Creating the NDPS Manager Object

To use your existing printers with NDPS, you must first create an NDPS Manager object using NetWare Administrator, and select the server and volume that are to host the printers. The NDPS manager NLM runs on the selected server, as do the NLMs for the individual printer agents. The queued jobs for each printer are stored on the selected volume, in subdirectories of the \NDPS directory. You must create an NDPS manager object for every server that is to host printers, whether the printers are directly connected to the server or not.

Once you have created the NDPS manager object, you load the manager program on the selected server using the following syntax:

```
LOAD NDPSM objectname
```

where *objectname* is replaced by the name and context of the object you just created.

From NetWare Administrator's NDPS Manager Details dialog box, you can activate or deactivate the NDPRM.NLM module on the server running the manager, select the users who are to be granted manager rights to the object, and access the list of printer agents controlled by this manager.

As with many of the new NetWare technologies that extend the NDS schema, no support is provided for the DOS-based NETADMIN utility. You can only manipulate the properties of NDPS objects with the NetWare Administrator utility.

Creating Printer Agents

In order to be used with NDPS, every network printer that does not contain an internal printer agent requires a software printer agent on a NetWare server. There are four ways of creating new printer agents for your existing network printers:

- By accessing the Printer Agent List in the NDPS Manager Details dialog box, using NetWare Administrator

- By creating an NDPS printer object in the NDS tree and selecting the New Printer Agent option

- By using the NDPS Manager screen on the server console

- By migrating queue-based print objects to NDPS using the NDPS Migration tool

To create a printer agent, you must specify the NDPS manager that will host the agent, the volume where print jobs are to be spooled, the gateway that will be used to access the printer (along with gateway-specific information such as an LPT port or a network interface card), and the drivers to be used for Windows 3.1 and Windows 95/98 clients.

Creating NDPS Printer Objects

To install a controlled access printer on your network, you must create an NDPS printer object in the NDS tree. When you do this, you can select an existing printer agent, create a new agent, or choose a public access printer from those advertised by the SRS. From the NDPS Printer Details dialog box, you can specify the users or groups that are to be granted access to the printer, and create print job configurations. However, the most useful screen is the Printer Control dialog box (see Figure 13.16), from which you can view the printer's capabilities and its queued jobs, as well as manipulate the printer's control panel.

Migrating Queue-Based Printers

NDPS includes a migration tool that enables network administrators to convert large numbers of traditional NetWare print elements into their equivalent NDPS objects. When you run DPMIGW3X.EXE from the SYS:PUBLIC directory of a server on which you have installed NDPS (for NetWare 4.*x*) or the Migration Wizard (for NetWare 5), the program scans the NDS tree for the standard NetWare printer, print queue, and print server objects. You can then select the objects migrated from those that the program finds.

Like the NetWare migration programs DS Migrate and MIGRATE.EXE, the NDPS migration tool stores the information that it discovers in a temporary directory, where you can modify it before any changes are actually made to your production environment. Because the standard NDS objects do not include all of the information required for NDPS, you must examine the discovered objects and supply values for certain properties, such as the printer type and the location of the drivers for the printer.

FIGURE 13.16

Using the NDPS printer object's Printer Control dialog box, administrators can interactively monitor the printer's functions.

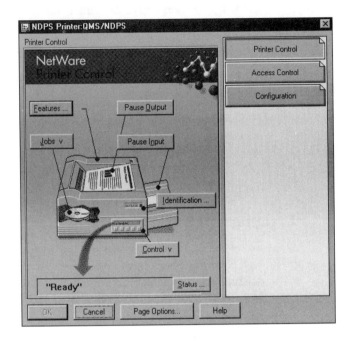

The migration process makes the following changes:

- Printer objects become NDPS printer objects.

- Print server objects become NDPS Manager objects with a printer agent for each managed printer.

- Operators and users of the print queue and print server objects receive the equivalent status in the NDPS printer and NDPS manager objects.

- Printer object notification information is registered with the event notification service.

The NDPS Migration program gives you the option of deleting the old print objects from the NDS database or leaving them intact. If you elect to leave the old objects in place, you must manually unload the PSERVER.NLM program from your servers so that the NDPS gateway can take control of the server port or the printer advertisement process.

NDPS Clients

Enhancements to the NetWare client, as well as the server, are required in order to use all of the features of NDPS. The latest versions of the NetWare Client32 for Windows 95/98/NT and DOS/Windows 3.1 include the NDPS files and the snap-in modules needed to extend the capabilities of NetWare Administrator. NDPS support is an optional feature that you must select during the installation of the client software.

The Novell Printer Manager program is installed to the SYS volume of the NetWare server during the NDPS installation process. The Windows 3.1 version, called `NWPMW16.EXE`, is placed in the `SYS:PUBLIC` directory and the Windows 95/98 version, called `NWPMW95.EXE`, is placed in `SYS:PUBLIC\WIN95`.

Summary

This chapter has explored the NDS relationships of traditional queue-based NetWare printing, as well as the newer NetWare Distributed Print Services (NDPS) technology. Since this book is about NDS, rather than about NetWare, some specifics of network printing were not examined if they had no NDS relationship. You should consult your NetWare manuals or one of the excellent Sybex Network Press NetWare books for the full details of network printing.

CHAPTER

14

NDS Clients

Networks come in two basic flavors: *peer-to-peer* and *client-server*. Peer-to-peer networking means that all of the computers on the network are considered equals and that generally each computer has resources that it shares with some or all of the other computers on the network. In client-server networking, the shared resources are controlled by computers called *servers:* file servers, database servers, print servers, Web servers, etc. In order to access the resources of these servers, though, it's necessary to run *client* software (thus, client-server networking).

Over the years, Novell has had four major iterations of client software, with each new one providing more services, flexibility, and ease of use. The first two predated NetWare 4 and NDS, and so, as you might imagine, they provide no NDS services. We'll briefly look at these two (surprisingly, still in use at some sites) which we'll call the *monolithic shell* and the *ODI shell* (we'll explain these terms in the next section). Then we'll spend most of the chapter looking at the *VLM requester* and the newest client software (introduced with NetWare 4.11) called *Client32*. Finally, we'll touch on client software for NetWare written by Microsoft and released with Windows 95/98 and Windows NT, as well as NDS clients for the Macintosh operating system.

The Shell Game

There were no provisions for networking in DOS up through a revision of version 3. (The revision introducing networking "hooks" was variously 3.1, 3.22, or 3.3 depending on the vendor releasing DOS: Microsoft's

MS-DOS, IBM's PC-DOS, Compaq's COMPAQ-DOS, or any of the other hardware manufacturers who embellished Microsoft's DOS before releasing it with their computers.) Network providers, including Microsoft, shipped client software which intercepted calls to the operating system, acting on the calls for networking while passing through the purely DOS calls. These programs were generally known as *shells*.

Technically, when the NetWare shell is loaded on a workstation, the shell intercepts activities on certain interrupts that applications use to talk to DOS services. These include Interrupts 21h, 24h, and 17h. To read a data file, for example, an application makes an Int 21h call to DOS to open a file with the indicated name. The NetWare shell intercepts the call and determines if the requested file is on a local drive or on a network drive.

If the request is for a local file, the shell passes the call to DOS and allows DOS to complete the request. If the file is on a network drive, the request goes through the shell's connection table, which defines information about the server and its location on the network. The shell then converts the request from a DOS request to an NCP request, and the network location information is used to build an IPX packet. IPX takes this packet and sends the request to the server. When the server sends a reply, the shell hands the data back to the application.

The Monolithic Shell

In order for computers to be clients of a NetWare network, Novell shipped what was called the NetWare shell with each version of the network operating system. When it was run, this program would remain in memory (called Terminate and Stay Resident, or TSR), intercepting calls to the operating system. Calls intended for the network would be rerouted to the server, while local calls would be passed through to DOS (see Figure 14.1). The shell program used to connect to the server was dependent on three variables: the version of NetWare, the version of DOS, and the network card installed in the computer. This was referred to in retrospect as the *monolithic shell* because everything—networking library, network card driver, network protocol—was included in a single executable program. There were few, if any, options for the user.

FIGURE 14.1

Architecture of the
monolithic shell

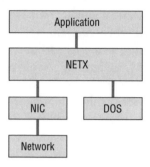

In the early days, when there was only a handful of different network cards, Novell shipped all of the available shells with the operating system. Up through the mid 1980s, this usually meant about 10 to 12 shells (1 version of NetWare × 2 versions of DOS × 5–6 different network cards) were available.

As networking became more popular, more manufacturers started shipping network cards. Faced with the possibility of having to ship dozens and dozens of different shells, Novell came up with a better solution. Rather than ship the shells as a compiled program, Novell shipped a precompiled version of the software for each version of DOS, along with a program to generate the shell. Each network card also had a precompiled module (some written by Novell, others provided by the card manufacturer). To create the client module, the network installer would run Novell's linking program (called GENSH, SHGEN, and WSGEN in different versions of NetWare) to tie together the correct DOS version of the shell with the correct network card driver. This created the monolithic shell: a single executable program, run at a client workstation that connected it to the network. Each new version of DOS and each new version of a network card driver required that a new shell be linked. This was tedious, at best, so Novell looked for a better way.

The ODI Shell

Working closely with Apple Computer Corp., Novell produced the Open Datalink Interface (ODI) specification. This broke the network driver out of the shell into three component parts: the actual card driver, called the Media-link Interface Driver (MLID); the Link Support Layer (LSL); and the protocol stack, a piece of software that understands the protocol (IPX/SPX, NetBEUI, TCP/IP, etc.) being used. The MLID consists of two parts, but they're linked together by the network card vendor before shipping. These parts are the Media Support Module (MSM) and the Hardware Support Module (HSM).

Novell provided the MSM that understood calls from the LSL and exposed a public application programming interface (API) which the HSM was written to. The HSM then translated the calls from the LSL (as handed off by the MSM) into calls to the network card hardware, and vice versa. Figure 14.2 shows the basic architecture of the ODI shell client.

F I G U R E 14.2

The basic architecture of the ODI shell

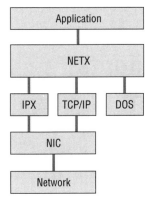

Part of the specification called on the MLID to read parameters from a plaintext configuration file (originally named SHELL.CFG, later renamed NET.CFG) containing such information as the network card settings (Interrupt request line, etc.). No longer was it necessary to relink drivers whenever an update was received or if parameters had to be changed.

At about the same time, Novell—responding to the pleas of network administrators everywhere—created a DOS-version-independent shell: NETX. It would work with any version of DOS, up to and including the current version at the time NETX was shipped. While it still required upgrading whenever a new version of DOS was introduced, it was a big improvement over the earlier days of strictly DOS-version-dependent shells.

Since almost every silver cloud has a gray lining, there was a downside. In place of the (relatively) small monolithic shell program, the network client now had to load NETX, one or two protocol stacks (IPX and possibly TCP/IP), the LSL, and the MLID. Because these all loaded in the low DOS memory space (that is, below the 640KB boundary) there was little room left for programs to run. And programs were beginning to use more RAM than ever.

Novell made an abortive attempt to create shells which used extended or enhanced memory (the RAM above 640KB). Called XMSNETX and EMSNETX, they were best known—when not actually crashing workstations—for slowing down network access.

There had to be a better way.

Post Shell Clients

The shell—NETX—was causing most of the problems people were seeing with Novell's client software; the ODI stack was working extraordinarily well. It was fast, efficient, and reliable. So the idea arose that perhaps the shell could be broken up into components also.

The Requester

But, asked some nameless Novell engineer, why use a shell at all? DOS now included hooks for what was called a *network requester*. By incorporating this technology, Novell could shrink the size of the client because it reverses the logic of passing programming commands. Instead of the shell having to decide which calls are for the network and which for DOS, DOS would decide and hand off network calls to the requester. All of the conditional code could be removed from the NetWare client (see Figure 14.3).

So a brand new client program was introduced, called *Virtual Loadable Modules* (VLM).

F I G U R E 14.3

DOS Requester (VLM)
architecture

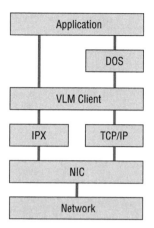

VLM Structure

VLMs were modularized: Each performed a specific function which, when taken together, did the work of the older NetWare shell. The ODI stack (MLID, LSL, Protocol) wasn't changed, but the client sitting on top of it now became a collection of modules, a number of which were optional. This meant, for example, that the printing VLM didn't need to be loaded unless you were actually going to use a printer. And the VLM engine looked for places in upper RAM (above 640KB) to put these modules as they were being loaded.

With the introduction of NDS, it was a simple enough task to just add an NDS VLM and keep on working; so the first version of NetWare to use NDS (NetWare 4.0) was also the first version to ship with the VLM requester as its client software.

The VLM client, though, also worked with NetWare 3.*x*'s bindery-based servers. This was a tremendous advantage when upgrading a network from version 3 to version 4. Without a client that spoke to both NDS and the bindery, it would be necessary to:

- Upgrade the server to NetWare 4

- Install all users into a (single) bindery context

- Upgrade client software

- Move users to the final position on the NDS tree

Instead, with the VLM client, you could first upgrade the client software, and then upgrade the server, putting users into their final position in the tree in one step.

VLM Problems

Mating Novell's networking requirements with Microsoft's DOS network requester API never produced a perfect fit. More and more code had to be added to the VLM client modules in compensation. Eventually, the VLM client grew to the point that it was using approximately 100KB of conventional memory and was slower than the NETX shell client. Third-party utilities written to the application programming interface (API) for NETX, which theoretically should have worked with VLM, didn't.

Microsoft's Windows 3.1 and Windows for Workgroups 3.11 were becoming common on users' desktops at about this time, with Windows 95 and Windows NT on the horizon. Users wanted a GUI (graphical user interface) version of LOGIN.EXE. Network throughput was also becoming an issue for administrators, and there was little more that could be done to make the requester or the client ODI stack more efficient.

It was time for new technology for both the network client and the network driver stack.

Client32: Today's Network Client

Novell's current client, initially referred to as Client32 (because it was a 32-bit application as opposed to the 16-bit shells and VLM) and now called simply "The Novell Client" (with different versions for DOS/Windows 3.1*x*, Windows 95/98 and Windows NT), takes advantage of the latest computer and operating system technology. It leverages the time and effort invested in server network drivers while combining the best aspects of a network requester with a network shell. It provides all of the functionality of NETX and VLM while adding additional features, dynamic memory management, and improved performance. Table 14.1 shows a comparison of features between Client32 and the VLM client.

	Feature	Client 32	VLMs
T A B L E 14.1 A Comparison of Features: Client32 versus VLM	Conventional memory required	4KB	100KB (est.)
	Point of login	DOS/ Windows 3.x/ Windows 95	DOS
	Provides automatic client update from the server	Yes	Yes
	Client side caching	Yes	35KB max
	Advanced NCP support	Yes	No
	ODI driver support	32-bit and 16-bit	16-bit
	32-bit NetWare Client API libraries	Yes	No
	16-bit NetWare Client API libraries	Yes	Yes
	NetWare Windows diagnostic tool (NWD2.EXE)	Yes	No
	Unattended install: Automatic Client Update (ACU)	Yes	Yes
	Windows install program (SETUP.EXE)	Yes	No
	DOS install program (INSTALL.EXE)	Yes	Yes
	Installs advanced client features	Yes	No
	GUI	Yes	No
	Login to multiple trees	Yes	No
	Searches and specifies a NetWare server	Yes	No
	Searches and specifies a NDS tree	Yes	No

TABLE 14.1 (cont.)	Feature	Client 32	VLMs
A Comparison of Features: Client32 versus VLM	Specifies context	Yes	Yes
	Specifies login script at login	Yes	Yes
	Drop-down list of the last used servers' trees and contexts	Yes	No
	Specifies login script variables at login	Yes	Yes
	Clears other connections at login option	Yes	Yes
	Login via NDS or bindery	Yes	Yes
	Saves settings on exit	Yes	No
	GUI for mapping of search drives	Yes	No
	GUI for updating environment variables	Yes	No
	NWUser	Yes	Yes
	Maps search drives via NWUser	Yes	No
	Positions search drive in path	Yes	No
	Limits options available to users in NWUser	Yes	No
	Leverages NLM technology at the client	Yes	No
	Supports NAL application management	Yes	Yes
	Allows selection of default capture parameters	Yes	No
	Multitree support	Yes	No
	Offers restore capture status	Yes	Yes
	Allows reconnection to servers	Yes	Yes

TABLE 14.1 *(cont.)*	Feature	Client 32	VLMs
A Comparison of Features: Client32 versus VLM	Allows reconnection to NDS tree	Yes	Yes
	Allows reconnection to drive mappings	Yes	Yes
	Restores open files	Yes	No
	Restores file locks	Yes	No
	Customizable configuration	Yes	Yes
	Online documentation/configuration help	Yes	No
	Dynamic updates	Yes	No
	Login to multiple trees	Yes	No
	Supports extended NDS schema: view additional objects	Yes	Yes
	Supports application object extensions via NetWare Application Launcher (NAL)	Yes	Yes
	Named Pipes	Yes	Yes
	NetBIOS	Yes	Yes
	Server Message Blocks (SMB)	Yes	Limited
	NetWare/IP	Yes (32-bit)	Yes
	NetBEUI	Yes	Yes
	IPX/SPX	Yes (32-bit)	Yes
	TCP/IP	Yes (32-bit)	Yes
	Large Internet Packets (LIP)	Yes	Yes
	Packet Burst	Yes	Yes

16-bit versus 32-bit Clients

Before examining Client32 in more detail we'll need to review a bit of background.

We hear the terms 16-bit and 32-bit tossed around regarding applications, operating systems, and networking clients, but they actually refer to the central processing unit (CPU) of the computer.

The original IBM PC and PCXT were based on the Intel 8088 and 8086 CPUs. These chips could address memory and process data in 8-bit (1 byte) chunks. Intel's 80286 chip was improved to allow addressing of 16-bit (double-byte or *word*) chunks but soon gave way to the 80386 (and later the 80486, Pentium, and Pentium II) CPUs, which could address 32 bits at a time.

Desktop operating systems lagged behind technologically, though, in moving to 32-bit operation. Windows 3.1, for example, is only a 16-bit system. In contrast, Novell had been relatively quick to move to 32-bit operation for the server beginning with NetWare 3. This early effort turned out to be significant to the development of Client32.

The advent of Windows 95 and Windows NT (following on the joint development effort between Microsoft and IBM, which led to OS/2) brought 32-bit operating systems (and 32-bit application support) to the desktop.

The Development of Client32

Several fundamental changes from earlier clients were made in the design of the Client32 requester. The new requester comprises two fundamental parts: the NetWare I/O Subsystem (NIOS) and client NetWare Loadable Modules (NLMs).

NIOS insulates the client modules from the host operating system by providing an OS abstraction layer that core modules can use to access system services. Instead of making OS calls to access system services, Client32 core modules make NIOS calls.

In addition, NIOS provides services to manage client NLMs, using dynamic, self-configurable parameters where possible. Figure 14.4 shows the basic architecture of Client32. (Compare this to Figures 14.1, 14.2, and 14.3.)

Novell also decided to leverage the large amount of work that had been done to optimize 32-bit server ODI network card drivers. When a new driver specification was promulgated for NetWare 4.11, it required drivers to be written in the C language (rather than the assembly language that had typically been used earlier). This meant that the same driver could now be used on both the server and the client workstation, and enabled through the newly developed NetWare Input/Output System (NIOS).

FIGURE 14.4

Client32's basic architecture

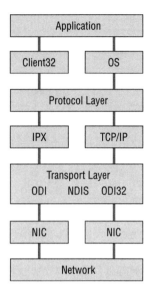

NIOS

NIOS is the first Client32 component that is loaded when a client wishes to attach to the network. It is essentially a DOS-extender program that creates a protected-mode, flat-memory environment for loading the other Client32 modules and drivers. You can think of NIOS as the client equivalent of Net-Ware's SERVER.EXE program, which runs first on a NetWare server to set up the protected-mode environment for the NetWare operating system. Where SERVER.EXE is a module launcher and memory manager rolled into one, NIOS is a module launcher that communicates with an extended memory manager (such as HIMEM.SYS) that is already loaded on the workstation.

After you load NIOS.EXE, you will not be able to unload it unless you reboot the workstation. However, once NIOS is loaded, it makes the Net-Ware client environment flexible and dynamic. You can load and unload the other Client32 modules and drivers at any time. Through the NWSETUP.EXE utility, you can dynamically allocate and deallocate memory for many of the NET.CFG settings.

By using operating system-specific application program interfaces (APIs), NIOS creates an extended-memory environment that allows 32-bit NLMs and LAN drivers that are running in protected mode to execute real-mode operations when necessary. In addition, NIOS manages real-mode to protected-mode context switches and provides hooks to real-mode interrupts. NIOS also provides a Windows transition architecture that allows environment-dependent modules to correctly handle transitions from DOS to Windows and from Windows to DOS.

NIOS is the only module that loads as an executable (EXE) file. All of the other modules are implemented as client NLMs and are loaded with the LOAD command from the STARTNET.BAT file.

NIOS and Memory Allocation

When loaded, NIOS communicates with HIMEM.SYS (or equivalent XMS extended memory manager) to find out how much extended memory is available. Upon initialization, NIOS takes about 25 percent of the available extended memory for its own file caching routines and other internal tasks.

Using a flat memory model, NIOS communicates with the extended memory manager to allocate memory for each of the remaining Client32 modules as they load. Over 99 percent of the NetWare Client32 software loads in extended memory. Client32 uses only about 4KB of memory for a *shim* in either upper memory blocks (UMBs, the RAM between 640KB and 1MB) or conventional memory. Usually NIOS can find 4KB available in UMBs and loads the *shim* (a bit of code that redirects calls to the actual location of the software) there. If NIOS cannot find 4KB of UMBs available, it will place the shim in conventional memory.

NIOS manages memory allocation for the communications protocols, LAN drivers, and other client-based NLMs that are loaded after it. These modules can use another 800KB to 1.3MB of extended memory, depending on the number of NLMs and types of LAN drivers you have loaded and how many NET.CFG parameters are set differently from their defaults. NIOS allocates this memory starting from the top of available extended memory and working downward.

Having only a 4KB real-mode footprint for the network connectivity software frees up conventional memory for DOS-based applications. This is especially beneficial for workstations that load multiple frame types and protocols.

NIOS Protocols and Drivers

The NetWare Client32's Link Support Layer (LSL) and protocol stack (IPX and TCP/IP) components are similar to their NetWare DOS Requester (VLM) counterparts. However, the NetWare Client32 components have been rewritten as client NLMs rather than as DOS executables. This way, the NetWare Client32 components can take advantage of the flat memory model that NIOS provides.

The NetWare Client32 software supports 32-bit LAN drivers as well as the older 16-bit ODI LAN drivers. Additionally, you can use drivers developed to Microsoft's NDIS specification (similar to ODI). You can thus choose from five basic sets of available LAN drivers:

- 32-bit ODI LAN drivers included with NetWare Client32

- Many of the 32-bit ODI Server LAN drivers included with NetWare 4.1 and above (generally, those written to version 3.30 or higher of the ODI specification)

- 16-bit ODI LAN drivers from previous NetWare client software

- 16- and 32-bit NDIS drivers

The 32-bit C-based versions of the LAN drivers usually have a filename that begins with C. For example, CNE2000.LAN is the C-based version of the NE2000.LAN server driver. Because these are NLM files, they are loaded using the LOAD command. Configuration settings such as frame type, interrupt, I/O port, and retries are specified in the LOAD command, just as they are with server drivers.

The Client32 Requester

The NetWare Client32 Requester (CLIENT32.NLM) takes the place of the NETX shell or the NetWare DOS Requester (VLMs) and has some of the characteristics of each—it's a hybrid of shell and requester. The Client32 Requester provides the internal tables and services necessary to track network resources, file caching, and automatic reconnection levels.

As with the DOS Requester, the NetWare Client32 Requester is a set of subcomponents, or modules. However, the modules are all contained within the CLIENT32.NLM file instead of being in separate files. Table 14.2 lists the modules contained in CLIENT32.NLM.

TABLE 14.2	Module	Name	Description
Client Modules Contained in CLIENT32.NLM	CONNMAN	Connection Manager	Used by Client32 to keep track of the connection tables and to store other connection information.
	TASKMAN	Task Manager	Keeps track of each task in the system, regardless of whether they are WINDOS, WIN16, or WIN32 applications or activities.
	FILEDIR	File and Directory	Handles all file system functions.
	PRINT	Printing	Sets up network printing capabilities for Client32.
	SESSMUX	Session Multiplexor	Supports NCP (NetWare Core Protocol) sessions attaching and accessing NetWare servers. Includes support for Microsoft's SMB (Server Message Block) sessions.
	NCP	NetWare Core Protocol	A child module that ties to the Session Multiplexor.
	NSMUX	Name Services Multiplexor	Coordinates activities between the child modules, or processes, that you load.
	NDS	Novell Directory Services	A child module to the Name Service Multiplexor module. Provides the name resolution and authentication processes for Directory Services connectivity.
	BINDERY	Bindery Services	Also a child module to the Name Service Multiplexor. It provides the name resolution and authentication processes for Bindery connectivity.
	MOCKNW	Mock NetWare	Catches raw NCPs sent from applications and redirects them to Client32 functions in order to take advantage of Client32's caching and automatic reconnection settings.

TABLE 14.2 (cont.)	**Module**	**Name**	**Description**
Client Modules Contained in CLIENT32.NLM	POLYPROC	Polyprocedure	Contains a set of generic miscellaneous routines that don't specifically fit into any of the other CLIENT32.NLM modules.
	NETX	DOS Interrupt 21h	Used to redirect all Interrupt 21h (NETX) function calls to redirector Client32 functions.
	VLMMAP	VLM Mapper	Used to redirect all DOS Requester (VLM) function calls to Client32 functions. The VLMMAP module is used to support applications and utilities that are written to NETX and DOS Requester APIs. The NetWare Client32 Requester is fully backward-compatible with the NETX shell and the NetWare DOS Requester, so NetWare-aware applications taking advantage of the earlier client APIs should run with no modification under the NetWare Client32. This compatibility is accomplished through the NETX and VLMMAP modules that are a part of CLIENT32.NLM.

Client32 and NDS

Client32 allows greater access to the power of NDS than ever before, offering several significant new features.

Multiple Tree Support A user may now authenticate to more than one NDS tree at a time. This capability is supported in the Provider, in GUI Login, and in NWCALLS.

Login and Authentication Done at the Requester All code for login and authentication has been moved to NDS. This is significant mainly for DOS applications, which will realize a savings in conventional memory when the large libraries are no longer statically linked into the login executable.

NDS Name Resolution Done at the Client   Name resolution will be done at the client when it is advantageous to do so. This will take some of the burden off the server, as well as allow the best NDS partition to be used when an object name is resolved to multiple addresses.

Simplified Connection Licensing   Licensing must be handled differently on NDS networks than on bindery networks. When the user authenticates to a NetWare 2 or 3 server in a bindery network, that user is automatically authenticated to file and print services as well. In NDS (NetWare 4 servers), the user can authenticate to Directory Services, but not necessarily to file and print services. Because Directory Services is a free service, no license is used until an actual license NCP is sent by an application.

In addition to separating licensing from authentication, the Client32 Requester is smarter about recognizing services that need to be licensed. It will license a connection automatically if certain NCPs are used, even if the issuing application does not request a license. This relieves applications of some of the burden of deciding exactly which NCPs require a license.

Microsoft Clients

In the mid-1980s, when it began shipping networking software, Microsoft chose IBM's NetBIOS protocol as the basis of its networking communication, enhancing it and christening it NetBEUI. (Novell's IPX/SPX was based on Xerox's XNS protocol.)

As networks expanded, though, they outgrew NetBEUI, which was not routable from one network to another.

Beginning with Windows NT 3.51, Microsoft offered a choice of using NetBEUI, TCP/IP, or a Microsoft-developed version of IPX called NWLink. By the time Windows 95 and Windows NT shipped, NWLink was Microsoft's preferred protocol for networking.

Microsoft Client for NetWare Networks

At the time Windows 95 (and Windows NT 4) was being developed, the competitive climate between Novell and Microsoft prevented them from working jointly on a NetWare client for the new operating system. Instead, each worked separately with the other's published API to develop its own client. Novell came up with Client32 for Windows 95 (see the earlier Client32 section of this chapter). Microsoft developed the Microsoft Client for NetWare.

Unfortunately, Microsoft used an older API (the one for NETX) which had no knowledge of NDS. As a result, the client that shipped with Windows 95 could only be used for NetWare 2.*x*, 3.*x*, and bindery mode 4.*x* networks.

Realizing its mistake, Microsoft quickly created the Microsoft Service for Novell Directory Services which was released six months after Windows 95 (but *did* ship with Windows NT 4 and Windows 98).

This client works adequately for a "plain vanilla" NetWare NDS network. It does not, however, support newer NetWare utilities and applications such as Z.E.N.Works, Novell Distributed Print Services (NDPS), or Border Manager, which require extensions to both NDS and the client. Some third-party utilities, written to the Novell client API, may also yield strange results (or none at all) when this client is used.

Macintosh Clients

Novell has supported the Macintosh operating system as a client since the release of NetWare 2.15. A strong selling point for the NetWare for Macintosh product was that it required no additional training for Macintosh users and no additional client software. It was implemented in such a way that the NetWare server emulated a Macintosh server and the client used the built-in AppleShare networking client to access it.

Don't bother looking on the NetWare 5.*x* CD-ROM for Macintosh clients; you won't find any. Novell has turned over development of Macintosh products to Prosoft Engineering, which has released NetWare 5 Services for AppleShare, a new set of NetWare Loadable Modules (NLMs) that provide AppleTalk services over a Novell network, as well as the NetWare Client for Mac OS. Get details at their website, `http://www.prosofteng.com/`.

The downside of this, of course, was that a Macintosh client was limited to doing only those things allowed by AppleShare. This trade-off (ease of use versus functionality) seemed to work until the advent of NetWare 4 and NDS. Because AppleShare had no understanding of NDS, Macintosh clients could only log on in bindery mode for versions 4.0 through 4.02 of Net-Ware. With NetWare 4.1, new client software (MacNDS) was released that fully connected the Mac to NDS. Recently, a new client for MacOS has been released that further integrates Apple's client into NetWare and NDS.

MacNDS

The MacNDS client was released with NetWare 4.1. It provides access to NetWare 4.1 NetWare Directory Services for Macintosh workstations running System 7.*x* operating systems. MacNDS does not provide Directory Services support for versions of NetWare for Mac prior to version 4.1, or on Macintosh workstations running System 6.

The MacNDS client software contains these main components:

- **MacNCP** MacNCP enables a Macintosh workstation to log in directly to a Directory Services tree and to connect to any server in that tree without the user needing to reenter their name and password for each server. It allows the user to specify a preferred user name, Directory tree, and Directory context for DS logins.

- **NetWare UAM** The NetWare User Authentication Method enables a Macintosh user to log in to a NetWare network, change their password, or log in to Directory Services via MacNCP. In a non-Directory Services environment, the UAM allows for NetWare encryption and longer names and passwords, as well as the processing of expired passwords.

- **MacIPX** MacIPX enables a Macintosh to communicate on the network using the IPX/SPX family of protocols (rather than its native AppleTalk protocol). MacIPX is required by MacNCP to access Directory Services.

- **NetWare Aliases** The NetWare Aliases extension enables you to create aliases to files and folders on NetWare servers. You can store the aliases on your Macintosh workstation and use it to quickly log in to a server and open a frequently used file or other service.

While MacNDS allowed the Macintosh to connect to NDS, MacNDS still couldn't fully participate and still required NetWare for Macintosh to be running on every server the Macintosh might attach to. As always, though, the Novell engineers were working hard to improve this situation.

NetWare Client for MacOS

Networking has become so common in the business world (and even in the consumer world—home networks are growing faster than business networks!) that it is no longer considered necessary to emulate an AppleShare server slavishly in order to ensure that Macintosh clients can easily participate in a NetWare network.

The NetWare client for MacOS allows the IS manager to remove NetWare for Macintosh, including the `APPLETLK.NLM`, `AFP.NLM`, and `ATPS.NLM`, while still allowing the Macintosh computers to fully participate in the network. This helps reduce the load on the server. Only one NLM, `MACFILE.NLM`, is needed. This NLM just takes care of the desktop database, and it uses very little server memory or CPU time. It's also no longer necessary to run two protocols on the server, because this client supports IPX. This makes the management of LANs and WANs easier. Because it uses IPX, there is a unique node number assigned to each client that is displayed in `MONITOR.NLM`. It also helps to eliminate the security risks associated with across-the-LAN File Sharing by not routing AppleTalk.

However, the Mac user can still access all AppleShare services by using the AppleTalk protocol simultaneously with IPX. None of the functionality of AppleShare networking is lost.

This client is fully NDS-aware, so it can be managed like any other NDS client object. It's also the first Macintosh client to use encrypted passwords and to allow passwords 128 characters in length.

The NetWare Client for MacOS offers a single login to all services in NDS. The user need enter their password only once, and the client then automatically authenticates to any servers or printers the user tries to use after login.

This client comes with a remote console application for the Mac OS. This allows the remote management of the server for backups and the loading and unloading of NLMs, etc.

For developers, the NetWare Client for MacOS supports the ability to log in to servers without using the Chooser—so they can write programs that can login to servers without requiring user intervention. Even though the user is not required to use the Chooser, the NetWare Directory Browser has a Macintosh look and feel.

The client is intelligent, and automatically senses the frame type (Ethernet 802.2, 802.3, Ethernet II, or SNAP) used on the network. IS managers can automate the process by creating preference files with a user's name and context already in them.

While the NetWare Client for MacOS no longer requires that servers run NetWare for Macintosh, you may still wish to run that software as a solution for small workgroups using Appletalk. This new client is designed for enterprise networks and large workgroups where Macintosh workstations make up a small percentage of the total workstations. It should be used where the Macintosh does not have access to NetWare servers because NetWare for Macintosh has not been installed. It should be used on WANs and LANs where AppleTalk is not being routed. Finally, it should be used whenever the user wants to have full access to the power of NDS.

Summary

This chapter has presented client software for NetWare networks in a historical context. We learned that the NetWare shell (NETX) could not access an NDS tree, and that PC clients required either the DOS requester (VLM) or Novell's newest client—Client32—in order to log in to an NDS tree.

We have looked briefly at client software from Microsoft intended to be used with NetWare networks and NDS. We then finished with an examination of the two NDS-enabled clients available for the Macintosh operating system: One requires that NetWare for Macintosh be running on the NetWare server, while the other allows connection to NDS trees without it.

NDS clients continue to evolve as both Novell and third parties add more functionality to NDS (which we'll see in the chapters that follow). Network administrators should periodically visit the Novell Web site (`http://www/novell.com/` and `http://support.novell.com`) for updates and upgrades.

PART

III

Exploiting Novell
Directory Services

C H A P T E R

15

NDS and Novell Products

Early on in the promotion of Novell Directory Services the company used the marketing slogan, "NDS Everywhere!" This phrase was apparently taken as a corporate mandate, because the intervening years have seen the spread of NDS to other operating systems (see Chapter 17), to a myriad of third-party products (see Chapter 16), and even to corporate programmers. But the most consistent spread of NDS is to almost the entire product line of Novell itself.

Generally, this increased popularity has taken the form of using NDS to store additional objects and properties (often by extending the schema). They can then be maintained and manipulated with the NWADMIN program through the use of snap-in modules, which are provided with the non-NetWare products. In this chapter, we'll look at Novell's non-NetWare products and explore how they use NDS.

GroupWise

GroupWise is Novell's entry in the workflow and information management category, a category that used to be referred to as *groupware*. It's an outgrowth of WordPerfect Office, which was kept by Novell when the rest of the WordPerfect product line was sold to Corel.

GroupWise Objects in NDS

GroupWise uses NDS as its master directory, or address book. This means GroupWise can use data which has already been defined on the network, so there is no need to enter common user information more than once. In addition, the administration user interface for GroupWise has been integrated with the NWADMIN utility. This gives users a single point of administration with an intuitive interface they are already familiar with.

GroupWise extends the NDS schema to add the object classes listed in Table 15.1.

T A B L E 15.1 GroupWise Object Classes	**GroupWise Object Class**	**What It Is**
	Domain	A directory object that contains a set of post offices, agents, and connectivity agents, and information about the way they link (pass data) to other domains in the system. A domain is the topmost object in the GroupWise object hierarchy. An important attribute of the domain is the path to the location of the administrator data file.
	Post Office	The location where user data is stored and accessed. An attribute of the post office object is the path to the location of the message databases and subdirectories. Another attribute identifies the users who access their data at the post office.
	User	A person who is authorized to use the GroupWise system. Each user object has a distinguished directory name and a GroupWise address which consists of the domain and post office the user belongs to, as well as the user's name.
	Resource	A nonuser object that can be scheduled. Meeting rooms and equipment are examples of resource objects.
	Distribution List	A list of users and/or resources that receive any message addressed to the distribution list.
	Library	A storage location for documents with an associated access list and profile attribute set. An attribute defines the locations where the documents will be stored.
	Agent	A process that works on a specific set of GroupWise data. The Post Office Agent delivers messages to the user data store, the Message Transfer Agent transports messages between domains and post offices, and the Administration Agent replicates information between the GroupWise directory databases and NDS.
	Connectivity Agent	An agent that provides conversion from GroupWise to another message or communication protocol.

The GroupWise Admin snapin adds the interface for all of the GroupWise object classes described above. It lets you edit GroupWise-specific objects and attributes in NDS and allows many GroupWise utilities to be accessed from the Tools menu in NWADMIN.

Directory Replication and Synchronization

GroupWise actually maintains its own database of users and resources, but the GroupWise directory is secondary to the global directory provided by NDS. That is, a subset of the information available in NDS (the GroupWise address book information) is replicated to the GroupWise directory and is kept synchronized with NDS. The fully replicated GroupWise directory is built on an indexed database to provide fast lookups for the GroupWise address book.

NDS is considered the "master directory," and pertinent data is replicated from NDS to the GroupWise directory. Data is never pushed from the GroupWise directory; it is always read from NDS and written to GroupWise (see Figure 15.1).

FIGURE 15.1

GroupWise data replication and synchronization

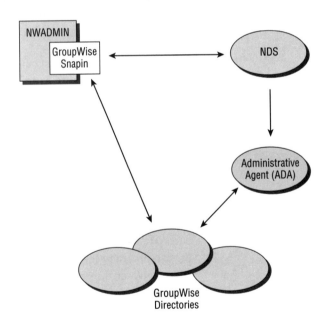

The GroupWise Administrative Agent (ADA) can be configured to synchronize objects from either the domain the database belongs to, specified domains, or a specified set of NDS Organizational Units.

There are two methods by which information is synchronized from NDS to a domain database. The first method is used when information is changed through the NWADMIN utility with the GroupWise Admin snapin running. In this case, the GroupWise snapin simultaneously writes changes to both NDS and to the GroupWise domain database.

In the second method of synchronization, the Administration Agent (ADA) checks NDS for changes that have occurred but are not reflected in the GroupWise directory. When a difference is detected, the data in NDS is used to update the GroupWise directory. This method detects changes made by NetWare administration products that are not using the GroupWise ADMIN snapin. It also detects changes made by any application that writes directly to NDS. ADA will never write to NDS, even if the GroupWise directory contains information that is not stored in NDS (in fact, it doesn't even check for this condition).

When an ADA is configured, the administrator defines the domains in which the ADA will perform GroupWise and NDS synchronization. Only ADAs that run on platforms with NDS access are able to participate in the NDS-to-GroupWise synchronization, but all ADAs participate in the GroupWise-to-GroupWise synchronization.

Administrative data is propagated by ADA from one domain's GroupWise directory database to other domain and post office databases. This model allows for simultaneous operation of GroupWise 4.*x* and GroupWise 5.*x* domains in an interconnected system. It also allows a GroupWise system to span NDS and non-NDS network nodes.

Because the GroupWise directory is replicated around all of the domains and post offices in the GroupWise system, domains can exist on platforms where NDS is not available and still participate fully in the GroupWise system. This means that existing domains on NetWare 3.*x* servers and on other network operating system platforms can continue to function as they have in the past.

A domain's type determines how it participates in the replication of GroupWise directory data. A GroupWise domain can be a primary, secondary, external, or foreign domain. The functions of these domain types are as follows:

- There can be only one primary domain in a GroupWise system. All directory updates must pass through this domain. Every change is sent to the primary domain from the originating domain. The primary domain then propagates the change to the rest of the system.

- A secondary domain participates fully in the replication of administrator data, but all changes made at the secondary domain are sent only to the primary domain for propagation to other secondary domains.

- An external domain is considered a separate GroupWise system. By default, it receives no administration data but can be configured to participate in a system's directory synchronization. The GroupWise administrator specifies which objects to replicate from the external domain, and the administrator of the external domain specifies which objects can be replicated.

- A foreign domain is an external non-GroupWise system. GroupWise does not replicate foreign domains because their directory format is unknown. Many foreign domains can participate in directory information exchange through a gateway to GroupWise. Foreign domains are provided so addresses from outside systems can be published in the GroupWise address book.

Other Uses of NDS by GroupWise

Other notable GroupWise administrator features that have an NDS aspect include the following:

- A browser view called the GroupWise View is added by the GroupWise ADMIN snapin to make it easy for an administrator to see only those objects that belong to the GroupWise system.

- Import/Export permits the importing and exporting of GroupWise and NDS data to an ASCII delimited file.

- Migration provides the ability to push information from an existing GroupWise system into NDS and create the correct objects so the system can be administered in NWADMIN.

- Administrative access control is available. In general, GroupWise administrative functions are intended to be executed from a privileged account and accessed through NWADMIN. A user's access to GroupWise administrative functions is determined by that user's NDS access rights to GroupWise objects and attributes.

- Administration of GroupWise agents. These agents are defined as objects in NDS and are configured using NWADMIN. Each agent type has its own set of configuration settings. The configuration of the Administration Agent (ADA) defines the domains in which the agent is responsible for synchronizing GroupWise with NDS. Storing the configuration in NDS allows configuration files to be modified from the administration interface, eliminating the need to manually edit configuration files at each agent.

Business Internet Services

Novell's Business Internet Services (BIS)—formerly known as NCS (Novell Connection Service)—is a collection of services enabling companies to securely connect to remote locations via the Internet. NCS was co-marketed with AT&T as a part of the phone company's Internet service provider (ISP) business. Now that many ISPs offer this service, the name has been changed to Business Internet Services.

BIS isn't something the average company can purchase; it's only available to ISPs. It is important to many businesses using NDS because by using an ISP that offers BIS, the following benefits can be realized:

- You can safely connect remote or mobile users to your network and stay current with all your dial-in hardware without the hefty upgrade costs.

- You can have an inexpensive connection between all your remote offices.

- You can manage all your sites from one location.

- You can route all your communications (voice and data) over one connection.

- You can use a public data network that you can securely move mission-critical data across.

- You can create a secure communications network that connects you to your customers, suppliers, vendors, and business partners.

Figure 15.2 illustrates the use of BIS to connect a company with its remote facilities, mobile users, customers, and vendors.

Novell has joined with a number of the world's leading Internet service providers to offer a global business-class Internet service that offers all of the above network services. ISPs with these types of network services provide your corporation with the capability to extend its intranet to your remote employees, branch offices, customers, and suppliers to form its own *extranet*. Novell Directory Services lies at the heart of these networks, allowing users and network administrators to more effectively manage and use network resources anywhere in the world.

F I G U R E   15.2

BIS facilitates secure connectivity over the public Internet.

BIS and NDS

Business Internet Services (BIS) is a group of technologies designed to give ISPs the ability to provide additional value to help you integrate your remote and mobile users, customers, suppliers, vendors and business partners into one large *extranet*. (An extranet is a virtual private network located outside of your company's intranet.)

In order to have a true extranet solution, you need to have a directory that manages relationships and security between users, businesses, and network resources on the Net. At the heart of BIS lies Novell Directory Services (NDS). Having a directory-enabled network makes it easier for you and your ISP to manage and secure network resources. It also makes it easier for users to work with the network, and it lowers your total cost of ownership.

Companies using BIS know that NDS helps create connections with high levels of security, reliability, scalability, and manageability, as well as having the advantages of being easy to use and inexpensive.

Security

Business Internet Services networks provide the same security through a public data network that you have on your local area network, because both are controlled by NDS.

All data transmitted is verified through a mechanism called Source Address Assurance, which guarantees that the sources of the data are genuine. All users are authenticated through NDS in a secure manner via an encrypted authentication exchange. Access to resources is controlled through NDS, allowing the full granularity of NDS security to be applied. Usage can also be audited. All dial-in users are authenticated in a way that ensures that client passwords are never transmitted in cleartext.

Manageability and Reliability

Management of an extranet system is technically demanding, especially if a company's network administrators and engineers have little experience with telecommunications technology. ISPs have extensive experience reliably maintaining wide area networks. Using NDS as a part of BIS allows you to manage your resources while the ISP maintains a reliable data network.

Scalability

NDS serves as a single point of administration and access for all network resources (people, servers, printers, peripherals, and so on), regardless of platform, protocol, or location. This allows easy network expansion and eliminates the need to re-engineer for each new location, protocol, or platform. With BIS-based services, the company can start small and ramp up as demand grows. Corporations use this business network to connect all of their remote branches.

Ease of Use

Because BIS is based on NDS, most end users do not even notice that it is there. They log on to the network in the usual way and gain access to all of the resources they are allowed to use. As a result, using BIS doesn't require much training.

Cost Effectiveness

Business Internet Services helps you reduce your total cost of ownership through the use of a public network, a setup that creates efficiencies of scale unavailable with proprietary systems. "Hidden costs" are avoided; there is no need for continual capital outlay for technology upgrades.

BIS can also reduce administration costs compared with what you would pay for an in-house solution, and from an everyday-network-administration point of view, making it possible to outsource network administration and services, if desired.

BorderManager

BorderManager has been described as the industry's first integrated family of directory-based network services that manages, secures, and accelerates user access to information at every network border. A border is defined as the point where any two networks meet, including points where a company's intranet meets the Internet.

The intranet/Internet border is not the only frontier where Border-Manager can help. For example, it could be used to secure employee payroll records from all internal and external users except the finance department, while still allowing authorized users convenient access via the company intranet.

What BorderManager Does

BorderManager allows customers—through a single point of administration—to manage their companies' security polices, to protect their confidential information, to monitor outbound Internet traffic, and to reduce WAN connectivity costs. And it does all this while leveraging customers' existing hardware investment in servers, desktop systems, and routers.

BorderManager isn't just a firewall. It has a whole set of integrated features, including:

- Advanced proxy cache service that significantly accelerates Web access performance, reduces network/intranet traffic, and offloads Web server workload by up to 90 percent.

- Virtual private network (VPN) services which deliver secure, encrypted connections over the Internet and reduce costs for expensive dedicated private lines.

- Firewall services, which provide increased security through three levels of firewall protection that include packet filtering (Level I firewall), circuit gateways (Level II firewall), and application proxies (Level III firewall).

- A network address translation (NAT) service that allows unregistered IP devices to connect to the Internet.

- Remote access and routing services that provide cost-effective, remote client dial-up connections to a company's network, and secure WAN routing services.

- Microsystems' Cyberpatrol, which offers category-based content filtering to help eliminate access to objectionable Web content.

BorderManager and NDS

BorderManager's single point of administration through NDS allows centralized, policy-based management of access privileges for inbound and outbound users. This significantly simplifies administration, improves security, and reduces administrative expenses.

NDS automatically replicates security data and controls access across the entire network. NDS automates network administration, reduces administrative errors, and ensures consistent user access to intranet/Internet resources.

User-level access controls allow organizations to define access privileges to the Internet by user, group of users, time of day, application, and content category.

BorderManager Authentication Services

With the global rush toward the Internet, remote access has become the wild new frontier for doing business. In this mobile world, NDS and BorderManager Authentication Services (BMAS) make sure that you won't be facing another hair-raising adventure as you go around the next bend.

BMAS manages the physical or hardware level of your network through modem banks, access routers, and access servers. Remote Authentication Dial-In User Service (RADIUS) is an emerging Internet Engineering Task Force (IETF) standard that has been adopted by Novell and many leading dial-in and router hardware vendors.

To get a better picture of how BMAS fits into your network, think of today's entire network as comprising:

- Physical devices like modem banks, access servers, and routers

- Operating systems such as IntranetWare, UNIX, and NT

- Applications that run over the network

- Services that improve how people work with the network and that transcend both the intranet and the Internet

- The intranet and the Internet—for doing business, not just for public advertising

NDS' flexible, powerful, secure directory service is what ties all the network levels together and makes the network easy to use and easy to manage.

Leveraging RADIUS

The purpose of the RADIUS Internet standard protocol (as defined by RFC 2058) is to provide security, authorization, and accounting services that can best be used by managing a single database of users. A single database allows for authentication as well as configuration information detailing the type of service to deliver to the user (SLIP, PPP, Telnet, rlogin, and so on).

With RADIUS Services from BMAS, NDS becomes the only directory required for both remote access servers and local network servers. It provides a centralized point of authentication and authorization to access or administer network resources.

BMAS' RADIUS Services dramatically simplifies the process of remote access. The user logs in with a common name (such as Jsmith) or Internet e-mail address. Their dial-in access password can be the same or different from their NDS password, and the user can access all assigned resources without entering other passwords. For network administrators, BorderManager Authentication Services enables one directory to do double duty as the directory for both remote users and the network as a whole. There's no unnecessary repetition when it comes time to add or modify user information.

BMAS allows deployment and management of multiple remote-access servers, a primary RADIUS server, and any number of backup servers. If the primary server fails, the access server will switch to a secondary RADIUS server. If a network link goes down, dial-in users can still be authenticated with the replicated information stored locally on any NDS server. The distributed and replicated nature of NDS enables BMAS to continue providing uninterrupted service 24 hours a day, seven days a week.

ZENWorks

ZENWorks (Zero Effort Networks, but no one ever calls it anything but "ZENWorks," or simply "ZEN") is a set of software components that can help control the cost of owning and operating a network. Some analysts have estimated the cost of maintaining workstations to be 78% of the cost of the network. This estimate takes into account the administrative activities required by a network, such as workstation configuration, software application installation, and troubleshooting—all the things ZEN allows you to do quickly, easily, and efficiently.

ZENWorks is made up of three major components: Desktop Management, Application Management, and Remote Management modules.

ZEN and Desktop Management

The Desktop Management component allows you to place network dependencies for users and workstations in NDS. Using these so-called "policy packages," you can control the look and feel of users' desktops, application delivery, printer configuration, and Novell client configuration. Users no longer rely on their local workstation configuration; they rely on ZENworks and NDS to provide that configuration wherever they happen to log in. Table 15.2 shows some of the features available with ZEN's Desktop Management module.

TABLE 15.2 ZEN Desktop Management Features	Feature	Description
	Directory-Enabled Policies	Policies and profiles ensure that users can roam from one network location to another while securely maintaining their familiar, personalized desktop interface and having access to the applications and network resources they require. For network security and efficiency, user login can also be restricted to certain machines through an exclusionary policy.
	Centralized Printer Management and Configuration	Users need not configure their printer, even when a new printer is added or the user moves to another PC. Instead, the network administrator can distribute any modifications across the network to the appropriate workstation.
	Extensible Policies	Administrators can create custom desktop policies and distribute them across the network through integration with NDS.
	Hardware and Software Inventory	Administrators can track the hardware and software installed on users' computers. DMI 2.0 compliance makes complete hardware and software inventory data available in an SQL database that is ODBC-compliant.
	Desktop Virus Protection	Virus protection prevents network problems that might otherwise disrupt user productivity.
	Reporting	Reports provide detailed inventories and track the success or failure of software delivery for troubleshooting.

ZEN and Application Management

ZEN's Application Management component gives users access to the applications they need. Applications can be configured in NDS and, using the Application Launcher or Application Explorer, you can deploy entire applications, upgrade existing software, and make changes to system files automatically and on demand through NDS. With ZENworks, you no longer have to visit each workstation to deploy new software. Table 15.3 enumerates some of the benefits of ZEN's Application Management module.

T A B L E 15.3 ZEN Application Management Features	**Feature**	**Description**
	Customized Software Distribution	Reduces costs and simplifies administration by automatically distributing and customizing software for each user
	Self-Healing Applications	Automatically repairs "broken" applications without making the user wait for onsite support
	Software Metering	Gives administrators the ability to better manage technology resources by automating auditing and metering of NDS-delivered applications
	Lights-Out Distribution	Delivers software to workstations where no user is logged in
	Criteria-based Distribution	Automatically checks workstations for pre-defined criteria before installing software
	Prompted Macros	Allows administrators to give users choices about their desktop environments
	Pre- and Post-Distribution Scripts	Allows administrators to run scripts or invoke actions prior to software distribution

ZEN and Remote Management

The Remote Management component provides timely user support when problems occur at remote sites. ZENworks provides this support through three applications:

- **Hardware and Software Inventory**   This application gathers information about the hardware and software configuration of user workstations, including internal information such as hard drive and video adapter characteristics.

- **Help Requester**   This application provides users with the name, e-mail address, and phone number of support contacts who can provide assistance. When problems arise, users enter "trouble tickets" from the Help Requester. These tickets are routed through your e-mail system to your Help desk.

- **Remote Control**   This application allows you to take control of a user's workstation to resolve most workstation problems without actually visiting the workstation.

LDAP Services for NDS

LDAP, Lightweight Directory Access Protocol, is discussed in depth in Chapters 2 and 3, which you should review if you're not already familiar with the protocol.

As the X.500 directory specifications were being developed, a directory access protocol (DAP) was formulated. The DAP protocol specification had a lot of overhead, and not many people developed clients or applications to DAP. A group of people at the University of Michigan realized that if they could reduce the overhead in the DAP specification, they could get the same directory information out quicker and with smaller clients. They named this new protocol specification the Lightweight Directory Access Protocol (LDAP-RFC 1777). LDAP is quickly becoming the standard for clients on the Internet and intranets to use to access directory information, no matter which directory system holds that information.

LDAP Services for NDS allows you to easily publish your organization's information to your intranet and to the Internet, while still maintaining control—through NDS—over who can access that information.

LDAP services is included with NetWare 5 and is an add-on for NetWare 4.*x*. NetWare 5.1 with NDS, version 8 (eDirectory), integrates LDAP directly into the directory service. No additional NLMs are needed.

Benefits of LDAP Services for NDS

LDAP Services for NDS is based on the IETF RFC 1777 LDAP version 2 protocol. It provides the following key benefits:

- A way to expose information stored in NDS to any LDAP-enabled browser or application

- Levels of security not implemented in the current LDAP 2 standard

- A method for managing LDAP users

Exposing NDS through LDAP

LDAP Services for NDS gives you the freedom to specify exactly the information you would like to expose to an LDAP client. You can identify the NDS information you want to publish using class and attribute mappings that define the relationship between objects in LDAP and NDS.

Levels of Security

LDAP Services for NDS supports most NDS security features and adds an LDAP access control layer that provides additional security features. These security features allow you to make certain types of directory information independently available to the public, to your organization, and to those groups or individuals that need to see the information.

LDAP Services for NDS provides two security layers that allow you to control the publishing of network information. They are called the *NDS access control layer* and the *LDAP access control layer*.

NDS Access Control   The NDS access control layer is always enabled and operates on the NDS server side of LDAP Services. The NDS access control layer can be accessed by the following LDAP connection methods: anonymous bind, proxy user anonymous bind, and NDS user bind.

LDAP Access Control   The LDAP access control layer is an optional layer that operates on the LDAP client side of LDAP Services for NDS. Access Control Lists (ACLs) are part of the LDAP access control layer. These access control lists specify the rights an LDAP client has to specific LDAP information. The following rights are maintained by the LDAP Server Object ACLs:

- **Search**   Allows clients to search for LDAP object attributes that are defined in the Access To list.

- **Compare**   Allows clients to specify LDAP object attribute values that are compared to the corresponding (mapped) NDS values.

- **Read**   Allows users to read the values of the object attributes defined in the Access To list. Read access also provides Search and Compare rights. In addition, you receive Search access with the Read access rights.

- **Write**   Allows users to change the values of the object attributes defined in the Access To list. Write access also provides Read, Search, and Compare rights.

LDAP Access Management

LDAP Services for NDS is also a management tool that allows you to enhance performance of LDAP client connections and moderate LDAP access activity. Some of the features that help you manage LDAP Services include the following, which can all be done via the NWAdmin program.

- **User E-mail Address**   The user e-mail address page contains a list of Internet e-mail addresses that are returned when an LDAP client requests a user's e-mail address.

- **Search Entry Limit**   The Search Entry Limit specifies the maximum number of objects for which the LDAP-enabled server will return data.

- **Search Time Limit**   The Search Time Limit specifies the maximum amount of time in seconds that the LDAP enabled server will use to return data.

- **Idle Timeout**   The idle timeout defines the maximum amount of time in seconds that an LDAP connection can be inactive.

- **Bind Limit**   The bind limit defines the maximum number of simultaneous LDAP binds or connections.

- **Log Event**   Tracks user NDS access activity such as trace function calls, LDAP request information, connection information, BER encoding, search filter processing, configuration file processing, LDAP ACL processing, client request summary, search response summary, error messages from all log options, and server console messages for LDAP.

- **Setting the Suffix**   The Suffix text box defines the Directory tree or subtree that the LDAP servers can access.

- **Setting the Referral**   The Referral text box specifies the URL of an alternate LDAP server that is to handle any requests that cannot be completed by the servers in this group.

Oracle for NetWare

While not strictly a Novell product, Oracle for NetWare was jointly developed by a team of Oracle and Novell engineers. As such, it combines all of the features of the Oracle Relational Database System (RDBMS) with the power of NDS to create a fully integrated system supporting a myriad of applications. The ease of use and administration that this provides is possible only through this integration.

Oracle integrates its database software with NDS to provide single sign-on and native naming capabilities to its users. The single sign-on feature automatically authenticates users to an Oracle database based on their operating system (NDS) login. No Oracle username or password is needed, and the login is secure. The native naming feature allows users to connect to an Oracle database by specifying the database object name in the directory tree instead of specifying an Oracle service name. These powerful capabilities make it easier to administer a multiserver, multidatabase network than would be possible without NDS.

Oracle and NDS

Oracle has created a new NDS class, Oracle Instance, and extended the NDS schema to include it. In addition, the User, Group, and Organizational Unit objects have added attributes that support Oracle security services.

Security Services

The standard Oracle operating system security features, including administrator authentication, user authentication, and role identification, have been enhanced by integrating Oracle with NDS.

Administrator Authentication   Oracle uses an NDS group to authenticate users connecting as SYSDBA (Database Administrator) or SYSOPER (System Operator). Members of the appropriate groups will be able to connect to Oracle as SYSDBA or SYSOPER and to start or stop the Oracle server. With NDS, administrators can assign these privileges to an NDS user or a group of NDS users through the NWADMIN utility.

User Authentication (Single Sign-on)   Oracle authenticates users connecting to a database instance from a secure operating system connection. A user is created using the user's operating system name plus an optional prefix. For example, an operating system user called LPROBINS would have an Oracle username of OPS$LPROBINS. With NDS, administrators can build a flexible mapping of NDS users to Oracle users. The following are some examples of what can be done.

- An NDS user connects as an Oracle user.

- A group of NDS users connect as one Oracle user.

- All NDS users in an Organizational Unit connect as one Oracle user.

The last example is a powerful feature since it allows an administrator to give database access to a new user in an organization by simply creating the user in the appropriate location in the directory tree.

Role Identification   When a user connects based on the user's operating system group membership, Oracle enables roles (which are similar to NDS roles in that the user or users assigned to the roles inherit certain rights granted to that role). Operating system groups must be named in a specific way for Oracle to recognize and grant the roles. For example, the group ORA_TEST_CONNECT_D indicates that the Oracle instance TEST should grant members of this group the CONNECT role by default. With NDS, administrators can build a flexible mapping of NDS groups to Oracle roles.

The Oracle Instance Object

Oracle extends the NDS schema to add the Oracle Instance object class. The Oracle Instance object is a regular NDS object which has an administration interface based on NWAdmin. The Oracle Instance object behaves as a native NDS object and is administered from the NetWare Administrator in exactly the same way as any other NDS object. Access to the Oracle Instance object is completely controlled by the usual access rights, as defined in the NetWare Administrator for other NDS objects.

Figure 15.3 shows the NetWare Administrator in browse mode on the NDS directory. The Oracle Instance object, lprobins-orcl, is shown at the bottom of the tree. This object is created in the usual way by selecting Object Create ➤ Oracle Instance.

FIGURE 15.3

The Oracle Instance object

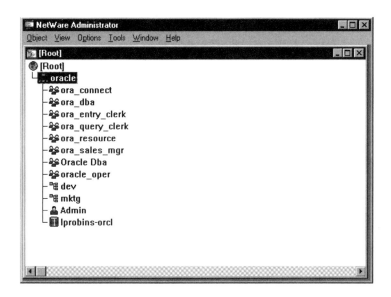

The Oracle Instance object acts as a mediator between the Oracle and NDS security domains. The Oracle Instance object is an object-oriented abstraction of the Oracle Instance in the directory tree. All configuration of operating-system-authenticated users and operating system role identification is done through this object. In fact, for the convenience of administrators, all possible Oracle user configuration operations can be achieved directly from this object.

Single Sign-On

Novell Single Sign-on is a new directory-based solution that eliminates the need for users to remember and input multiple passwords. Novell Single Sign-on extends the NDS schema to support a "SecretStore" in NDS. When a user authenticates to NDS and launches an application, the application password is sent to and kept in the SecretStore. From then on, the user logs in only once and NDS provides the application password to the application—all in the background.

NDS also handles mandatory password changes. For example, if Lotus Notes is configured to require a password change every 60 days, when the password expires, NDS prompts the user for a new password and automatically provides the old password in the "old password" field (the NDS password remains unchanged). The user can enter a random password, NDS then replaces the old Notes password in SecretStore with the new one, and the user never has to remember an application password—only the NDS password.

Applications must be enabled for Single Sign-on. The first release includes support for Lotus Notes, Entrust applications, PeopleSoft applications, and host emulation products from Attachmate and Wall Data. Novell also provides a toolkit which can be used to enable your in-house applications for Single Sign-on.

ScheMax

ScheMax was acquired by Novell through the purchase of Netoria software. This NDS utility provides network administrators an effective way to manage the NDS schema, add new classes and attributes, easily create NWADMIN snapins without programming, deliver NDS content to users, and set NDS attribute entry policies.

The schema can be modified, with new classes and attributes added or deleted. Easy to use wizards are included for simplifying the process even further. Attribute additions can be modeled offline without actually extending the schema, and the changes can be tested before being applied to the live NDS tree.

Class Information objects are created to allow new or unmanaged classes to be managed by NWADMIN. Using ScheMax you can now create, delete, and manage objects of an unmanaged or new class.

Summary

In this chapter, we've explored Novell's use of NDS with its other products. Among the uses they make of NDS are:

- Security

- Authentication

- User profiles

- Object location

- Object configuration

These uses are accomplished by extending the NDS schema and adding snap-in modules to the NWAdmin utility.

It can be expected that Novell will continue to make use of NDS—with both NetWare and other operating systems—to provide the best possible ease of use and ease of administration.

CHAPTER
16

Third-Party Products

As you can imagine, the adoption of Novell Directory Services by third-party vendors has been widespread. Many vendors have developed software that works with NDS and simplifies its use, while others have introduced software to manage, diagnose, and troubleshoot NDS itself. Still others have found ways to leverage the directory to improve their applications or even create entirely new categories of applications.

Most backup software vendors, such as Computer Associates and Seagate, incorporate NDS into their products because backing up the directory tree is as important as backing up data. Other packages, such as Bind-View EMS, work with NDS, recognize NDS objects, and help manage them. There's a growing list of vendors who use the directory to extend their applications reach, such as Dragon Systems' Naturally Speaking Enterprise or Business Layers' ePrivision Suite.

We'll look at all of these, but most important to this book are those utilities that diagnose NDS problems and allow you to troubleshoot the directory.

These tools can be divided into three categories: tools that help you migrate and organize your data from bindery-based NetWare (as in NetWare 2.*x* or 3.*x*), tools that help you manage NDS, and lastly, tools that help you diagnose, troubleshoot, and solve NDS problems.

The goal of this chapter is to let you know about the third-party utilities that exist so that you can manage your directory tree more easily.

Migration Utilities

When Novell was developing NetWare 4 and NDS, it teamed up in a partnership with a company called Preferred Systems (PSI). PSI was known for creating migration utilities. PSI's product, DS Standard NDS Manager, allows network managers to create a mirror copy of their NDS tree that is available for manipulation before the migration process. This back-end database ensures that mistakes, as well as planned events, are made to an offline copy rather than to a "live network." It also helps with migrations from NetWare 2.*x* or 3.*x* networks to NetWare 4.*x* and 5.*x* networks. PSI was purchased by Cheyenne, which was itself bought by Computer Associates, the current DS Standard vendor.

In August 1993, Novell incorporated parts of DS Standard into NetWare 4—including its find and replace characteristics, its migration templates, and its tree management features—and called it DS MIGRATE.

In addition, DS Standard helps with object support and the migration of large numbers of users via its UIMPORT capabilities. It contains a wizard-like Assistant, troubleshooting tips, "how to" examples, and case studies that guide the user through the migration from NetWare 3.*x* to NetWare 4.*x*/5.*x*, as shown in Figure 16.1. It offers the capability to print detailed object reports, change logs, and the directory tree.

F I G U R E   16.1

Computer Associates' DS Standard assists you in migrating from NetWare 3.*x* to NetWare 4/5.

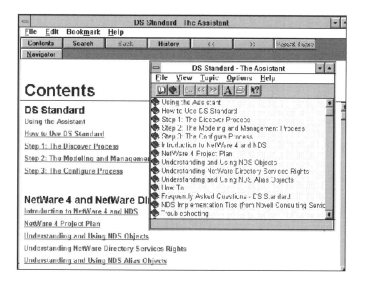

 DS Standard is compatible with LANDesk from Intel and ManageWorks from Digital.

Using DS Standard, you can discover your network, model the migration path, and configure the new system. In the process, you may consolidate bindery-based servers, design NDS trees, apply new naming conventions, merge the objects from several servers to a single server, and clean up your bindery data. Filters allow you to create queries for certain information, such as object type or property settings, and use Boolean logic and calculated fields to analyze the data.

DS Standard requires Windows NT Workstation, Windows 3.1, Windows for Workgroups 3.11 or Windows 95, and at least a 386/33 machine with 8MB of RAM and 26MB of disk space. It is year 2000 compatible.

NDS Managers

Two companies have made a market of organizing and managing the Novell Directory Services environment. They are BindView Development of Houston, Texas, and NetVision of Orem, Utah. BindView has been around for several years, and first created tools to manage the NetWare bindery for NetWare 2.*x* and 3.*x*. NetVision is the result of the efforts of some ex-Novellians who saw that there was more to managing Novell Directory Services than first appeared and that there were more opportunities for managing it than Novell was taking advantage of.

BindView Development's BindView EMS

BindView EMS is BindView Development's Windows-based utility for managing NetWare and Windows NT networks. It consists of four parts: one module for managing bindery-based NetWare, one for NDS-based NetWare, one for managing Windows NT, and an unrelated module for software and hardware inventory.

The BindView EMS/NOSadmin for NetWare lets you look at your NDS tree and analyze, manage, and report on the information you gather from it (see Figure 16.2). With BindView EMS/NOSadmin for NetWare, you can perform back-link analysis to optimize NDS traffic, analyze trustee and effective rights to determine if rights have been set correctly, and expose potential security threats. You can view your NDS database; view schema and attribute class definitions; and gather information about containers, including total objects, intruder detection information, organizational roles, and user template information.

BindView EMS/NOSadmin for NetWare contains perhaps the best reporting on NDS information. Any administrator would be wise to use it before migrating, changing servers, or performing any operation where directory information is at risk. With BindView EMS, you can report logical information about users, invisible objects, file servers, files and directories, print queues, and volumes.

BindView EMS is licensed on a NetWare server and user-object basis. The management console requires Windows 3.*x* or higher, 12MB of RAM, 40MB of disk space, and a 486/33 processor or higher, with a super VGA adapter.

FIGURE 16.2

BindView EMS can be used to manage NDS objects.

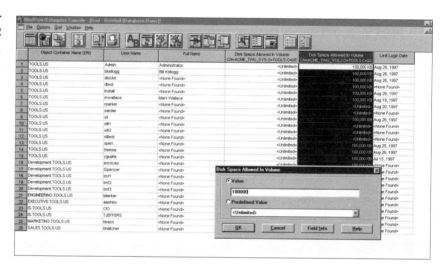

It contains an additional two snap-in modules: BindView EMS/NOSadmin for Windows NT and BindView EMS/NOSadmin for NetWare 3, which allow you to manage Windows NT and NetWare 3.*x* concurrently from the same management console. An additional snap-in module, NETinventory, allows you to gather and report on hardware and software characteristics of DOS, Windows, Windows 95, OS/2, and Windows NT workstations.

NetVision's Synchronicity for NetWare 3

NetVision's Synchronicity for NetWare 3 not only brings directory-style management to NetWare 3.*x*, it also allows servers to be managed collectively rather than as single entities. Synchronicity for NetWare 3 used NWAdmin to manage the network.

Synchronicity for NetWare 3 supports NetWare 3.11 and 3.12. NWAdmin provides the user interface to managing NetWare 3.*x* users, with the exception of the ability to manipulate file and directory rights and NetWare 3.*x* print servers. It supports an unlimited number of NetWare 3.*x* servers, unlike Novell's NetSync utility, which only supports 12 servers. Also unlike NetSync, Synchronicity supports bidirectional synchronization (3.*x* bindery to NDS and NDS to 3.*x* bindery).

NetVision's Synchronicity for NT

NetVision's Synchronicity for NT, shown in Figure 16.3, allows you to manage Windows NT Server- and Workstation-based networks along with your NetWare 4/5 networks and NetWare 3.*x*. It has a single management console and, with other NetVision products, allows you to form a metadirectory, which integrates many diverse directories into a single directory.

It offers bidirectional directory synchronization between Windows NT domain directories and NDS, and allows management via NWAdmin. Bidirectional synchronization is important because it allows Windows NT domains to be resynchronized with NDS if the NT primary or backup domain controller goes down. Users of Synchronicity for Windows NT can also use NT User Manager for Domains to update NT domain information. Synchronization of the new information will appear in NDS.

Synchronicity for NT is compatible with Windows NT 4, but does not allow you to manipulate file and directory rights in Windows NT.

NetVision's Synchronicity for Notes

NetVision's Synchronicity for Notes integrates Lotus' Domino Directory with Novell Directory Services so managers can manage them from a single management console. It supports Lotus Notes 4.0 and the Domino servers. It allows managers to add, modify, or delete Domino and Lotus Notes users

F I G U R E 16.3

Synchronicity for NT
allows you to manage
Windows NT networks
as NDS objects.

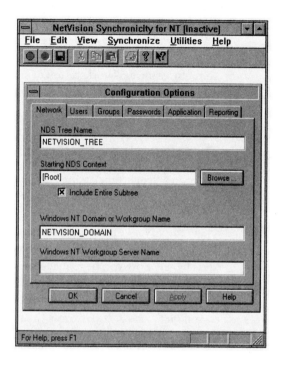

from NWAdmin, and handles the synchronization between the two. Synchronicity for Notes does the following:

- Supports hierarchical naming by joining Notes certifier IDs with NDS contexts of new user accounts

- Manages certifier ID and user ID files

- Preserves your investment in Novell Directory Services

Synchronicity for Notes is built on the same framework as other Synchronicity products: it uses the NetVision Global Event Services, a snap-in module for NWAdmin, and a synchronization agent, which runs on the Windows NT Workstation.

When Synchronicity for Notes is installed, any version of the NWAdmin snapin allows the integration of Notes accounts into NDS. It can synchronize events made in Notes with NDS and updates NDS about Notes changes on a scheduled basis or every few minutes. Synchronicity for Notes is compatible with other Synchronicity products, including Synchronicity for NetWare and

NT. It requires NWAdmin, NetWare 4.1 or above, Lotus Notes 4.0 or above, a Windows NT Server or Workstation synchronization agent, and 5MB of hard disk space on the Notes Server, the NetWare server, and the NWAdmin console. Domino can run on any platform, including AIX or OS/2.

It requires the NT workstation or server to be running the NetWare Client for NT, which you can download from `support.novell.com/home/client/winnt`.

NetVision's Synchronicity for Exchange

NetVision's Synchronicity for Exchange, an additional product in NetVision's line of Windows NT and NetWare interoperability products, allows users to manage Microsoft's Exchange Directory Service within an NDS architecture. Network managers can create Microsoft Exchange users and link them to NDS. When an NDS object changes, the Exchange user's properties change. Both can be managed through NWAdmin or through a NetVision snapin.

Synchronicity for Exchange works concurrently with Synchronicity for NT and NetWare 3. It performs the bidirectional synchronization of the NDS and Exchange directories, including password synchronization. Pricing starts at about $700 per 50-user license.

NDS Utilities

The applications covered in this section are less full-featured than the NDS manager programs listed earlier. They concentrate on either one or just a handful of NDS-related tasks.

Computer Associates' AuditWare

Computer Associates' (CA) AuditWare is a Windows-based reports and security analysis utility. It allows you to set and control access privileges for your NDS tree (see Figure 16.4). AuditWare consists of three parts: the Enforcer, which compares objects, the Assistant (a group of White Papers and troubleshooting tips), and the Object Rights Expert, which lets you analyze the Access Control List.

FIGURE 16.4

Computer Associates'
AuditWare can be
used to analyze
network security and
print reports.

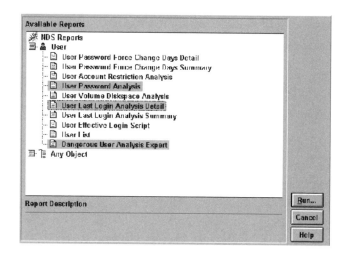

AuditWare lets you view potentially dangerous users, determine who has access privileges, and report on them. It allows you to set filters to show empty groups, objects with aliases, users with personal login scripts, and more.

AuditWare for NDS requires Windows NT, Windows 3.1, Windows for Workgroups 3.11, or Windows 95, a 386/33 or higher machine, 8MB of RAM, and 34MB of hard disk space.

Darwin Collins' NDS Utilities

Darwin Collins has several utilities for NetWare administration. They are:

- N4UTL148.ZIP contains N4OBJECT.EXE, which lets you display attribute names and values of specified objects.

- N4OBJMGR.EXE, which lets you add, move, rename, and delete user objects.

- N4ATTR.EXE, which lets you modify the values of attributes, such as passwords, group membership, and grace logins.

- N4EXPIRE.EXE, which lets you return the batch error level on the number of days until a user's password expires; N4GROUP.EXE, which lets you return the batch error level depending on whether a user is a member of specified group object.

- N4DSPACE.EXE, which lets you set and view space restrictions for user objects or for subdirectories.

- N4PA135.ZIP, which lets you reset user passwords and view the directory tree.

- NLOG125.ZIP, which is a contextless and distinguished nameless login program. With NLOG125.ZIP, users can log in without knowing their full network name or context.

All of the Darwin Collins tools are available at http://www.novellfans.com/n4util.asp.

DreamLAN Utilities from Peter Kuo

DreamLAN Network Consulting Ltd. (http://www.dreamlan.com/) is the vendor of Peter Kuo's Novell Directory Services (NDS) ToolKit for NetWare. This collection of NetWare Loadable Modules (NLMs) and DOS-based utilities lets you manage your network more easily and effectively. It also helps you assist your users in accessing your network more easily.

Of significant interest is the MakeSU utility, which allows you to recover from the loss of ADMIN access (such as a forgotten password, malicious user, etc.) to NDS.

JRB Software's JRButils

JRButils 5.00 consists of bindery-based, as well as NDS, utilities. From http://nz.com/webnz/JRBSoftware/, you can download 55 NDS utilities that help you manage a network more easily. This release includes three new programs: DELPROP, SCANPROP, and SERV_CMD. DELRPOP lets network administrators delete single properties from any bindery object. SCANPROP allows you to list the type property for any bindery object. SERV_CMD lets clients issue certain console commands on NetWare 4.x servers, such as mounting or dismounting volumes, adding namespaces, or listing SET commands.

PY Software

PY Software (`http://www.kagi.com/yellow`) offers two utilities: NDS List and LAN Show.

NDS List 1.1 gives you a list of network objects in real time, showing their place in the network. It tracks changes and shows the object's name, where it resides on a NetWare server or on the directory tree, its full name, its network address, and a list of the object's NetWare connections. It can monitor IPX addresses, list the speed of IPX packets, and display detailed IPX information.

LAN Show lets you view the state of computers, printers, and file servers on the network. It tells you if the object is logged in to the network or not. With LAN Show you can also create a list of user's rights to resources.

Click:VISION Manager

Long time NetWare developer John McCann has recently released a new NDS utility called Click:VISION Manager (`http://www.visualclick.com/`).

Click:VISION Manager is essentially a software development environment. But there's no programming involved. A few mouse clicks let you design applications that you can distribute to other users to enable them to interact with NDS in just the way you want them to.

For example, suppose you'd like your help desk personnel to be able to reset user passwords for users who forget them. A few mouse clicks give the proper rights to the help desk group, assign all users as the target, and limit the action to change password. In less than five minutes, the screen is drawn with a dropdown list of users, an entry box for the new password, and a button to click to change it. That's it. Give all help desk personnel access to this and they can change passwords—without all of the complexity (or possible security problems) associated with giving them access to the NetWare Administrator console.

If you need to allow some help desk personnel to reset intruder lockout status, as well as to be able to change passwords, just call up the password changer application (described above), add another button to reset intruder lockout, change the permissions on the operator (so that they can access the intruder lockout attribute) and you're done. Maybe two more minutes.

And that's just a tiny subset of the things you could do with Click:VISION Manager. You can design your own utilities to cut through the wealth of information in NDS so that you can hone in on what's important. You can create forms and report screens for others without having to give them access to objects and properties that they could compromise. Click:VISION Manager is easy, it's quick and it will save you time.

NDS Troubleshooting: Netpro

Netpro's DS Expert is a real-time utility that lets you view your directory tree. It notifies you of potential problems and gives you troubleshooting tips (see Figure 16.5). Via a Windows client, you can gather statistical information that helps you optimize your NDS design. It alerts you to errors as they occur and will tell you where to find them. DS Expert Agents, installed on NDS servers, send alerts and respond to thresholds. DS Expert also has a DSTRACE console that is capable of analyzing DSTRACE operations. NetPro's DS Expert consists of an NLM and a monitor.

You can download an evaluation of DS Expert from www.netpro.com. DS Expert costs about $1,300 for a two-server license. Additional server licenses are available for about $500 per server.

FIGURE 16.5

NetPro's DS Expert lets you troubleshoot NDS operations.

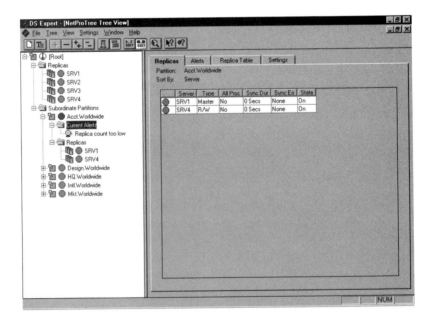

DS Expert also includes a software distribution and version control utility and can pass to SNMP consoles and ManageWise. You can download free evaluation software from NetPro's site on the Web at `www.netpro.com`.

Other Companies with NDS-Aware Programs

Many other utilities are available that operate with NDS. The following sections cover products from some of Novell's partners.

NOTE Contact information for the vendors of the products covered in this section is listed in Appendix B.

Callware

Callware of Sandy, Utah, makes computer telephony products and is the first telephony vendor to exploit NDS and to allow a single administrative console for NetWare/voice integration.

Cheyenne, a Division of Computer Associates

Cheyenne Software, Novell's largest Independent Software Vendor (ISV), makes networking solutions for backup, virus protection, and fax services. All these applications are NDS-aware and NDS-compliant. ARCserve for NetWare allows you to back up NetWare 3.*x* and 4.*x* environments; FAXserve for NetWare allows inbound and outbound faxing and support for NDS, using direct inward dialing and DTMF. Inoculan for NetWare provides antivirus protection for NetWare 3.*x* and 4.*x*, as well as Windows 3.1 and 95, DOS, Windows NT, and Macintosh clients.

Hewlett-Packard

Hewlett-Packard's JetDirect print server is NDS-enabled and allows users to configure printers as remote printers, in queue server mode, or in NDS queue server mode.

Intrusion Detection

Intrusion Detection's Kane Security Analyst (KSA), provides security assessment for NetWare 3.x, 4.x and 5.x. With KSA, you can look at user account restrictions, monitor the system, view access control, secure data confidentiality, and view password strength.

Lanovation

LAN Escort from Lanovation is a software distribution package for NetWare 3.x and 4.x, which allows network managers to remotely install applications, printers, and Windows environments to a user's desktop (see Figure 16.6). It integrates with the NetWare Application Launcher, and applications can be duplicated to multiple servers at once or to NDS containers. It supports bindery emulation as well as NDS.

The LAN Escort management console requires a 386 or faster computer running Windows 3.1 or Windows 95 with 4MB of memory and 2.5MB of disk space. The server requires NetWare 3.11, 3.12, or 4.1 or higher.

FIGURE 16.6

LAN Escort from Lanovation lets you automatically distribute software to NetWare 3.x or 4.x desktops.

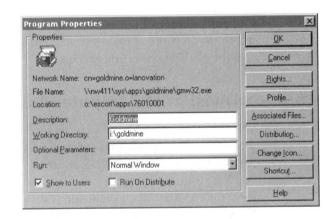

Motorola

Motorola Air Apparent for NetWare is an NLM-based wireless communications package that lets users receive e-mail through their alphanumeric pagers. It integrates with NDS so that the administrator doesn't have to worry about having a separate directory of pager numbers and users.

Oracle

Oracle7 Workgroup Server incorporates NDS technology to provide ease-of-use and point-and-click GUI tools in a comprehensive database manager. See Chapter 15 for more information about this joint effort by Oracle and Novell.

Seagate

Seagate's Palindrome Backup Director and Backup Exec are backup and restoration software packages for NetWare and Windows NT networks. They are fully NDS aware.

Symantec

Norton AntiVirus for NetWare, which uses NDS, allows you to configure a single server or a group of servers from a workstation for virus protection.

Summary

This chapter has introduced a number of NDS-aware and NDS-compliant software packages. In reality, we've only scratched the surface of the many utilities, tools, and applications that enthusiastic third-party developers have created to leverage the success of NDS. A more complete listing of companies is available in Appendix B. Information about others can be found on the CD that accompanies this book.

CHAPTER
17

NDS for Other Platforms

If NDS ran only on a NetWare platform, it would still be the most widely used directory service in the world. But Novell understands that there are other platforms for network services, other platforms that need directory services for security and authentication.

In the fall of 1999, Novell revamped their strategy for NDS running on non-NetWare platforms with the launch of NDS eDirectory and NDS Corporate Edition. NDS eDirectory is a stand-alone directory service running on multiple platforms. By adding NDS Corporate Edition, NDS replaces and/or synchronizes the native directory service on multiple non-NetWare platforms, including Windows NT, Solaris, Linux, Tru64 Unix and Windows 2000. Not affected by this change were the previously released NDS for AIX and NDS for OS/390, which were jointly developed by Novell and IBM. At the time this book went to press, Novell and IBM still had not decided which direction NDS on IBM platforms would take.

This chapter will look at each of these products, their similarities and differences, and their implementation methods.

NDS eDirectory

Novell eDirectory is, essentially, a stand-alone edition of NDS version 8. Novell has identified three major markets for the product: Internet service providers (ISPs), application service providers (ASPs), and independent software vendors (ISVs). Network administrators and enterprise networks are the target for NDS Corporate Edition.

eDirectory and ISPs

Internet service providers need to track lots of information about their customers. Names, account numbers, subscription start and end dates, credit card numbers, types of service, and many more factors are involved. Each of these factors, though, can be reduced to just another directory object or attribute, and that's where Novell hopes to have the edge over the myriad of solutions in use before the release of eDirectory.

As a sweetener, Novell also released the new Novell Internet Messaging System (NIMS), an electronic mail platform designed for ISPs and based on eDirectory. Those who buy NIMS get eDirectory "thrown in" at no charge. Since NIMS supports all major mail access protocols (SMTP, POP3, IMAP4) and can be accessed by most major mail clients—GroupWise, Exchange, Outlook, Notes and more—as well as through a Web browser interface, it's an enticing package for those providing subscription-based access to the Internet.

eDirectory and ASPs

Application service providers need to, if possible, track users even more closely than ISPs. Using eDirectory, they can do that as well as store user preferences within the directory. This gives those ASPs using the system a decided advantage over ASPs who choose to store user preferences on the user's computer. Using eDirectory, the ASP can allow the user access from any network-connected computer, and always present the application customized for that user.

eDirectory and ISVs

In a bold move, Novell offered free copies of eDirectory to software vendors who could redistribute it with their directory-enabled applications. This is the same model Novell used for Btrieve distribution, and it went a long way toward making Btrieve the ubiquitous database system it is today.

eDirectory Functionality

The directory in eDirectory is identical to that which ships with Netware 5.1. The only difference is that some utilities and some schema objects that are only relevant to an enterprise network (such as printing, for example) are not included.

The schema could be easily extended to include these, of course, while the utilities shipped with NetWare (or with NDS Corporate Edition) would work as well with eDirectory. Everything in this book, with those few exceptions, is just as relevant to eDirectory as it is to Netware-based NDS.

eDirectory will not, however, replace the network directory service you're currently using. If that's what you want to do, you'll need NDS Corporate Edition.

NDS Corporate Edition

Novell took the success of NDS for Windows NT along with the anticipated success of NDS for Solaris and scrapped the brand names in favor of NDS Corporate Edition (NDS-CE). Additional platforms—including Windows 2000, Linux, and Tru64 Unix—are planned for NDS-CE with others being evaluated.

NDS-CE replaces the directory service on a given platform by redirecting all access to NDS. While this varies slightly by platform, the user interface, utilities, and methods are as close to being identical from platform to platform as the underlying operating system allows.

The following sections look at the implementation of NDS Corporate Edition for Windows NT and Solaris.

NDS Corporate Edition for Windows NT

NDS-CE for Windows NT allows a network manager to manage Windows NT domains as part of a directory tree. NDS-CE for NT provides single login and a single point of administration for the entire Windows NT network, while still allowing a network manager to use the User Manager for Domains utility or NWAdmin as the primary tool for administering users. In addition, NDS-CE for NT is accessible by Internet protocols such as the Lightweight Directory Access Protocol (LDAP) and the Hypertext Transfer Protocol (HTTP), allowing it to be adapted for use with intranets, the Internet, and extranets.

Windows Domain Management

The management of domains, which were developed for workgroups, is extremely complex. Domains can be managed through several domain models that require trust relationships to establish the administrative and communication links among them. These trust relationships may be as simple as a one-way link between two domains or as complex as two-way trust relationships between each of 300 domains.

If you wish to be able to manage a Windows NT Internetwork as you would a NetWare network, so that each user has potential access to all the resources on the Internetwork, you need to establish two-way trust between each and every one of the NT domains. Or if you wish to manage the Internetwork as a single entity rather than as 50 separate domains, you need to create trust relationships. For example, consider that you have a modest-sized network of 50 Windows NT domain controllers. To manage each of the 50 servers as a single network with a single login and a single administration tool, you need to create 50×49, or 2,450, separate trust relationships, hardly an easy task.

How NDS-CE for NT Works

NDS-CE for NT consists of a single DLL that redirects information from Windows NT domains into the NDS tree. In Windows NT, information is sent from the SAMLIB.DLL file to the SAMSRV.DLL file via remote procedure calls. The SAMSRV.DLL accesses the Security Accounts Manager (SAM), the repository of domain information.

NDS-CE for NT replaces the SAMSRV.DLL with an enhanced version that also directs information to NDS. Domains are treated as group objects—they contain information about the domain as well as information about individual users. Network managers can assign users to domains without regard to their position in the NDS tree. They only need to create a single-user object and assign it to multiple domains without having to establish trust relationships.

When NDS-CE for NT is installed, all passwords can be migrated. No changes to client workstations are required. Only machines acting as Primary (PDC) or Backup Domain Controllers (BDCs) are affected. Because it uses Microsoft APIs, NDS-CE for NT allows Windows NT to use NDS for NT services such as Microsoft Exchange, Systems Management Server, SQL Server, or any other NT Service that uses the domain model.

NDS Corporate Edition for Solaris

NDS for Sun's Solaris operating system is similar in structure to NDS for Windows NT, replacing Solaris' traditional authentication methods. Any Unix application running on Solaris that takes advantage of the operating system security is automatically integrated with NDS security, enabling a single password to network resources and applications.

Solaris' Authentication and Security

User accounts in the UNIX operating system have been traditionally managed using etc/passwd, etc/group, and other local system files. This is fine for a small organization with a small number of servers, but is not scalable for organizations that have hundreds of UNIX workstations and servers distributed throughout their organization.

Sun Microsystems, Inc. provided a solution called NIS, which allows the user, group, and other per-server databases to be stored in a master server and replicated to other servers in the organization. Though NIS is available for most flavors of UNIX, it is difficult to administer. The network administrator has to create and modify user accounts on a single server only (similar to Windows NT's Primary Domain Controller) and use NIS tools to reflect the change to all the other servers. NIS uses a flat database that is not scalable for enterprise-wide deployment. It is also difficult to administer because all the administration is centralized.

The improved version of NIS, called NIS+, replicates the servers incrementally and has a hierarchical name space that improves flexibility. But it continues to retain the master-slave replication architecture, which is difficult to administer. NIS+ is not as widely deployed as NIS.

How NDS-CE for Solaris Works

NDS-CE for Solaris installs a Read/Write replica of NDS on the Solaris server. This local replica on the Solaris server is indistinguishable from, and is administered exactly like the replicas on, a NetWare server.

Each Solaris system is then reconfigured (automatically) to use NDS for authentication and to access user account information. A Pluggable Authentication Module (PAM) provider intercepts the system entry requests to authenticate the users and redirects them to NDS. A Name Service Switch (NSS) provider is deployed to intercept all database accesses and redirect them to NDS. The PAM and NSS replace those used by Solaris' native NIS or NIS+ systems.

The pam_nds and nss_nds modules use the Directory Client (DClient) to access information from the NDS database. The DClient finds the nearest NDS server and sends the requests to this server. If the NDS replica is locally installed on Solaris, the DClient requests will be resolved locally and will not have to travel on the wire.

NDS-CE for Solaris extends the NDS schema to include the Solaris user and group attributes. Because NDS is an organization-wide repository, Solaris accounts can be administered like any other NDS object using NetWare Administrator.

A tool is provided for easy migration to NDS of existing Solaris users in the /etc/passwd, NIS, and NIS+ databases. This helps administrators to move existing user accounts on Solaris systems to NDS. The administrator can control the NetWare semantics to be adopted for the Solaris user accounts that are migrated to NDS. The password of the user account is also migrated.

NDS for AIX and S/390

Novell and IBM have partnered to create an NDS solution for IBM's mainframe and mid-range operating systems. This is, however, based on NDS version 7—not on eDirectory (a.k.a. NDS version 8). While Novell is hoping to talk IBM into porting eDirectory to the AIXC and s/390 platforms, no agreement had been reached as we went to press.

NDS for AIX is similar in structure and design to NDS for Solaris or NDS for Linux, replacing the Unix-based security and authentication services of the IBM OS while enabling full control of a mixed network of NetWare and AIX hosts from Novell's NWADMIN utility.

NDS for S/390, officially called Novell Network Services for OS/390, is an integrated part of the OS/390 Security Server and can be chosen at any time to become the authentication and security provider for the operating system. Enterprises with S/390 systems and NetWare enterprise networks gain all of the S/390 reliability and scalability benefits by placing NDS replicas on the IBM hosts and administering all users and objects from the NetWare platform.

Summary

In this chapter you've learned that NDS is the directory of choice for the majority of network users around the world. NDS is available, of course, on NetWare but also on most major UNIX platforms as well for Windows NT domains.

CHAPTER

18

The Future of NDS

 started this book (back in Chapter 1) using a telephone book as an example of a directory. It's an easy-to-understand metaphor, so much so that many people today define directory services as a sophisticated phone book for the network. I hope that this book has shown that directory services in general, and NDS in particular, are far more than that.

Today's heterogeneous networks include client computers, file-, application-, and communication-servers, gateways, hubs, routers, and printers. They also include applications such as databases, Web servers, groupware, e-mail, and document management. Add the many people who use these resources from varying locations and you have a fairly complicated network, yet NDS manages it all with ease.

Now consider all the devices that will be networked in the near future, such as copy machines, fax machines, PBXs, security systems, heating and air conditioning systems, and cellular phones. These resources will need to be accessible from anywhere in a totally connected global network. Fortunately, NDS will be ready.

In this chapter, I want to look into the future and see what Novell has planned for NDS. Additionally, I'd like to go out on a limb (Look! A tree joke!) and speculate about other possibilities.

Novell's Goals for NDS

In 1997 Novell published a road map for NDS services to be rolled out over the following few years. A quick list of Novell's goals related to NDS were:

- Short Term (1 year)

  - Establish NDS as the industry *de facto* standard for network directory services.

- Integrate all the layers of the network through standards integration, partnerships, and internal development.

- Long Term (3–5 years)

    - Build a NetWare-sized business on NDS-based services.

    - Make NDS integration part of the decision criteria when deciding whether to buy network applications.

    - Be the leader in directory standards definition.

The 1-year goals, established in mid-1997, have already been met. The 3–5 year goals are well on their way to completion. While the goals are stated in rather general terms, there is also a plan in place to accomplish them. Novell is using aggressive and straightforward tactics to achieve these goals.

First, all of Novell's product line has been integrated with NDS (see Chapter 15). Novell has also provided development programs and tools for the entire industry. Equally important is the use of standards and industry partnerships.

Novell has a number of different subscription plans for developers, including a free online service. If you're interested in developing software to work with NDS, point your browser to `http://developer.novell.com/brochure/`.

Implementing Novell's Goals Using Standards

Novell has recognized that one of the major drawbacks to NetWare over the years was its proprietary nature. Having learned their lesson, Novell has developed NDS with standards in mind because standards help to make development happen more quickly and increase the likelihood that products will be accepted by industry.

Enhancing Standards

When published standards fall short, Novell has committed to enhancing the standards and working to get industry adoption of the specifications. NDS use of LDAP and RADIUS are a good example of this.

Creating Standards

Where a need for a standard exists but there are no standards, Novell has committed to working cooperatively to create one for the industry. The Java Naming Directory Interface (JNDI), originally spearheaded by Novell and adopted by the industry and SunSoft, offers one good example. Another is the unprecedented industry grouping called DSML.ORG.

DSML.ORG   In June 1999, Novell joined with every major directory service vendor—including Microsoft, IBM and Netscape—to endorse and energize a new standard for the exchange of directory information. XML (extensible Markup Language) is quickly becoming the de facto standard for Web page design because of its ease of use and—as the name implies—extensibility. DSML (Directory Services Markup Language) is planned as a subset of XML focused on directory services. Going far beyond LDAP, DSML will allow the exchange of information among directories and applications—including legacy applications—with little or no additional programming needed. From this, Novell will develop a product (due in late 2000) called DirXML.

DirXML   While NDS for Windows NT, NDS for Solaris, NDS for Linux and NDS for AIX/System 390 have all been very successful products (see Chapter 17), Novell recognizes that developing interfaces for every possible operating system and application is far too labor (and dollar) intensive to be worthwhile. Using DSML, however, Novell will create a new product that will interact with and synchronize with other directory services and applications.

DirXML will be a virtual depository for directory information. That is, rather than store objects within NDS which are imported from other systems, only pointers to the information will be stored. Thus, administrators of the other systems continue to work as they always have done, while NDS administrators and applications always have the latest, most up-to-date information available within the directory.

Implementing Novell's Goals Using Partnerships

Where it is impossible to implement a standard, Novell has promised to work toward industry adoption through contractual partnerships and to become the *de facto* standard. The many UNIX OS vendors integrating, distributing, and supporting NDS testify to the great success Novell is having with partnerships. If there are great business opportunities but partnerships are not yet possible, Novell will build the solution better and faster than the competition, as NDS for NT has shown.

Future Novell Products

Novell has already outlined some possible future uses for NDS to be developed either in-house or in partnerships with other companies. Some aspects of these future products have been released (although the full product range has not yet been implemented).

NDS, Intranets, and the Internet

One possible implementation is using NDS to automatically publish timely information to the local intranet or the Internet to keep vendors, customers, suppliers, and sales representatives up to date with current organizational information.

Using the existing NetWare Web Server, NDS objects and information can be accessed via any standard Web browser. For example, a selective list of attributes and useful information about employees could be published directly to the Internet as part of a company Web site directly from NDS without having to use an HTML editor. Any modifications to NDS objects or attributes would automatically update the published Web pages. Deleting a user from the directory would automatically remove all information about him or her.

Not far behind Web publishing comes the management of other traditional and nontraditional network objects, such as IP management with Domain Name Service (DNS), Dynamic Host Configuration Protocol (DHCP), and Lightweight Directory Access Protocol (LDAP). Much of this functionality will come with the next release of Novell's ManageWise network management platform as well as with the release of NetWare 5.1 in early 2000.

NDS and Your Daily Life

What about using the directory interface through a television to monitor a security system, lights, and thermostat in a vacation home? Or how about starting or monitoring a car through a wireless connection?

The capability to manage and organize these devices is already part of the directory structure of NDS. Currently, there are over 45,000 independent NDS developers creating directory-enabled applications. Novell believes the application space for directory browsers and management applications is fast becoming filled—if it is not already filled. Vendors will need to make innovative use of the directory to differentiate their products from others in the marketplace.

A Future Scenario

Imagine if you will...

It's 7 a.m. on Monday morning, and you awake to a loudly ringing alarm (or music, or a voice telling you it's time to get up). Wandering into the kitchen, you pour a cup of coffee (it's set to brew so that it's just ready as you walk in) and head over to the computer.

You enter your password, watch as you're connected to "the network" in a few seconds, then start scanning the newspaper, which is delivered on screen. Since it's Monday, the first thing you want to see are the previous day's National Football League scores—so the sports section is presented first. As you cycle through the pages on screen, the sections are presented in the order that you've indicated earlier you prefer to view them.

Now click the shower icon and head into the bathroom. You can simply climb into the shower because you know the water temperature is set to the exact temperature you prefer (rather cooler than your spouse's preference).

You might want to check your calendar for the day before getting dressed. (You do dress differently for meetings than for pulling cable, don't you?)

With the temperature outside running around 18 degrees (the display is right there on your monitor), you press a few buttons to start your car and warm it up. Once the heater is working, an alarm sounds to tell you the car is ready.

After getting into your toasty warm car, you log in to the dashboard terminal and answer "yes" when it asks if you'll be going directly to work. (It knows that's where you normally go at this time on Monday).

You're then greeted with an alert pointing out that due to a 12-car pileup, the freeway is closed. Fortunately, the terminal can also pull up an alternate route that—although a bit longer—will get you to the office at a reasonable time. Once you accept this, an e-mail is automatically sent to everyone you had scheduled an 8:00 a.m. meeting with, telling them it's postponed until 9:30 a.m. (The scheduling application determined that this was the next available time for everyone involved.)

When you get to the meeting, you log in to the computer in the meeting room and (in a few seconds) your presentation is being shown on the large flat-screen monitor mounted on the wall. Your prerecorded comments are playing through the speaker system, and are synchronized perfectly with the slide show. When other people at the meeting ask questions at the end of the presentation, you quickly supply answers based on the supporting documentation available to you on the computer.

Later in the day, you're reminded (by that same scheduler) that you should send your mother a birthday present. You're presented (on screen) a catalog of stores whose products your mother likes. You pick a store, then decide that a sweater would be nice. You're presented with a list (and pictures) of sweaters that are a blend of silk and cashmere in various shades of blue (your mother's preferences). Picking one, you type in instructions for the sale: bill to your Visa card, ship to your mother, enclose a card saying "Happy Birthday." No need to enter the details; they're already on file.

You finally finish the proposal you've been working on for two weeks and forward it to your boss for approval (using an "urgent" message, of course!). Twenty minutes later, you get the approval you need (digitally signed by your boss) and publish the proposal, which is quickly replicated to all of the necessary servers on your global network. Interested managers are immediately notified that it's available for them to read.

Oops! There's another flashing alert on your screen and an alarm is ringing! There's a problem with a server in the Chicago office. It has shut down! Fortunately, the other servers in its cluster take over the user load, but you need to have someone look at it right away.

Searching the directory for hardware technicians in Chicago who are working this afternoon, you see one name pop up. You click on the telephone number and hear your phone start dialing. Uh-oh. The technician is away from his desk, but his local telephony server reroutes the call to his beeper, putting in your phone number. In a few minutes, he calls back to inform you that the problem has already been fixed, because the network management application also notified him (as the technician on duty) when the hardware trouble began.

It's almost time to go home, but first you need to pick up some things at the grocery store. Click a few buttons on your computer to order milk, orange juice, bananas, shampoo, and laundry detergent. Once again, no need to enter any additional information—your brand and size preferences are already known. Indicate on the order that you'll pick them up in 20 minutes, and you're ready to leave the office.

You drive to the pickup window at the grocery store and log in to the terminal. In seconds, your order is delivered to you.

Arriving home, you find that the lights are on and the television is showing your favorite program. There's a small icon blinking on the TV screen indicating that there's an urgent message for you. When you log in to the computer again, you find there's e-mail from your brother-in-law. Your sister had the baby (a girl!) who looks big and beautiful (she's got red hair!) as you can tell from the enclosed picture. Better send some flowers!

How Did They Do That?

All of the activities described in the preceding section can be done today with existing technologies. The only "futuristic" part of the scenario is the connectivity between the activities. That connectivity requires a directory service: one which is global in scope and which contains information about you, your friends and relatives, and the many objects in your life. (These are objects like your car, your television, your coffee maker, etc.)

That directory also needs to have the capability to interact with your schedule, your e-mail, and all the other computer applications you may use throughout the day. It further needs to know about computers, hosts, and networks that contain information relevant to you: the news, global positioning, traffic reports, shopping services, and the like.

The directory needs to support a high degree of security (look at all of those financial transactions) and authentication. At the same time, it needs to do this with the benefit of a single signon—you really don't want to enter a password every time you interact with a computer application.

A Global Directory?

We don't foresee a single tree holding information about every person and every object in the world. While Novell has demonstrated a very large-scale tree (see the sidebar, *The Two-Million-User Tree*), it wouldn't be efficient to put the entire world in one tree. With NDS version 8, Novell has demonstrated a tree with over one billion objects, but that's still not enough to hold the entire world.

What is possible, though, is to have multiple private directories linked to one or more public directories through an NDS technology called *DirXML*. DirXML allows an administrator to expose parts of a local, private directory to a different, public directory. Someone accessing the public directory sees only one tree, consisting of the public objects and those exposed from the private directories.

The Two-Million-User Tree

Novell engineers built a two-million-user NDS tree to show the incredible extent to which the Novell directory is scalable. While few enterprises would ever need a directory tree of this size, Novell engineers felt that it was important to let current and potential customers know that no matter how large their directory needs might be, NDS could handle them—and could do so with ease.

The idea of building a two-million-user NDS tree originated with a large Novell customer who wanted to know if NDS would scale to 300,000 potential user accounts in a single directory tree. Novell engineers decided to up the ante by building a fully functional million-user NDS tree, which later evolved into a two-million-user tree.

The objectives required that the network design have the following characteristics:

- Be IP-based, to accommodate the latest Internet/intranet technologies

- Be composed of server and network hardware widely used in enterprises today

- Have all shipping server and NDS code—no beta or special products or patches

- Meet standard NDS design guidelines as defined by Novell Consulting Services

- Require no "tweaking" of either NDS or server parameters

- Be highly fault tolerant to network and server outages

The million-user NDS tree was up and fully functional in three days.

The Novell engineers created the one million user accounts in approximately 25 hours using eight Pentium Pro 200 MHz machines. They then synchronized the one million users' accounts to 16 additional servers (three replicas per partition) over the course of 11 hours.

During the directory synchronization process, the 100 MBps Ethernet network utilization never exceeded 2 percent. Each of the eight primary NDS servers held 125,000 user accounts. The NDS database files on each server were approximately 320MB. The NDS design required less than two hours of planning to achieve both a scalable and a fault-tolerant NDS design for one million users.

After gathering the necessary information for the million-user tree, Novell engineers added one million more user accounts, bringing the total user accounts to two million. Each of the eight primary NDS servers now held 250,000 user accounts. The NDS database files on each server were approximately 640MB. In terms of replication, synchronization, managing the directory, and login speed, NDS performance was on par with the million-user tree.

What do you do with a two-million-user NDS tree? Unless you have two million users, not much. However, on all networks large and small, users log in and log out, servers are brought up and down, and administrators manage the users and resources. The two million-user tree proved that these "real-world" operations can be undertaken with just as much confidence on a huge global network as they can on smaller installations.

What Needs to Be Done?

As I said, all of the technologies for the scenario described earlier already exist. NDS can be scaled and trees can be federated to encompass huge amounts of data. Through the use of protocols such as LDAP, older legacy systems and otherwise inaccessible proprietary systems can be "persuaded" to expose and export the necessary data that they contain.

What is needed are interfaces to the objects (lights, automobiles, and appliances) and applications which are NDS-enabled. Novell is working toward this through the mechanisms outlined in the first part of this chapter, but there are many opportunities for others to jump right in and provide the applications and interfaces necessary. Novell has provided all the tools needed for these developments; all that is required is the inspiration to create world-class software.

What Can You Do?

As a network administrator, information systems manager, corporate executive, or network user, there is a way that you can help to bring about the scenario I've described. Simply insist on NDS and NDS-enabled applications for all your computing needs. I believe that NDS—and only NDS—is the path to this future. It must be. Why else would I have spent a year writing this book?

Summary

This chapter has presented the future of NDS based on the road map Novell has drawn and the authors' vision of an NDS-enabled world.

Most information technology futurists, pundits, gurus, and gadflies agree that directory services is the single most important factor in bringing the world together online. Populating the directory with all of the people and objects worldwide won't happen overnight. It won't happen this century. But soon, very soon in historical time, the changes will occur. I believe that NDS will be the directory service of choice to provide this connectivity.

CHAPTER

19

Programming for NDS

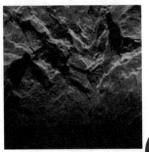

One of the key benefits of using NDS in your environment is its extensibility. Earlier in this book, we have discussed schema extensions and tools for extracting information from NDS. The most powerful tool of all, however, is a programmer. Tools are available to program NDS in a number of environments, including:

- C
- Java
- Delphi
- ActiveX components
- Open Database Connectivity (ODBC)
- Novell Script
- NetBasic

In this chapter, we will look at these different environments and provide a foundation for learning to program NDS.

NDS Programming Concepts

Before diving into the different environments available for programming NDS, there are some basic concepts you need to understand about how programs interact with NDS. Visual Basic, for example, hides much of the complexity of programming NDS. Conversely, when programming in C, these concepts are not hidden, increasing the complexity of programming for

NDS—and at the same time providing much more flexibility. Even when programming in the easiest environments, though, it is important to understand how things work in order to more effectively diagnose problems in your code. We will discuss these requirements based on the C development environment, as all of these concepts are exposed through that development environment.

Request and Reply Buffers

NDS communications between a client program and the server are handled through a buffer. In general, when your program requests an NDS operation, a *request buffer* is created and sent off to the server. The server then replies with a *reply buffer* containing the results of the operation requested. For example, when you use NLIST to request the value of a user's full name, NLIST creates a request buffer containing the request for the full name and sends the request to the server. The server processes the request and then replies with a buffer containing information that includes the requested information.

If you ever worked with NetWare 2.*x* or NetWare 3.*x* bindery programming, you will know that this is very similar to how bindery requests were handled. At the lowest levels, NDS uses a similar structure to the bindery request/reply formats.

Fortunately, this is all mostly hidden in each of the environments we will talk about later. Understanding how the buffers are built, though, is important when trying to figure out what went wrong with a function call.

Memory Management

Memory management is significant with many NDS calls in the C portion of the Novell Developer Kit. In many cases, you could allocate a static character array, but to provide more flexibility in your program, you will want to dynamically allocate and free memory instead. Even in the simplest of programs, it works out better if you learn to allocate memory dynamically rather than statically.

For many C programmers, this may represent a change in thinking. While the functions to dynamically allocate memory are in the standard

C libraries, many C programmers prefer to allocate static chunks of memory in the variable declaration section of their code, rather than allocating it on the fly. Part of the reason many programmers use static arrays is because you need to remember to free the memory when you've finished with it; otherwise, your program will likely develop a "memory leak."

Because memory management can make your program more complex, it is important to plan your development accordingly. If you have to pass information between functions, make certain that you remember where the memory was allocated and where you need to free it. If you call a function recursively, keep in mind that if you allocate memory in the recursive part of the program, it will all need to be freed at some point.

In this same vein, the Novell Developer Kit libraries for NDS are written to the *large* memory model. When programming in C, you must specify at least this memory model. Using a tiny, small, or medium memory model will not work. This is partly because the RSA encryption library components are only available in the larger memory models.

Context Handles

When dealing with NDS function calls in C, a context handle is used to maintain information about the operation being used. The context handle contains the current context information for your operation, but also contains a number of flags that define how naming is presented and how your functions are executed.

Context handles contain a number of *keys* which are used to change aspects of the behavior of the context handle, and thus the behavior and formatting of information passed to the NDS function call. Table 19.1 shows the different keys that can be used when creating or modifying a context handle.

These keys are set in C using the functions NWDSCreateContextHandle() and NWDSSetContext(). When using the latter function, you must first get the context handle you wish to modify using NWDSGetContext().

In other languages, such as when using the ActiveX controls for Visual Basic, context handle management is not even part of the API set.

Each of the context handle keys has a number of flags associated with it to change the behavior of NDS function calls. Tables 19.2 through 19.9 describe the flags and other information each key uses and what they affect.

T A B L E 19.1	**Context Handle Key**	**Usage**
Context Handle Keys	DCK_FLAGS	Controls how name information is returned
	DCK_CONFIDENCE	Controls the replica type an NDS operation uses
	DCK_NAME_CONTEXT	Sets the current context
	DCK_LAST_CONNECTION	Contains the connection that processed the last request
	DCK_TREE_NAME	Contains the current tree name
	DCK_DSI_FLAGS	Determines the entry information returned about objects
	DCK_NAME_FORM	Used to select dot or slash name format
	DCK_NAME_CACHE_DEPTH	Used to improve performance of resolve name operations

T A B L E 19.2	**Key**	**Meaning When Set**
DCK_FLAGS	DCV_DEREF_ALIASES	Causes aliases to be dereferenced; return values will be of the aliased object rather than the alias itself.
	DCV_XLATE_STRINGS	Translate Unicode strings to the local codepage.
DCK_FLAGS	DCV_TYPELESS_NAMES	Return names without the type. For example, the name CN=Jim would be returned as simply Jim.

T A B L E 19.2 *(cont.)*	**Key**	**Meaning When Set**
	DCV_CANONICALIZE_NAMES	Return a fully distinguished name rather than a relative distinguished name.
	DCV_DEREF_BASE_CLASS	Return the base class of an object that has been aliased rather than the alias class itself.
	DCV_DISALLOW_REFERRALS	Force a server not to refer to another server to retrieve information. If a referral is needed and this flag is set, the call will fail.

T A B L E 19.3 DCK_CONFIDENCE	**Value**	**Meaning**
	DCV_LOW_CONF	Perform requested operation using any readable replica.
	DCV_MED_CONF	Perform requested operation using any writable replica.
	DCV_HIGH_CONF	Perform requested operation using the master replica only.

T A B L E 19.4 DCK_NAME_ CONTEXT	**Usage**
	Used to set the current context added to object names when the DCV_ CANONICALIZE_NAME flag is set.

T A B L E 19.5 DCK_LAST_ CONNECTION	**Usage**
	Used to retrieve the name of the server used for the last operation. The value of this key can change during a single request, depending on which servers are used to find the information requested.

T A B L E 19.6	**Usage**
DCK_TREE_NAME	Used to retrieve the name of the current tree. For an application that allows multiple tree authentication, multiple context handles should be used to control which tree is being used for the current operation.

T A B L E 19.7	**Flag**	**Meaning when set**
DCK_DSI_FLAGS	DSI_OUTPUT_FIELDS	ORed bitmask of the other DSI keys.
	DSI_ENTRY_ID	Returns the entry ID of the object on the server the operation was performed on.
	DSI_ENTRY_FLAGS	Returns information about the state of the object. See Table 30-xxx for more detail on this.
	DSI_MODIFICATION_TIME	Returns the modification time of the object in seconds since 12:00 A.M. 1/1/1970.
	DSI_MODIFICATION_TIMESTAMP	Returns the modification of the object in seconds since 12:00 A.M. 1/1/1970 as well as the replica number that the operation originated from and the even type for the most recent modification.
	DSI_REVISION_COUNT	Returns a count of the number of times the entry has been modified.
	DSI_CREATION_TIMESTAMP	Returns the timestamp for the object creation time in seconds from 12:00 A.M. 1/1/1970, as well as the replica number where the creation took place and the NDS event type for a creation event.

TABLE 19.7 *(cont.)*	Flag	Meaning when set
	DSI_BASE_CLASS	Returns the base class used to create the entry. This can be used to get the information on object classes more quickly than other methods.
	DSI_ENTRY_RDN	Returns the partial name (relative to the context handle's context) of the entry in the format specified by the keys DCK_NAME_FORM and DCK_FLAGS. If these flags are not changed from the defaults, the format is a typeless dotted format.
	DSI_ENTRY_DN	Returns the full distinguished name of the entry in the format specified by the keys DCK_NAME_FORM and DCK_FLAGS. If these flags are not changed from the defaults, the format is a typeless dotted format.
	DSI_PARENT_ID	Returns the entry ID of the object's parent object in the database on the server the operation is performed on.
	DSI_PARENT_DN	Returns the full distinguished name of the object's parent object.
	DSI_DEREFERENCE_BASE_CLASS	Returns the base class of an object referenced by an alias if the DCV_DEREF_BASE_CLASS flag is set.
	DSI_SUBORDINATE_COUNT	Returns the number of objects that are subordinate to the object.

T A B L E 19.7 *(cont.)*	**Flag**	**Meaning when set**
	DSI_PARTITION_ROOT_ID	Returns the entry ID of the root object in the partition the object is in. This entry ID is for the database on the server the operation took place on.
	DSI_PARTITION_ROOT_DN	Returns the full, distinguished name of the partition root object for the object.
	DSI_PURGE_TIME	Returns the oldest purge time for a partition object. The time is returned in seconds from 12:00 A.M. 1/1/1970.
	DSI_REPLICA_TYPE	Returns the replica type used for the most recent operation.
	DSI_REPLICA_NUMBER	Returns the replica number used for the most recent operation.
	DSI_REPLICA_STATE	Returns the state of the current replica.

T A B L E 19.8 DCK_NAME_FORM	**Flag**	**Meaning**
	DCV_NF_PARTIAL_DOT	Use dotted notation and relative names. For example, Jim.IT.B123A.
	DCV_NF_FULL_DOT	Use dotted notation and full distinguished names. For example, Jim.IT.B123A.MSP.XYZCorp.
	DCV_NF_SLASH	Use slash name format. Slash name format can only use full, distinguished names. For example, \TEST_TREE\XYZ-Corp\MSP\B123A\IT\Jim.

T A B L E 19.9	**Usage**
DCK_NAME_ CACHE_DEPTH	Used to set the number of entries cached for resolve name requests

Unicode

The last concept we will cover is the use of *Unicode* character sets. As discussed earlier, NDS stores its string information in a two-byte character set called Unicode. This allows NDS to store string information for languages that use special accented characters, letters specific to the alphabet, or even complex information such as Kanji or traditional Chinese characters. Because Unicode is a two-byte string format, you need to convert localized strings into Unicode format for storage in NDS, even if you use English as the primary language your program is used in.

Because of the Unicode requirement, any program that manipulates or reads NDS information must initialize the Unicode tables and also must have the local codepage files available.

From a C programming standpoint, this means calling the NWCallsInit() function, which does a number of things, including initializing the Unicode tables.

Newer versions of the Novell Developer Kit (NDK) include the ability to automatically translate the Unicode data into the local codepage; this is done through the context handle, using the key DCK_FLAGS to set the DCV_XLATE_STRINGS flag. With the latest NDK, this is the default behavior when creating a context handle with the NWDSCreateContextHandle() function call.

In Visual Basic, since you do not have to create the context handle, the default setting is used to translate strings to the local codepage.

The second part of making sure this works is that you have the Unicode files located in a directory where the application can find them; typically, this is in the NLS subdirectory under the directory where the application's executable file is found. For example, if your program file is located in C:\NDK\SOURCE, you must have a copy of the Unicode files in C:\NDK\SOURCE\NLS.

Iteration Handles

Because information stored in NDS is virtually unlimited in size, there has to be a way to retrieve information that is larger than the size of the buffer it is retrieved to. For this purpose, Novell included the concept of an *iteration handle* in NDS programming. An iteration handle allows you to control the information retrieved and restructure the entire buffer based on the fragments received. Another use for iteration handles is to allow you to abort particularly long operations if the amount of information retrieved is larger than the maximum buffer that can be allocated.

Use iteration handles to prevent problems with reading too much information at a time. In some cases, getting a class definition can result in a –649 error because the largest buffer available is not large enough to handle the size of a class definition.

Task-Oriented Programming in C

There are three basic operations that are central to nearly all NDS programming: reading information from NDS, searching for information in NDS, and writing information to NDS. In addition, there are two additional operations that unlock the power of programming for NDS: manipulating the schema and manipulating objects.

In this section, we will look at each of these five tasks using the C programming language. For these tasks, the operations are similar in C to the implementation in other languages. As discussed earlier, using C provides the greatest flexibility in implementation, but it also increases the complexity of the program somewhat because the APIs do very little of the work.

Reading Information from NDS

Reading information from NDS is a relatively simple matter. Once you have initialized the buffer, context handle, and iteration handle, you make a call to read the requested information. Once the information is read from NDS, you then process the reply buffer to retrieve the attribute information you requested.

The following code fragment provides a sample for retrieving the Last Name attribute for the specified user:

```
ccode = NWDSAllocBuf(DEFAULT_MESSAGE_LEN, &attrNames);
if (ccode < 0)
{
     printf("NWDSAllocBuf returned: %04X\n", ccode);
     return ccode;
}
ccode = NWDSInitBuf(dContext, DSV_READ, attrNames);
if (ccode < 0)
{
  printf("NWDSInitBuf returned %04X\n", ccode);
  NWDSFreebuf(attrNames);
  return ccode;
}
ccode = NWDSPutAttrName(dContext, attrNames, "Surname");

if (ccode < 0)
{
  printf("NWDSPutAttrName returned: %04X\n", ccode);
  NWDSFreebuf(attrNames);
  return ccode;
}

ccode = NWDSAllocBuf(DEFAULT_MESSAGE_LEN, &outBuf);

if (ccode < 0)
{
  printf("NWDSAllocBuf returned: %04X\n", ccode);
  NWDSFreebuf(attrNames);
  return ccode;
}

do
{
  ccode = NWDSRead(dContext, objectName, DS_ATTRIBUTE_
VALUES, FALSE, attrNames, &iterHandle, outBuf);
```

```
  if (ccode < 0)
  {
    printf("\nNWDSRead returned: %04X\n", ccode);
    NWDSFreebuf(attrNames);
    NWDSFreebuf(outBuf);
    return 1;
  }
}while(iterHandle != -1L);
```

This sample code reads the attribute value for the *Surname* attribute, which is the attribute name that stores the last name for a user.

Once the buffer is read using the NWDSRead function, we haven't actually manipulated the output yet. We read each buffer in the end of this code fragment, but we do nothing with the results.

To process the results, the last "do" loop can be changed to actually process the results returned from the buffer. This change could look like this:

```
do
{
  ccode = NWDSRead(dContext, objectName, DS_ATTRIBUTE_
VALUES, FALSE, attrNames, &iterHandle, &outBuf);

  if (ccode < 0)
  {
    printf("\nNWDSRead returned: %04X\n", ccode);
    NWDSFreebuf(attrNames);
    NWDSFreebuf(outBuf);
    return 1;
  }

  ccode = NWDSGetAttrCount(dContext, buf, &attrCount);

  if (ccode < 0)
  {
    printf("\nNWDSGetAttrCount returned: %04X\n", ccode);
    return ccode;
  }
```

```
    for (i = 0; i < attrCount; i++)
    {
    ccode = NWDSGetAttrName(dContext, buf, attrName,
&valCount, &syntax);

      if (ccode < 0)
      {
        printf("\nNWDSGetAttrName returned: %04X\n", ccode);
        return ccode;
      }

      printf("\nAttribute Name : %s", attrName);
      printf("\nAttribute Value(s):\n");

      for (j = 0; j < valCount; j++)
      {
        ccode = NWDSComputeAttrValSize(dContext, buf, syntax,
         &attrValSize);

        attrVal = (void *)farmalloc(attrValSize);

        ccode = NWDSGetAttrVal(dContext, buf, syntax, attrVal);

        if (ccode < 0)
        {
          printf("\nNWDSGetAttrVal returned: %04X\n", ccode);
          return ccode;
        }

        printf("%s\n ", attrVal);

        free(attrVal);
      }

  }while(iterHandle != -1L);
```

The code added above is fairly generic, and should work in many cases. This code would result in the output:

```
Attribute Name:  Surname
Attribute Value(s):  Jones
```

Searching for Information in NDS

Frequently when looking for information to read, a search is required to locate objects that meet a certain criteria. For example, you might want to search for users who have the value "Jones" in the *Surname* attribute.

The function *NWDSSearch* is the function that is used to perform searches within NDS. Just as the NLIST command (discussed in Chapter 12) allows you to specify a number of things (including search criteria, how much of the tree to search, and the object class being searched for), the NWDSSearch function also allows you to build a search buffer that contains the same type of information.

The NWDSSearch function uses a buffer that uses tokenized input to delimit the search parameters. Very complex searches can be built, if you have the patience to build the buffer the way it needs to be built.

Building the buffer for our search would involve the following code:

```
ccode = NWDSAllocBuf(DEFAULT_MESSAGE_LEN, &searchFilter);

if (ccode < 0)
{
  printf("NWDSAllocBuf returned: %04X\n", ccode);
  goto ExitFunction;
}


ccode = NWDSInitBuf(dContext, DSV_SEARCH_FILTER, searchFilter);

if (ccode < 0)
{
  printf("NWDSInitBuf returned: %04X\n", ccode);
  goto ExitFunction;
}
```

```
ccode = NWDSAllocFilter(&cur);

if (ccode < 0)
{
  printf("NWDSAllocFilter returned: %04X\n", ccode);
  goto ExitFunction;
}

/* Object Class = User */

ccode = NWDSAddFilterToken(cur, FTOK_ANAME, "Object Class", SYN_CLASS_NAME);

if (ccode < 0)
{
  printf("NWDSAddFilterToken returned: %04X\n", ccode);
  goto ExitFunction;
}

ccode = NWDSAddFilterToken(cur, FTOK_EQ, NULL, 0);

if (ccode < 0)
{
  printf("NWDSAddFilterToken returned: %04X\n", ccode);
  goto ExitFunction;
}

ccode = NWDSAddFilterToken(cur, FTOK_AVAL, "User", SYN_CLASS_NAME);

/* And */

if (ccode < 0)
{
  printf("NWDSAddFilterToken returned: %04X\n", ccode);
  goto ExitFunction;
}
```

```
ccode = NWDSAddFilterToken(cur, FTOK_AND, NULL, 0);

if (ccode < 0)
{
  printf("NWDSAddFilterToken returned: %04X\n", ccode);
  goto ExitFunction;
}

/* Surname = Jones */

ccode = NWDSAddFilterToken(cur, FTOK_ANAME, "Surame", SYN_CI_STRING);

if (ccode < 0)
{
  printf("NWDSAddFilterToken returned: %04X\n", ccode);
  goto ExitFunction;
}

ccode = NWDSAddFilterToken(cur, FTOK_EQ, NULL, 0);

if (ccode < 0)
{
  printf("NWDSAddFilterToken returned: %04X\n", ccode);
  goto ExitFunction;
}

ccode = NWDSAddFilterToken(cur, FTOK_AVAL, "Jones", SYN_CI_STRING);

if (ccode < 0)
{
  printf("NWDSAddFilterToken returned: %04X\n", ccode);
  goto ExitFunction;
}

/* End Expression */
```

```
ccode = NWDSAddFilterToken(cur, FTOK_END, NULL, 0);

if (ccode < 0)
{
  printf("NWDSAddFilterToken returned: %04X\n", ccode);
  goto ExitFunction;
}
```

Once the buffer is set up, then you can allocate a buffer for the results and call NWDSSearch to perform the search. The results are returned to the results buffer, which can then be processed the same way you would process a read command.

Writing Information to NDS

Writing values to attributes in NDS is referred to as a modification operation. The function called to make the change is NWDSModifyObject. As with the search operation, modification requires a bit of setup before the actual modification can take place.

The amount of setup required for modification of an attribute value is relatively small. As with the other operations, buffers need to be allocated. Supposing we wanted to modify the fax number for a user object, the relevant code would be as follows:

```
ccode = NWDSPutChange(dContext, inBuf, DS_ADD_VALUE, "Facsimile
Number");
if ( ccode < 0 )
{
  goto Freebuf;
}


ccode = NWDSPutAttrVal(dContext, inBuf, syntaxID, "801-555-1212");
if ( ccode < 0 )
{
  goto Freebuf;
}
```

```
ccode = NWDSModifyObject(dContext, objectName, NULL, 0, inBuf);

if ( ccode < 0 )
  printf("\nNWDSModifyObject returned %04X", ccode);
```

All that's needed with the NWDSModifyObject call, as seen in this code fragment, is that you put the modification information in the buffer with NWDSPutChange and then put the attribute value with NWDSPutAttrVal. Once these two steps are taken, you can commit the change with NWDS-ModifyObject and the change is made.

Schema Operations

Manipulation of the NDS schema is where the real power is in NDS programming. Through extensions to the schema, you can add new object types or attribute types to create new uses for the directory. While not everything benefits from being directory-enabled, there are things that derive significant benefit from being directory-enabled.

There are four functions that are useful for modifying the NDS schema:

- NWDSDefineAttr

- NWDSDefineClass

- NWDSRemoveAttrDef

- NWDSRemoveClassDef

Before we talk about these functions, however, we need to examine rules for modifying classes in NDS.

NDS classes can be added, but must be derived from another class type. Even if a new class has nothing in common with other classes (such as the Person or Device classes), it must always derive ultimately from the Top class. This class adds essential components to your object class in order to make the object a real class in NDS. The only class with no parent classes (or "super" classes) is Top itself.

A *base class* is a class that is defined in a default installation of NDS. The *User class* is an example of a base class. Base classes can have additional attributes added to them, but once those new attributes are associated with a base class, they cannot be removed.

Removal of a user-defined class can be done only after all objects of that class type have been deleted from the NDS tree. Similarly, an attribute definition can be removed only after it has not been associated with any classes in the tree. When removing NDS attributes, the classes must be deleted first—which is why extensions to base classes cannot be removed.

Modifications of the schema should be treated as if they are non-reversible, even though in many cases they can be removed from the tree. Consider a schema modification to be a major change in your environment and treat it accordingly. Use a test environment to test your extension before adding it to a production environment, especially if you are modifying a base class.

Creating new attributes involves the use of the Attr_Info_T structure, defined as follows:

```
typedef struct
{
  nuint32 attrFlags ;
  nint32 attrSyntaxID ;
  nint32 attrLower ;
  nint32 attrUpper ;
  Asn1ID_T asn1ID ;
} Attr_Info_T;
```

The different elements in the structure are used to define different properties of the attribute, as described in Table 19.10.

When creating a new attribute, all that is necessary is to fill in the attribute information structure and then call NWDSDefineAttr.

Similarly, when creating a new class, the structure Class_Info_T is filled in and then a call is made to NWDSDefineClass.

```
typedef struct
{
  nuint32 classFlags;
  Asn1ID_T asn1ID;
} Class_Info_T;
```

The Class_Info_T structure is defined in Table 19.11.

T A B L E 19.10 Attribute Information structure elements	**Element**	**Use**	**Example**
	attrFlags	Used to define properties of the attribute.	DS_SIZED_ATTR
	attrSyntaxID	The identifier for the type of data used.	SYN_CI_STRING
	attrLower	Lower bound for the attribute. With numeric syntaxes, this is a lower boundary; for strings, it is a minimum length.	2
	attrUpper	Upper bound for the attribute. With numeric syntaxes, this is an upper boundary; for strings, it is a maximum length.	50
	asn1ID	ASN.1 identifier for the attribute. In most cases, this structure is set to zero.	0

T A B L E 19.11 Class Information structure elements	**Element**	**Use**	**Example**
	classFlags	Used to define properties of the class.	DS_CONTAINER_CLASS
	asn1ID	ASN.1 identifier for the class. In most cases, this structure is set to zero.	0

Manipulating Objects

Object manipulation is the process of adding, deleting, renaming, or moving objects. NDS programming opens up the ability to customize these routine tasks in order to make your administrative environment more efficient.

Adding, deleting, renaming, and moving objects are tasks that most administrators perform on a daily basis. While the NetWare Administrator program allows you to use templates for customized creation of user objects, through programming for NDS you can customize these everyday tasks and free up additional time to take on other projects.

Imagine, for example, being able to customize the movement of large numbers of user objects from one location to another, automating the movement of the user object and updating attributes in the user to reflect a new server, home directory path, profile login script, or other attributes.

Or imagine being able to automatically check for users who have not logged in for a certain number of days, disable those accounts, update an attribute, and then automatically delete the user object if the account is no longer active.

Fortunately, the NDS API set includes calls for the object-level operations in these examples. We have already talked about updating attributes in the section *Writing Information to NDS*, but by combining these operations with additional operations, repetitive tasks that take days to complete can be completed in just a few minutes.

Adding Objects to NDS

Adding objects to NDS involves filling a buffer with a minimum of the mandatory attributes and object class, followed by calling the NWDSAddObject function. As with all NDS function calls, a context handle needs to be created and the current context should be set to the context the object is to be created in.

For example, the following code would create the user JimH in the container O=Home:

```
ccode = NWDSAllocBuf((size_t)DEFAULT_MESSAGE_LEN, &buffer);
if(ccode)
{
  printf("\nNWDSAllocBuf returned %04X", ccode);
  freecontext(context);
}
```

```
ccode = NWDSInitBuf(context, DSV_ADD_ENTRY, buffer);
if(ccode)
{
  printf("\nNWDSInitBuf returned %04X", ccode);
  freebuf(buffer, context);
}
ccode = NWDSPutAttrName(context, buffer, "Object Class");
if(ccode)
{
  printf("\nNWDSPutAttrName returned %04X", ccode);
  freebuf(buffer, context);
}
ccode = NWDSPutAttrVal(context, buffer, SYN_CLASS_NAME, "User");
if(ccode)
{
  printf("\nNWDSPutAttrVal returned %04X", ccode);
  freebuf(buffer, context);
}
ccode = NWDSPutAttrName(context, buffer, "Surname");
if(ccode)
{
  printf("\nNWDSPutAttrName returned %04X", ccode);
  freebuf(buffer, context);
}
ccode = NWDSPutAttrVal(context, buffer, SYN_CI_STRING,
"Henderson");
if(ccode)
{
  printf("\nNWDSPutAttrVal returned %04X", ccode);
  freebuf(buffer, context);
}
ccode = NWDSAddObject(context, ".JimH.Home", NULL, 0, buffer);
if(ccode)
{
  printf("\nNWDSAddObject returned %04X", ccode);
  printf("\nUnable to create user");
}
```

As with the search function, the buffer called `buffer` in this code fragment contains a type of tokenized information defining attribute values as well as the class name. If the buffer did not contain the mandatory attribute Surname, the creation would fail with an error −609.

Deleting Objects from NDS

Deleting objects from NDS is a relatively minor operation involving a call to the NWDSRemoveObject function. The NWDSRemoveObject function requires just a context handle and an object name relative to the context stored in the context handle.

Deleting objects is a non-reversible operation. You will want to be sure your program is coded properly to ensure it deletes the correct object, especially if you have objects in multiple contexts with the same name.

When deleting objects, it is normally considered a good idea to set the context to the context the object is in rather than using a relative distinguished name. Using an RDN requires that you know the target relative to the current context, and can lead to mistakes. By forcing the context in your context handle to be the context that the object is located in, you eliminate the ambiguity of trying to resolve a name to a context other than the current context.

If you want to preserve a context, use the NWDSDuplicateContextHandle to create a duplicate context handle that you can then change to the context of the object to be deleted.

Renaming and Moving Objects in NDS

Renaming and moving objects in NDS is also a matter of a single function call, once the context handle management is completed. There are three functions that can be used for renaming and moving objects. The functionality of these three functions is similar, with two of them allowing an object move and an object rename to happen within a single function call. Table 19.12 provides an overview of what each of these three functions can be used for.

T A B L E 19.12 Functions for renam- ing and/or moving objects	**Function**	**Used for**	**Limitations**
	NWDSModifyRDN	Rename	Used only for renaming objects
	NWDSModifyDN	Rename, Move	Requires the use of full DNs to operate
	NWDSMoveObject	Rename, Move	Unable to store the old object's name if used in a rename operation

The function NWDSModifyRDN is used to rename the object.

This function contains a total of four parameters. As with other NDS function calls, the first parameter is the context handle to be used for the operation. The second and third parameters are the old and new names of the object being renamed. The fourth is a *boolean* value used to determine whether the old name of the object is to be retained or not. If the name is retained, it is retained in another attribute.

The functions NWDSModifyDN and NWDSMoveObject are capable of both operations. The differences between these two functions are limited to how the source and destination are specified and whether the old name can be saved or not.

With the NWDSModifyDN function, the source and destination parameters specify the full DN of the source and destination names. This function is capable of saving the old object name if the naming attribute is a multi-valued attribute.

The NWDSMoveObject function uses an RDN for the source object, a DN for the destination container, and a third parameter to specify the new RDN for the object. This function does not allow you to save the old object name.

Programming in Languages Other than C

While this chapter has focused on programming in C, there are several other languages that you can use to program NDS. In this section, we will look at a number of these languages, including Java, Delphi, ActiveX components for Visual Basic and Active Server Pages, the NDS ODBC driver, Novell Script, and NetBasic.

Java

Java is the development environment Novell has been pushing towards since the release of NetWare 5 in September of 1998. NetWare 5 included the fastest Java Virtual Machine to date. Novell introduced the concept of *servlets* as server-based applications designed to perform specific functions. These servlets can be accessed through a Web page in much the way a Perl script would be.

Programming NDS in Java involves the use of the NDS Java Bean, which abstracts the X.500 naming intricacies from the programmer, allowing fairly rapid development of Java-based applications.

The Java Bean interface to the directory allows you to perform many NDS operations, including:

- Adding Objects

- Deleting Objects

- Filtering Objects

- Listing Objects

- Manipulating the NDS Schema

Java development is rapidly becoming a preferred development environment because of the cross-platform portability of Java code.

Delphi

For rapid development, Delphi is a very popular environment as well. The Novell Developer Kit includes primitives for Delphi equivalent to the C functionality, allowing Delphi developers to leverage their knowledge in Delphi programming without sacrificing functionality of the Novell Developer Kit's C libraries.

ActiveX/Visual Basic

Development using the ActiveX components for NDS is an extremely popular environment because of the ease of development, particularly by non-programmers.

The ActiveX components can be used in either a Visual Basic environment or in an Active Server Page environment with Web servers running Microsoft's Internet Information Server (IIS) product.

The ActiveX component has evolved over the past short time to include features such as partition/replication management, allowing for rapid development of point solutions for NDS.

Because of the ability to extend IIS capabilities with ActiveX controls, it is possible with the ActiveX control to develop a Web-based front end into management of NDS tasks. This allows for specialized features such as the development of a password change service under NetWare 4 that can be used with any station running a Web browser.

Open Database Connectivity (ODBC)

The last additional development environment we will look at is the use of the NDS ODBC driver. This driver is not so much a development tool directly as a tool that allows you to gather information using non-development tools.

The ODBC driver enables you to view the NDS tree as if it were a number of tables that can be queried using standard query methods, such as Structured Query Language. Any application that can use 32-bit ODBC drivers can utilize this tool for directory database query and modification.

To configure the ODBC driver, download it from the Novell Developer Web site at `http://developer.novell.com/cgi-bin/download/odbc.exe` and install the package.

The current implementation of the NDS ODBC driver is an "early access release" technology, meaning that it is still going through the development phase. As such, it still has some challenges for implementation. As of this writing, the driver only supports read operations when used as a linked table. Imported tables would support write, but will not write back to NDS.

Integration with tools like Microsoft Access and Microsoft Query is also in need of work. Given some time, though, this should turn into a valuable tool for reporting against NDS and—hopefully—for managing NDS.

Novell Script

The Novell Script tool is another early access release product that will allow Visual Basic Script-compatible programs to run in a NetWare server environment. Novell Script requires the Java Virtual Machine in order to function, and its intended use is for scripting Web server back end components to interface with a Web server such as NetScape's Enterprise Server for NetWare.

NetBasic

NetBasic, from HiTecSoft of Scottsdale, Arizona, is a server-based development environment that can be used for stand-alone development or Web development.

There are two versions of NetBasic available. The first version comes with NetWare and is a language that is processed at run time—in effect, it is a very powerful scripting language that gives you a lot of control right at the server console.

The second version is a compiler version, available from HiTecSoft only. The compiler version allows you to compile NLM code from NetBasic scripts. The advantage of compiled code is that it runs faster and has fewer dependencies than the scripting version does.

Both versions allow a lot of flexibility in developing NDS-aware applications. Because NetBasic is built on the Novell NMX component technology, additional functionality can be added to the language through the NMX Component Developer Kit. This kit, which is available from Novell, allows a C programmer to extend the NetBasic language by developing additional components that can be used by the NetBasic language.

For more information on NetBasic, see HiTecSoft's Web site at http://www.hitecsoft.com or the Novell developer pages at http://developer.novell.com.

APPENDICES

APPENDIX

A

Glossary of NDS Terms

A

Access Control List Objects in Novell Directory Services contain a property called ACL that lists objects that have been assigned trustee rights to the object.

access rights Each file and directory has access rights assigned to it that control how users may use it. For example, a user may modify (M) a file but may not delete (D) it.

ACL *See* Access Control List.

Admin A "super user" account initially assigned to the person installing NetWare. Admin has all rights to all objects in NDS by default, but it can be limited by an Inherited Rights Filter.

Alias object An alias is a pointer to another object in the tree, which may reside in another container. Each object in the directory tree may have an alias associated with it.

attributes Each object has attributes assigned to it that describe properties associated with it. File and directory attributes exist that affect the actions a user may take on network files and directories. An NDS object's attributes vary depending on the type of object it is. Typically, NDS objects' attributes are called *properties* so that they are not confused with file attributes.

B

backlink A directory services attribute or property that the directory uses to tell the locations of the external references to a property. When you create an external reference, a backlink is also created. The background process maintains and verifies the backlink regularly.

Bindery object restriction A directory services attribute of the type integer. It indicates that a bindery object cannot be represented by a directory object.

bindery   Versions of NetWare through 3.2 rely on a flat-file database called the bindery. The bindery consists of entries that control a user's access to files and directories, workstations, printers, and applications. A bindery exists on each server. In NetWare 4.*x*/5.*x,* the bindery has been replaced by Novell Directory Services.

bindery emulation   A service of NetWare 4.*x*/5.*x* that allows management of objects in NetWare 2.*x* and 3.*x* networks under Novell Directory Services. Also referred to as *Bindery Services*.

bindery emulator context   Another name for the bindery context.

bindery queue objects   Print queues created by PSERVER (or other utilities) as bindery objects in a server's first bindery context.

C

chaining   A method of name resolution in which a server requests information about an object from other servers. In chaining, Server 1 will ask Server 2 for information on the object. If Server 2 does not have information, it will report back to Server 1 and keep looking. It will ask Server 3, Server 3 will ask Server 4, and so on until Server 1 has an answer.

classes   An NDS object can be defined as an instance of an object class. Examples of classes are: User, Printer, Print Server, NCP Server, Alias, and so on.

CN   Stands for the Common Name.

Common Name   Every Directory Services object has a name that is unique within its context in the directory structure. This is called Common Name when it refers to users, nodes, or servers.

container objects   An instance of a class used to organize the directory tree. Container objects may contain other containers as well as leaf objects. Organizations, Countries, and Organizational Units are examples of container objects.

container   Used in Novell Directory Services to group objects. It may contain leaf objects or other containers, and it normally represents a logical or physical organizational level within a company, such as a department or a division. There are four types of containers: Organizational Unit (OU), Organization (O), Country (C), and Locality (L).

context   The context represents the user's current location in the Novell Directory Services tree.

Corporate Edition   NDS for non-NetWare operating systems.

Country object   The Country object is used in trees that cross country boundaries. For example, in a multinational company, the country objects may be US, FR, and GB. Country object names are defined by the International Standards Organization and follow a standard naming convention defined by the organization.

D

device   The device class is a noneffective class. It is a super class for such effective classes as Computer and Printer. As a noneffective class, it is not possible to instantiate an object of class *Device*.

Directory Map object   A pointer to a server drive path normally used to map drives in login scripts or batch files. This is done so that login scripts need not be changed when a drive path changes—it is sufficient to change the directory map object.

Directory schema   *See* schema.

directory tree   *See* tree.

Distinguished Name   Each object in NDS has a unique name that identifies it, based on its location in the directory tree. This is a combination of the object's Common Name and the Distinguished Name of its container.

DN   *See* distinguished name.

DS.NLM   This NetWare Loadable Module is run when the server is booted. It is the Directory Services NLM.

DSMERGE.NLM   Administrators use this NLM to merge two NDS trees or to rename a tree.

DSREPAIR.NLM   This NLM repairs the directory database and replaces BINDFIX in NetWare 3.*x*. It can also give status on replication and be used for troubleshooting and problem determination.

E

eDirectory   Stand Alone NDS for web sites and applications.

effective class   Any class whose instantiation (an object) can actually be created in the tree. An example of an effective class is the User class.

effective rights   Effective rights pertain to what a user can do in the directory tree and are controlled by the Inherited Rights Filter, the trustee assignment, and the security restrictions specified. They consist of two types of rights: object rights and property rights. Object rights determine what a user can do with objects; property rights control a user's access to that object.

G

group object   An object consisting of a list of several user objects. It is used to associate users from different containers.

L

leaf object   Represents entities on the network such as nodes, users, printers, or groups. Leaf objects are organized in containers. Some of the more common leaf objects are Bindery Object, Computer, Group, NetWare Server, Print Server, User, and Volume.

Locality   A container class that defines where objects are located in an organization unit.

login script   A series of commands executed each time a user logs into the network.

N

name resolution   *See* tree walking.

Naming attribute   The attribute that identifies an object.

NDS   Novell Directory Services (NDS) is the global naming system introduced in NetWare 4.*x*. It has been adopted by other vendors. It contains information about the network, including the objects in the network. See also eDirectory and Corporate Edition.

NETADMIN   NETADMIN is the DOS-based version of NWAdmin, which is used to manage NDS objects.

noncontainer objects   *See* leaf object.

noneffective classes   Used to define other classes, but cannot be instantiated in the tree. An example of a noneffective class is the Organizational Person class.

O

O   The abbreviation and notation for Organization, usually the top of the Directory Services hierarchy (under [Root], but may be subordinate to Country or Locality).

object   An object has both properties and values, and represents different components of the directory tree, such as users. Objects may also be root, container, or leaf objects.

object ID   Each object on a server has a unique four-byte object ID.

object rights Each object on the network has rights associated with it that control what that object can do. These rights are Browse, Create, Delete, Rename, and Supervisory.

object supervisor rights With this right, the user has all rights to the object and all of its properties.

P

partition Logical parts of the tree. (Replicas are the copies of the data in those logical parts.) A logical subset of a directory tree used to provide better management or security. The data in a partition is called a replica.

PARTMGR The DOS-based NDS utility that lets you manage partitions.

primary time servers NDS servers are classified as primary time servers, single reference time servers, reference time servers, or secondary time servers. The primary time server helps other servers determine the network time.

property rights Each object has property rights that apply to it and that tell it what it may do with a property. Property rights are Add or Delete Self, Compare, Read, Supervisor, and Write.

R

RDNs *See* Relative Distinguished Names.

Read-Only replica A replica type that is updated by other servers in the replica list, but does not update those other servers.

Read/Write replica A copy of the Master replica that may be used to change the makeup of a tree.

reference time servers   Used to help determine the network time, but they differ from primary time servers in that they use an external time source to determine it. While reference time servers participate in time synchronization, they do not adjust their time except in response to the external time source.

Relative Distinguished Names (RDNs)   Since it is often tedious to refer to objects by their distinguished names, a Relative Distinguished Name is used. The RDN is a partial name that identifies an object by its relationship within the current context.

replica   A copy of a partition that allows a backup of the information in the partition and also creates a local source for the partition. The four partition types are: Master, Read/Write, Read-Only, and Subordinate Reference.

replica ring   A list of all the replica pointers in a partition.

root   The top of the directory tree, represented by the globe in NWAdmin.

root server   The root server is the first server installed in the directory tree.

S

schema   The list of definitions for all object types in the tree.

secondary time servers   A type of server that does not help determine the network time. Secondary time servers receive it from a primary or single reference time server.

single reference time servers   Servers that determine the network time and represent the only server on the network that determines the time. Small networks ordinarily use a single reference time server. Single reference time servers are not compatible with reference or primary server types.

subordinate references   A replica type that contains a copy of a partition root object that is used only for treewalking.

subtree administrator   An object that is responsible for part of the directory tree.

super classes   An object is an instantiation of an object class. An object class is created from another class, called its *super class*. Objects may inherit directly from only one super class. For example, the User class has the Organizational Person class as its immediate super class; the Organizational Person class inherits attributes from the Person class, which in turn inherits properties from the Top class. The Top class is the only class that does not inherit any attributes from a super class.

synchronization   The process of maintaining the integrity of the data in a partition across multiple servers.

T

tree   The NetWare directory database is organized as a tree that has leaves (leaf objects), a root, and containers.

tree walking   The process of resolving the location of an object within the tree.

typeless names   A method of naming which does not include the object type. If the object type is included, it is called a *typeful name.* CN=JOHN.OU=MARKETING.O=ABC is a typeful name. JOHN.MARKETING.ABC is a typeless name.

APPENDIX

B

NDS Vendors

For this appendix, I'd hoped to present a listing (a "directory," if you will) of companies who sell NDS utililities, or software that integrates into an NDS system. But in today's business world—with companies rapidly starting up, merging, and quietly disappearing—no printed list could hope to be accurate (see Chapter 1 for a discussion of the directory model).

For an up-to-date listing of providers of directory utilities and applications, point your Web browser to `http://vquill.com/ndsbook/vendors.htm` where I maintain the "Complete Guide to NDS Vendors."

Index

Note to the Reader: Throughout this index **boldfaced** page numbers indicate primary discussions of a topic. *Italicized* page numbers indicate illustrations.

G

H

I

O

What's on the CD?

On the CD provided with *Mastering Novell Directory Services*, you'll find a collection of the most useful and dynamic products available for maximizing the full potential of NDS. Here are the various shareware and evaluation products featured on the CD:

- WebTrends AuditTrack
- Intrusion Direction Kane Security Analyst
- BlueLanceLT Auditor+
- NetPro DS Analyzer
- BindView EMS
- Adobe Acrobat Reader
- Console Manager for NetWare demo
- NLMAuto Professional demo
- QView Pro
- REXXWARE demo
- TaskMaster demo

There is additional software available on the Sybex Web site: www.sybex.com. Click Catalog and search for this book.

NOTE Contact information and complete installation instructions for the programs can be found in the readme file located in the root directory of the CD.